DYNAMICS
OF WORLD POLITICS

DYNAMICS
OF WORLD POLITICS

STUDIES
IN THE RESOLUTION
OF CONFLICT

EDITED, WITH AN INTRODUCTION
AND CASE STUDY BY

Linda B. Miller

Center for International Affairs
Harvard University

PRENTICE-HALL, INC., Englewood Cliffs, New Jersey

PRENTICE-HALL INTERNATIONAL, INC., *London*
PRENTICE-HALL OF AUSTRALIA PTY. LTD., *Sydney*
PRENTICE-HALL OF CANADA, LTD., *Toronto*
PRENTICE-HALL OF INDIA PRIVATE LTD., *New Delhi*
PRENTICE-HALL OF JAPAN, INC., *Tokyo*

FOREWORD

The idea for this book developed as I taught courses on international relations at Barnard College, Columbia University. As I searched for appropriate readings, I found that existing anthologies usually contained fragmentary offerings of modern and classical theorists or a mélange of outdated policy statements. In many cases, editors had compiled vast quantities of disparate material calculated to discourage students seeking a unifying approach rather than an encyclopedic one. Moreover, the great majority of these texts have tended to reinforce an artificial separation of international law and organization from the study of world politics, thereby weakening the links between the sub-disciplines of international relations.

The present volume attempts to correct these deficiencies. It is both comprehensive and selective. Recognized authorities deal with the increasingly significant theme of conflict-resolution from varying perspectives in sophisticated, readable analyses. The book should be of equal interest to those concerned with post-war diplomatic history, contemporary world politics, or international law and organization. The first three essays in each part assess the general strengths and weaknesses of a particular mode of accommodation and conflict-resolution. The three case studies illustrate the underlying principles discussed in the critiques that precede them.

The individual selections were chosen for their value in illuminating aspects of the international political milieu rather than as examples of diversified theoretical approaches. The contributors have viewed their subject from the vantage point of somewhat specialized training and experience, yet the participating scholars, lawyers and diplomats share a number of common concerns. All are aware that the importance of the techniques they discuss varies with the nature of the international system under study. As a group, the essayists are concerned with the structure of the contemporary world, the relationships of the actors, the distribution of power, and the kinds of tension in world politics.

In weighing the significance of technological, economic, or ideological forces that cut across the system and affect the goals pursued by the actors in novel ways, the authors are seeking to explain vital tasks performed by the processes of international relations that affect these goals. The accommodation of competitive political interests and the resolution of conflict are the tasks that concern the contributors. Their central focus is the global system, but their essays treat sub-systems of international relations where relevant. Of necessity, an empirical emphasis pervades the essays, although they are not limited to pure description. Some notion of a world order consonant with moral values is to be found in several of the contributions, implicitly if not explicitly, but a consensus on ideal types or models does not emerge.

I edited the essays and wrote the introduction and case study while I was Research Associate at the Center of International Studies, Princeton University in 1966-1967. Although the Center itself did not support the project, several of its members were extremely helpful in its preparation, and followed its progress with interest, especially Oran R. Young, Mohammed Guessous, Richard A. Falk, and Gabriella R. Lande. William C. Olson of Columbia University and Stanley Hoffmann of Harvard University provided trenchant comments on the introduction and the general conception of the work. The reactions of my Barnard classes served as a worthy guide in the selection of essays. James Murray of Prentice-Hall was a consistently constructive and amiable editor. June Traube of the Princeton Center was a patient and reliable typist.

The volume will serve its main purpose if students and teachers of international relations are stimulated to challenge the arguments advanced in the essays.

L.B.M.

CONTENTS

PART II

INTERNATIONAL LAW

PART III

INTERNATIONAL ORGANIZATION

TO MY STUDENTS

EDITOR'S INTRODUCTION

For theorists, as for policy-makers, the evolution of the postwar international system has created unusual hazards. While the need for conceptualization and theory in world politics is accepted, there continues to be widespread disagreement on the validity of various approaches to the subject. The so-called "great debate" between the "scientists" and the "traditionalists," reminiscent of the "realist vs. idealist" controversy, is but one indication of the prevalent uncertainty about the appropriate scope and method of the field.[1] Despite the persistence of confusion in the study of international relations, an inquiry into the prospects for accommodation or conflict-resolution can tell us much about the international system, since "the nature of world politics depends largely on the choices made by the actors among available techniques of war or negotiations, among conceivable types of law, groupings and organizations, or among possible methods of economic transformation."[2]

Some observations on the distinctive features of the contemporary international system as a setting for conflict and changing perspectives on diplomacy, international law, and international organization will serve to place the essays in context.

THE CONTEMPORARY INTERNATIONAL SYSTEM
AS A SETTING FOR CONFLICT

A comparative study of international systems suggests that certain types of conflict are not only more prevalent in particular systems, but also more acceptable to the actors. The existing state of technology helps to shape the political objectives of the basic units in a system and also the relationship of the members. In turn, this relationship may affect the acceptability of various kinds of conflict and the development of particular modes of accommodation and conflict-resolution. Thus certain similarities and differences between the European state system and the contemporary international system are instructive.

The basic units of the European system, as it evolved in the eighteenth, nineteenth, and twentieth centuries, were individual, independent nation-

---

[1] For two examples of this literature, see Hedley Bull, "International Theory: The Case for A Classical Approach," *World Politics*, XVIII (April 1966), 361–77; and Morton A. Kaplan, "The New Great Debate: Traditionalism vs. Science in International Relations," *World Politics*, XIX (October 1966), 1–20.

[2] Stanley Hoffmann, ed., *Contemporary Theory in International Relations* (Englewood Cliffs, N.J.: Prentice-Hall, Inc., 1960), p. 183.

1

states, sovereign, territorial entities which were self-contained, centralized, and self-reliant for purposes of defense.[3] Other units in the system comprised a number of semi-sovereign entities or dependencies, controlled by larger states. Power in the European state system was distributed more or less evenly among the larger units, whose leaders enjoyed the common understanding that the international system *qua* system would survive the outbreak of war. Smaller states were sought as allies when the larger powers engaged in direct conflict.

Rapid economic and technical change undercut the separateness of the individual units and destabilized the European system. A notable degree of interdependence, based on trade, developed between the great powers in the years prior to World War I, but it failed to promote unity among rival units. Statesmen used personal diplomacy, alliances, conferences, legal norms, and rudimentary forms of international organization to regulate their relations with each other. New units could be admitted to the system by peaceful means. Yet when conflicts among the basic units developed in Europe or outside the continent—in Asia, Africa, or the Middle East—they could be resolved acceptably by violent means. The policies of self-extension adopted by the basic units helped to make the system a more open one as lesser units were colonized. But the European leaders attempted to maintain legal and political distinctions between Europeans and non-Europeans.

The role of war underwent important changes in the system's evolution. Throughout the eighteenth and nineteenth centuries, war performed a regulatory function and permitted an acceptable adjustment of interests. But the technological advances in weaponry that made annihilation of one or more units possible, in world wars, marked the end of the system's capacity to dominate international affairs. Neither the European concert nor the League of Nations constituted a central enforcing agency; the system remained a decentralized one throughout its history. The principle of a balance of power, as a policy consciously pursued by statesmen, operated to preserve the identity of the basic units and to prevent the hegemony of one unit over the others.

In contrast to the European system, the contemporary international system is a global one, comprising a variety of state and non-state actors with differing capabilities and interests. In many cases, the basic units are of larger geographical dimensions than their European counterparts and they are not "penetrable." Power is distributed unevenly, with greater distinctions between the ranks of large and small units. The system as a whole is heterogeneous, with units displaying varying norms of conduct and values of state behavior. Leaders share no certainty that the system *qua* system will survive direct confrontations. The superpowers have displayed an inherent inability to project themselves outward permanently; in their innovative peacetime coalitions they have encountered increasing resistance

---

[3] See John Herz, *International Politics in the Atomic Age* (New York: Columbia University Press, 1959), part 1.

to their leadership from middle rank units. States have employed economic and propaganda techniques in new ways since 1945. As in the European state system, the effective control of force remains on the national level and governs the expectations of the actors, yet the influence of smaller states has been enhanced in the ideological and other contests that preoccupy the larger units.

The status of war in the contemporary system is ambiguous. The development of nuclear weapons has rendered traditional military conflicts unacceptable. Moreover, "insofar as these weapons have made great-power wars too dangerous, they have altered—and *perhaps* revolutionized—the relationship between members of the international system. Conflict, rather than being eliminated, has been concentrated in areas where nuclear weapons cannot be used effectively or where the stakes involved would not justify their use. In addition, conflict has been transferred from the formal military level to the level of political, economic, and paramilitary confrontation."[4]

Colonial wars, post-colonial breakdowns of law and order, proxy wars, and other types of internal conflict have become surrogates for the large-scale interstate wars of the European system. But interstate conflicts between smaller powers, especially in Asia, Africa, and the Middle East are frequent. Although the superpowers and others have engaged in competitive interventions with uncertain rules, states have shown a predilection for negotiated settlements and refrained from pressing their interests to the point of nuclear exchange.

Given the acceptable range of conflict in the contemporary system, more limited in one sense than in the European system, yet more complex in other respects, the difficulties in measuring national power have increased. The political value of national military power has declined as disadvantages to its use for foreign policy objectives have increased.[5] The traditional catalogue of material resources does not explain which increments of power or capabilities may be most *relevant* in the particular types of conflict that characterize the contemporary system.

The transfer of conflict to the level of political, economic, and paramilitary confrontation has coincided with the decolonization process. A large number of weak new states, with unstable political structures and uncertain economic viability, has been introduced into a system already riven by great power conflict. As a result, new demands have been placed on the larger states whose aid is sought for developmental purposes and also on the existing international institutions which often serve to legitimize the new states' entry into the system. Disputes, ostensibly between states, reveals overlapping tensions of global proportions—between rich and poor, white and non-white.

In diplomatic arenas where competing governmental interests are pressed,

---

4 Robert L. Rothstein, "Alignment, Nonalignment, and Small Powers: 1945–1965," *International Organization*, XX (Summer 1966), 407.

5 Klaus Knorr, *On the Uses of Military Power in the Nuclear Age* (Princeton: Princeton University Press, 1966), p. 37.

especially in international organizations, racial and ideological considerations affect the disposition of economic and political issues.

Like its European predecessor, the contemporary system has developed no central enforcing agency, no "manager of power." Instead, contradictory patterns of state behavior are evident, some reinforcing a traditional nation-state system, others appearing to strengthen an international society composed of larger units, perhaps supranational communities. Despite the erosion or, some would argue, the obsolescence of the state's economic and security functions, the nation retains a psychological importance as a focus of individual loyalties. Interdependence is more apparent than real, for only where "a firm expectation of peace"[6] has developed, as in Western Europe since World War II, have states forged strong institutional links that may transcend an intergovernmental character.

The contemporary international system thus combines several unique features—nuclear weapons and post-colonial tensions—with others derived from earlier systems, in a fashion that renders accommodation and conflict-resolution by established methods particularly difficult.

CHANGING PERSPECTIVES ON DIPLOMACY, INTERNATIONAL LAW AND INTERNATIONAL ORGANIZATION

The origins of the techniques of accommodation and conflict-resolution discussed in this volume may be traced in early Western international systems, and some roots are to be found in ancient Eastern civilizations.[7] When units in these systems, for example the Greek city-states, found it desirable to regulate their interactions on an orderly basis, forms of diplomacy, law, and international organization evolved. In all systems, convenience has played a significant role in the shaping of diplomatic styles, legal norms, and institutional structures for cooperative ventures. Many contemporary diplomatic practices and legal conceptions have a long history. Alliances, truces, commercial treaties, and conferences were highly developed by the Greeks, as were standards of arbitration, the treatment of aliens and the conduct of war. Yet despite the timeless quality of some of the political issues that entail the use of these techniques, the size and type of the basic unit have influenced the particular forms of diplomacy, law, and organization that have developed in different systems. Although it is evident that the accommodation of competitive interests and the resolution of conflicts

---

[6] Kenneth Waltz, "Contention and Management in International Relations," *World Politics,* XVII (July 1965), 739.

[7] Interesting comparisons between Eastern and Western systems are presented in George Modelski, "Kautilya: Foreign Policy and International System in the Ancient Hindu World," *American Political Science Review,* LVIII (September 1964), 549–60; and in Joel Larus, ed., *Comparative World Politics* (Belmont, California: Wadsworth Publishing Co., 1964).

are important tasks in any international system, they are of special urgency in the present era when the survival of the system is challenged.

It may be helpful for purposes of analysis to differentiate accommodation and conflict-resolution. Through accommodation, actors may come to accept the legitimacy of divergent interests or goals; through conflict-resolution, specific disputes or controversial issues may be settled by interested parties. But often distinctions between the two are blurred, by both participants and observers. Moreover, usage of the terms varies greatly, as the essays attest. Such imprecision reflects the fluidity of the contemporary system in which instances of "pacific non-settlement" and "non-pacific settlement"[8] are numerous.

Changing perspectives on diplomacy, law, and international organization are apparent in the attitudes of both policy-makers and scholars. Diplomacy, once narrowly construed as the art of negotiation, is now understood to include the policies of states as well. Both the goals pursued by the actors and the tactics and strategies employed to realize them concern statesmen and commentators. Relations between states no longer constitute the entire diplomatic field, nor is Europe the diplomatic center of the world. Since 1945 new negotiating situations have gained prominence, for example the large multilateral conference that focuses on economic aid and development or on arms control and disarmament. There are new forums for bargaining, among them, regional organizations and the U.N., and new diplomatic styles. Diplomacy is global, intense, and continuous rather than episodic. The demands of diplomacy have created the need for personnel who are equipped to represent the interests of states in technical or scientific fields and in the councils of international institutions. The demands of contemporary diplomacy are especially difficult for the newer states, which often lack trained élites but wish to participate actively in world politics.

There is renewed interest, on the part of scholars, in analyzing diplomacy theoretically. What is the relationship between violent conflict and negotiations? For what types of agreement do governments negotiate? For what kinds of interests do they bargain? What "rules," if any, can be derived from the study of national styles of statecraft? What side effects do states seek in negotiations? Comparative studies of international systems, past and present, may yield stimulating answers to these questions. Only a few lines of inquiry can be indicated here.

Clearly the prevailing pattern of power in a given system and the character of the relationship between key members are consequential factors. In the period of cabinet diplomacy, the bargaining reputation of a state depended upon its availability as a partner to as many countries as possible. No relationship was considered permanent and no moral opprobrium was attached to shifting alignments. Quite different standards prevailed in the first two decades of the cold war. The polarization of power in the international system, climaxed at the end of World War II by the emergence of

---

8 See Inis L. Claude, *Swords into Plowshares,* 3rd ed. (New York: Random House, 1964), p. 216.

the United States and the U.S.S.R. as superpowers, helped to rigidify diplomacy. Losses for one side were interpreted as gains for the other. The ideological enveloping of every policy matter affected the conduct of diplomacy in serious ways. For both sides, the status quo came to appear reliable, if ultimately unsatisfactory. The ambivalent attitudes of American and Soviet leaders toward any negotiations with each other resulted in the postponement of accommodation on particular issues which might have been negotiable, for example, nuclear-free zones in developing areas.

A gradual loosening of bipolarity, more extensive in non-military affairs but also apparent in the military sphere, has created opportunities for less rigid diplomatic postures. The efforts to woo the smaller states and to keep formal allies in line that consumed the time and attention of American and Soviet leaders throughout the 1950's proved disappointing. In recent years, the emergence of alternate poles of attraction (France and China come to mind at once), a development the superpowers could not prevent, has enabled the United States and the U.S.S.R. to explore their coincident interests more thoroughly. The test ban treaty of 1963, one result of the renewed probing of mutual concerns, demonstrated the usefulness of formal procedures and practices in giving effect to the converging policies of adversaries. The possibility of superpower leadership in resolving sub-global conflicts should not be discounted, in view of the Soviet role in negotiations after the India-Pakistan conflict of 1965. Yet, as the Tashkent agreements exemplify, such diplomatic enterprises may do nothing more than restore a precarious *status quo ante*.

Existing diplomatic techniques can be adapted to changing power configurations in the international system. Diplomacy that proceeds by way of concession and concludes in compromise is a salient mode of accommodation and conflict-resolution when the actors permit it to be, in bilateral relations or in multilateral contexts.

Like diplomacy, international law and organization are techniques employed by statesmen in world politics and academic subjects studied by scholars. Postwar developments have affected the status of international law and organization from both perspectives. Far-reaching alterations in the international system have demonstrated the irrelevance of legal codes or institutional structures posited in a vacuum. Conceptions of international law and organization nurtured in the period of the European state system, positivist conceptions emphasizing the dominance of sovereign states, are no longer adequate for the contemporary system in which the older meanings of sovereignty and independence have eroded. The sociological concerns that animate a number of observers who are attempting to revitalize the study of international law and organization within the broader context of world politics are documented in the present collection of essays.

Among the changes in the international system that require incorporation into legal doctrine and state practice are 1) the emergence of new non-Western state actors who reject doctrines inherited from the colonial era that appear prejudicial to their political, social, and economic advancement, and 2) the emergence of nonstate actors, especially regional and general international organizations, and subnational actors, particularly private economic corporations and individuals, whose relations with state actors require some measure of regulation. The traditional preoccupations of international law and organization with the regulation of state behavior is shifting in response to the needs of the contemporary system. The direction of change is difficult to plot exactly, but certain trends are discernible.

In the writings of scholars and in the rhetoric of policy-makers, increasing attention is being accorded to 1) the pertinence of legal procedures and intergovernmental institutions in promoting accommodation and resolving conflicts, and 2) the usefulness of international agreements endorsed by the U.N. or regional groupings to assist in the control of potentially destructive technological developments. Yet there is abundant evidence that the assessments of scholars and policy-makers diverge on such critical issues as the desirable and feasible roles for international law and organization in managing national uses of force or the redistribution of natural resources. Often there appears to be little common ground between statesmen who continue to employ international law and organization as techniques for the rationalization of national policy positions, and scholars who argue for centralized institutions that may contribute to world order by establishing or clarifying permissible and impermissible norms.

Are there any points of contact between statesmen who decline to submit disputes involving vital interests to existing international tribunals and scholars who assert the law-creating function of United Nations resolutions? Despite the different perspectives of observers and policy-makers, there are uses of international law and organization relating to the changed political milieu that suggest links between theory and practice. Notable among these uses is the increasing importance of multilateral treaties to express the consent of diversified members of the international society in areas of regulation where the perceived need for accepted norms outweighs parochial interests. A second use of international law and organization that may enhance the value of these techniques to political decision-makers directly affects the prospects for accommodation and conflict-resolution. In times of crisis, the fact that international organizations exist (whatever jurisdictional problems may arise subsequently between regional and global institutions, or between these organizations and states) allows communication between the actors.[9] Moreover, the articulation of claims and counter-claims couched in legal terminology may facilitate the conciliatory attempts of third parties by placing limits on the stakes of conflict.

It is too soon to argue that such uses may lead to substantial modification or to a transformation of the international system. Often the combined uses of diplomacy, international law, and international organization, far from eliminating tensions, may seem to exacerbate them. The disposition of the South West Africa case in the International Court of Justice, the accompanying diplomatic moves within the U.N., the O.A.U., and outside the

---

[9] This argument is stressed in William D. Coplin, "International Law and Assumptions about the State System," *World Politics,* XVII (July 1965), 615–34.

international organizations, suggest that these techniques remain of little efficacy in the absence of concentrated pressures to alter the political wills of interested parties. Similarly, the protracted civil strife in Cyprus illustrates the severe limitations of existing techniques in an era of destabilizing change.

But the ambivalent attitudes of states toward international law and organization as modes of accommodation and conflict-resolution need not prevent the gradual evolution of convergent interests on a variety of political or economic issues. These interests, when strengthened by accommodating diplomatic postures, may foster a tolerable, if partial, world order.

PART I

DIPLOMACY

CHAPTER ONE

PEACE STRATEGIES
OF DETERRENCE
AND ACCOMMODATION

Arnold Wolfers
Washington Center of Foreign Policy Research

Arnold Wolfers' critical assessment of "peace strategies" clarifies the contribution of utopian and domestic policy proposals to the maintenance of international order. In explaining the relationship of deterrence to the distinctive processes of accommodation and conflict-resolution, Wolfers is careful to avoid conventional wisdom. His conceptions of international stability and national security are grounded in a theory of world politics that emphasizes practical approaches to the existing milieu rather than drastic system transformation. His realistic appraisal of general and complete disarmament serves as a useful corrective to sweeping generalizations on its virtues. The essay gains in importance because Wolfers does not confine his attention to transient phenomena in the postwar era. He stresses the "core values" that affect the goals and perceptions of policy-makers in all historical periods.

Reprinted from *Discord and Collaboration*. Baltimore: Johns Hopkins University Press, 1962, pp. 133–47. By permission.

...Policies dealing with peace, or with the prevention of war, occupy a prominent place in the foreign policy of most nations much of the time. It would be distressing if this were not so, particularly now that war threatens unprecedented destructiveness and, at least in the case of unrestricted war between two nuclear powers, has ceased to be a rational instrument of policy.

Despite the widespread public clamor for peace and the unending stream of official professions of peaceful intent, it is often said that peace itself is never the actual goal of foreign policy. This contention rests on the misapprehension that in order to qualify as a goal, peace would have to be regarded as an absolute value for which all other values would be sacrificed. But few objectives, even the protection of such a core value as territorial integrity, are absolute in this sense: Czechoslovakia, for example, ceded much of her territory to Hitler in 1938 in order to save the rest. Peace too competes with other values, with justice in one instance, with honor in another. It may therefore be sacrificed if avoiding war would require resigned acceptance of intolerable injustice or the violation of solemn pledges. As a rule, only a nation facing defeat will "buy" peace at the extreme price of an unconditional surrender which means placing itself and all it values at the mercy of the enemy. Between this contingency and the opposite extreme at which a nation prefers war to making any sacrifice —or actually cherishes war as a value in itself—lie the wide range of choices by which nations decide what losses to incur or what gains to forfeit in order to restore, preserve, or consolidate peace.

It stands to reason that peace is valued most by nations for whom war and violence can promise nothing but loss and destruction. The more satisfied nations are with the established order, or the weaker they are compared to their potential enemies, the more they can be expected to be "peace-loving," i.e., willing to make sacrifices to preserve the peace. But even powerful dissatisfied countries will sometimes be found on the peace-loving side; the restraint of these countries, which are capable of contesting the *status quo* through force but instead accept the conditions that provoke their dissatisfaction, is all the more praiseworthy.[1] Of course, under present nuclear conditions such resignation is not difficult for countries that could not hope to change the *status quo* except by resort to a war of devastating self-destruction. Germany's resignation to partition, at least for an indefinite

---

[1] George Kennan suggests that Americans, particularly, are prejudiced in favor of the *status quo* and peacefulness. He points out that "to the American mind, it is implausible that people should have positive aspirations, and ones that they regard as legitimate, more important to them than the peacefulness and orderliness of international life," and goes on to say that "we tend to underestimate the violence of national maladjustments and discontents elsewhere in the world." *American Diplomacy, 1900–1950* (Chicago: University of Chicago Press, 1951), p. 96.

time, or the resignation of the United States to Moscow's continued rule over Eastern Europe can be better explained by their realization of the costs of the alternative to peace than by either a passionate desire for peace or a condemnable indifference to the injustices of the *status quo*.

The varying value different men and nations attach to the blessings of peace and to the lives and property that war would destroy are not irrelevant in accounting for their respective propensity to resort to war, whether offensively, to change the *status quo*, or defensively, to preserve it; but if, in times ahead, the readiness to initiate war should decline, it will be less for greater love of peace or greater indifference to unjust conditions than for greater fear of nuclear destruction. Evidence of this has not been lacking since the dawn of the nuclear age. In places such as Indochina, Suez, Tibet, and Goa, where the danger of nuclear weapons' being used, or of escalation of war to the nuclear level, was considered small, nations and factions within nations have demonstrated no unusual restraint in the resort to violence and even less in the use of threats of war—not all bluff— for purposes of both deterrence and blackmail.

When governments do concern themselves with the promotion of peace, they are faced with a wealth of suggestions and an ever growing volume of literature on how peace can be attained or made to endure.[2] Most of the advice on peace addressed to the problem of how to order the world— legally, politically, and militarily—to make wars among nations impossible fails to spell out how national governments responsible for the security of their countries could go about creating such an order.

The plans of exponents of world government offer the most striking example of the dichotomy between the ideal and the practical peace strategy. In maintaining that a world authority enjoying a monopoly of military power would make war impossible, they are stating a truism. The important question is whether national governments are in a position to replace the multistate system with a single sovereign power possessing unchallengeable authority over the entire political world. To affirm this as a practical possibility the exponents of world government point out, correctly, that sovereign nations have on occasion merged their independence into a union or federation with others, forfeiting their separate control over military forces and thus their ability to resort to war. This argument fails to consider, however, the amount of amity and mutual confidence necessary among nations to make their merger conceivable. Wherever peace is endangered and conflict and enmity reign as they do, for instance, in the cold war today, peace through world government—and thus its greatest purpose, the elimination of the danger of nuclear war—presupposes that the two opposing power blocs agree on its establishment. Such agreement,

---

[2] See the elaborate and useful bibliographies and research proposals published by the Institute for International Order (11 West 42 Street, New York 36, New York). These include the quarterly bibliographical publication *Current Thought on Peace and War,* and five "Research Designs for Peace." Also prominent in the field of nonutopian peace research is the Center for Research on Conflict Resolution of the University of Michigan, which publishes the quarterly *Journal of Conflict Resolution.*

however, as mentioned earlier,[3] assumes willingness on the part of the opposing blocs to place their countries in the hands of an authority wielding a monopoly of power over which their opponent might later manage to gain control.

Here lies the utopian joker. If ever the United States and the Soviet Union gained such boundless confidence in each other, no world government would be needed. For a nation to favor world government even in the absence of such mutual confidence, on the ground that the envisaged constitutional or legal provisions and commitments would make it impossible for the other nation to seize control, would be to demonstrate an almost inconceivable degree of ignorance on the part of responsible leaders about the limits of the power of law under conditions in which a deeply rooted consensus on major issues and a genuine community among the parties are conspicuously absent.

Some other well-known peace proposals or panaceas for peace are similarly utopian in that they lie beyond the range of practical policies open to the "powers that be." Peace would be safer, for instance, if human nature could be changed so as to bring all statesmen to value peace more than anything their countries could hope to attain or defend by a resort to force. Similarly, there would be no danger of war if all governments could be made to abide by a rule of law prohibiting war's initiation. The question is how governments interested in peace could effect not only in their own people but also in their opponents the radical switch in psychology and behavior that would be required. If the answer is that nations who failed to change the nature of their citizens or went to war in violation of the law should be punished by the ones who have been reformed, the result still would be war even though it would be called enforcement of the peace, police action, or military sanctions.

Yet another set of ideas about peace is put forth with at least implicit advice that they be made the basis of national peace policies, in this case policies of a domestic type. As was mentioned earlier,[4] many of the social scientists who have digressed from their chief field of interest and competence into the field of relations between nations have treated international war as an event originating in the minds of psychoneurotic men characterized by abnormal aggressiveness, dogmatism, or hatred of other peoples. From this assumption—of which, to my knowledge, no empirical verification has ever been attempted—it follows that the prevention of war calls for measures designed either to cure the unbalanced minds of the men who are in a position to initiate war, to prevent such men from attaining power, or, best of all, to combat the causes of psychoneuroses within the society itself.

I do not propose to inquire here into the validity of the underlying psychological thesis, which reminds one of the similar ethical thesis ascribing

---

[3] See *Discord and Collaboration,* Chapter 8, "The Balance of Power in Theory and Practice."

[4] See *ibid,* Chapter 3, "The Determinants of Foreign Policy," and especially fn. 3 thereto.

all initiation of war to the action of evil men. No doubt many wars have been the work of mad of vicious men; but I would argue that the Hitlerian wars of the "mad Caesars" are the exception rather than the rule. Yet even if the "neurosis thesis" were correct, it is hard to see how governments to whom it might appeal could go about eliminating the disease or seriously reducing it even at home, if one considers the number of neurotics in every nation from whose ranks future "mad Caesars" and their followers could be drawn. It is impossible, moreover, to envisage how these same governments could hope to affect the incidence and influence of men of a neurotic type in countries other than their own. Probably the promotion of non-aggressiveness in some countries would merely strengthen other countries that are more inclined toward war and therefore opposed to the suggested reforms or therapy. The result would be a unilateral psychological disarmament and a dangerous undermining of peace efforts based on deterrence.

Leaving aside, then, both utopian and domestic policy proposals recommended as peace strategies, I shall turn to the practical ways in which governments concerned with peace can express their concern in a manner compatible with the pursuit of the nation's interests as traditionally conceived. They can express this concern and indeed have done so again and again by measures designed to promote peace. Three different objectives of such measures can be distinguished: first, the restoration of peace after it has been broken, or "peacemaking"; second, the preservation of peace by prevention of war; and third, the consolidation or stabilization of peace.

If it had not been amply proved before that peacemaking is one of the most ticklish tasks of diplomacy, the two world wars should have removed all doubts. Even if both sides become keenly interested in ending hostilities, they often continue to fight because there is more at stake for them than peace, the price of which in terms of other values may change with every turn of the war. Moreover, even within the camp that sees a chance of victory there is frequently passionate controversy between those who advocate a punitive peace and those who prefer to settle for a conciliatory peace. The goal of both factions is an "enduring peace," but the proper road to that goal is not clear. Those who would continue the fight may be sincerely convinced that only total defeat will deter the enemy from ever renewing the war; those who advocate reconciliation hope thereby to remove some of the dissatisfactions that originally provoked the resort to force. Because the kind of order established at the close of a war may become the chief cause of a subsequent war, one would wish that more of the "peace research" to which scholars are dedicating themselves would focus on the problems raised by peacemaking.

Policies designed to preserve the peace form a regular and often predominant part of the foreign policy of nations that consider themselves exposed to military attack. If they see no way to change the intention of the would-be attacker, and are unwilling to surrender to such an attack, they must seek to prevent it. This means engaging in a policy known as deterrence; it is designed to frighten off the opponent or to dissuade him from carrying out his intention to fight. Nuclear deterrence is only one form of this policy, but one in which the means of causing fright are particularly awesome. If effectiveness means no more than that hostilities are avoided or postponed, deterrence can be an effective peace strategy. But while the opponent has been prevented from carrying out his aggressive intentions, neither his intentions, nor his means of putting them into practice, nor the underlying conflict between the opponents has been altered. Peace remains no less precarious for having been preserved in this fashion and may continue to be what today is called the cold war.

Because governments concerned with peace are interested in going beyond the mere prevention of open hostilities, much of their foreign policy or peace strategy is aimed at consolidating and stabilizing the peace. Since as in the case of the restoration of peace, deterrence is not, or not by itself, sufficient, consolidation calls for accommodation in its broadest sense. Deterrence, to preserve the peace, and accommodation, to consolidate it, then, are the chief peace strategies of nations, and they usually can be pursued simultaneously. While they may at times get into each other's way, neither strategy is likely in the long run to achieve satisfactory results alone. Nations that have neither the means to deter nor the means to accommodate their opponents must rely on others for their protection from war. They are incapable of any policy that would deserve the name of peace strategy, although they may mistake professions of peaceful intent or the advocacy of sweeping universal schemes for peace, such as total disarmament, as substitutes for such a strategy.

Deterrence through military power is as old as the multistate system itself: *si vis pacem para bellum* was a classic commentary. It is a prominent aspect of the balancing of power process because it defines the purpose of the balancing operations of countries seeking to prevent the initiation of war by their opponents.[5] Most of the discussion on deterrence lies beyond the scope of the present study which concerns international politics without extending into the field of military policy and strategy.[6] The relationship between deterrence policy and peace preservation deserves some consideration here, however. It is often claimed that preparations for war (for that matter, preparations for any coercive action), which are inherent in all military deterrence, increase rather than reduce the danger of war. For this reason the United States has been criticized for an alleged overemphasis

[5] For further consideration of this point see *ibid*, Chapter 8, "The Balance of Power in Theory and Practice."

[6] The present author has contributed to the discussion of military and especially nuclear deterrence in the following articles: "The Atomic Bomb in Soviet-American Relations," in *The Absolute Weapon*, ed. Bernard Brodie (New York: Harcourt, Brace & World, Inc., 1946); "Could a War in Europe be Limited?" *The Yale Review* (Winter 1956); "Europe and the NATO Shield," *International Organization*, No. 4 (1958); "Limits on Disengagement" in *East-West Negotiations*, published by the Washington Center of Foreign Policy Research, 1959; "Nuclear Restraint: A Two-Edged Sword," *Marine Corps Gazette* (May 1960); and by his part in the report of the Washington Center of Foreign Policy Research to the Committee on Foreign Relations of the United States Senate entitled, "Developments in Military Technology and Their Impact on United States Strategy and Foreign Policy" (December 1959), of which he was a coauthor and the responsible editor.

on deterrence and thus on military preparedness or "positions of strength." There is some truth in the contention that what is intended to deter an opponent may instead provoke him and thus lead to the war it was supposed to prevent. This may happen even when there is no unnecessary sabre-rattling and no lack of communications between the parties. No government can ever be certain that a build-up of forces and weapons systems by the other side is not a preparation for offensive action, or that it will not turn into such preparation even if not originally so intended. Under nuclear conditions a strong suspicion on this count might even trigger a pre-emptive strike.

Yet, however serious the risks inherent in polices of deterrence, particularly when the full intensity of nuclear brinkmanship is reached, the alternative involves risks of far more ominous proportions. It means placing oneself at the mercy of an actual or potential opponent, who as a rule will not fail to justify to himself, if not to others, actions designed to take advantage of his superiority. Instead of being provoked, opponents are being tempted here by the lack of resistance they expect to meet.

But while deterrence is indispensable, it can be accepted as the sole peace policy only when chances of accommodation at a tolerable price are nonexistent. After all, at best deterrence can affect the underlying dispute only by "laying it on ice" for a more or less prolonged period. Occasionally such postponement of hostilities may allow the old conflict to be superseded by new preoccupations and consequently to fade away. Some people in the West, for instance, cherish the hope that during a prolonged Soviet-Western stalemate, Red China will develop into a major threat to the Soviet Union and that this will induce Moscow eventually to lose interest in communizing the West. As a rule, peace resting on deterrence alone, whether it be deterrence of only one party or mutual deterrence, leaves nations in a state of conflict and thus in the precarious position of sitting on the lid of a boiling kettle. This is particularly true in an age troubled both by fanatical demands for change and by profound fears for the security of national core values.

Accommodation is no more a panacea for peace than is deterrence. It takes two to accommodate just as it takes two to make war. If one side cannot be deflected from the demands that produce conflict and, therefore, threaten violence no matter what compromises the other is in a position to offer, the only remaining alternatives to war are either deterrence or surrender. But even if successful, accommodation cannot guarantee enduring peace and it may, in fact, have an unstabilizing effect. There is no way of telling in advance whether concessions will satisfy the other side or merely whet its appetite. If accommodation takes the form of unequal or unilateral concessions, it becomes "appeasement" in the invidious sense the term has taken on since Munich, which implies that it will call forth new demands. To point to the dangers of the chain reaction or domino effect of such appeasement does not mean, however, to rule out accommodation by unilateral concession under all circumstances. To give up untenable positions with a view to creating better chances of effective deterrence and accommodation further in the rear, as belligerents frequently have done with success, may be the lesser of two evils.

Leaving aside the case of unilateral concessions, accommodation aims at compromise in which the difference between the parties is split at a point acceptable to both. Most of the work of diplomacy and of international organizations such as the United Nations consists of efforts at accommodation. Not only do parties to disputes rarely offer inflexible resistance to accommodation, which usually requires direct negotiation at some point, but "third parties" that are prepared to get into the act if given an opportunity are even more rarely lacking, although the role of the mediator is known to be neither easy nor thankful. Their overriding incentive is to moderate or resolve conflict between others before it erupts into violence and destroys the peace, the benefits of which all parties share. Left to their own devices, conflicting parties engaged in measuring their respective strength encounter great difficulties initiating a policy of accommodation because they become exposed to the suspicion of weakness. This explains why the mediator almost invariably is a crucial figure in accommodation.

The question of what makes a successful mediator deserves much more attention than it has received. A reputation for impartiality may be only one characteristic of the suitable mediator, but it is indispensable; therefore the present lack of genuinely neutral countries or of individuals in these countries recognized as neutral by both sides—Khrushchev has even denied that there can be such individuals—seriously reduces the chances for effective mediation and thus for peace through accommodation. The United Nations, though in many respects an ideal mediator, is no substitute for individuals or individual nations with a reputation for impartiality: it cannot set up acceptable mediatory boards or committees unless at least chairmen can be found who are recognized as neutrals by both parties.

The most serious obstacle to any accommodation that is not merely a verbal cloak for the surrender of one party is the depth of the gulf that separates parties whose conflicts constitute a threat to the peace. It would be defeatist, however, provided a balance of coercive power is maintained on all levels of confrontation, to assume *a priori* that maximum demands and counter-demands cannot be whittled down and compromised or that the issues are as indivisible as the political labels used to characterize them would indicate. Of course, mediation and negotiations may fail, as they have frequently failed in the past. But while their failure should serve as a warning to those who would sacrifice or jeopardize deterrence for the sake of the more "peaceful" road of accommodation, nations with a vital stake in the prevention of war have strong reason to wish to meet their opponents part way whenever there is any chance of resolving conflict by agreement. Those seeking change may be induced to accept less than they originally demanded—or to resign themselves to no change at all—particularly if a determined and credible show of counterpower or the odium of initiating violence makes the price of forceful change appear high. It may prove more difficult to induce a nation defending its established rights and possessions to negotiate away any part of the *status quo* both because the use of force in response to an attack is unlikely to provoke moral condemnation and because the impression of weakness is deeply feared as a threat to the security of all of a nation's rights and possessions. Stringent advance commitments to take or to hold add further obstacles to peaceful change. Yet without such change nations can hope at best for the "peace" of a tenuous stalemate or truce.

No mention has been made so far of arms control or disarmament as instruments of peace strategy, although in the public mind they hold a key position among such instruments. Disarmament proposals are not necessarily utopian, although of course they may be. On many occasions nations have cut back their armaments unilaterally, often because the danger to their security declined, sometimes because they could no longer afford to continue their previous military efforts. But only in rare cases have limitations and reductions of armaments been agreed upon, either tacitly or formally, by two or more nations. This phenomenon calls for some explanation here because of its discouraging implications for a peace strategy of agreed disarmament.

Arms control agreements, if they turn out to be practical, can bridle an arms race that aggravates tensions by heightening the fear of both accidental and offensive war. The dangers arising from a nuclear arms race are particularly serious because a nation might strike preventively if it foresaw a change in its relative power position arising from technological advantages gained by its opponent in the field of decisive weaponry. The most formidable practical obstacle to arms control agreements is the justified fear that mutual reduction or abolition of military establishments will destroy an existing distribution of military power on which deterrence rests. It can be taken for granted that no nation locked in conflict with another will consent to a change in its relative military power position by an arms control agreement, yet the difficulties posed by the technical problem of making reductions proportional in their effect on the power of the opposing parties tends to defeat even the most serious efforts at accommodation in this field.

The question has been raised whether general and complete disarmament would not obviate the need for proportionality. If both sides reduce their forces to zero how, it is asked, can one of them then increase its relative military strength—remembering that by the terms of the agreement it retains none? Here, however, the problem of reliable inspection is raised, in a most acute form. As others have pointed out, instability would be vastly increased under nuclear conditions if one side could gain a monopoly of nuclear power merely by hiding a limited number of warheads and missiles in contravention of an agreement. Nor is this the sole objection to total disarmament as a peace strategy. Under the best of circumstances it would take time to cover the road to total disarmament. Every step in the process, therefore, raises the same problem of proportionality as is encountered in the case of less than total disarmament or arms control measures. Then too, nations considering the total elimination of military forces and weapons must ascertain whether such elimination would leave intact their remaining relative power position. The country with superior capability for coercion short of war, or for more rapid rearmament, would by total disarmament improve, and under certain circumstances, decisively improve, its relative power position.[7]

It can be concluded that tacit or formal agreements for the proportional reduction of military power if faithfully carried out would tend to consolidate the peace by reducing the dangers inherent in an arms race, although in leaving the underlying conflict unresolved, such agreements could not by themselves eliminate the precariousness of peace nor would they make efforts at accommodation beyond the field of armaments superfluous. Total disarmament, however, presents such difficulties under nuclear conditions in terms both of proportionality and inspection that it can be ruled out as impractical and relegated to the category of utopian schemes.

---

[7] For an imaginative exploration of problems that total disarmament would not solve, see T.C. Schelling, "The Stability of Total Disarmament," Study Memorandum Number 1, Special Studies Group, Institute for Defense Analyses, Washington, D.C. (October 6, 1961).

CHAPTER TWO

NEGOTIATING SKILL:
EAST AND WEST

Fred Iklé

Massachusetts Institute of Technology

In a deft and entertaining analysis of recent diplomatic encounters between representatives of Western governments and the Soviet Union, Fred Iklé dispels clichés that often characterize the discussion of negotiating styles. His assertion that Western talents are best expressed in dealings with "friendly nations" and within international organizations, while Soviet skills are perhaps superior in adversary relationships is borne out by relevant examples from diversified negotiating situations. Iklé's portrait of the compleat negotiator is an appeal for improved techniques that will enhance the salience of diplomacy in the resolution of conflict. His account of recurring weaknesses and blunders is a sober reminder of diplomacy's limitations in promoting accommodation between states in a decentralized and competitive international system.

Reprinted from *How Nations Negotiate*. New York: Harper and Row, 1964, pp. 225–55. By permission.

It is meaningful to contrast the Soviet style of negotiation with that of Western governments, for there are enough unique characteristics to set the two apart. But between the styles of Western governments the differences are normally overshadowed by those between individual negotiators. In the current era something like a national style emerges in the West only in a case such as De Gaulle's France, where the particular style of the man at the top is executed in detail by a centralized government with disciplined and experienced officials.

Western diplomats differ of course in their training and cultural traditions. These differences may find some reflection in their methods of negotiation, but usually they are not pervasive enough to produce a distinctly recognizable negotiation style. More important are the differences in government structure determining the domestic constraints under which each negotiator must operate. These, however, vary from issue to issue. An example of a somewhat more constant national characteristic is the high sensitivity of American diplomats to public opinion, which might derive both from cultural factors and the particular features of American political life. French diplomats are prone to elaborate historical-philosophical themes as a background to their negotiating strategies, perhaps because their education puts such stress on the composition of synthesizing essays. German and American negotiators at times place a greater emphasis on legal aspects than the diplomats of most other Western countries, probably because of the important role that lawyers play in the conduct of foreign policy in Bonn and Washington.[1]

HOW SHREWD ARE SOVIET NEGOTIATIONS?

Soviet foreign policy has been highly successful in the last twenty years, if measured by the expansion of the Communist-controlled area and by

[1] Kenneth W. Thompson stresses this point for the American diplomatic style in *American Diplomacy and Emergent Patterns* (New York: New York University Press, 1962), pp. 37–38. Charles W. Thayer also believes that one can scarcely distinguish different styles of diplomacy among the great powers, except for the Soviet style— *Diplomat* (New York: Harper & Row, Publishers, 1959), pp. 83–84. Harold Nicolson, however, maintains that there are certain constant characteristics that distinguish the practice of negotiation by such powers as Great Britain, Germany, France, and Italy. As a good Englishman, Nicolson of course finds that the British type of diplomacy "is on the whole the type which is most conducive to the maintenance of peaceful relations"; but as not such a good historian he forgets 1914 and the 1930's when he writes that the British diplomatist "almost always succeeds" (*Diplomacy*, pp. 144, 131). Raymond Aron contrasts the methods by which the British and the French negotiate with the United States: the British try to influence American policies through discussion and public opinion, the French through obstructions (i.e., the threat of "no-agreement")—*Paix et Guerre entre les Nations*. (Paris: Calmann-Lévy, 1962) pp. 461–63.

Russia's newly won influence in many parts of the world. Yet the combined military and economic strength of the West has remained superior to that of the Communist camp during this same period of expansion. Small wonder that many people think Soviet negotiators are far shrewder and more skillful than their Western opponents and the conferences with the Russians are traps to be avoided rather than opportunities to be sought.[2]

Undoubtedly, Soviet negotiators have certain advantages over their Western adversaries because they are backed by an authoritarian government. Western capitals, and Washington in particular, cannot develop a negotiating position on a major issue without letting the public in on some of the internal controversies. This gives Soviet delegates valuable intelligence about the strength with which Western positions are held. Moscow, of course, permits no leaks about any differences that might exist between, say, Gromyko and Malinovsky over how to approach the West on disarmament or on Berlin. Its fall-back positions remain secret, not only from newspapermen but frequently also from its own delegations. Western diplomats often complain about this wall of secrecy that makes it so difficult to find out how firmly a Soviet position is held and what sort of modifications in the Western position might lead to agreement.

Moreover, Soviet diplomats need not feel constrained by domestic public opinion as much as Westerners do. The public in Communist countries is normally poorly informed about negotiations. Knowing their lack of influence on foreign affairs, Soviet citizens hardly attempt to make their views heard—or even to formulate a view of their own. This permits Soviet diplomats to choose their negotiating tactics with greater freedom. Only in the long run, perhaps, do Communist leaders require some domestic backing for their foreign policy.

Soviet negotiators enjoy a further advantage in that they can support their long-term strategy and day-to-day tactics with fully coordinated propaganda machinery, whereas Western countries speak always with many voices. Frequently at conferences the Russians delight in citing statements by Western opposition leaders, scientists, or journalists to refute a position of a Western government.

In short, Soviet negotiators seem to command all that is required for carrying out the most cunning strategies: complete secrecy in planning, freedom from domestic interference in execution, and the coordinated support of a powerful authoritarian regime. Given all these advantages, have Soviet negotiators really shown proportionate cunning and skill? An examination of their record, comparing some of their opportunities with the results they actually obtained, is in order.

The Marshall Plan, to take one case, will long be remembered as one of the most successful and farsighted programs of American foreign policy. What is almost forgotten is that the Russians were initially invited to participate. After Marshall's historic speech in June, 1947, British Foreign

2 Apart from additions and changes, this section has appeared as an article in the *New York Times* (Dec. 9, 1963), Magazine section. © 1962 by The New York Times Company. Reprinted by permission.

Secretary Bevin quickly seized the initiative, met with his French colleague Bidault, and asked Moscow to join in a conference at which Europe would work out its answer to the American offer. Stalin sent Molotov to Paris with a delegation of eighty-nine aides.

What did the skillful Soviet negotiator make of this decisive opportunity? He did not try to postpone West European recovery and European-American cooperation by more than five days!

True, Bevin made it clear that he would not be delayed by Soviet stalling. But why did Molotov make it so easy for Bevin? Why did he reject outright the American offer for a coordinated recovery program, instead of accepting it in principle and then discussing the details latter? Why did he fail to exploit the suggestion made by some groups in the West that the United Nations should play the leading role in European recovery? Or he could have shown some interest when Bidault (conscious of pressure on his government by the powerful French Communist Party) made a last-minute effort to save the conference. With reluctant agreement from Bevin, Bidault's proposal attempted to meet some of the Soviet objections by emphasizing that the organization for European recovery would not interfere with a country's internal affairs. Yet Molotov would not give an inch, and the conference broke up. Thus Russia lost its chance to delay or influence an integrated West European recovery.

To realize the enormity of this Russian blunder, we must recall that the implementation of the Marshall Plan was not assured at that time. On the one hand, U.S. Congressional support was far from certain. On the other hand, there was considerable European backing for Russia's participation. Prior to the conference which brought Molotov to Paris, an editorial in the London *Times* said: "The strongest argument which could be placed in Mr. Marshall's hands for delivery to Congress would be the firm hope of a sound integration of the whole European economy effected by all the countries which are to benefit from American aid, and led by Britain, France, and the Soviet Union." Similarly, the *Economist* proposed that the United Nations Economic Commission for Europe be used—"in spite of its shortcomings"—as the machinery to administer Marshall aid: "Might it not therefore be the course of wisdom to reach a compromise between the Russian and the Western views?"[3]

Khrushchev showed himself an equally unskillful negotiator with his

---

[3] The *Times* (London, June 24, 1947); the *Economist* (June 28, 1947). A French diplomat noted in his diary just a few days before Molotov's final *nyet:* "With a little Machiavellism, the Soviets ought to...insert themselves in the preparatory plan because their accession would immediately provoke its failure." (Jacques Dumaine, *Quai d'Orsay: 1945–51* [Paris: Julliard, 1955] p. 204.) And two years later McGeorge Bundy reflected: "How much of the original impetus of the plan would have survived if Molotov had really sat down at Paris, deployed the enormous retinue he took with him (and one still wonders what they were doing there if this notion was not considered) and cooperated in form but not in fact?" In the mood of 1949 Bundy goes on to ask: "And if we are grateful, are we perhaps also safe for the present, from the effects of a policy of deceptive friendliness by Russia?" [In "The Test of Yalta," *Foreign Affairs* (July 1949), pp. 627, 629.]

tactics on the Berlin issue, though his mistakes were of a different kind from Stalin's and Molotov's. As noted before, Khrushchev spoiled his bargaining reputation by repeating again and again his threat to sign a peace treaty with the Communist regime in East Germany, each time specifying the period within which he would do so but doing nothing each time his bluff was called. An explicit threat with a time limit can be a potent weapon; however, prudent negotiators use it only when they are fully prepared to carry it out or are certain that they will not be challenged. A time limit makes it all too apparent if they are caught bluffing, and this damages the credibility of their threats in the future. History recounts few examples of a senior statesman who squandered and blunted his power to use such threats so completely as Khrushchev did.

This was not Khrushchev's only blunder. When he broke up the summit meeting in May, 1960, he spoiled a unique opportunity to extract concessions from the United States. Only a few days before he flew to Paris to meet with Eisenhower, Macmillan, and De Gaulle, he was able to denounce the United States roundly for the U-2 flights, causing major repercussions in the whole world and skillfully trapping the U.S. government in a lie. On the first day in Paris, Khrushchev played his cards well; with righteous indignation he asked for an apology from the President, which he must have known he could not get. But he did get the promise that the U-2 flights would be discontinued, while Macmillan and De Gaulle pleaded with him to start the summit meeting.

What a reversal of roles, after Khrushchev had been calling for a summit conference so long! What a chance for Khrushchev to drop the demand for apology grudgingly, as if making a generous concession, and then to confront the Western statesmen and ask for reciprocal concessions!

Khrushchev chose another tactic. He put on his rambunctious show in Paris, throwing away his dignity and his trump card. In the end it was, in a sense, he who apologized—two days later in East Berlin. To the glum East German Communists who had expected the long-announced peace treaty, he said the existing situation would have to be preserved until another summit meeting could take place.

Later, Khrushchev hinted that he had anticipated the failure of the Paris summit meeting but that his colleagues wanted him to go all the same. Perhaps Khrushchev realized that his earlier expectations were too optimistic and that the Western powers would not abandon Berlin completely. But this was a poor reason for bringing back from Paris even less than he could have gotten. Had he chosen a shrewder tactic, generously "forgiving" the U-2 incident, the Western powers could not have broken up the meeting without making at least some concessions—perhaps quite substantial ones.

According to a recent Soviet handbook on diplomacy:

> [Communist diplomacy] is invariably successful in exposing the aggressive intentions of the imperialist governments. . . . It does this from the tribunes of diplomatic conferences, in official diplomatic statements and documents, as well as in the press. [This] is one of the important methods of socialist diplomacy by means of which it mobilizes democratic social opinion and the

masses of people all over the world against the aggressive policies of the imperialist governments.[4]

Yet, when faced with some unusual opportunity for mobilizing "the masses of people all over the world," Soviet diplomacy is not "invariably successful." Along came the issue of atmospheric nuclear tests in the spring of 1962, for example. For the previous six months the United States had confined itself to underground testing, although the Soviet Union had resumed nuclear tests in the atmosphere the summer before. But in March, 1962, the American government decided the self-imposed handicap was too great, and President Kennedy announced twelve days before the disarmament conference convened that the United States would soon have to resume nuclear testing in the atmosphere. He promised, however, that if the Soviet Union would accept a treaty with appropriate controls, "sign it before the latter part of April, and apply it immediately..., there would be no need for our tests to begin." Some people feared that the Russians might take advantage of that offer and make some last-minute concessions which would trap the American government into further negotiations whose only result would be postponement of its tests.

As it turned out, the Soviets were far too clumsy. Whatever their real aims, they failed to delay the U.S. tests, they did not inflict a propaganda defeat on the West, and they did not get a control-free ban against underground nuclear testing. Although at the time they probably preferred to remain free to resume their own tests later in 1962 rather than to commit themselves at once to test cessation under a treaty, they must surely have been interested in making propaganda gains and in increasing dissension between the United States and neutralist nations. For this, they had some real opportunities.

They could have encouraged the interest the British negotiators showed in a further reduction of the inspection system. "We are ready to negotiate upon any proposals for an adequate minimum of international verification," said the British Foreign Secretary Lord Home. "We are flexible and ready for reasonable compromise." *Nyet*—no international verification at all, was the Soviet reply.

Opportunity for the Soviets to make some political and propaganda gains became even greater when the eight neutral nations proposed their compromise plan for a test ban. That plan essentially accepted the Soviet position that there should be no foreign inspectors in Russia but added an "international commission" to evaluate the data from national systems. The commission could, in a vaguely defined way, call on a suspected country to furnish more information and *perhaps* arrange an on-site inspection. Obviously, the United States had some serious reservations about the proposal but refrained from rejecting it.

At that juncture, Premier Khrushchev could have announced dramatically that he was not only ready to accept the neutrals' proposal but

[4] *Diplomaticheskii Slovar* (Moscow: State Publishing House for Political Literature, 1960), I, 466.

also that he would consent to combine it with the "best elements" of the Western draft, provided President Kennedy kept his word and did not start atmospheric tests, now that a treaty could be signed "before the latter part of April." Had the President rejected this outright, beginning the tests a few days later, he would have met with a worldwide storm of protest and probably with serious disagreement from Macmillan. On the other hand, had the President postponed the tests, Khrushchev would not have been committed to any treaty he did not want. As the Western negotiators were urgently trying to nail down a specific treaty text (while the expensive task force in the Pacific was kept waiting), the Soviet negotiators could have become evasive or simply have stuck to the neutrals' proposal until American patience ran out. In the end, the United States might have been forced to resume atmospheric tests with a propaganda loss far greater than it actually suffered in April, 1962.

The Soviet negotiators were not imaginative enough to try for these almost riskless gains. To be sure, they urged negotiations on the basis of the neutrals' proposal, but they refused to accept obligatory international inspection (although, without detailed specifications, "international inspection" is just a vague phrase). And while they made some threats to discourage the American tests, they failed to couple them with a dramatic offer.

Another tactical mistake of Soviet negotiators is that they often fail to exploit an "extortionary" demand before it has become obsolete. After World War II they maintained their opposition to the cession of the Saar to France, apparently in the hope that France would have to ransom the Saar from the Soviet veto at a high political price. As late as 1947 it looked as if this tactic would work. Secretary Byrnes expected that "Russia will maintain its opposition to the cession of the Saar until the final hours and then seek to secure, in exchange for agreement, French support on some other question."[5] The Soviet negotiators missed this final hour. Instead they unwittingly made possible the transfer of the Saar to Germany and thus contributed to Franco-German reconciliation.

Related to the mistake of letting an "extortionary" demand become obsolete is the failure to revise an unacceptable demand in time to make gains through a compromise. For example, in 1945 Stalin faced Turkey with a double demand. As we have seen, he not only requested a revision of the Montreux Convention but also asked for a slice of Turkish territory and a Russian base in the Straits. Originally, the United States was willing to support a revision of the Montreux Convention in Russia's favor, Great Britain was ready to go along, and Turkey would probably not have been able to resist by herself.

But Stalin's additional demands for a slice of Turkish territory and a base stirred up British and American opposition. As a result, Stalin failed at the Potsdam Conference to consolidate any gain regarding the Straits. All he obtained was American and British consent to "recognize" the need

[5] *Speaking Frankly,* p. 170.

for revision of the Montreux Convention. It was agreed that the next step should be the subject of direct conversations between the three powers and Turkey. But then in 1946 Stalin made the fatal mistake of renewing *all* his demands against Turkey. This aroused American opposition, and a year later Turkey received full American support under the Truman Doctrine. When in 1953 the Russians at last withdrew their demands for Turkish territory and a base in the Straits, what good was this belated concession? Turkey was now firmly in NATO, and the Western support for changing the Montreux Convention had long since evaporated.

The mistake of clinging to unacceptable demands for too long is related to the self-defeating way in which the Russians sometimes negotiate a tie-in. The tactic of a tie-in will not work if the opponent is asked to surrender more than he expects to receive. When the French negotiators at Brussels linked their consent to the Second Stage of the Common Market with an agreement on agriculture, they managed this tie-in successfully, because the sacrifices they asked of the Germans for the common agricultural policy were not such as to outweigh German interest in continued progress of the Common Market. But when Russian negotiators tried to obtain more influence in the United Nations Secretariat, they totally mismanaged the tie-in tactic. As dicussed earlier, they tried to tie their consent to a successor for Dag Hammarskjöld to their demand for a "troika." A troika, however, would have canceled all interest the United States and other United Nations members had in replacing Hammarskjöld, whereas a more modest Soviet demand (such as for a "troika" of Deputy Secretaries) might have been accepted, particularly if it had found favor with the uncommitted nations. (In fact, the Western nations did accept some changes in the UN Secretariat in favor of the Afro-Asians.)

We can find some common elements in the shortcomings of Soviet negotiators. They often ask for a whole loaf where they could get half a loaf—and wind up with nothing. They fritter away the credibility of their threats and the value of their promises, the two key tools for every diplomat. They cannot find the right dosage of demands and inducements. Curiously, they walk out of negotiations when they should stay in, while at other times they keep on talking in violation of their own deadlines. They insult those whose good will they ought to cultivate, and become self-righteous and rigid where they ought to be ingratiating and inventive. They fight furious battles against an empty phrase or a vague principle, although they are past masters at twisting the meaning of words and at utilizing agreements-in-principle for their own ends.

In short, the shrewd and skillful negotiating style of the Soviet government turns out to be a myth. However, Western diplomats should not be too sanguine about Soviet blunders, for many of these blunders are simply a failure to take advantage of Western vulnerabilities. On such occasions the East-West performance resembles that of two novice chess players. If one player leaves his queen unprotected and the other fails to take it, neither can be called a master.

Moreover, the very idiosyncrasies of Soviet negotiators that account for their blunders can also work to their advantage. If they are careless in having their bluffs called, they are also carefree in trying to gain through bluffing. If they miss many a chance to obligate the West by being a little more generous, they correspondingly feel no obligations to be generous where it would hurt them. And if they do not have the French dexterity in managing a tie-in so as to come out ahead, their rigidity also prevents them from becoming entangled in an exchange where they are left holding the short end. It is true, sometimes they are so stubborn that they cling to an unacceptable demand until they have missed the opportunity for a profitable compromise. But at other times, they are stubborn enough to repeat what seems to be an unacceptable demand until the opponent has changed his evaluations and accepts all or most of what they asked for. Sometimes, certainly, they are too obtuse to force Western governments into a substantial concession by beguiling Western opinion with a small concession of their own. At other times, nonetheless, this obtuseness saves them from disaster, when they can salvage a crucial position only by defying public opinion throughout the world.

Contrary to a popular image in the West, Soviet negotiators are bold rather than shrewd, brazen rather than cunning. It is not the skills attributed to a Talleyrand that the West must fear from Communist diplomats, nor are the Russians brilliant disciples of Machiavelli. What the West must beware of is the brazenness that allowed Stalin to negotiate for his East European empire while the Germans were at the gates of Moscow, the boldness that permitted Khrushchev to make this empire "unnegotiable" while trying to negotiate for Communist control over West Berlin and for the retention of his troops (if not missiles) in Cuba.

WESTERN TALENTS

Dante's description of Heaven may strike us as somewhat lackluster and contrived in comparison with the rich detail and vividness of his Hell. Whoever has tried to describe Heaven will understand why even a Dante might fail. Certainly, for as mundane a topic as negotiating skill, Hell is much easier to paint than Heaven.

Perhaps the faults of negotiators can be more readily identified than their virtues, because in diplomacy failure usually makes news while success is undramatic. Perhaps the weaknesses of our negotiators stand out more sharply because they are spiced with our frustrations, whereas their strengths seem so bland since they are taken for granted. Perhaps the Faustian devil in all our souls, which makes us sooner tire of one page of praise than of a hundred pages of criticism, beguiles us into thinking that in any comparison of virtues and vices, the vices alone tell an interesting story.

It seems natural to evaluate the diplomatic talents and faults of Western governments primarily by comparing them with those of the Soviet government, because among modern negotiating styles the principal distinction is that between East and West. Actually, the Western fortes show up mainly in negotiations with other Western governments but are of little value with

Communist opponents; and conversely, the Western faults are harmful in dealing with Communist diplomats but less serious in negotiations within the West. That is to say, the talents of Western diplomacy are largely confined to negotiations with more or less friendly nations, whereas its weaknesses show up in coping with an adversary.

An important talent of Western diplomats that Communists largely lack is the ability to negotiate within the framework of an international organization and to take advantage of international institutions for settling disputes. Through various alliances, Western nations are able to coordinate their activities and to maintain an effective unity in policy execution, even though they might never be fully agreed on all the details of a policy or on a unified doctrine. In fact, it is precisely because they do not insist on a unity of dogma that they can negotiate their differences so as to avoid both schism and *diktat*. The Warsaw Pact cannot embrace Yugoslavia, and for all practical purposes it now excludes Albania. But NATO was able to survive the Suez crisis, it has lost neither Greece nor Turkey so far in spite of their quarrel over Cyprus, it contains such diverse nations as Norway and Portugal, and unless Paris and Washington descend to the negotiating methods used between Mao Tse-tung and Khrushchev, NATO will also be able to weather the American-French dispute.

Western diplomats are skillful also in dealing with conflicts in isolation. Within an alliance tied by an intimate fabric of military, commercial, financial, and cultural relations, they understand how to negotiate about a conflict in one of these spheres without impairing their relationship in the other spheres. This means they must be willing not to bring in other matters even when this might strengthen their case.

Related to the adeptness with which Western diplomats negotiate within international organizations is their capacity for utilizing rules of accommodation. Many rules are observed among Western allies as a matter of routine, thus preserving a tradition of reciprocation that is both efficient and profitable in the long run. Perhaps their familiarity with constitutional procedures in domestic affairs helps Western officials to work with and benefit from an accommodating style in international affairs. Of course, this presumes a mutual and lasting willingness to use restraint in making gains at the expense of the other parties. When this restraint breaks down, all the short-run accommodations nevertheless proffered become gratuitous losses.

Negotiation in this *esprit communautaire* is greatly facilitated through legal arrangements which set limits to the parties' expectations and thus to the range of conflict over which they bargain. It is also helped by common institutions that can take on a mediating function or provide experts to settle terms of agreement through the "deductive method." And as Jean Monnet pointed out, the life of institutions is longer than the life of people, so that institutions can, if they are well constructed, accumulate and transmit the wisdom of succeeding generations.[6] In the case of negotia-

6 Jean Monnet, *Les Etats-Unis d'Europe Ont Commencé* (Paris: Laffont, 1955), p. 22.

tions between France and Germany, for example, the special relationship based on the rapport between De Gaulle and Adenauer is already a thing of the past. But the collaboration based on the common institutions in Brussels has survived, and in the long run it may well turn out to be the principal driving force for Franco-German unity.

As with Soviet diplomacy, however, the idiosyncracies that account for Western negotiating skill are, on other occasions, responsible for Western weaknesses. Most of the Western talents cannot weather highly antagonistic situations.

WESTERN WEAKNESSES

The following inventory of Western weaknesses is illustrated mostly with examples from American and British diplomacy. Perhaps other Western negotiators—be they French or Finnish, Turkish or Italian—might protest that this portrait does not fit them. But since the diplomacy of the United States (and to a somewhat lesser extent that of Great Britain) plays such a leading role, American or British weaknesses are certainly highly relevant for the West.

Letting the Opponent Determine the Issues

In a news conference on July 12, 1962, Secretary of State Rusk complained, when talking about the Berlin issue, that "the other side seems not to want to talk about a great many things which are of interest to us, the permanent peace settlement for Germany as a whole, for example, or arrangements with respect to Berlin as a whole, because they have simply said that certain matters are just not discussable." One of the newspaper correspondents present thought he had detected something new. He started fishing for more: "You have now reintroduced the elements of an all-German settlement and of a Berlin accord that involves all of Berlin. Is this perhaps an interesting outcome of your recent European trip?" But the Secretary retreated quickly: "No, I didn't intend to make that much news with that remark. I was reflecting on the general attitude of the West over a considerable period of time.... The West has been trying to...find a permanent satisfactory German settlement which would bring peace to Central Europe. But that has not been pursued because, as you will recall, I did say that was the kind of thing that the other side has not been willing to discuss. They say, 'This is not discussable. Now let's talk about your position here in West Berlin.' "[7]

And what does the West do? It talks about its position in West Berlin and agrees that East Berlin and Eastern Europe are not discussable.

It is, of course, often impossible to prevent the opponent from making an issue out of something that one would prefer to have left alone. And if

---

[7] *Department of State Bulletin* (July 30, 1962), pp. 172–73.

the opponent can make no-agreement unpleasant enough, it may even be desirable to negotiate about such issues. But this does not mean that one must abstain from raising other issues where the tables would be turned. The neutralization of Laos was an unavoidable issue. Because the Communists committed more force than the United States was willing to commit, they could have achieved an outcome favorable to them without an agreement. Likewise, the neutralization of South Vietnam has become an issue for the United States, in part because of the difficulty of achieving a military victory and in part because of De Gaulle's attempt to gain influence at the expense of his American ally. Yet the West scarcely tries to make an issue out of the neutralization of North Vietnam. During the Laos Conference of 1961–62, the neutralization of North Vietnam was never seriously raised as an issue, and in connection with the possibility of a negotiated settlement for South Vietnam it was raised only belatedly and rather gingerly. For example in his press conference of February 1, 1964, President Johnson said that if there was a proposal from any side to neutralize both North and South Vietnam, "the United States would consider it sympathetically." Why not *make* a proposal for a neutral North Vietnam and press for it?

Similarly, it may be impossible for the United States to prevent the notion of returning Okinawa to Japanese control from persisting as at least a latent issue. There seems to be no need, however, to accept as a law of nature the point of view that the return of the Soviet-held Kuril Islands to Japan is no longer an issue.

To compare the case of the Panama Canal Zone with that of the formerly Finnish port of Petsamo is instructive. In both cases there is the same overwhelming disparity of strength between the country in possession of each of the areas (the United States and the Soviet Union) and the country that claims or might claim the area (Panama and Finland, respectively). In both cases the country in possession acquired permanent sovereign rights through a clearcut treaty (although Stalin showed more foresight than Teddy Roosevelt in not leaving Finland "titular sovereignty" over Petsamo). And the difference in the history of the two treaties is not such that the renegotiation of one should be an obvious issue whereas the renegotiation of the other is never mentioned. The Soviet-Finnish treaty ended a war, it is true, in which Finland had joined in an attack on the Soviet Union. But the Soviet Union had attacked Finland and taken territory from her only fifteen months earlier, whereas Panama owes its existence as a nation independent of Colombia to Theodore Roosevelt's intervention.

It can be said, of course, that little Finland is anxious not to make an issue out of the return of Petsamo (although without this port Finland has no access to the Arctic Sea), because she would rather live in peace with Russia and because she has not the faintest hope of ever getting Petsamo back anyway. But this is precisely the point. The Finns know that Soviet negotiators would not permit them to make an issue out of Petsamo;[8] the

---

[8] Actually the Russians did relent on other issues. For example, in 1962 the Finns succeeded in getting permission to lease the Saimaa Canal, which they had lost in the peace treaty with Russia.

Panamanians know that it is quite profitable to make an issue out of their treaty with the United States.

The tendency to let the opponent determine the issue shows itself not only in the selection of subjects for negotiation but also in the terminology adopted and the concepts used. This may be a more serious consequence, for it can affect the thinking of negotiators without their being aware of it.

An interesting illustration is the development of the concept "colonialism." Western negotiators talk and think of "decolonization" only in reference to areas in Africa, Asia, or Latin America that have been colonized by a Western country. When referring to Eastern Europe, on the other hand, they talk in terms of "stabilization," or at best "liberalization," and it is a rather rare occasion when they bring up the very recent colonization of Tibet or the nineteenth-century colonization by Russia of vast areas in Central Asia. Western diplomats maintain that it would be futile to make an issue out of Tibet or Uzbekistan or to compare the desirability of self-determination for Angola with that for East Germany. The Western effort to win the support and friendship of Afro-Asian nations, it is argued, would not be helped by raising such issues, because the Afro-Asians do not wish to become involved in the East-West "cold war" but are only interested in those manifestations of colonialism that are part of their own experience.

Western negotiators who think this way seem to forget that whether or not a subject seems relevant to one's own experience depends on how it is presented. When the U.S. government consented in December, 1962, to the removal of the Hungarian question from the UN agenda and to having the position of a UN Representative on Hungary abolished, it merely intended to abandon what seemed like a useless irritant against the Soviet Union. But unintentionally, it confirmed the view of the Afro-Asian nations that colonialism in Hungary had nothing to do with the colonialism they were fighting.

Mental associations are formed by repetition. If the West consents to the removal of the Hungarian question from the UN agenda (which has a long and growing list of other colonial issues) and almost never raises such issues as the fate of the Asian Muslims in Soviet Uzbekistan, it teaches the Afro-Asians to associate "colonialism" only with those issues in which it is the accused party.

Shy About Counter-Demands

Western negotiators assume that it would be clearly improper not to be flexible. It is widely felt in the West that concessions ought to be reciprocated and that compromise is the ideal way of reaching agreement. At the same time, Western governments (except France under De Gaulle) are reluctant to refuse negotiation if confronted with a redistribution demand. However, if one engages in redistribution negotiations while observing the rule of flexibility, there is only one way of avoiding a net loss: to make counter-demands. But this, Western negotiators are reluctant to do.

Counter-demands are requests for a redistribution in one's favor, either on an issue related to the one raised by the opponent or possibly on a quite unrelated issue. They are essential, not only to permit oneself to be flexible without incurring a net loss, but also to protect oneself against mediators who simply split the difference between the opposing proposals—as most mediators are wont to do. How, for example, would U Thant have mediated the Berlin negotiations? "There are various other issues like Berlin," he said on December 2, 1962, "on which it may become imperative to reach solutions on the basis of compromise and the principle of give-and-take on both sides."

On those rare occasions when Western negotiators do confront the opponent with a counter-demand, they tend to convey a lack of conviction— almost as if they acted with a bad conscience. They do not push the counter-demand with the same vigor that the opponent puts behind his initial demand, nor do they repeat it anywhere nearly as often.

For example, after the Soviet demands against West Berlin in November, 1958, the Western allies, in their notes of December 31, 1958, hinted at a counter-demand for the areas now in East Germany which were evacuated by the Western troops:

> The Soviet Union has directly and through its [East German] puppet regime...consolidated its hold over the large areas which the Western Alliance relinquished to it. It now demands that the Western Alliance should relinquish the positions in Berlin which in effect were the *quid pro quo*. The three Western Powers are there as occupying powers, and they are not prepared to relinquish the rights..., just as they assume the Soviet Union is not willing now to restore to the occupancy of the Western Powers the position which they had won in Mecklenburg, Saxony, Thuringia, and Anhalt and which, under the agreements, of 1944 and 1945, they turned over for occupation by the Soviet Union.[9]

But little has been heard of this potential counter-demand since.

Similarly, after the Berlin wall went up, the Western allies occasionally suggested that freedom of circulation should be restored in all Berlin in accordance with the Four-Power Agreements. But this has remained a wish rather than a demand, and even the wish was quickly suppressed when it met with the expected Soviet rebuff.

The reluctance to make counter-demands is not confined to East-West negotiations. The United States made no counter-demands, for example, in the negotiations with Panama after the riots in the Canal Zone in January, 1964. It is true that the incident touching off these riots can be blamed on the American side (the refusal of American students to observe the U.S.-Panamanian agreement on flags). But afterwards, mobs from Panama attacked the Canal Zone, and sniper fire from *outside* the Zone caused casualties among U.S. forces. As President Johnson pointed out, the

---

9 U.S. note to the Soviet Union of Dec. 31, 1958. *Department of State Bulletin* (Jan. 19, 1959), p. 79.

role of the U.S. forces "was one of resisting aggression, and not committing it."[10]

Resisting aggression? The negotiations were opened with Panamanian charges of U.S. aggression, and the United States made no demands of its own. One wonders whether American interests might not have been better protected, and the negotiations actually facilitated, had the U.S. government immediately come forth with a series of counter-demands. For example, Washington might have requested that Panama take steps to prevent a recurrence of mob attacks on the Canal Zone; it might have raised the question of compensation for the property destroyed; and it might have hinted that the violence by Panamanian mobs made it inadvisable to offer further concessions, inasmuch as the flag incident would not have occurred had the United States refused to accept Panamanian flags in the Zone a number of years ago. In short, Washington could have assumed the posture of the aggrieved party instead of meekly accepting the role of the accused. By abstaining from any counter-demands, the U.S. government might actually have done a disservice to the Panamanian government, because for domestic reasons the Panamanian government needed to win concessions from the United States, and counter-demands would have allowed Washington to concede more.

Western negotiators give various justifications for not raising counter-demands or for abandoning them so meekly. Counter-demands, it is said, would widen the area of conflict. This is of course true when they are first raised. Indeed, it is the purpose of counter-demands to prevent the area of conflict from lying entirely on one's own side of the fence. But later, counter-demands may facilitate agreement by putting some pressure on the opponent and permitting greater flexibility in one's own position.

Another justification for avoiding counter-demands, which is used primarily in the United States, is that Congress and the public would object if the counter-demand were later dropped in exchange for the withdrawal of the opponent's original demand. This justification is weak for three reasons. First, effective negotiation requires a willingness to become committed and to occasionally absorb the cost of breaking one's commitment. Second, the objections to dropping counter-demands can often be avoided by identifying one's counter-demands as such. Where this is feasible, the public will accept, if not urge, that they be dropped as soon as the opponent withdraws his original demand. Third, there is something disingenuous in arguing that Congress or the public would not accept the withdrawal of counter-demands. Unless the negotiator also refuses to be flexible, he is in fact implying that a concession on a counter-demand would be noticed, whereas a concession at the expense of the status quo could be concealed.

As a result of their shyness about counter-demands, Western negotiators frequently miss opportunities for making tie-ins. (Unlike the counter-demand in redistribution negotiations, which wards off the opponent's demand, the counter-demand in a tie-in is used to gain some objective by

[10] President Johnson's statement of Jan. 23, 1964.

making the fulfillment of a demand by the opponent conditional on the fulfillment of one's own demand.)

In the postwar negotiations with the Soviet Union on European problems, the Western powers were anxious to work out a treaty for re-establishing Austria's independence. In 1946 the Western powers and the Soviet Union negotiated the peace treaties with Bulgaria, Romania, Hungary, and Italy, about which the Russians were just as anxious. The Soviet Union wished to conclude peace treaties with the three Balkan states in order to solidify and formalize Communist control, and it wanted a peace treaty with Italy in order to obtain Italian reparations.

While these peace treaties were being negotiated, Secretary Byrnes tried in vain to bring up the Austrian treaty. At the first session of the Council of Foreign Ministers meeting in April, 1946, Byrnes asked that the Austrian question be included on the agenda, but Molotov immediately objected, saying he was not ready to give it consideration at this time. Byrnes tried again in April and at the next session of the Council of Foreign Ministers in June. At this latter session, Molotov contended that it was inadvisable to consider the Austrian treaty because the parties would have their hands full with the treaties under consideration. As Secretary Byrnes recalled in his memoirs, Molotov exclaimed: "May God help us to complete the work on the treaties which are now before us." And then Byrnes continued in his memoirs: "Since it was clear that Mr. Molotov was lending little assistance, I could only reply that I hoped, indeed, that God would do so."[11]

But this was not the only reply Byrnes could have given. He could have firmly refused to discuss any other treaties unless the Austrian treaty were included. Since the Soviet Union still had considerable interest in these other treaties, the tie-in might have worked.

A more recent example of neglecting a tie-in is provided by the British negotiations with Egypt in 1954, concerning the Egyptian demand for the withdrawal of British troops from the Suez Canal area ahead of the time specified in the Anglo-Egyptian treaty. Surely, the British negotiators must have thought about the possibility that Egypt might want to nationalize the Canal. Yet, they did not attempt to tie guaranties against nationalization to the withdrawal of their troops. They were of course under American pressure to give in to the Egyptian demand, and even if they had obtained an Egyptian promise against nationalization, it might later have been broken. Nonetheless, by tying in their counter-demand at that time, they might have accomplished one of two things. With an Egyptian promise against nationalization, British intervention against a breach of this promise would have been easier to justify at home and harder to oppose by the United States (and Egypt, knowing this, might well have kept the promise). If, on the other hand, Egypt had refused to give such a promise, the British-Egyptian conflict would have come to a head at a time far more favorable to Britain: there would have been no need to attempt a landing of troops in the Suez Canal Zone, for the troops were still there.

---

11 *Speaking Frankly*, p. 164.

Afraid of Making Unacceptable Proposals

Related to the shyness about counter-demands is the aversion of Western negotiators to push proposals that they consider unacceptable to the opponent. This aversion applies to major poisitions only, not to proposals on some details within a larger position. On details, Western diplomats of course frequently make demands which they expect to be unacceptable—only in order to have room for concessions when seeking a compromise.

As noted before, Communist negotiators are more willing to exert themselves for unattainable goals. Or perhaps they are more aware of the fact that what the opponent will ultimately accept is in part a function of what is being proposed to him. Sometimes they even admit that they do not expect their proposals to be accepted. Khrushchev once wrote to Macmillan: "In sending this message [suggesting a German peace treaty and withdrawal of foreign forces], I ask myself the question, what will be your reaction? Will you accept our proposals? I will tell you frankly, I have no belief in this because I do not believe in the wisdom of those circles which now determine the policy of the Western powers. It seems that the time is not yet ripe. . . ."[12]

Various reasons may account for the aversion of Western diplomats to unacceptable proposals. They may feel that it would look foolhardy to advance such proposals. They may fear they would needlessly antagonize the opponent. Or they may think that they could be accused of not negotiating "in good faith."

The notion that one should not push unacceptable proposals has for Westerners almost the quality of a moral rule, even where this "moral" way of negotiating comes in conflict with the morality of one's negotiating position. Paradoxically, this rule—far from facilitating negotiation—may sometimes destroy the possibility for negotiating at all. On certain issues, Western diplomats prefer to avoid negotiation altogether because they would either have to push unacceptable proposals or take the initiative in proposing an outcome that would be inferior to no-agreement.

What these Western negotiators overlook is that by refusing to press a certain proposal because it seems unacceptable, they may actually make it so or at least maintain it so. They strengthen the opponent's commitment by conveying to him that he is not expected to yield. And they forgo pressures that might erode the opponent's evaluations.

Western diplomats could learn a lesson from their colleagues in the new African states. There are several similarities between the posture of the new African states with regard to their grievances about the Union of South Africa and the posture of the Western powers with regard to their grievances about Eastern Europe. The goals that the Africans favor—abolishing apartheid and wresting Southwest Africa's independence from the Union of South Africa—are now totally unacceptable to the government of South Africa. Likewise, the goals that the Western powers favor in Eastern Europe are now totally unacceptable to Moscow: self-determination in the Soviet Zone

---

12 Letter to Macmillan of April 12, 1962.

of Germany and independence in Eastern Europe such that, say, the Hungarians could choose neutrality as they tried to in 1956. The African states have nowhere near the military and economic powers needed to force the government of South Africa to give in. In the same way, the local populations in East and Central Europe do not have the power to force Moscow to give in (as demonstrated on June 17, 1953, and in October, 1956). If South Africa were to be defeated by a full-scale Soviet intervention, this might bring an East-West war into the heart of Africa. And if the West attempted a full-scale military intervention against Soviet control in Eastern Europe, this, correspondingly, would probably lead to an East-West war in the heart of Europe that might well become nuclear.

The difference between the African negotiators and the Western ones is that the Africans keep pushing day after day their proposals for abolishing apartheid or detaching Southwest Africa from the Union, whereas Western negotiators act in the belief that self-determination for the Soviet Zone of Germany or full independence for Budapest is out of their reach, if not out of the question. The Africans feel confident that the trend of history is in their favor, regardless of the present imbalance in power. The Western powers either do not look for a favorable trend (they settle for "stabilization"), or they hope for internal "liberalization" (a trend which would permit them to continue their passive role). Thus they forget that historical trends are shaped by the expectations of men and that these expectations can be shaped, in part, by pushing unacceptable proposals.

But what about the objection that unacceptable proposals will make a favorable outcome even less likely by provoking the opponent and exacerbating his feelings of hostility? There is, of course, no pat answer to this familiar risk. The choice between modesty and aggressiveness depends on the merits of the issue and on the prospects for changing the opponent's attitudes. It is not a foregone conclusion that relations with the opponent will become more difficult if he is being confronted with unacceptable proposals. Westerners often wish that the Soviet Union were more of a "status quo power"—that is, interested in preserving only its present influence and possessions, not in adding to them. Is it not possible to stimulate such an interest more by challenging the Soviet stake in the status quo than by guaranteeing it?

Denying Oneself Available Threats

From April, 1939, until the announcement of the Hitler-Stalin pact on August 21 of that year, the British and the French tried to negotiate an agreement with Russia against the likelihood of German aggression. This was not an easy assignment, since the Poles, Romanians, and Baltic states— the potential victims of Hitler's next move—were adamantly opposed to automatic Soviet assistance, fearing (not unreasonably as shown by later events) that once Soviet armies entered their countries to fight the Germans, they might never leave.

According to a Foreign Office memorandum of May 22, 1939, the British in their own right were not sanguine about negotiating with Moscow: "Even though we may not be able to count implicitly on the Soviet Government either honestly wishing to fulfill, or being capable of fulfilling, their treaty obligations, nevertheless, the alternative of a Soviet Union completely untrammelled and exposed continually to the temptation of intriguing with both sides. . .might present a no less, perhaps more, dangerous situation than that produced by collaborating with a dishonest or an incompetent partner."

Nor did the British have much confidence in the strength of their negotiating position. On July 20, 1939, William Strang, the British emissary in Moscow, reported to London:

> Our need for an agreement is more immediate than theirs. Unlike them we have assumed obligations which we may be obliged to fulfill any day; and some of the obligations we have undertaken are of benefit to the Soviet Union since they protect a good part of their Western frontier. Having committed ourselves to these obligations, we have no other policy open to us than that of building up the Peace Front. The Russians have, in the last resort, at least two alternative policies, namely, the policy of isolation, and the policy of accommodation with Germany.[13]

By assuming that they had "no other policy open" to them, the British denied themselves the capacity to threaten. Scarcely nine months before, the same British government and the French had signed an agreement with Hitler at Munich, in violation of their commitment to Czechoslovakia and excluding the Soviet Union, permitting the Germans to expand eastward while keeping peace in the west. If the Soviets were as suspicious as Strang reported they were in his dispatch from Moscow, it should have been easy for the British to make the Soviets suspect that unless they showed more interest in reaching agreement on the Peace Front, there might be another Munich which would bring the German army up to the Soviet border. The British seem to have forgotten that a threat has to be credible only to the opponent; it does not have to be agreeable to oneself or satisfy all one's commitments. Who can say whether hints of such a threat would not have led to an Anglo-French-Soviet agreement before Stalin signed the pact with Hitler? The puzzling thing is that the British never even considered whether or not they should make use of it.

Western negotiators have no particular difficulty in using threats that are merely an extension of warnings (i.e., when the threatened action is an addition only to the action that would be taken anyhow in one's self-interest if the opponent failed to comply). Such threats Western negotiators often use to good effects, and, in contrast to Khrushchev's negotiating style, they wisely prefer to leave them implicit, where feasible, instead of making explicit threats.

On those occasions, however, when the Western negotiator could make an

<hr>

[13] E. L. Woodward and R. Butler, eds., *Documents on British Foreign Policy 1919–1939* (Third Series), V, 646; VI, 422.

effective threat only by envisaging a radical departure from his basic policy, he often denies himself the capacity to threaten, even though these occasions are frequently decisive junctures in important negotiations. Of course, if you are pursuing certain aims through negotiation, it is not an inviting prospect to contemplate a complete reversal of your policies in conflict with your present aims—merely for the purpose of hurting your opponent. But your opponent may not know how attached you are to your present policies and how unlikely such a reversal is. Just because you do not wish to switch to the opposite policy does not mean that you should guarantee to your opponent that you will not do so.

Such self-denial is desirable only in dealing with close allies or trustworthy friendly nations, when it is more important to maintain the opponent's long-term confidence than to exert pressures by threatening a reversal of one's joint policies or a reversal even of the alliance itself. Where this long-term confidence is lacking, nothing is lost by letting your opponent fear that you might do an about-face unless he becomes more accommodating. In 1942, to cite a previous example, Churchill was won over to Eden's idea that Stalin should be granted territorial gains in Eastern Europe in exchange for a pact with Great Britain. Churchill changed his mind not because he felt confident about Stalin's long-term policies but for precisely the opposite reason: he feared Stalin might make another deal with Hitler.

American negotiators have deprived themselves of threats on a number of occasions because they did not want to envisage reversing a basic policy. In the Far East as in Europe, the United States has adhered to the policy of leaving the Communists certain sanctuaries—areas where it will not interfere—to avoid a direct great-power conflict, to reduce the risks of expanding hostilities, and occasionally to preserve Western sanctuaries as a *quid pro quo*. Much as this may have been a wise policy, it was foolish to guarantee to the opponent in every instance that this policy would not be reversed.

The Korean armistice negotiations might have ended faster or on terms more favorable to the West had Peking been left in greater doubt whether or not the Chinese mainland (then exceedingly vulnerable) might be attacked from the air or the sea. At least the threat should have been kept alive that the United Nations forces would try to regain part of North Korea. On February 3, 1951, months before the armistice talks had even started, the State Department declared (according to the *New York Times*) "that the restoration of peace in Korea would not be helped by 'speculation' about whether U.N. forces would or would not cross the 38th Parallel if they reached it in a new offensive." The restoration of peace might indeed have been helped if just such speculation had been encouraged very loudly in Washington!

Again, in the negotiations for the neutralization of Laos in 1961, the Americans would have been in a stronger bargaining position if they had not deprived themselves so much of their capacity to threaten. When the American negotiators set out to attend the Laos Conference, Washington could simply have expressed mild interest in neutralization. Instead, the

United States gave obvious signs that it would pursue nothing but neutralization and make no more attempts, for instance, to include Laos in a
Western alliance. Nor were the Communists given much reason to fear an
expansion of hostilities into their sanctuary in North Vietnam.

The Russians, by contrast, do not give the United States the comfort of
curtailing their capacity to threaten. One reason why the United States is
cautious in asserting itself in Panama or in helping anti-Communist forces
in Cuba is the fear that the Russians might intervene, either by supporting
local opposition or with action elsewhere. Khrushchev likes to encourage
speculation about Soviet intervention rather than to snuff it out. Even
after his retreat in the 1962 Cuba crisis, he promised to intervene in Cuba
if the United States ever acted against Castro.

But when asserting themselves on Eastern Europe, the Russians have no
American threats to worry about. In October, 1956, while the Kremlin
leaders formulated plans to crush the Hungarian Revolution, they might at
first have been somewhat worried that the West would help the Hungarians.
Then, as the West continued no negotiate only for propaganda effects in
the United Nations, this risk must have looked increasingly smaller. And, as
if to assure everyone that the United States all along had been negotiating
merely for side-effects, President Eisenhower guaranteed to the Russians
that as long as they maintained superior local force, their sanctuary in
Eastern Europe was under no threat from the West, either at that time or
on any similar occasion in the future. "Nothing, of course, has so disturbed
the American people as the events in Hungary," he remarked in his press
conference on November 14, 1956. "Our hearts have gone out to them, and
we have done everything it is possible to, in the way of alleviating suffering.
But I must make one thing clear: the United States doesn't now—and never
has—advocate open rebellion by an undefended populace against force
over which they could not possibly prevail."

Robert Murphy's account of the atmosphere in the U.S. State Department during the Hungarian Revolution is much to the point. There were
"fears of terrible reprisals" by the Soviet army against the Hungarians, but
no thought seems to have been given as to how the United States might
instill some fears into the Soviet leaders when they debated whether to order
military intervention. There was much concern that "the Russians were
trying to blame Americans for the human slaughter" [*sic!*]—this concern, in
fact, prompted the Eisenhower statement just quoted—but little concern that
the United States migh be blamed for having lost all interest in the liberation of Eastern Europe. The idea of flying supplies to the Hungarians was
conveniently dismissed by the argument that Austria opposed any overflights,
but how many planes would Austria have shot down? And the suggestion
of *threatening* American intervention was equated with the *certainty* of
war. Although it is obvious that "the American people did not desire to go
to war against the Soviet Union," would the Russian leaders have desired
to go to war against the United States if offered a more attractive compromise settlement? During the Cuban missile crisis in 1962, President
Kennedy could also have argued that the American people did not "desire"

to go to war against Russia and confined himself to negotiating for ephemeral side-effects in the United Nations.[14]

We can detect some underlying characteristics that the weaknesses of Western negotiators have in common. There is a somewhat passive attitude toward conflict, a tendency to avoid conflict rather than to win it and a readiness to quit while gains might still be made. Where the West has to negotiate from weakness, it often lacks the self-confidence and boldness to push for success; where it can negotiate from strength, it is frequently too squeamish to exploit its advantages. More fundamental, however, is the tendency to overlook the fact that negotiation changes evaluations. He who mistakes his eroding evaluations for the trend of history can be made to believe that slowing down his retreat is a gain, that preventing further enemy advances must be the limit of his ambitions, and that trying to recover what has been lost would be utter recklessness.

THE COMPLEAT NEGOTIATOR

The compleat negotiator, according to seventeenth- and eighteenth-century manuals on diplomacy, should have a quick mind but unlimited patience, know how to dissemble without being a liar, inspire trust without trusting others, be modest but assertive, charm others without succumbing to their charm, and possess plenty of money and a beautiful wife while remaining indifferent to all temptations of riches and women.

It is easy to add to this garland of virtures, but difficult in the real world to judge a good negotiator from a bad one. One cannot evaluate a negotiator merely by asking how close he came to realizing the aims of his government; for if he came close, he may owe his success to modest aims or favorable conditions rather than to his skill. Nor can one be sure that he has done well just because his gains and losses compare favorably with those of the opponent; for it is an essential task of negotiators to change the evaluation of gains and losses.

Frequently one judges a negotiator by comparing the results he obtained with results he might have obtained had he acted differently. In doing so, however, one should distinguish between errors in negotiation, on the one hand, and errors in prediction and foreign-policy planning, on the other. Furthermore, one has to allow for domestic constraints which limit the alternatives that the negotiator could have chosen. Even though a skillful negotiator will guide and strengthen his domestic support, he cannot escape these constraints completely.

[14] Robert Murphy, *Diplomat among Warriors* (Garden City, N.Y.: Doubleday & Co., 1964), pp. 428–32. Murphy's pages merely reflect State Department thinking during those days. Had Murphy been in charge of the Hungarian crisis, he might have acted differently. His memoirs suggest that he did not usually share the Western weakness of denying oneself available threats (e.g., his recommendation to challenge the 1948 Berlin blockade on the ground, pp. 316–17).

On occasion, the outcome of an international conference seems predetermined by the balance of military strength, by economic factors, or by other forces beyond the negotiator's control. For example, George Kennan argued that the establishment of Soviet military power in Eastern Europe and the entry of Soviet forces into Manchuria did not result from the wartime conferences of Moscow, Teheran, and Yalta, but from the military operations during the concluding phases of the war when the Western democracies were not in a position to enter these areas first.[15] One can surely agree with Kennan that only a limited range of alternatives was open at these conferences. But one should question how narrow this range actually was and whether the negotiators did not take for granted bounds that they drew themselves.

Imagine, for instance, a reverse of the situation in Iran and in Korea— that Iran was the country divided into a Communist North and a pro-Western South but that Korea was unified under a government friendly to the West. If this were the situation today, we would probably feel that the Western democracies could have done nothing to prevent the Russians from staying in Northern Iran (an area they occupied first, after all!) but that in Korea the West had a better chance to keep the country unified and friendly (obviously! Russia having entered the war against Japan so late and Korea being more accessible to American military strength than Iran).

Many of the clichés about the perfect negotiator might be revised rather than discarded. A good negotiator should be *realistic,* yes, but not in the sense of accepting an outcome as being determined by the balance of forces without trying to re-interpret this "balance" in his favor. Instead of taking a situation for granted, he should be realistic in recognizing that his opponent's evaluations as well as his own are constantly adrift, that issues are not created by Nature but by himself and by his opponent, and that there are ways of negotiating from weakness as well as from strength.

A good negotiator should also be *flexible*—not by being without a firm position but by utilizing both firm and flexible proposals. He should be flexible in his tactics by discriminating between occasions when it pays to adhere to rules of accommodation and when it does not. He must distinguish situations where it would be disastrous to make a threat, from others where it is essential to threaten or even to bluff. He must know when to humor the personal quirks of his opponent and when to ignore them. He must be willing to disregard propaganda losses at one time and to negotiate merely for propaganda at another time. He must be prepared to follow domestic opinion at home as well as to encourage a new consensus both in his government and in his country.

And a good negotiator should be *patient*—though not primarily in order to sit in Geneva for months at a time hearing the opponent repeat speeches

---

[15] George F. Kennan, *American Diplomacy, 1900–1950* (Chicago: University of Chicago Press, 1951), p. 85. Regarding Europe, Kennan conceded that "the postwar line of division between East and West might have lain somewhat farther east than it does today, and that would certainly be a relief to everyone concerned" (*ibid,* p. 87).

and repeating his own. He should be patient in working for seemingly lost causes, because by doing so he may slowly change the opponent's views and objectives. He should be patient to live with conflict and uncertainty and know that he may have succeeded even if (or precisely because) his negotiations failed. Above all, he must maintain the will to win.

CHAPTER THREE

COALITION DIPLOMACY
IN A NUCLEAR AGE

Henry A. Kissinger

Harvard University

The advent of nuclear weapons has placed new demands on the theory and practice of coalition diplomacy. The calculation of national interests has become a more complex process as risks and costs are perceived in a different relationship. Periodic shifts in strategic doctrine reflect not only changing technical capabilities but also varying psychological and historical attitudes among alliance partners. Henry A. Kissinger's argument for strengthened consultation within the Atlantic alliance rests on an awareness of the desirability of flexible procedures. Kissinger's proposals suggest ways in which diplomacy can ease if not eradicate intra-alliance tensions. His call for a high level political body to coordinate foreign policy objectives and military needs is especially timely in the aftermath of French disaffection with NATO's organization and command structure.

Reprinted from *Foreign Affairs* (July 1964), pp. 525–45. By permission.

For several years now disputes have rent the Atlantic Alliance. They have focused on such issues as nuclear strategy and control, the organization of Europe and the nature of an Atlantic Community. However, the most fundamental issue in Atlantic relationships is raised by two questions not unlike those which each Western society has had to deal with in its domestic affairs: How much unity do we want? How much pluralism can we stand? Too formalistic a conception of unity risks destroying the political will of the members of the Community. Too absolute an insistence on national particularity must lead to a fragmentation of the common effort.

One does not have to agree with the methods or policies of President de Gaulle to recognize that he has posed an important question which the West has yet to answer. There is merit in his contention that before a political unit can mean something to others, it must first mean something to itself. Though de Gaulle has often acted as if he achieved identity by opposing our purposes, our definition of unity has occasionally carried overtones of tutelage.

There is no question that the abrupt tactics of the French President have severely strained the pattern of allied relationships which emerged after the war. But no one man could have disrupted the Alliance by himself. Fundamental changes have been taking place in the nature of alliances, in the character of strategy and in the relative weights of Europe and the United States. A new conception of allied relationships would have been necessary no matter who governed in Paris or in Washington. The impact of particular statesmen aside, a farsighted policy will gear itself to dealing with these underlying forces. It will inquire into the degree to which objectives are common and where they diverge. It will face frankly the fact that different national perspectives—and not necessarily ignorance —can produce differing strategic views. It will examine the scope and limits of consultation. If this is done in a new spirit on both sides of the Atlantic, a more vital relationship can take the place of the previous U.S. hegemony.

II. THE CHANGE IN THE NATURE
OF ALLIANCES

Since the end of World War II an important change has taken place in the nature of alliances. In the past, alliances have been created for three basic reasons: 1) To provide an accretion of power. According to the doctrine of collective security, the wider the alliance, the greater its power to resist aggression. 2) To leave no doubt about the alignment of

45

forces. It has often been argued that had Germany known at the beginning of both World Wars that the United States—or even England—would join the Allies, war would have been averted. 3) To provide an incentive for mutual assistance beyond that already supplied by an estimate of the national interest.

To be sure, even before the advent of nuclear weapons, there was some inconsistency among these requirements. The attempt to combine the maximum number of states for joint action occasionally conflicted with the desire to leave no doubt about the collective motivation. The wider the system of collective security, the more various were the motives animating it and the more difficult the task of obtaining common action proved to be. The more embracing the alliance, the more intense and direct must be the threat which would produce joint action.

This traditional difficulty has been compounded in the nuclear age. The requirements for tight command and control of nuclear weapons are to some degree inconsistent with a coalition of sovereign states. The enormous risks of nuclear warfare affect the credibility of traditional pledges of mutual assistance.

As a result, most of the theories of nuclear control now current within the Western Alliance have a tendency either to turn NATO into a unilateral U.S. guarantee or to call into question the utility of the Alliance altogether. American strategic thought verges on the first extreme; some French theorists have hinted at the second.

As for the United States, official spokesmen have consistently emphasized that the European contribution to the overall nuclear strength of the Alliance is negligible. European nuclear forces have been described as "provocative," "prone to obsolescence," and "weak." For a considerable period after the advent of the Kennedy Administration, some high officials held the view that on nuclear matters the President might serve as the Executive Agent of the Alliance. Since then the United States has made various proposals for nuclear sharing, the common feature of which has been the retention of our veto over the nuclear weapons of the Alliance.

However sensible such schemes may appear from the point of view of the division of labor, they all would perpetuate our hegemony in nuclear matters within the Alliance. Allies are considered necessary not so much to add to overall strength as to provide the possibility for applying power discriminately. In these terms, it is not surprising that some allies have considered their conventional contribution as actually weakening the overall strength by raising doubts about the *nuclear* commitment of the United States.

According to the contrary view, alliances have lost their significance altogether. The French theorist, General Gallois, has argued, for example, that nuclear weapons have made alliances obsolete. Faced with the risk of total destruction, no nation will jeopardize its survival for another. Hence, he maintains, each country must have its own nuclear arsenal to defend itself against direct attack, while leaving all other countries to their fate.

This formula would mark the end of collective security and would be likely to lead to international chaos. Under conditions of growing nuclear power on both sides, it would be idle to deny that the threat of nuclear retaliation has lost some of its credibility. The Gallois theory would, however, transform a degree of uncertainty into a guarantee that the United States would *not* come to the assistance of its allies, thus greatly simplifying the aggressor's calculation. Moreover, in order to protect itself in this new situation, each country would need to develop not only a nuclear arsenal of its own but also foolproof procedures for assuring the Soviets that a given nuclear blow did not originate from its territory. If Gallois is right, and each country is unwilling to risk nuclear devastation for an ally, it will also want to prevent itself from being triggered into nuclear war by a neighbor. Thus each country will have a high incentive to devise methods to protect itself from a counterattack based on a misapprehension. The Gallois theory would lead to a multiplication of national nuclear forces side-by-side with the development of methods of surrender or guarantees of non-involvement.

When views such as these carry influence on both sides of the Atlantic, it is no accident that much of the debate on nuclear matters within NATO turns on the question of confidence. We tend to ask those of our allies possessing nuclear arsenals of their own: If you trust us, why do you require nuclear weapons? Our nuclear allies reply: If you trust us, why are you concerned about our possession of nuclear weapons? Since the answer must inevitably emphasize contingencies where either the goals or the strategy would be incompatible, the debate on nuclear control within NATO has been inherently divisive.

The concentration of nuclear power in the hands of one country poses one set of problems; the range of modern weapons raises another. In the past, a threatened country had the choice either of resisting or surrendering. If it resisted, it had to be prepared to accept the consequences in terms of physical damages or loss of life. A distant ally could be effective only if it was able to bring its strength to bear in the area of conflict.

Modern weapons have changed this. What each member country wants from the Alliance is the assurance that an attack on it will be considered a *casus belli*. It strives for deterrence by adding the strength of a distant ally to its own power. But, equally, each state has an incentive to reduce damage to itself to a minimum should deterrence fail. The range of modern weapons provides an opportunity in this respect for the first time. In 1914 Belgium could not base its defense on a strategy which transferred to Britain the primary risks of devastation. In the age of intercontinental rockets this technical possibility exists.

Part of the strategic dispute within the Alliance, therefore, involves jockeying to determine which geographic area will be the theater of war if deterrence fails (though this obviously cannot be made explicit). A conventional war confined to Europe may appear relatively tolerable to us. To Europeans, with their memory of conventional wars, this prospect is not particularly inviting. They may find a nuclear exchange which spares their territory a more attractive strategy and the threat of nuclear retaliation a more effective deterrent. The interests of the Alliance may be indivisible in an ultimate sense. But this does not guarantee the absence of sharp conflicts on methods to reach these objectives.

In short, the destructiveness and range of modern weapons have a tendency to produce both extreme nationalism and neutralism. A wise alliance policy must take care that in dealing with one of these dangers it does not produce the other.

The nature of alliances has changed in yet another way. In the past, one of the reasons for joining an alliance was to impose an additional obligation for assistance in time of need. Were each country's national interests completely unambiguous, it would know precisely on whom it could count; a formal commitment would be unnecessary. Both the aggressor and the defender would understand what they would confront and could act accordingly. Wars could not be caused by a misunderstanding of intentions. They would occur only if the protagonists calculated the existing power relationships differently.

Traditionally, however, the national interest has not been unambiguous. Often the aggressor did not know which countries would ultimately be lined up against it; Germany in 1914 was genuinely surprised by the British reaction to the invasion of Belgium. Occasionally the defenders could not be certain of the extent of their potential support—as was the case with the Allies in both wars regarding U.S. participation. Historically, the existence of an understanding on this point, tacit or explicit, has often been the determining factor in the decision to go to war. In the decade prior to World War I, the staff talks between Britain and France, which led to the transfer of the French fleet to the Mediterranean, were one of the key factors in Britain's decision to go to war in August 1914. (Thus the talks achieved one objective of traditional alliances: to commit Britain to the defense of France. They failed in another: to make the opposing alignment clear to the potential aggressor.)

One of the distinguishing features of the nuclear period is that the national interest of the major powers has become less ambiguous. In a bipolar world, a relative gain for one side represents an absolute weakening of the other. Neither of the major nuclear countries can permit a major advance by its opponent regardless of whether the area in which it occurs is formally protected by an alliance or not. Neutral India was no less assured of American assistance when the Chinese attacked than allied Pakistan would have been in similar circumstances. In these conditions, the distinction between allies and neutrals is likely to diminish. A country gains little from being allied and risks little by being neutral.

This inevitably results in the weakening of allied cohesion, producing what some have described as polycentrism. But polycentrism does not reflect so much the emergence of new centers of actual power as the attempt by allies to establish new centers of decision. Polycentrism is virulent not because the world has ceased to be bipolar, but because it essentially remains so. Far from doubting America's military commitment to Europe, President de Gaulle is so certain of it that he does not consider *political* independence a risk. He thus adds American power to his own in pursuit of his policies.

No matter how troublesome a major ally may be, it cannot be allowed to suffer defeat. France's policy is made possible by our nuclear umbrella— a fact which adds to the irony of the situation and the annoyance of some of our policy-makers. Our frequent insistence that in the nuclear age an isolated strategy is no longer possible misses the central point: for this precise reason allies have unprecedented scope for the pursuit of their own objectives. And the more the détente—real or imaginary—proceeds, the more momentum these tendencies will gather. We live in a curious world where neutrals enjoy most of the protection of allies and allies aspire to have the same freedom of action as do neutrals.

These conditions turn coalition diplomacy into an extraordinarily delicate undertaking. Appeals which were effective in the past either work no longer or turn counterproductive. Thus the warning that certain European actions might lead the United States to withdraw is bound to have consequences contrary to those intended. If believed at all, it demonstrates that there are at least *some* contingencies in which the United States might abandon its allies, thus magnifying pressures for European autonomy.

The scope for real Third Force policies is vastly overestimated. Realism forces close association between Europe and the United States whatever the vagaries of individual statesmen. But it has happened often enough in Western history that an underlying community of interests was submerged by subsidiary rivalries. Ancient Greece foundered on this discord. Western Europe nearly tore itself apart before it submerged its rivalries. And now the Atlantic area faces the challenge of how to combine common action with a respect for diverse approaches to the central problem.

III. THE ABSTRACTNESS AND NOVELTY OF
MODERN POWER

The destructiveness of modern weapons gives the strategic debate unprecedented urgency. The speed with which they can be delivered complicates the problem of command and control in a way unimaginable even a decade and a half ago. Doctrinal and technical disputes occur within each government. It is not surprising, then, that they should rend the Alliance as well.

The novelty of modern weapons systems gives the disputes a metaphysical, almost theological, cast. Never before in history has so much depended on weapons so new, so untested, so "abstract." No nuclear weapons have been exploded in wartime except on Japan, which did not possess means of retaliation. No one knows how governments or people will react to a nuclear explosion under conditions where both sides possess vast arsenals.

Moreover, modern weapons systems are relatively untested. During the debate in this country over the nuclear test-ban treaty, a great deal of attention was focused on the adequacy of our warheads. In fact, the other components of our weapons systems contain many more factors of uncertainty. The estimated "hardness" of Minuteman silos depends entirely on theoretical studies. Of the thousands of missiles in our arsenal, relatively few of each category have been thoroughly tested. There is little experience with salvo firing. Air-defense systems are designed without any definite knowledge of the nature of the offense. A high proportion of the phenomena discovered in nuclear testing have been "unexpected."

The situation is further complicated by the fact that the purpose of modern weapons is deterrence: to prevent—by a particular threat—a certain course of action. But deterrence is primarily a psychological problem. It depends on the aggressor's assessment of risks, not the defender's. A threat meant as a bluff but taken seriously is more useful for purposes of deterrence than a "genuine" threat interpreted as a bluff. Moreover, if deterrence is successful, aggression does *not* take place. But it is impossible to demonstrate why something has not occurred. It can never be proved whether peace has been maintained because NATO pursues an optimum strategy or a marginally effective one. Finally, the longer deterrence lasts the more color will be lent to the argument that perhaps the Communists never intended to attack in the first place. An effective NATO deterrent strategy may thus have the paradoxical consequence of strengthening the arguments of the quasi-neutralists.

Even if there is agreement about the correct weapons system, there may be disagreement about how it can best be coupled with diplomacy to produce deterrence. How does one threaten with solid-fuel missiles? As these are always in an extreme state of readiness, how then does one demonstrate an increase in preparedness such as historically served as a warning? From a technical point of view it is highly probable that missiles can perform most of the functions heretofore assigned to airplanes. The shift to missiles and the elimination of airplanes envisaged by the former Deputy Secretary of Defense Roswell Gilpatric[1] makes a great deal of sense technically. But has adequate attention been given to the kind of diplomacy which results—particularly in crisis situations—when the retaliatory threat depends on solid-fuel missiles in underground silos? During the Cuban missile crisis, dispersing SAC planes to civilian airports proved an effective warning. What will be an equivalent move when our strategic forces are composed entirely of missiles?

These questions do not permit clearcut answers. Yet they are at the heart of many of the disputes within NATO. The United States has held the view that deterrence was best achieved by posing a credible threat. And it has related credibility to whether the risks, if deterrence failed, were tolerable. The Europeans for a variety of reasons have generally been of a different opinion. They have maintained that deterrence depended on posing the most extreme risks. They have been prepared to sacrifice a measure of credibility in favor of enhancing the magnitude of the threat.

---

[1] "Our Defense Needs: The Long View," *Foreign Affairs* (April 1964).

This debate has been inconclusive because it ultimately depends on a psychological, not a technical, judgment.

The controversy originated in an attempt by the United States in 1961 to change the relative weight to be given to conventional and nuclear weapons in NATO doctrine. The method of effecting this change was not new—though it was urged with new insistence. NATO had been presented many times before with American blueprints and had seen its consultative role limited to discussing the technical implementation of an American conception. What gave the dispute its particular urgency was that the advent of a new, highly analytical American Administration coincided with the growing strength and self-confidence of Europe and the deliberate policy of President de Gaulle to assert a more independent role.

In the process, many of the issues that had been obscured in the previous decade by the curious, somewhat one-sided nature of the transatlantic dialogue came for the first time into sharper focus. This highlighted a difference in perspective between the American and the European conception of NATO which had existed since its beginning.

When the Korean War raised the spectre of Soviet military aggression, both sides of the Atlantic made a serious effort to turn NATO into a more effective military instrument. However, given the enormous disparity in military and economic strength between the United States and Europe, the primary concern of the European countries was to commit the United States to their defense. They saw in NATO above all a means to obtain American protection, by which was meant American nuclear protection.

However, the Europeans had too much experience with the tenuousness of formal commitments not to strive for more tangible guarantees. This led to pressures for the stationing of American troops in Europe. European reasoning was similar to that ascribed to a French marshal in 1912 when he was asked how many British troops he wanted for the outbreak of a European war. He is reported to have replied: "We need only one, who we will make sure is killed on the first day of the war." In the nuclear age, the price of a guarantee has risen to something like five divisions.

With so many American troops permanently stationed in Europe, it was only sensible to try to give them some meaningful military mission. Even during the period of the doctrine of massive retaliation, NATO forces were larger than the prevailing strategic concept seemed to demand. Indeed, the number was somewhat inconsistent with it. Despite our commitment to a retaliatory strategy, we constantly pressed for a European contribution of ground forces. The Europeans, though they agreed to a succession of NATO force goals, never really believed in the doctrines used to rationalize them. Rather they saw in their military contribution a form of fee paid for United States nuclear protection. The Europeans agreed to our requests. But they tried to see to it that their actual contributions would be large enough to induce us to keep a substantial military establishment in Europe, yet not so high as to provide a real alternative to nuclear retaliation. They were opposed to giving the conventional forces a central military mission; but they also resisted any hint of American withdrawal.

This ambivalence was brought into the open by the shift in United States strategic doctrine in 1961. The American attempt to strengthen the forces for local defense had the paradoxical consequence of bringing to the fore the issue of nuclear control which for many Europeans had always been the crux of the matter. For the first time, U.S. strategic views were publicly challenged, at first hesitantly, then even more explicitly. Europe had now gained sufficient strength and confidence so that the mere enunciation of an American policy no longer guaranteed its acceptance. The peremptory way in which the United States proceeded only sharpened the controversy. And France added fuel to the flames by giving European misgivings their most extreme formulation.

But if French policy has deliberately sharpened conflicts, the United States' tendency to turn an essentially psychological issue into a technical one has unintentionally exacerbated disagreements beyond their intrinsic significance. Our spokesmen often leave the impression that disagreement is due to the ignorance of our allies, and that it is destined to yield ultimately before extensive briefings and insistent reiteration. Faced with opposition, we are less given to asking whether there may be some merit in the arguments of our allies than to overwhelming them with floods of emissaries preaching the latest version of our doctrine.

But the real problem is not that the Europeans fail to understand our quest for multiple options. They simply reject it for themselves. When the issue is Asia or Latin America, Europeans favor an even more flexible response than we do; with respect to the defense of Europe, their attitude is more rigid. As long as the United States retains ultimate control over nuclear weapons, the European incentive is bound to be exactly the opposite of ours. Rather than permit a "pause" for "appreciating the wider risks involved," Europeans prefer to force us to make our response as automatic as possible.

This problem has little to do with whether the United States could afford to give up Europe. It is rooted in the nature of sovereignty and made acute by the destructiveness of nuclear weapons. Robert Bowie, one of the most eloquent spokesmen of the dominant school of U.S. thought, criticized British nuclear policy before the Assembly of the Western European Union as follows: "Britain has retained its national command structure and the right to withdraw them at its option. This means that they *certainly* could not be counted on by any of the others to be available in case of need."[2] [Italics supplied.] If this concern is real regarding British nuclear forces, which are, after all, assigned to NATO, it must be even stronger regarding U.S. strategic forces which remain under exclusive American control.

The problem can then be summed up as follows: Exclusive U.S. control of nuclear strategy is politically and psychologically incompatible with a strategy of multiple choices or flexible response. The European refusal

[2] Proceedings of Western European Union Assembly, Ninth Ordinary Session, December 3, 1963.

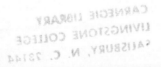

to assign a meaningful military mission to conventional forces in Europe is incompatible with the indefinite retention of large U.S. forces there. If the United States prizes a conventional response sufficiently, it will have to concede Europe autonomy in nuclear control. If the Europeans want to insist on an automatic nuclear response, a reconsideration of our conventional deployment on the Continent will become inevitable. Refusal to face these facts will guarantee a perpetuation of present disputes and increasing disarray within NATO.

The United States-European dialogue on strategy is confused further by the nature of the intra-European debate. Many of those who applaud our views do so for reasons which may not prove very comforting in the long run. We must be careful not to take every agreement with us at face value. Acquiescence in our opinion can have two meanings: It can represent either a sincere commitment to Atlantic partnership or disguise a neutralist wish to abdicate responsibility. For the American nuclear umbrella, now sometimes exploited by President de Gaulle for his own purposes, can also be used—and more dangerously for the West—to support policies amounting to neutralism. In many countries it is the leaders and groups traditionally most committed to national defense who have developed views on strategy which challenge American concepts; while some of those most ready to accept U.S. strategic hegemony have in the past been the least interested in making a serious defense effort. We may therefore have to choose between our theories of nuclear control and Atlantic cohesion, between the technical and the political sides of Atlantic policy.

IV. DIFFERENCES IN HISTORICAL PERSPECTIVE

Some of the strains in Atlantic relationships have resulted from factors outside anybody's control. Many reflect the growth in Europe of the very strength and self-confidence which American policy has striven to promote since the end of World War II. Others have been caused by the tactics of President de Gaulle, whose style of diplomacy is not really compatible with the requirements of coalition. We share the responsibility through too much insistence on technical solutions and too little allowance for the intangibles of political judgment and will.

But perhaps the deepest cause of transatlantic misunderstandings is a difference in historical perspective. Americans live in an environment uniquely suited to an engineering approach to policy-making. As a result, our society has been characterized by a conviction that any problem will yield if subjected to a sufficient dose of expertise. With such an approach, problems tend to appear as discrete issues without any inner relationship. It is thought that they can be solved "on their merits" as they arise. It is rarely understood that a "solution" to a problem may mortgage the future—especially as there is sufficient optimism to assume that even should this prove to be the case, it will still be possible to deal with the new problem when it materializes.

But Europeans live on a continent covered with ruins testifying to the fallibility of human foresight. In European history, the recognition of a problem has often defined a dilemma rather than pointed to an answer. The margin of survival of European countries has been more precarious than ours. European reasoning is likely to be more complicated and less confident than ours. This explains some of the strains in Atlantic relationships. Americans tend to be impatient with what seems to them Europe's almost morbid obsession with the past, while Europeans sometimes complain about a lack of sensitivity and compassion on the part of Americans.

In the fall of 1963, our newspapers were filled with derisory comments about French manœuvres then taking place. The scenario of these manœuvres supposed that an aggressor force was attacking France through Germany. France's allies had surrendered. As the aggressor's armies were approaching her borders, France resorted to her nuclear weapons. It is, of course, easy to ridicule this scenario by contrasting the small size of the French bomber force with the magnitude of the disaster envisaged. But the crucial issue is not technical. It arises from the fact that France has undergone shattering historical experiences with which Americans find it difficult to identify. The scenario of the French manœuvres recalled importantly— perhaps too rigidly—France's traumatic experience of 1940, when foreign armies attacked all along the Western front and France's allies collapsed. The British Fighter Command remained in England; the fact that this critical decision was wise does not affect the basic psychological point. Moreover, the French disaster came at the end of two decades in which France almost single-handedly shouldered the responsibility for the defense of Europe while her erstwhile allies withdrew into isolation or offered strictures about France's obsession with security. The nightmare that some day France might again stand alone goes far deeper than the obstinate ill will of a single individual.

A comparable problem exists in Germany. Washington has at times shown signs of impatience toward the German leaders and their constant need for reassurance. Secretary Rusk has been reported more than once to be restless with what he has called the "pledging sessions" which the Germans seem so often to demand. However, insecurity is endemic in the German situation. A divided country with frontiers that correspond to no historical experience, a society which has lived through two disastrous defeats and four domestic upheavals in 40 years, cannot know inward stability. The need to belong to something, to rescue some predictability out of chaos, is overwhelming. The memories of our allies should be factors as real in the discussions of our policy-makers as the analysis of weapons systems.

The importance of this difference in historical perspective is compounded by the continuing disparity in strength between the two sides of the Atlantic. While it has become fashionable to speak of Europe's newfound equality, it is important not to take it too literally. Europe *has* gained in strength over the past decade and a half. It can and should play an increasingly responsible role. But for the foreseeable future we are likely to be by far the stronger partner.

It is important to be clear about this because it requires us to show unusual tact and steadiness. Many of our allies have been guilty of unilateral actions far more flagrant than ours. But when we act unilaterally, disarray in the Alliance is almost inevitable. Drastic changes in U.S. strategic doctrine or action without adequate consultation—such as the removal of I.R.B.M.s from Italy and Turkey or the withdrawal of troops from Germany—create either a sense of European impotence or increase the pressure for more autonomy. Bilateral dealings with the Soviets, from which our allies are excluded, or about which they are informed only at the last moment, are bound to magnify Third Force tendencies. When our allies resist such U.S. policies and practices, it is not necessarily because they disagree with our view but because they are afraid of creating a precedent for unilateral changes in other policies. (Even statements of substantive disagreement may be a smokescreen for deeper concerns.) Moreover, many allied leaders who have staked their prestige on certain U.S. policies can suffer serious domestic consequences if we change them drastically.

Thus the voice of Europe reaches us in extremely distorted form. President de Gaulle sharpens all disputes and even creates them in pursuit of his policy of independence. But some other leaders do not give full expression to their disquiet because they do not want to undermine further the solidarity on which their security is thought to depend. Whereas France exaggerates her disagreements, some other countries obscure theirs. Thus the dialogue with Europe is often conducted on false issues, while real issues—like the future of Germany, or arms control, or the role of tactical nuclear weapons—are swept under the rug in order not to magnify the existing discord.

We, in turn, are faced with the problem that technology and political conditions are changing so rapidly that no policy can be maintained over an indefinite period of time. How to shape policies that are responsive to change while maintaining the confidence of our allies? The future vitality of the Western Alliance depends on understanding the possibilities and limits of the consultative process.

V. THE LIMITS AND PURPOSES OF CONSULTATION

The always difficult problem of coalition diplomacy is magnified by three factors:

1. The fact that the two superpowers are committed to the existing balance provides their European allies with wide scope for purely national actions.

2. The internal workings of modern government are so complex that

they create a variety of obstacles to meaningful consultation. Nations sometimes find it so difficult to achieve a domestic consensus that they are
reluctant to jeopardize it afterwards in international forums. The tendency
of the United States to confine consultation to elaborating its own blueprint
reflects less a quest for hegemony—as some of our European critics occasionally assert—than a desire to avoid complicating still further its own
decision-making process.

3. As governments have found in their domestic experience, access to the
same technical data does not guarantee unanimity of understanding. In an
alliance of states very unequal in size and strength, and with widely varying
histories, differences are almost inevitable. And they are likely to be made
all the more intractable by a technology of unprecedented destructiveness
and novelty.

Thus consultation is far from being a magic cure-all. It will not necessarily
remove real differences of geography, perspective, or interest. Nevertheless,
an improvement in the consultative process should be one of the chief
concerns of the Alliance.

The dominant American view has been that consultation would be most
effective if there were a division of labor within the Alliance according to
which the United States retained control over nuclear weapons while
Europe specialized in conventional forces. Similarly, it has been suggested
in Great Britain that the independent British nuclear deterrent could be
given up in return for a greater voice in American policy.[3] The proposed
NATO Multilateral Force on which the United States increasingly stakes
its prestige is basically a device to make its nuclear hegemony acceptable.[4]

In other words, the thrust of our policy is to create a structure which
makes it physically impossible for any of the allies (except the United
States) to act autonomously. This raises the following problems: a) How
effective will consultation based on such premises be? b) Is such a system
as useful for the long-term political vitality of the Alliance as it is for the
conduct of a general nuclear war?

With regard to the first of these, any process of consultation must be
responsive to the following three questions: Who has a right to be con-
sulted? Whose voice carries weight? Who has enough competence?

These three levels are not necessarily identical. Many agencies in our
own government have a right to express their views, but not all carry the
same weight. When some of Britain's Labor leaders suggest that they want
a greater voice in our decisions in return for giving up British nuclear
weapons, the answer has to be: Like whose voice? Like that of the Arms
Control and Disarmament Agency? Or the Joint Chiefs of Staff? Or the
State Department? Or the Commerce Department? In our interdepart-
mental disputes, clearly, the outcome often depends on the constituency

[3] See Patrick Gordon Walker, "The Labor Party's Defense and Foreign Policy,"
Foreign Affairs (April 1964), pp. 391–98.
[4] For the author's view on the NATO Multilateral Force, see "NATO's Nuclear
Dilemma," *The Reporter* (March 28, 1963).

which the agency or department represents. The weight given to advice is inevitably related to the competence that it reflects.

If the United States retains indefinitely an effective monopoly of nuclear power, we would probably find in time that Europe simply does not have sufficient technical competence for its views to carry weight. And this in turn is likely to breed irresponsibility on both sides of the Atlantic. A right of consultation without the ability to make a serious judgment may, in fact, be the worst possible system. Over a period of time it is bound to reduce Europe's voice in Washington; while in Europe it must produce a sense of impotence or extreme nationalism. Indeed, it may enable neutralists to focus all Europe's anti-nuclear sentiment against the United States. Some European autonomy on nuclear matters—preferably growing out of existing programs—seems therefore desirable.

The emphasis placed on a unitary strategic system for the Alliance has reversed the proper priorities. The real challenge to the consultative process is less in the field of strategy than in diplomacy. The ability to fight a centrally controlled general war is useful; but the ability to devise common policies in the face of a whole spectrum of eventualities is much more important.

If the Alliance cannot develop procedures for a common diplomacy—or at least an agreed range of divergence—it seems contradictory to insist on a system of unitary strategic control. When NATO has proved unable to develop even a common trade policy toward the Communist world, it is not surprising that countries are reluctant to entrust their survival to a NATO ally, however close. Policies on a whole range of issues such as Suez, the Congo, negotiating tactics over Berlin, or the defense of Southern Arabia have been unilateral or divergent. The United States is now in the curious situation of staking a great deal of its prestige on establishing the NATO Multilateral Force and a system of unitary strategic control while East-West negotiations on the war in Southeast Asia or arms control are dealt with more or less unilaterally.

In reassessing these priorities, it may be important to ask how unitary a system of control for strategy and diplomacy is in fact desirable. What kind of structure is more vital in the long run: An Atlantic system that automatically involves all partners? Or one that permits some autonomy? On many issues—particularly East-West relations—united action is essential. With respect to others, some degree of flexibility may be desirable. Over the next decades the United States is likely to find itself increasingly engaged in the Far East, in Southeast Asia, and in Latin America. Our European allies will probably not consider their vital interests at stake in these areas. President de Gaulle's views on this subject are far from unique in Europe, even if his methods are.

If the Atlantic system is absolutely centralized, policy may be reduced to the lowest common denominator. The Soviets may use our involvements elsewhere to blackmail Europe. This, combined with the lack of interest among Europeans in the issues involved, may strain the Alliance beyond the breaking point. On the other hand, if Europe is accorded some capacity for autonomous action—military and political—its concern would be no greater, but the temptation for Soviet adventures might be reduced. Put positively, a structure which permits a variety of coordinated approaches toward the new nations could enhance the vigor of our policies, the self-confidence of our allies, and the long-term vitality of the Alliance. Paradoxically, the unity of the Atlantic area may well be furthered by a structure which grants the possibility of autonomous action while reducing the desire for it.

VI. WHAT STRUCTURE FOR THE ATLANTIC AREA?

The most delicate problem faced by the United States in its Atlantic policy, then, is to promote cohesion without undermining the self-confidence and the political will of its allies. Formal structures can help in this effort. But when they become ends in themselves they may cause us to beg the key question by the very terms in which we state it.

Some of the current theories of Atlantic partnership run precisely this risk. According to the dominant U.S. view, shared by such wise Europeans as Jean Monnet, there is only *one* reliable concept of Atlantic partnership —that described by the image of "twin pillars" or a "dumbbell," composed of the United States and a united Europe organized on federal lines with supranational institutions. This is, of course, one form of Atlantic partnership. But is it wise to stake everything on a single approach? History is rarely such a linear and simple process.

Every European state is the product of some process of integration at some time over the past four centuries; and Germany and Italy achieved unity less than one hundred years ago. European history suggests that there is more than one way to achieve integration. In Italy, it came by way of plebiscite and annexation abolishing the individual states. In Germany, unification occurred under the aegis of one state but as the act of sovereign governments which remained in existence after unity was achieved. The resulting structure clearly did not lack cohesiveness.

Moreover, how valid is a concept of European integration which is rejected by *both* France and Great Britain? In the outrage over Britain's exclusion from the Common Market, it has not always been noted that Britain's view (shared by both major parties) of the organization of Europe is almost identical with that of France. Both countries would find it difficult, if not impossible, to commit themselves now to a federal structure and common parliament. It only adds to the irony of the situation that many of the most ardent advocates of Britain's entry into the Common Market both here and in Europe are also dedicated proponents of a federal Europe. How do they propose to reconcile these two objectives?

The may be various roads to European cooperation. The one traced by the Fouchet Plan—calling for institutionalized meetings of foreign ministers and sub-cabinet officials—is not the least plausible, and indeed it is the one most consistent with British participation. It has the advantage of producing some immediate progress without foreclosing the future. It would also permit a more flexible arrangement of Atlantic relations than the "twin pillar" concept now in vogue.

While the United States should welcome any European structure that reflects the desires of the Europeans, it would be unwise to stake everything on one particular formula. A very rigid conception of Atlantic partnership can easily fail to do justice to the richness and variety of relationships possible within the Atlantic context. Is it really possible or useful to lump the countries of Europe together on all issues? Are they always inherently closer to one another than any of them is to the United States? Do the Dutch inevitably feel a greater sense of identification with the French, or the British with the Germans, than either does with the United States? If we separate the question into political, military, or economic components, is the answer always uniform and does it always point in the same direction? Would it not be wiser to retain some flexibility? There is a grave risk that too doctrinaire an approach will produce either a collapse of political will or, more likely, a new and virulent form of nationalism, perhaps even more intense than the nationalism of the *patries*. A Europe largely constructed on theoretical models might be forced into an anti-American mold because its only sense of identity will be what distinguishes it from America. Our bent for structural remedies sometimes blinds us to the fact that institutions produce their own momentum and that this cannot be foreseen from the proclamations of their founders.

In assessing our own Atlantic policy, we must cut through slogans to such questions as: Is it wise to insist that the only road to European unity is by institutions unacceptable to both France and Britain? Is the best way to solve the strategic problem by staking our prestige on a device— the Multilateral Force—which compels us to oppose the existing nuclear programs in Europe while bringing a host of presently non-nuclear countries (among them Germany, Italy, Greece, and Turkey) into the nuclear business, occasionally with only their reluctant assent? Can it be in the interest of NATO, of the Federal Republic, or of the United States, to make Germany the senior European nuclear partner in the Multilateral Force and to create an institution which can rally all anti-U.S., anti-German, and anti-nuclear sentiments against us?

European history teaches that stability is unattainable except through the cooperation of Britain, France, and Germany. Care should be taken not to resurrect old national rivalries in the name of Atlanticism. The United States should not choose a special partner among its European allies. The attempt to woo one, or to force European countries to choose between us and France—a tendency which despite all disavowals is real—must magnify the European nationalism which French policy has already done so much to foster.

Our concern thus returns to the somewhat out-of-scale figure of President de Gaulle. A sense of frustration resulting from his policies, and even more from his style, has caused many to see him as individually responsible for the failure to realize many deeply felt objectives. This is not the place to attempt an assessment of his character. Conceivably he is as petty, as animated by remembered slights, as some of our commentators suggest. It is also possible that a man so conscious of his historic role has larger purposes. At any rate, we will not know until we have had a real dialogue with him. In a period of détente with Soviet Russia, is it impossible to conduct a serious conversation with a traditional ally? President de Gaulle has repeatedly expressed his willingness to coordinate strategy rather than to integrate it. We should make new efforts to explore what he means. His 1958 proposal of a Directory is not acceptable when confined to Britain, France, and the United States. Do we know his attitude toward a wider forum?

Irritation with de Gaulle's tactics does not change the fact that in his proposals of 1958 for a Directory he put his finger on perhaps the key problem of NATO. In the absence of a common foreign policy—or at least an agreed range of divergence—the attempt to devise a common strategy is likely to prove futile. Lord Avon and Dean Acheson have come to the same conclusion. The time seems ripe to create a political body at the highest level—composed perhaps of the United States, the United Kingdom, France, the Federal Republic, and Italy—for concerting the policies of the nations bordering the North Atlantic. Such a body should discuss how to implement common Atlantic purposes and define the scope of autonomous action where interests diverge. It should also be charged with developing a common strategic doctrine.

Conceivably this could end the sterile scholastic debate over the relative benefits of integration as against coordination. It might heal a rift which if continued is bound to hazard everything that has been painfully built up over 15 years. Both the United States and France are able to thwart each other's purposes. Neither can create an alternative structure—France even less than we. As in a Greek tragedy, each chief actor, following a course that seems quite reasonable, is producing consequences quite different from what he intends.

This should not happen. The problems will become insuperable only if technique is exalted above purpose and if interest is too narrowly conceived. The West does itself an injustice by comparing its disagreements to the rifts in the Communist bloc. In the Communist world, schisms are inevitable and unbridgeable. Western societies have been more fortunate. Their evolution has been richer; they have forged unity by drawing strength from diversity. Free from the shackles of a doctrine of historical inevitability, the nations of the West can render a great service by demonstrating that if history has a meaning it is up to us today to give it that meaning.

CHAPTER FOUR

CASE STUDY : CONTROLLING
THE RISKS IN CUBA

Albert and Roberta Wohlstetter

University of Chicago

The Cuban missile crisis is a case study *par excellence* of shifting power configurations in world politics. The Wohlstetters' penetrating review of the 1962 confrontation illuminates the motives of American, Soviet, and Cuban leaders whose actions shaped the outcome of the direct conflict between the superpowers. The bargaining tactics and strategies employed by small non-nuclear powers and large nuclear powers attest to the importance of "appearances" as well as "realities" in international politics. The Cuban crisis amply demonstrates both the pertinence of intermediate responses and the possibilities of miscommunication. Since certain basic questions of timing and intention remain unanswered, caution must be exercised in judging the long-term effects of the crisis. Diplomacy rather than international law and organization was the chief mode of accommodation and conflict-resolution used by the primary actors. The OAS, NATO, and the UN served as forums in which policy positions could be explained, and legal formulations allowed the actors to place limits on the stakes of conflict and their uses of force. Interpretations of the missile crisis may vary, but its value for the study of diplomacy's strengths and weaknesses is assured.

I

The environment in which smaller powers face large ones has, it is clear, changed drastically. The intensive development of nuclear and other modern weapons and the vast expansion of communications linking remote parts of the world have on the one hand increased the level of violence possible in a world conflict, and on the other seem to have made minor and local violence a worldwide public concern. It is not easy, however, to trace the implications of this changed environment. Public light on local violence does not pass with equal speed in both directions through the Iron and Bamboo Curtains. Though one striking movement of our time has been the multiplication of realigned, non-aligned, and partly aligned nations and their use of many international forums, shifting modes of rivalry and cooperation continue to be dominated by the two principal centres of force: a many-centred East against a not-very-completely allied West. Overwhelming nuclear capabilities, in spite of the many hopeful or ominous predictions of rapid diffusion during the last twenty years, and in spite of the search for independence by the United Kingdom, France, China, and possibly others, still are concentrated in the United States and the Soviet Union.

How does the threat of great power violence increase the risks for the smaller powers? And how might the smaller powers affect the nuclear risks? In a contest between the great powers does the very size of their weapons of destruction inhibit, as it is said, any use of force? What is the role of non-nuclear force? And what are the uses of great power bases on foreign soil?

It is much easier to ask these questions than to answer them; and too much to hope that an analysis of the crisis over the Russian bases in Cuba can provide the answers. However a look at this crisis may illuminate a little the issues and so at least help make the questions more precise. All of the questions at any rate were raised in Cuba. There the two big powers and a small one were engaged in a three-cornered partial conflict (and partial cooperation); and nuclear weapons and their future, if not immediate, launching from these Russian bases outside the Soviet Union were at the very heart of the matter. It is frequently said that we were very close to nuclear war, that Russia and the United States played a desperate game of "chicken" with the risks nearly out of control. Threats and warnings were signalled, and not always understood. And we now hear that the resolution of the crisis will affect all future risk-taking, that the crisis was a "turning point."

It is perhaps worth one more look then at this much inspected event, to see how some of the standard sayings about constraints and risks in the use of force apply. What were the interests and what were the dangers in the various policy alternatives open to each of the three powers directly engaged? And how did they affect allies less directly engaged?

II. THE VIEW FROM CUBA

From the standpoint of Cuba the basing of nuclear weapons there had some clear values. Mr. Theodore Draper,[1] an acute analyst of the development of Castro's Cuba, suggested rather early that Cuba may have invited the Russians to put their bombardment missiles there. Castro himself has fluctuated between attributing the idea to the Cubans and to the Russians. On our count, out of some half a dozen major mentions, the score is about even.[2] Whoever got the idea first, strategic bases in Cuba would have had their uses for Castro as well as for Khrushchev. For one thing there was the prestige; modern weapons impress neighbours and can raise the political status of the country which harbours them, especially if the neighbours are misinformed or uninformed. The prestige, to be sure, is precarious, as the United Kingdom, in spite of its great scientific competence, has found, first with *Blue Streak,* then with *Skybolt,* and now with the recently aired difficulties in the *Valiant* and TSR-2 programmes. However, in the less developed countries and even in secondary industrial powers, arms may be valued more for their flourish than their actual power. It seems that the sheer magnitude of the capabilities of the United States and the Soviet Union has outclassed the nuclear potential of others in ways that were quite unexpected by those who predicted nuclear weapons would be equalizers on the world scene. Yet France and China would scarcely agree, and a less developed country like Cuba might place a sizeable symbolic value on being only the host to nuclear installations.

For another thing, the symbol had its important domestic uses. Within Cuba the presence of these bases, while essentially alien and forbidden to Cuban citizens, reinforced and confirmed Castro's defiance of the northern colossus, made more persuasive his warnings of an American invasion, and distracted attention from gathering difficulties at home. These difficulties had been political as well as economic. 1962 had witnessed an open break in March between Castro and the old guard Communists, followed by a purging and reorganization of Cuba's single political party.[3] A severe drop (the first of several) in the sugar harvest from the preceding year (from 6.8

---

[1] Interview, December 6, 1962.

[2] Claude Julien, *Le Monde,* March 22 and 23, 1963; followed by Castro's denial to *Prensa Latina,* March 23, 1963; Jean Daniel, "Unofficial Envoy: An Historic Report from Two Capitals," *The New Republic* (December 14, 1963), pp. 15–20; Herbert Matthews, "Return to Cuba," *Hispanic American Report,* Special Issue (January 1964), p. 16; Juanita Castro, Speech to the World Affairs Council, Los Angeles, February 8, 1965.

[3] The ori (Integrated Revolutionary Organization), now purs, a fusion of the Cuban Communist Party and Castro's own 26 July Organization.

to 4.8 million tons) was among the early results of an ill-conceived attempt to diversify agriculture quickly at the expense of Cuban comparative advantage. Troubles had also begun to plague the industrial programme. The Cuban planners had left out of their plans the provision of raw materials for the factories they ordered, and were discovering to their dismay that in many cases it cost as much to import the raw materials as to buy the finished products abroad. An extraordinarily rapid collectivizing and stratification of farms and even small commercial and manufacturing enterprises, at a pace unequalled in Russia, Asia, or middle Europe, had begun to affect production incentives and to require a large increase in managerial skills; meanwhile Cuba had been losing professionals through emigration. As these internal threats to the Revolution appeared, distraction may have been welcome.

In any case the move had international relevance for the future of Castro's variety of Communism, particularly in Latin America. The missile installation was seen by the Cubans as a great and unprecedented gesture of protection and solidarity by the most powerful country in the Communist world. Inevitably some of this power might be expected to rub off on Castro. By increasing his prestige, it could be expected to serve as an aid in his programme for spreading insurgency throughout Latin America. And it suggested that, like Castro's own communism, successful coups on the same model might be protected against counterrevolution and external attack. One of Castro's explanations for accepting Moscow's offer of long-range missiles could also support this interpretation. It was, he said, "not in order to assure our own defence, but foremost in order to reinforce socialism on the international plane."[4]

Speeches in September and early October, 1962, by Cuban Communist leaders hammered at the theme, "Cuba is not alone," and Castro's public expressions of thanks to the Soviet Union were emotional to an extreme. Read today, with our present knowledge of the timing of arrangements to install the rockets, these pre-crisis speeches seem to contain implied threats of rocket fire against the United States in case of an invasion, and an identification of Cuba's fate with the final catastrophe, *Goetterdaemmerung.* Castro explained on April 20, 1953, the second anniversary of Playa Giron, "When the missiles were installed here, it was no longer a problem of six or seven divisions, it was...a problem (for the United States) of having to confront the risk of a thermonuclear war." In a recent interview with Barnard L. Collier he made this more explicit. "The missiles were very logical to us. We were running the danger of conventional war. . . . The conventional war would be most dangerous to us. We would be destroyed alone."[5]

4 Claude Julien, *Le Monde,* March 22, 1963, reporting an interview which took place in January of that year. Castro repudiated some statements of this interview, but in view of Julien's reputation as an accurate journalist and some of the confirmable details of the setting and circumstances, there is much to suggest this account is authentic. The role of long-range missiles in his insurgency programme has been confirmed by his sister, Juanita Castro, in a talk on February 8, 1965, to the World Affairs Council, Los Angeles.

5 *New York Herald Tribune,* August 17, 1964.

Cuba was not alone in another sense, because the missile bases supplied hostages. They were a visible symbol that Russia was "contracting in," just as their withdrawal, Castro feared, might make it easier for the United States to underestimate the Soviet Union's solidarity with Cuba. Castro's statement to Collier suggests that the rationalization he had given earlier to the French reporter, Jean Daniel, for accepting missiles hardly represented his actual motives and estimates. To Daniel he had implied that if Russia extended only conventional military aid, the United States would not be deterred from invading, even though Russia would, in spite of American doubts, actually retaliate with thermonuclear weapons and so touch off world war;[6] Russian nuclear missiles in Cuba, however, would deter a U.S. invasion and therefore prevent nuclear war altogether. To Collier, on the other hand, Castro made clear that he himself did not believe the Soviet Union would retaliate with nuclear weapons in the event of U.S. conventional attack, and that if Cuba were to go down he would prefer that it be destroyed not alone, but on a grand scale along with a good deal of the rest of the world. As he said, "For us the danger of a conventional war and a world war were the same, the destruction of Cuba."[7]

The presence of the missiles meant that the Soviet Union was more obviously engaged—in Castro's phrase, "highly compromised"—in the fate of Cuba. Though not, as it turned out, irretrievably; not at any rate when Russia was caught in the process of installation. If a substantial number of missiles had been installed and made operational before discovery, forcing withdrawal might have been somewhat harder. The quarantine of missiles and ground support equipment on their way to Cuba would, of course, no longer have been open to the United States. Something less focussed on the actual process of installing missiles would therefore have been necessary; perhaps a more general blockade or a still broader and more violent measure. Moreover, though this is arguable, it might have been somewhat more difficult psychologically for the Russians to withdraw immediately after the installation of the missiles than during the process. Perhaps this difficulty would have faded rapidly with time; after some years surely withdrawal would again be easier. In any case, Chairman Khrushchev was caught *in flagrante,* in a difficult position to maintain.

In the event of conflict between the United States and Cuba, a considerable number of Russian missiles and bombers, at least twenty odd thousand Russian troops,[8] and, still more, Russian prestige would have been

---

[6] According to Daniel's account of Castro's beliefs (*The New Republic,* December 14, 1963, p. 18), Russia "recognized that if conventional military aid was the extent of their assistance, the United States might not hesitate to instigate an invasion, in which case Russia would retaliate and this would eventually touch off a world war." Russia therefore decided to install the missiles, and Castro accepted them as a matter of "honor." The passage just quoted was omitted from the *New York Times* version of the interview, but appears in the original in *L'Express,* December 6, 1963.

[7] *New York Herald Tribune,* August 17, 1964.

[8] The estimate by President Kennedy in January, 1963, was 16,000 to 17,000 in Cuba, after a withdrawal of 4,500. Press Conference, January 25, 1963, as reported in the *New York Times* (January 26, 1963). The official American figure for the crisis period has stayed around 22,000. Castro now claims the number was much larger.

put in jeopardy. To avoid Russian casualities in some of the attacks that might have been made at the end of October (for example, the non-nuclear bombing of Cuban bases manned by Russian forces) there would have had to be extreme selectivity in the American attack; or evacuation by the Russians on receipt of explicit warning; or some combination of the two. Russian forces in Cuba then, like American forces in Europe, though to a very much lesser extent, would have been hostage to the Cubans in the event of an attack by the United States. This point should not be pushed too far or regarded simply in formal terms. The United States forces which are hostage in Europe number now perhaps 350,000 men and many of their dependents. By comparison, a Russian force of 20 odd thousand, is a token. Nonetheless, a distinctly visible token. As Castro puts it today, "The Soviet Union is seriously compromised in the world with Cuba. That is important. It is like the U.S. in Berlin."[9] But he observes that the "compromising" was even more serious with the surface-to-surface missiles in Cuba.

It was not simply the presence of Soviet troops in Cuba, but their manning and guarding of the long-range rockets that seems to have faced the United States with a dilemma in October 1962. If the United States undertook some hostile action against Cuba, would it dare leave these lethal weapons alone? Would it not have to destroy them? And would this not bring Russia's intercontinental missiles down on the United States?

The line of argument suggested by these questions without a doubt is plausible. However, it persuades mainly by its vagueness. The precise circumstances and nature of the United States action and the risks to the Russians of their own alternative responses need to be specified, and these are only some of the things which would require examination. We shall not assess how the risks would have looked in connection with the various actions open to the United States, if the installations had been completed. We shall ask: What were the risks involved in the actions taken by the United States and in alternatives it considered during the process of the missile installation by the Russians? Much has been said about this, but how close *were* we to the brink?

Whether or not the Russians might have used their medium and inter-mediate range missiles located in Cuba or their intercontinental missiles based at home in retaliation against an attack on Cuba, desperate action by the Cubans themselves was another matter. Could the Cubans have used the Russians' missiles based in Cuba? If the surface-to-surface missiles had been in their charge, they may well have been more tempted than the Russians to use them. At least the threat to use these missiles against the United States in any of a number of circumstances might from the stand-point of the Cubans have had a considerable appeal. For one thing, the Cubans know less about the consequences of nuclear exchange: these are sobering, as Chairman Khrushchev used to keep telling Chairman Mao; and there is no reason to suspect that Khrushchev's successors—or ultimately Mao's—would be less sober. (Familiarity breeds respect.) For another, we

---

9 Interview with Barnard Collier, *New York Herald Tribune,* August 19, 1964.

are told, the Cuban Communists and the Russian ones are rather different. We even had some hints from Chairman Khrushchev on this subject. The Cubans are southerners, impulsive, romantic revolutionaries; and they would put their own fate (or at least that of the current Cuban government) at stake in an American attack or an American-supported resistance. The Russians are northern and more controlled (though there are those embarrassing nineteenth-century Dostoievskian Russians); they are disciplined Bolsheviks (whose character was formed in conscious contrast to such Dostoievskian Russians); and for all of their twenty odd thousand, clearly much less intimately engaged in Cuba.

Whatever faith we attach to these contrasting characterizations, we have some actual observations on the contrasting behaviour of Chairman Khrushchev and the Cuban Communists. Or more exactly, we can at the least contrast how the Russians behaved in the crisis and how the Cubans say they would have behaved. In the clutch the Chairman was eminently cautious and controlled about the triggering of Russian missiles in Cuba. The Cubans on the other hand suggested considerably more abandon. Che Guevara apparently had a beady eye on New York, and said later that he would have pulled New York down with Cuba. "If the rockets had remained, we would have used them all and directed them against the very heart of the United States, including New York, in our defence against aggression. But we haven't got them, so we shall fight with what we've got. In the face of an aggressor like the United States, there can be no solution other than to fight to the death, inflicting the maximum damage on the enemy."[10]

This sort of threat might be compared with that posed by a small nuclear power, according to General Pierre Gallois and other enthusiasts for the spread of nuclear weapons. In the writings of these theorists the precise service performed by nuclear weapons for the small powers is seldom very clear. If one of the two major powers planned a nuclear first strike against a small nuclear power, such as Cuba might have become, or for that matter, a secondary industrial power like France, the small power's arsenal might not offer much of a deterrent. To deter a first strike, a nuclear force must be able to survive it. And a second strike capability is a more complicated matter than enthusiasts for diffusion have understood.

However, sometimes the use of nuclear weapons by a small power is contemplated as a response to lesser attacks by the great power: a massive retaliation theory, in short, with the smaller power appearing in the role of miniature massive retaliationist. Such nuclear retaliation against a non-nuclear move by a great power would of course be suicidal. The small power is not likely to have a genuine second strike capability against Russia or the United States; if these countries are careful, it is still less likely to have a "preclusive" first strike capability, that is, an ability to prevent the

10 Interview, November 28, 1962, with a London *Daily Worker* correspondent, reported in the *Los Angeles Times*, December 11, 1962.

great nuclear power from retaliating. From a responsible leader of a smaller power, then, the threat of a miniature massive retaliation might not be very convincing. It is not clear that Guevara, for example, who has a reputation for disciplined intelligence, would be as abandoned in fact as he claims in retrospect. After all, Chairman Khrushchev tried to sound rather reckless in advance of the crisis. In mid-September of 1962 he called the attention of the governments of the world and world opinion to "the provocations which might plunge the world into the disaster of a universal world war with the use of thermonuclear weapons..." "Bellicose reactionary elements of the United States have long since been conducting in the United States Congress and in the American press an unbridled propaganda campaign against the Cuban Republic, calling for an attack on Cuba, an attack on Soviet ships carrying the necessary commodities and food to the Cuban people, in one word, calling for war." "...one cannot now attack Cuba and expect that the aggressor will be free from punishment for this attack. If this attack is made, this will be the beginning of war."[11] In short, interception of Russian ships carrying arms to Cuba would mean the start of World War III.

On the other hand, some leaders in small countries have earned a reputation for recklessness. Guevara's uncompromising speed in nationalizing industry, and immediate full implementation of what he regards as Communist principles, have an element of ruthlessness and lack of realism which is not the same as recklessness, but which should make us thoughtful. And it may be that Castro himself could convince us with a suicidal threat. The "Venceremos" (We shall win) with which all Cuban letters now are signed might be hollow, but Castro might just mean the "Patria o Muerte" (Fatherland or Death) which precedes it.[12] He has had a long personal history of near suicidal defiance of big forces; his casual and disastrous assault on the Moncada barracks on July 26, 1953; his landing on the *Gramma* in Oriente in 1956, announced in advance to Batista, calamitous not only to most of his companions but to the inhabitants who expected him two days earlier; to say nothing of some hair-raising student escapades. "Frente a Todos" (Against Everybody) has been his slogan.[13] One can understand that more than the traditional guerrilla doctrine of protecting the leader might have influenced Fidel's subordinates to keep him home in the headquarters of the Sierra Maestra when they went out on a raid. When he was in charge, casualties were prohibitive. His own life has been charmed, but not that of his followers. It should give any prospective father

11 *New York Times*, September 12, 1962. (Soviet Government Statement released by *Tass*.)
12 He describes the Cubans manning the surface-to-air missiles today in precisely these terms. They are "disciplined and fatherland-or-death types" (Speech, January 21, 1965). If he had surface-to-surface missiles, he might very well man them with the same "types" and, at the least, almost certainly so describe them.
13 "Frente a Todos" is the title Fidel gave to his reply in Mexico in 1955 to charges against him of corruption and usurpation of power by the Ortodoxo Party and other groups fighting Batista in Cuba.

figure—or even a brother figure, Russian or otherwise—considerable pause.[14]

Castro in charge of nuclear rockets might be convincingly reckless.[15] It is precisely this case which would appear to be intolerable to both of the two opposing great powers. It is clear that a persisting threat by Cuba to use nuclear weapons in response to unspecified or vaguely specified non-nuclear moves by the United States would be very hard for the U.S. to bear. But it would also raise grave problems for the Soviet Union. Russia would have every motive to preclude or stop such a threat or, if this were not possible, to separate herself as clearly as could be from the threatener.

From the standpoint of the Cuban people, a miniature massive-retaliation policy would place them in double jeopardy. It would raise the stakes and conjure up the possibility of nuclear destruction either before or after a Cuban move. However, the hazards to Cubans were increased considerably even by the presence of Russian-controlled missiles.

The issue of Russian control is raised very acutely by the nightmare vision of Cuba pulling Russia down along with New York. No doubt with exactly this in mind Mr. Khrushchev made every attempt to assure Mr. Kennedy that there was nothing whatsoever to worry about from those romantic Cubans. Good, solid, stolid, sensible Russians were guarding the safety catches on the missiles in Cuba: "The means which are located on Cuba now, about which you are talking and which as you say concern you, are in the hands of the Soviet officers. That is why any possibility of accidental usage of those means, which might cause harm to the United States, is excluded."[16] During the crisis as well as earlier, Chairman Khrushchev indicated that he subscribed to the analysis of the Cubans as temperamental southerners. "The Cubans are very volatile people, Mr. Khrushchev said, and all of the sophisticated hardware provided for their defence was entirely under the control of Soviet officers...and it would never be fired except on his orders as Commander in Chief of all of the armed forces of the Soviet Union."[17]

[14] Fidel's actual father had trouble. When Fidel was 13 years old he organized a strike of sugar workers against his father, and later when he was 18, his mother reports in a biography written with one of Castro's sisters, that she permitted him to call his father an exploiter and a landlord, one of "those who abuse the powers they wrench from the people with deceitful promises." While the father reacted in rage, Fidel apparently still expected (and received) his financial support even after his marriage, demanded $1,000 to buy weapons for the Moncada attack, left the house finally with $100. Castro's vilification and attack of big forces may have aimed at a continued dependence rather than an absolute break in relations. The United States turned out to be a less tolerant father, withdrawing economic support, intending damage, and even inflicting some, when Castro carried on too long, too noisily, too roughly.

[15] Some European analyses of the crisis suggest that Castro and the Cubans differed from Khrushchev in that the Cubans do not believe in nuclear threats in response to less than nuclear attack. The claim cannot survive an examination of Castro's and Guevara's speeches. Such suicidal nuclear threats were not only contemplated by Castro, but might be more persuasive issuing from him than from Khrushchev.

[16] October 27, 1962, message to President Kennedy, published in New York Times October 28, 1962.

[17] Interview with W. E. Knox, American industrialist, "Close Up of Khrushchev During a Crisis," New York Times Magazine, November 18, 1962, described as taking place "a little more than three weeks ago."

Of course this raises some interesting questions. How sure could Khrushchev be? What about the use of force by Castro to jump Big Brother ("Frente a Todos")? Mightn't he try to get hold of Russian nuclear weapons for use against the United States and so ultimately to ensure the engagement of Russia? (To say nothing of the rather grandiose plans he has expressed for spreading his revolution beyond the Andes.) That, we may surmise, was what a good many of those 22,000 Russian troops were there to prevent: they were there to see that the weapons and in particular the warheads, if they were on the island, would be totally inoperable when seized. Newspaper reports have made clear that the Russian bases were heavily guarded and the Cubans, with the possible exception of a few of the elite, never got near the weapons.

But could these Russian forces be relied on? We know that the Russian troops in the satellites wavered during the revolts in Eastern Europe in the 1950's. The Russians have since rotated their security forces more frequently. However, seeing to it that nuclear weapons would not fall into the hands of irresponsible Cuban users is a much simpler job than preventing sympathetic collusion between rebels and an occupying force. It requires only a very small elite force whose loyalty could be relied on. And the loyalty of even a random sample of Russians might be trusted here: letting Cubans get hold of these weapons would mean placing all of Russia and a good deal else in jeopardy. In any case, there are more sophisticated methods of assurance available. The United States, on July 5, 1962, announced that it was initiating a programme to install electronic locks (the Permissive Action Link) on its weapons to protect them against unauthorized use. These locks would require release from a central source, possibly very distant. Analogous remote keys conceivably could be held in Moscow itself. And while there is no public evidence whatsoever of mechanical or electronic devices so used in the Soviet Union, a tight political control seems most probable, given the structure of Soviet society; physical possession of these potent weapons would be dangerous in the hands of a dissident internal faction. The interests of the larger powers clearly coincide in preventing unauthorized firings by their own citizens. And both want to keep the keys out of the desperate hands of a smaller power. In the event it was the interests of the major powers that dominated.

So far we have treated the crisis mainly from the viewpoint of the small power. How did these missile bases figure in the calculations of the big powers?

III. THE VIEW FROM THE SOVIET UNION

Much ink has been spilled over whether the Soviet move into Cuba had a purely political significance for the Russians, or whether Soviet bases in Cuba had also a military worth to them. But Soviet objectives can be both political and military; these purposes are not separate, and neither the political nor military is very simple or pure. If the "purely political" is somewhat nebulous, the "purely military," a kind of art-for-art-'s-sake, has no meaning at all.

The leaders of the Soviet Union in any case, when they address the Communist world, have never made the separation. In fact, the shift in the balance of forces, which according to Mr. Khrushchev had come drastically to favour the Socialist countries, was clearly linked in his pronouncements to the development of Soviet military power, and was accompanied by a drum fire of rocket threats against the United States and all of the countries in which the United States bases its military forces. And this supposed shift in military power is not unrelated to a vision of a future, totally Communist world, whether this be single or many-centred. Many American and British writers recently have assured us that the Soviet Union is a *status quo* power, a "have" or satisfied power. This is all very well, but Chairman Khrushchev did not seem to know it. The *status quo* he was looking for seemed to be, as he had told it to Walter Lippmann, the *status quo post* rather than *ante* a major transformation. And there is no evidence that Khrushchev's successors look on the matter more comfortably for the West. To say that they would prefer this to be a peaceful transformation and indeed believe that it may well be, does not exclude latent military power as a major element in the expected transformation. Otherwise one would have to count every acquiescence to a threat of force as a peaceful change. Latent or actual Communist military force monitored the early take-overs in Eastern Europe at the end of the war and prevented a reversal of the revolutions in 1953 and 1956. The possibility of its use defined the rules of behaviour both for internal opposition and outside aid. The possible use or threat to use military force is an operative element in many political transformations. In any case, it is apparent that the military build-up in Cuba had a considerable number of entwined political-military functions.

First it should be recalled that the introduction of strategic bombardment vehicles, MRBM's, IRBM's, and IL 28's, capped a vast piling up, started considerably earlier, of active defences and ground forces which could be used to defend Cuba against internal as well as external attack, and the building of a base in Cuba which could serve as a centre of weapons transfer and material aid to insurgency in Latin America. From the standpoint of the Soviet Union the purposes of such a build-up partially coincide with some of the Cuban interests we have sketched. The important split between the Russians and the Red Chinese is not accurately represented as an ideological contrast between the foreswearing of any use of revolutionary violence by the Russians and its reckless advocacy by the Chinese. There are of course important differences in national interests. But the Chinese are considerably less reckless and the Russians more flexible and opportunistic than the conventional picture suggests.

Specifically for the Russians, the military build-up was in part a reaffirmation of the relationship between Russia and Cuba, a healing of wounds after the rift in March, 1962, that had resulted in the flight of Escalante, the old line Communist Party bureaucrat. It was a visible demonstration to those who were unaligned or falling out of line that for a small power to line up with the Soviet Union even near the centre of American power was safe, that a changeover to communism would not be reversed and that the power of the Soviet Union was committed as safeguard against any threat of reversal. More than this, by successfully defying the United States, forcing it to accept this major move into Cuba, the Soviet Union could powerfully influence the expectations of the rest of the world most obviously those of the Latin Americans, but also those expectations and hopes that affect the outcome in Berlin and in more remote regions of Southeast and Southern Asia. And the expectations affected were specifically about relative strength and the will to use that strength. The large-scale Russian introduction of nuclear bombardment vehicles would have appeared also directly to answer the persuasive official American analyses of U.S. superiority published in 1961 and 1962. The tendencies toward division within the Communist world only reinforced some of these purposes. For the move was a Soviet blow in competition with the Chinese for leadership of the Socialist countries, and for leading the way in transforming the uncommitted world—and eventually that part of the world now committed to what they regard as the wrong side.

We have been discussing functions objectively served rather than Soviet conscious motivation, which must necessarily remain obscure.[18] If, for example, the move had been successful, if the Soviet Union had gone before the United Nations to defend it, and the United States had acquiesced in the accomplished fact, it might have served any or all of the preceding military-political functions. On the other hand, if the success had been less complete, if the United States had not acquiesced, Soviet withdrawal might then have exacted as a price American withdrawal from some of its military bases on the territory of allies. The tentative skirmishing in the Khrushchev-Kennedy correspondence on the Turkish-Cuban base swap indicated one line of Soviet interest. But elimination of military bases is a directly military as well as a political fact. This has been somewhat obscured, because the significance of overseas bases themselves for the 1960's has been understood only in a rather cloudy and sometimes quite erroneous fashion in the current Western discussions. How about the Cuban bombardment bases themselves? Some commentators have stated in rather unqualified fashion that they had essentially no military worth.[19]

Perhaps the first thing to be said is that it is not very sensible to talk with great confidence on these subjects. Responsible judgment here is difficult even with complete access to privileged information. The classified data are uncertain, the public data still more so, and few of the commentators have looked carefully at the quantitative implications of even

---

18 There are several discerning analysts of this complex and uncertain Soviet motivation; we have found especially useful the balanced and original treatments of Nathan Leites and Helmut Sonnenfeldt.

19 See, for example, *The New Republic* (November 3, 1962), pp. 3ff; *The Reporter* (November 22, 1962), pp. 21ff; *The Bulletin of the Atomic Scientists,* Vol. 19 (February 1963), pp. 8ff.

the public data. Many who doubted the Russians would install bombardment vehicles in Cuba simply took at face value Chairman Khrushchev's
statement that such weapons would add nothing to the capabilities provided
by their intercontinental rockets. And then when it was clear that Khrushchev had gambled a great deal on precisely such installations, they persisted
in dismissing their military significance. As we have already suggested,
such bases have a variety of functions, but Khrushchev's gamble should at
least have raised some doubts in the minds of those who dismiss their
strategic value out of hand.

Part of the confusion comes from the fact that the military value of
these Russian installations was not likely to consist in their efficiency as an
addition to the Russian deterrent to American nuclear attack. Because of
their proximity, their known position, and their lack of shelter, warning,
or protected reliable communications, they would not have been hard to
eliminate in an opening blow, nor would they have severely complicated
an attack by a large reliable missile force;[20] and so they were not likely
to be an economic way to increase a Russian second-strike capability. The
more likely strategic value concerned their significance for a possible
Russian preclusive first strike, as weapons that, in case of need during a
grave crisis of escalation, would help to blunt an American retaliation.
Resolution of such an issue would involve a detailed analysis of the entire
complex mechanism of American retaliation, as it existed in 1962, including
not merely the vehicles (that is, the missiles and aircraft), their physical
disposition, their protection and degree of readiness, but also the system
for commanding and controlling their response and penetrating enemy
defences. For good reason, data on this subject are not publicly available.
And overall statements on capability by public officials necessarily must be
designed not simply to convey information to the public, important though
that is, but also to limit information to the enemy and to affect his estimates
favourably to ourselves. A resolution of this complex issue cannot therefore
be made one way or the other. Even the much simpler partial question,
the comparative vulnerability of our bombardment vehicles to distant as
distinct from close, land-based attack, is necessarily shrouded with secrecy.
Recognition of these limitations on analysis in the beginning of wisdom.

Take the partial problem of protecting the vehicles against the initial
blow, from far off or nearby. This is a quantitative matter demanding more
than the standard caution. The probability that a vehicle will survive
depends among other things on the number of attacking vehicles, their
reliability, their average aiming accuracy, the kiloton yield of their nuclear
warheads, and the degree of resistance of the vehicles under attack. This
dependence moreover is not simply linear. The number of weapons, for
example, required to destroy a vehicle sheltered to a sufficient degree will

---

[20] During the 1950's the belief was widespread that even very vulnerable unprotected bases, if widely separated, would present insuperable coordination problems
for a missile attack. This belief is examined critically and in technical detail in
"On the Value of Overseas Bases" by Albert Wohlstetter, RAND Paper P-1877
(January 5, 1960).

within relevant limits vary as the square of the average aiming accuracy. That is, double the inaccuracy and four times the number of attacking vehicles are required; triple the inaccuracy and nearly ten times the number of attackers are needed. Requirements are sensitive also to yield and degree of resistance, though less so. Changes in requirement are something less than proportionate to changes in yield or resistance: they vary as the two-thirds power: if a shelter is 8 or 27 times harder, the number of attackers required for a given probability of destruction would increase by factors of 4 or 9 respectively. But the average inaccuracy, for example, of even our own weapons can only be uncertainly estimated with complete access to classified tests. Our estimates of the performance of Russian weapons must be still more uncertain. Estimates are in any case not public and are frequently misrepresented with great confidence in the press. Moreover they change rather rapidly. A careful reading of the public press will confirm that the publicly stated average inaccuracies of bombardment missiles have decreased in the last few years by very large amounts; public estimates have been divided by at least five. Yet a factor of 3 reduction in inaccuracy can lower requirements to destroy hard targets by a factor of 9; a factor of 5 reduction, by 25. Even estimates of the number of vehicles of various types in the Russian force, we know from experience, have been in error. And the errors have not always been in one direction. The Cuban example illustrates some of the uncertainties. Here in a small area close by, under the most intense and continuous air reconnaissance, we counted some 30 missiles; and the Russians removed 42.[21] These comments suggest the limits of our own discussion.

The point to be made then is that some of these sensitive performance characteristics for the offensive vary with distance and improve significantly with close proximity: the important parameter of guidance accuracy, for example. Reliability is another performance characteristic which can improve with the simplified missiles possible at close range. A typically blithe argument assessing the military worth of Cuban bases states that while accuracy is improved in the shorter ranges, on the other hand, bomb yields are necessarily smaller. Unfortunately, as we have indicated, changes in accuracy affect requirements much more sensitively than changes in yield. And, what is more, there is no law of nature suggesting that a missile payload declines at shorter ranges. For a given thrust, other things being equal, the opposite is true. It is possible to throw larger payloads at shorter distances. All of this is relevant for an exclusive choice between distant and close-in attack.

However, the second point to be noted is that *in the short run* this was not the choice open to the Russians. In the long run they could choose to build intercontinental missiles and base them in Russia, say, or spend an equal amount of resources for missiles based in Cuba. But in the years 1962 and 1963 the Russian bombardment force capable of reaching the United States

21 "...we never knew how many missiles were brought into Cuba. The Soviets said there were 42. We have counted 42 going out. We saw fewer than 42." Roswell L. Gilpatric, ABC's *Issues and Answers* telecast November 11, 1962.

was sharply limited. The missiles they sent to Cuba were a net addition to this force, since, based in Russia or in one of the European satellites, they could not reach the United States. Moreover the number of MRBM's—48— and IRBM's—apparently between 24 and 32—which were already installed or on the way[22] was quite sizeable in relation to the public Western and American government estimates of the Russian intercontinental missile force and approximately equalled the Institute of Strategic Studies' estimate of 75 Soviet ICBM's.[23]

Third, our short-run need not be so short as to stop in mid-December, 1962—the time the Department of Defence indicated as the operational date for the IRBM's of 2200 nautical mile range. In fact, it appears that the Russians had in addition to the roughly 75 medium and intermediate range missiles shipped to Cuba in 1962, hundreds more that could acquire by location in Cuba the ability to bomb American targets. The ISS estimate suggests a force of MRBM's alone ten times as large as the total number of MRBM's and IRBM's emplaced in Cuba, and beyond this, a growing total force of IRBM's. Further shipments of medium and intermediate range missiles could have been installed in Cuba, if the United States offered no interference, with the same impressive speed that characterized the installation of the first 75. The MRBM's were activated "with the passage of hours." (For example, two sets of photographs separated by less than 24 hours, displayed an increase of perhaps 50 per cent in the amount of equipment.[24] There has been almost universal agreement on the logistic efficiency of the Soviet operation.) Such a change in location might have corrected at a stroke what appears to be a great imbalance in the composition of the Russian strategic force: it is heavily weighted towards attacking European theatre targets and by comparison neglects American forces based outside Europe, though these make up the principal retaliatory strength of the alliance.

Fourth, the axis of attack from Cuba outflanked the Ballistic Missile Early Warning System. Unlike submarine launched missiles, of the range estimated to be available to the Soviet Union, these Cuban-based missiles would have covered essentially all of the United States, with little or no warning.[25] The coordination problems for the Russians are less severe

22 On the CIA and DOD public accounts, there were 48 MRBM's which launch positions had been prepared (there were 24 launchers). For the IRBM's, 17 erectors were counted on the way out, with the 17th reckoned by the Americans as a spare. Briefing, February 6, 1963, by Mr. John Hughes, Special Assistant to General Carroll, reprinted in *Department of Defence Appropriations for 1964*, U.S. Congress, House of Representatives 88th Session, Part I, Washington, D.C., 1963.
23 "The Military Balance," 1962–1963.
24 According to a Defence Department spokesman, October 22, 1962.
25 Doubts about this coverage persist in some European and American analyses. They appear to be based on a poorly reasoned uncritically sceptical commentary by Roger Hagan and Bart Bernstein, "The Military Value of Missiles in Cuba," *Council for Correspondence Newsletter* (November 22, 1962). Hagan and Bernstein relied on newspaper and magazine accounts of intelligence data that themselves confused the MRBM's and IRBM's installed in Cuba with the shorter range T–1 and T–2, and they misread the public statements about the expected operational date and number of the IRBM's.

than were suggested by some writers at the time of the crisis, and in fact on the whole before attacking it is easier to communicate at a great distance with land-based missiles than with distant submerged submarines. All of the above is in the short or fairly short run. For a long run in which the Russians were free to spend resources, to build new ICBM's based in Russia or new medium or intermediate range ballistic missiles based in Cuba, the choice this opens up to them cannot be dismissed out of hand. As some of the commentators suggested, the shorter range missiles are cheaper. If they are drastically cheaper for a desired level and type of performance, they would offer the Russians a significantly larger destruction capability for a given budget. Some long-run mixture of close and distant basing then might be optimal for a Russian force, providing their decision makers with an improved option in a crisis to strike first.

In sum, Cuba offered to the Russians the means for a very large and immediate expansion of the forces capable of hitting elements of the American retaliatory force based in the United States. Moreover further large increments were readily available. The effect of such a rapid increase in power on the actual military balance could not be lightly dismissed; and the political uses of even an apparent change seemed evident.

IV. THE VIEW FROM THE UNITED STATES

The sudden installation of a sizeable number of nuclear bombardment vehicles in Cuba, and the long-term prospects of such a base very near American shores, offered much foundation for sober thought about significant alterations in the military balance. This balance is not a simple one-dimensional matter and neither were the effects of such an installation. However, as we have already indicated, the Russian military build-up touched many problems of defence other than the preservation of a United States second-strike capability in the event of a thermonuclear war. It affected the political and military stability of Cuba and Latin America. And President Kennedy was acutely conscious of the political effects of even the *appearance* of a vast Soviet increase in military power. "The Cuban effort," he commented after the crisis, with Russian deception in mind, "has made it more difficult for us to carry out any successful negotiations, because this was an effort to materially change the balance of power...not that [the Soviets] were intending to fire [the missiles]....But it would have politically changed the balance of power. It would have appeared to, and appearances contribute to reality."[26]

One of the least understood aspects of the crisis from the standpoint of American as well as Russian interests concerned the role of overseas bases. It was the building of a Russian overseas base of course that prompted the crisis. Our discovery of the installation was preceded by Khrushchev's

---

26 *Washington Post,* December 18, 1962. The right contrast with mere appearance is not a steady intent to fire, but a contingent choice in future crises.

public deprecation of its utility, his statement that it would add nothing to his long-range rockets based in the Soviet Union. In Western discussion, during the crisis and since, of concessions or disengagements, the possibility of giving up American bases overseas was prominent. The issue was somewhat blurred by the focus on the Turkish-based *Jupiters*, whose removal had been planned before the crisis and ironically was delayed by Soviet demand for their removal during the crisis itself. For good reason. Whether or not the *Jupiter* installations were useful, it was apparent that their removal under pressure would be a very different thing from the dismantling of the *Thors* in England, initiated sometime before because they were not worth their keep. (In fact one of the writers of this essay had written a series of critical analyses of the *Thors* and *Jupiters* beginning in 1957; but was clear that October 1962 would have been a poor date for a change.) In any case, the deficiencies of the *Thor* and *Jupiter* bases should not be taken as an example of the general worthlessness or for that matter of the lessening value of overseas bases.

In the West, liberal and conservative opinion sometimes meet on common ground in the depreciation of the role of overseas bases in the 1960's. Suggestions that modern developments in missilery make them unnecessary might be quoted from the surviving massive retaliationists, but also from *The Liberal Papers*.[27]

Such suggestions are a vast over-simplification of the military implications of current and future states of the art of war. It is true that the deterrent function of some American weapons in a big thermonuclear war was much more dependent on overseas bases when the predominant part of the U.S. force was the short-legged B-47. However, thermonuclear war is not the only problem of national and alliance defence or of the defence of non-aligned powers. U.S. defence programmes have stressed more and more the threat of non-nuclear, conventional, and unconventional warfare—moreover, thermonuclear war itself is a lot more complicated than this deprecation of overseas bases suggests.

In brief, overseas bases have vital roles in a possible central war in the 1960's and 1970's—both for deterrence and for limiting damage in case deterrence fails. They do dilute and can dilute even more Soviet offensive preparations by posing the need to set up a *variety* of defensive barriers. They are an important source of continuing information on the enemy. They can be made to complicate the design of his attack—for example, with the extension of the present bomb alarm system. Under several plausible contingencies of outbreak they can help spoil his attack. All this for a thermonuclear war.

---

[27] "The United States may find that it will no longer need bases around the periphery of the USSR and Communist China, and that instead, pending effective arms reduction, it should place its chief reliance on long-range missiles to be delivered from its own territory." *The Liberal Papers*, James Roosevelt, ed. (Garden City, New York: Doubleday and Co., 1962), p. 268.

And, "The question would then arise whether the security of Japan would be more effectively safeguarded by the use of United States long-range missiles in case of an emergency than by the presence of American troops and/or weapons on Japanese territory," p. 269, *ibid.*

But even more obviously today, overseas bases have a dominant role in non-nuclear wars. They affect the speed with which the West can react and the cost and size of reaction to aggressions in remote parts of the world. The role of Japan in fighting the Korean war, the movements in May 1962 from various stations to Thailand, and later movements of weapons from Thailand in support of the Indians in their battle with the Chinese all illustrate the continuing importance of overseas bases.

For the Russians also overseas bases in the 1960's and 1970's might conceivably come to have an important role. And this role would have principally to do with non-nuclear internal and external wars. Dr. Guy Pauker suggested a while ago that the massive Russian military aid to Indonesian or other overseas base areas might be the only way Russia has of influencing events in Southeast Asia directly rather than through the agency of its quarrelsome Chinese sometime partner and rival. Whatever the case for the Soviet Union, recent American policy unambiguously requires distant logistic support. The explicit shift in the last four years to stress conventional and unconventional non-nuclear war makes it more necessary than ever, and yet the importance of overseas bases seems to be less and less understood. Perhaps the recent troubles in India and Malaysia, with the demands they may place on British bases east of Suez as well as some American ones, will make their worth more generally appreciated. Less than nuclear contests remote from one or both of the great powers may nevertheless engage their interests in conflict, but such contests are hard to influence without overseas bases.

Our discussion of Cuba suggests that not all the interests of the United States conflict with those of the Soviet Union. Mr. Khrushchev and Mr. Kennedy were both clear about their mutual interest in keeping Castro's finger off a nuclear trigger. On the other hand, the view from the Soviet Union indicates that, in spite of talk about "overriding" interests of both sides in avoiding nuclear war, there are many fundamental points at issue between the great powers. And while there is hardly a doubt that both sides would be worse off in the event of a nuclear war, and that they do and should spend considerable energies and resources in avoiding it, the dubious note in the phrase "overriding interests. . ." is struck by the adjective "overriding." It suggests that the opposing interests are negligible, well understood, and easily resolved or likely to be resolved in the near-term future, if only, we are told, the politicians are sincere.

President Kennedy did not take the Soviet build-up in Cuba as an act unrelated to the future of the world. He related it to Chairman Khrushchev's desire to see the world transformed, to sponsor struggles of liberation, and to revise what the Russians regard as "abnormal" situations, such as West Berlin. In his October 22 speech announcing the American blockade of arms shipments to Cuba, President Kennedy warned that any hostile acts at other points on the globe (he mentioned West Berlin specifically) would meet with equal American determination, and he called upon Mr. Khrushchev to "abandon this course of world domination."

The encounter over this small island, then, on the American view, had to do with the future of the world. However, in this encounter, not only

Cuba, but the rest of the aligned and non-aligned world—the OAS, NATO, China, the United Nations—were subordinated to a passive role. The chief actors were the opposing nuclear powers. Castro could obstruct, delay, and complicate the resolution of the issue, but in the end he was hardly able to affect it centrally. Members of the OAS and NATO were apprised of the President's decision to institute a quarantine a few hours before it was announced to the public, and the actual signing of the Presidential proclamation of quarantine, was delayed to obtain the formal approval of the OAS members. These friends of the United States without exception rallied to its support and in the week of unrelenting pressure to get the missiles out, their consensus played a part. To assess its importance one should contemplate what might have been the effect of dissent. Can we be sure that a welter of doubts and alternative proposals might not have altered Khrushchev's esimate of the singleness of American resolve? If it had, the crisis might not have ended where it did.

Mr. Khrushchev had worse luck in this dealings with some of his allies. But in the end it was President Kennedy's and Chairman Khrushchev's decisions that determined events. The difficulty in sharing such momentous decisions raises important domestic issues in a democracy, but it has even more obvious problems for allies whose fate may be affected by those decisions.

Nonetheless what transpired was by no means a game of nuclear "chicken," as the advocates of unilateral disarmament suggest; both President Kennedy and Mr. Khrushchev showed acute consciousness and care about the risks.[28] (Some sober and excellent analysts accept the analogy of "Chicken," but the differences seem to us more significant than the identities. Bertrand Russell, who introduced the parallel in the 1950's as a paradigm of international behaviour today, meant precisely to suggest the recklessness of the statesmen, and the triviality and childishness of what was at issue—a kind of loss of face with the other children in the neighbourhood.) Nor was Cuba a case in which there was no danger of military action. There were possibilities of escalation, of the spread and intensification of violence. The risks of nuclear war are never zero. But the President was aware also of the risks of escalation in *inaction*. Inaction in Cuba would have invited, for example, a spiralling series of actions over Berlin.

From the timing of Mr. Khrushchev's move in Cuba it seems likely that he was conscious of the relation between Cuba and a climax to East-West disagreements over Berlin. President Kennedy at any rate was explicit about the connection. Retreat from a prominent public and formal stand that the United States had taken as recently as mid-September would

---

[28] Hysteria was manifest among those who thought of the decision makers of the great powers as hysterical or insane. Two ladies of the Campaign for Nuclear Disarmament in London left abruptly for Ireland; a famous American scientist left Washington for Geneva; and a contributor to the Council for Correspondence left his teaching job and his wife and children to take off for Australia. See *Encounter* (January 1963). Review of the British press on Cuba, see *Council for Correspondence Newsletter* (November 1962).

have invited Mr. Khrushchev to believe that the United States would retreat also in Berlin. (This might also have come to be the belief of the allies of the United States.) However, the risks that Mr. Khrushchev would have undertaken in Berlin are, for a variety of reasons, considerably larger than the risks he undertook in Cuba. The government of the United States had tried to make it clear that if the Soviet Union moved on Berlin or on the Central European front, then NATO in spite of local Communist superiority, would throw into the breach a very large conventional force, including perhaps a half dozen American divisions. If these were destroyed or in danger of destruction, it is evident that the risks of an American nuclear response would be raised enormously.

One cliché and over-simple view that seems to have a special appeal in crisis has it that the threat of force or the use of a low level of violence, including even a partial blockade, leads naturally to higher levels of violence. But in Cuba a very rudimentary and limited use of force, reversed the direction, started it down. There was in fact at no time during the crisis any suggestion on the part of President Kennedy and his immediate staff that this was a careless game of bluff, in which they incautiously might let a war get started by chance or unauthorized acts. On the contrary there was every attempt to resist the acts of desperation proposed from both the left and the right. "We have been determined," President Kennedy said on October 22, "not to be diverted from our central concerns by mere irritants and fanatics." Newspaper accounts during the crisis and a Senate Report published at the end of January, 1963, stressed the extreme concern of the President and his executive committee with even the minute details of actions taken at the lowest levels of government.[29] There was no dearth of management of the crisis.

Some of the statements of President Kennedy and even more those of Chairman Khrushchev may be a little misleading in this respect. In the case of Mr. Khrushchev, up to a certain point he may have wanted to convey an impression of recklessness. When confronted with the threat of having a Russian freighter boarded and searched, he asserted that this "would make talks useless" and bring into action the "forces and laws... of war";[30] it would have "irretrievably fatal consequences."[31]

In other words he was indicating to President Kennedy that interception of a freighter would involve thermonuclear massive retaliation, either as a deliberate act of the Russians or because he would not be able to restrain and control his own forces. Not he, but the laws of war would be in

[29] Senator Henry M. Jackson (Democrat, State of Washington), *Los Angeles Times,* January 29, 1963, and "The Administration of National Security: Basic Issues" for the Committee on Government Operations, 1963.

[30] Message to President Kennedy on October 27, 1962: "you, in your statement, said that the main aim is not only to come to an agreement [but also to] undertake measures to prevent a confrontation of our ships and thus aggravate the crisis and thus [ignite the fires] of a military conflict in such a confrontation, after which any talks would be already useless as other forces and laws would go into action, the laws of war." *New York Times,* October 28, 1962.

[31] *Ibid.*

charge. After the crisis had receded, moreover, Chairman Khrushchev was anxious to represent his retreat as a statesman's action to save the world from the imminent peril, "the direct threat of world thermonuclear war which arose in the Caribbean area."[32] "If one or the other side had not shown restraint, not done everything needed to avert the outbreak of war, an explosion of irreparable consequences would have followed."[33] He made more than a suggestion after the event that the danger of recklessness arose from "the ruling circle of the United States who are rightly called 'madmen.' The madmen insisted and insist now on starting a war as soon as possible against the Soviet Union."[34] Mr. Khrushchev's open and bitter contest with the Chinese and Albanian Communists also required pointed reference to the imminent dangers of thermonuclear war. However, at the peak of the crisis and in fact in the same letter in which he tried for the last time to suggest an inevitable and uncontrollable thermonuclear response to the interception of a Soviet freighter, Chairman Khrushchev made it very plain that he was in careful, thorough, and self-conscious charge of the decision on whether or not to respond with nuclear weapons. It was here in fact that he in particular stressed that the Cuban missiles were under his control. And in the following day he emphasized again that "the Soviet government" will not allow itself to be provoked."[35] Finally in his *post-mortem* speech to the Supreme Soviet on December 12, 1962, he indicated that both the Russian and American "sides displayed a sober approach, and took into account that unless such steps were taken that could help overcome the dangerous development of events, a third World War might break out." The madmen in the ruling circle of the United States then were very sober lunatics; and the sober Russians understood that.

Some of President Kennedy's statements in the crisis and after may also have overstated the likelihood of a nuclear exchange. He was appropriately anxious to express the gravity of his concern about such a catastrophe. Theodore Sorensen makes clear that President Kennedy was aware of the pitfalls of public utterance at this time. "His warnings on the presence of Soviet missiles in Cuba had to be sufficiently sombre to enlist support around the world without creating panic here at home."[36] And so on October 22, 1962, he talked of the world "at the abyss of destruction." In his acceptance of Mr. Khrushchev's retreat on October 28, 1962, he seemed also to accept the validity of Mr. Khrushchev's earlier threat of uncontrollability. "Developments, were approaching a point where events could have become unmanageable." Though control was evident in every one of his moves, President Kennedy's statements did not stress in words that he was in con-

---

[32] Speech of December 12, 1962, to the Supreme Soviet, *New York Times,* December 13, 1962.
[33] *Ibid.*
[34] *Ibid.*
[35] Message to President Kennedy of October 28, 1962.
[36] *Decision-Making in the White House* (New York: Columbia University Press, 1963), p. 47.

trol. It has therefore been possible to misconstrue just what were the risks in the crisis.

The matter is of great importance. The fact that Cuba could be isolated makes a great contrast with the problem in Central Europe. But even on the Central European front American policy differs markedly from that of a dictator who uses a reputation for irresponsibility and apparent willingness to usher in *Goetterdaemmerung* for even minor agains. Threats of uncontrollability should be administered by prescription, against special dangers, and in small doses. Its use except *in extremis* is not compatible with a reputation for being both sane and meaning what one says.

In fact the main risks were of a local, non-nuclear action involving the United States and Russian forces. The possibilities of isolating a limited conflict have seldom been clearer. The situation is very different from Berlin. Remote islands are better than enclaves in satellite territory in this respect. Cuba, surrounded by water rather than East Germans, very distant from the centre of Russian conventional power, did not represent, nor was it contiguous to, any interests that the Soviet Union had dominated for many years. How likely was Chairman Khrushchev to launch missiles at the United States to retrieve a gamble for a quick expansion of this Communist foothold in the Western Hemisphere, itself a windfall? Retreat in fact has not even meant the loss of the foothold.

What was threatened was a local non-nuclear action, a measure of very limited violence, only the boarding of ships. On the staircase of ascending steps in the use of force there would have been many landings, many decision points, at which either side could choose between climbing higher or moving down. The United States' nuclear retaliatory force would have made a Soviet missile strike against the United States catastrophic for Russia. But the United States also had an immense local superiority in conventional forces. The Soviet Union clearly would have lost the nonnuclear exchange. Chairman Khrushchev stepped down to avoid a clash of conventional forces in which he would have lost. To avoid this level of loss he would have had irresponsibly to risk very much higher levels.

Some distinguished American analysts tell us that our local superiority in conventional force was an inessential convenience affecting our selfconfidence, but not Khrushchev's. Without a deep psychoanalysis of the former Chairman, this would be rather hard to prove or disprove. However, so bald a separation of the determinants of decision on the two sides seems most implausible. Each side strained to affect the anticipations of the other by act as well as word, and its own expectations depended in part on how it read the other's. The American leadership knew that Khrushchev had no basis for confidence in the outcome of any clash with conventional arms in the Caribbean; and a world to lose if he resorted to nuclear weapons.

Inevitably, the question of how nuclear and how conventional arms figured in forcing Khrushchev's withdrawal was much disputed once the crisis had passed, although it is doubtful whether many of the disputants changed their views as a result either of the crisis or the post-crisis debate.

Witnesses at the Congressional hearings in the following spring at any rate interpreted events according to their predispositions.[37] Those who had held before the crisis that a strategic nuclear threat can credibly and safely deter all but rather minor border incursions testified that "strategic superiority" was the major factor forcing Khrushchev's withdrawal. Those who had believed that nuclear force—in particular a clearcut second-strike nuclear capability—is vital, but inadequate as a response to an important range of provocations, took the withdrawal as illustrating "the cutting edge" of the conventional sword. This single encounter where the United States had both the capability to dominate in a conventional conflict and also to inflict overwhelming nuclear damage could not demonstrate once and for all that conventional superiority will always have a major utility; still less could it show that it might easily be dispensed with. Witnesses such as Secretary McNamara who valued and had greatly increased useable conventional capability in the preceding two years, were in charge of controlling the risks during the crisis. They deployed and prepared to use a vast conventional force, including several hundred thousand men poised for invasion. While continuing to deter nuclear action by the Russians, they prepared a mounting sequence of threats short of nuclear war. The dispensability of these moves can only be conjectured. Relying on more desperate threats might have worked, but would clearly have been a greater gamble.

The relevance to Berlin of the Cuban crisis was, as we have said, immediately recognized by the President and the other members of the EXCOM, for a retreat in Cuba would have been evidence of a likely retreat in Berlin. But our firmness in Cuba cannot conclusively show the opposite. Some Americans are concerned to play down our conventional superiority in Cuba lest it suggest, illogically to be sure, that we would be firm *only* where we have conventional superiority. But for us as for the Russians the stakes as well as the risks are larger in Berlin.

Not that the risks were small in Cuba. The menace of actual conflict between American and Russian forces even in battle with conventional weapons was emphasized by the long history of debate on the massive retaliation theory. As General Maxwell Taylor's account makes clear, much of the doctrinal dispute among the Joint Chiefs had taken the form of a seemingly scholastic argument over the definition of "general war."[38] "General war" had been defined as a conflict between the forces of the United States and those of the Soviet Union, and the definition assumed and made explicit that nuclear weapons would be used from the outset. The definition was an attempt to enforce by semantics, so to speak, a belief that any hostile contact between American and Russian troops would bring immediate nuclear devastation, and so to discourage such a contact. But in Cuba it was apparent that conventional attack on the Russian missile

---

[37] *Military Procurement Authorization, Fiscal Year 1964*, Committee on Armed Services, U.S. Senate, 88th Congress, First Session, 1963, pp. 507, 896 and *Passim.* Cf. also *Hearings on Military Posture*, House Armed Services Committee, 1963.

[38] *The Uncertain Trumpet* (New York: Harper & Row, Publishers, 1960), pp. 7ff, 39, 117.

bases was one of the alternatives contemplated and that therefore the United States was separating the decision to do battle with the Russians from the decision to initiate a nuclear war. Decisions to board Russian ships were even more obviously kept distinct from a nuclear decision.

Chairman Khrushchev was right in his later assertion that the United States and the Soviet Union were both in full control of their nuclear forces.

V. CONTROL AND AUTOMATIC STAIRS

We stress the point only because, in this respect, some of the American official statements made at the height of the crisis did less than justice to American policy. Any suggestion that the United States could not control its responses even in boarding a Russian freighter, would be bound to raise disturbing questions at home. And under some circumstances it would be self-defeating. If Chairman Khrushchev had thought that American decision makers themselves believed their next move would push events out of control, that they had, in the legal phrase, the last clear chance to avoid nuclear war, he might very well have doubted the desperate move and so have been rather less deterred and less alarmed than the American public and America's allies. He might have found it inconceivable that the American President would deliberately let matters get unmanageable. In fact, well before the Cuban crisis the President and Secretary MacNamara and Secretary Rusk had declared, and their subordinates had elaborated, a thoughtful doctrine of controlled response, up to and including the conduct of a nuclear war. Yet, as we have mentioned, President Kennedy's statement of October 22, excellent as it was on the whole, focussed, for understandable reasons, on "the abyss of destruction." And in attempting to get across the essential message of the American nuclear guarantee for neighbours in Latin America, it indicated that "any nuclear missile launched from Cuba against any nation in the Western Hemisphere" would evoke " 'a *full*' retaliatory response upon the Soviet Union." (our italics). This does not sound like a controlled response. The attempt, it appears, was to say that the United States would respond to a missile against its neighbours as it would respond to one against itself. This latter policy would leave open the possibility of controlled reaction. The United States has made clear that a single nuclear missile launched against the United States need not trip an uncontrolled "full" response.

However, it was even more important to make clear, and in American behaviour it was evident, that the United States did not exclude the possibility of control in the non-nuclear spectrum. In fact it insisted upon it. It responded in a carefully limited way to an aggression which involved the installation, but not the firing, of a nuclear weapon. Against such a move the Cuban crisis demonstrated the relevance and the adequacy of the lowest non-nuclear moves in an ascending series of non-nuclear threats and actions: the threat to board and search freighters for military equipment, a single actual boarding of a chartered Lebanese ship, the imposition of a selective economic blockade, a general blockade, the threat or the actual use of bombing with high explosives against strategic missile bases, the threat or actual use of paratroops, and so forth. The later steps in the sequence never had to be more than latent. But one of the reasons the limited American threat worked was that the United States was willing to take the next steps, if necessary, and had the power to do so—to make each next step less profitable for the Soviet Union.

Before the crisis, the alternatives for policy were discussed in terms of a few bare possibilities: a pure American military invasion, a total blockade, or doing nothing. In the crisis it appeared the world was richer in alternatives than had been conceived by extremists of the left or right. There is a good deal between doing nothing and all-out nuclear war, and an appropriate intermediate response could make a nuclear war less rather than more likely. President Kennedy observed that these alternatives became apparent in the course of five days of discussion, that without this time for hammering out alternatives, he might have chosen less wisely and more extremely.[39] The history of this crisis should be an important corrective for the loose assumption that the only time available for decision in the nuclear age is 15 minutes—a magic number supposed to represent the time from radar intercept to impact of an ICBM following a least energy path.

Professor Richard Neustadt, who has written most perceptively about the use, the limits, and the risks of using American presidential power, has taken the Cuban missile confrontation to illustrate the President's extreme awareness of the new dimensions of these risks, of the fact that somewhere in a succession of decisions he may make one that can neither be reversed nor repaired.[40] It has probably always been true that at some time in a sequence of diplomatic acts, warnings of possible military actions, and military acts themselves, statesmen have felt "things in the saddle," events taking over. It then becomes extremely unlikely that adversaries will back away from the contest or its intensification. Even though the new level of violence is likely to leave both of them worse off than *before* the sequence of threats and pre-war manœuvres had started, nonetheless, there may be some point of no return in the sequence. At that point the outcome may appear to be better than the risk of stopping. The fact that today decisions taken in crisis might precipitate a disaster on a scale without precedent in history is sobering.

There is a sense of course in which any large scale war does enormous, irreparable harm. Population growth and economic recovery after the war replace the lives lost, the wealth annihilated, and the suffering only in a statistical sense that ignores precisely who died and what treasures were

[39] *Washington Post*, December 18, 1962.
[40] *Administration of National Security. Hearings Before the Sub-Committee on National Security Staffing and Operations of the Committee on Government Operations*, U.S. Senate, 88th Congress, 1st Session. Part I (1963), p. 76ff.

destroyed. Some nuclear conflicts might start by miscalculation and end by being quickly brought under control, and conceivably could do less material damange than World War II and I. Nonetheless such a standard is terrible enough and a nuclear war could be enormously worse. This new sense of the possibility of irreparable harm says a good deal about the psychological burden of the Presidency. And not only the Presidency. The Chairman of the CPSU explicitly referred to the "irreparable" consequences of a failure in restraint by either side. It makes clear why neither Nikita Khrushchev nor John Kennedy behaved like the irrational juvenile delinquents who are sometimes presumed to occupy the seats of power today, strapped by their seatbelts in a carefree game of chicken.

Where the alternative is to be ruled by events with such enormous consequences, the head of a great state is likely to examine his acts of choice in crisis and during it to subdivide these possible acts in ways that make it feasible to continue exercising choice. This sort of behaviour does not fit an increasingly popular and professional picture which has it that political leaders may be thoughtful, responsible, and close to reality in between crises, but overreact passionately during the crises themselves. However, there is a good deal of professional evidence as well as common sense opinion to indicate that, as Dewey put it, when any thinking is going on, it is likely to be because there has been some trouble. Routine experience may lead us imperceptibly to ignore a slowly changing or suddenly new reality, but we do sometimes rise to a challenge with heightened alertness and an increased sense of responsibility, especially on matters of great moment. The behaviour of the decision makers in the Cuban crisis at any rate provides a counter example to a good many pessimistic predictions derived from studies by behavioural scientists concerned with reducing international tension.[41]

A process of escalation is usually thought of simply as an increase in violence growing out of a limited conflict in which an adversary may act to stave off his loss or an opponent's prospective success. The aspect of "escalators" that inspired its use in this connection, we suspect, is the fact that moving stairways carry a passenger on automatically without any effort of his will. However, as we have suggested there are down-escalators

---

[41] Generalising from 1914, some studies predict that as tensions rise in a crisis, decision makers will tend to decide emotionally rather than by calculation. The range of alternatives they see will narrow and they will be less able to assess the likely consequences of each possible choice. They will see less time before the enemy strikes and this will lead to still greater tension, to a tendency to value early action and dislike delay, to depreciate the dangers of violent action and the rewards of non-violent action, and to accept suspicions and fears as facts. These predictions are necessarily somewhat vague. None of them, however, appears to have been borne out by the behaviour of decision makers in the missile crisis. See *Content Analysis, a Handbook with Applications for the Study of International Crisis* by Robert C. North, Ole R. Holsti, M. George Zaninovich, and Dina A. Zinnes, Northwestern University Press, 1963, Appendix B, for the hypotheses derived from 1914 and contrast with materials derived from the Cuban crisis and presented by Holsti, North, and Brody in *Peace Research Society (International) Papers*, Vol. 2, Oslo (1965).

one can decide to get off or to get on, to go up or down, or to stay there; or take the stairs. Just where automaticity or irreversibility takes over is an uncertain but vital matter, and that is one of the reasons a decision maker may want to take a breath at a landing to consider next steps. It is apparent from President Kennedy's own descriptions of the Cuban crisis as well as Mr. Sorenson's that he gave enormous value to the cautious weighing of alternatives made possible by the interval of almost a week; to the five or six days mentioned for hammering out the first decision. And the decision made was precisely one that left open a variety of choices. Finally, the availability of less desperate choices than acquiescence or holocaust had been prepared before the crisis by the deliberate policy of preserving options, developing a force capable of flexible response.

One way in which the overhanging possibility of an irreversible disastrous decision might operate today is to bring on an immobility that, paradoxically, reduces the alternatives to a few extremes. The irreversible sequence might be started then by a desperate act to avoid the loss that looms in the extreme of retreat. But there is more than one way to arrive at a paralysis and gross reduction of choice. The opposite path, proceeding on the perception that commitment is inevitable, can advance commitment to a much earlier stage than necessary in the process of coercion and resisting coercion. This is the danger inherent in threats of massive retaliation. That war can be so massive a disaster tempts us to use the threat of this disaster to paralyze an adversary bent on aggression; but it may end in our own paralysis. The Cuban missile crisis at any rate illustrated an intensive search among alternatives to find a threat that could be executed with a minimal risk, and a slowly ascending sequence of threats which could not be challenged by the Soviet Union without making its position still worse.

There is an important class of situations in which a crisis may be precipitated as the result of an unfounded or exaggerated mutual distrust. These are cases where, in the words of the most brilliant analyst of such reciprocal fears, "people may vaguely think they perceive that the situation is inherently explosive, and respond by exploding."[42] But some of the time guns go off because we do not know they are loaded; grenades explode because we think they are duds; or enemies attack because we are so sure they will not attack that we are unprepared for it. The Cuban missile crisis should remind us of these equally important situations in which an excess of trust or self-confidence causes the trouble, and a sharp awakening to the possibilities of explosion helps bring the trouble under responsible control. Tactics of deception typically attempt to induce trust where it is not warranted. Khrushchev and Gromyko during the prelude to the crisis simply lied. And the traditional confidence man feeds on the gullibility and wishfulness of his target: "Never give a sucker an even break" evokes a long history of cases where it is not mutual distrust that is explosive, but fond belief on the one side, a willingness to exploit it on the other, and a

42 T. C. Schelling, *The Strategy of Conflict*, p. 208.

violent sense of outrage by the victim at having his innocence exploited. But the victim need not explode. He can carefully signal the danger to his adversary.

The resolution of the missile crisis may be regarded as in the main a brilliant example of a successful communication of a precise and firm intention. However, in some of its aspects, and especially in its generation, the crisis illustrates the possibilities of miscommunication. Under other circumstances, such miscommunication might not have had so fortunate an ending. Moreover, the misunderstandings do not fit one current wishful stereotype: that our troubles stem only from our failure to realize how like us our adversaries really are. Our estimates and those of the Russians, just before the missile confrontation, resembled each other mainly in that they each too easily assumed an identity in modes of thought and valuation. They illustrate rather the difficulty one always has in breaking out of the circle of one's own notion of what is normal in national behaviour.

The missile crisis was precipitated by some poor Russian and American estimates of each other's willingness to take risks. The American leaders did not believe the Russians would be foolhardy enough, in the face of President Kennedy's explicit warning against it, to put into Cuba missiles which were capable of hitting the United States. The Russians on the other hand did not think the Americans would risk a direct confrontation.

The false estimates on both sides did not concern whether the United States had clearly warned the Russians not to put in place in Cuba surface-to-surface missiles with a significant capability to hit the United States. They had to do with Russian disbelief that the President would act in case they ignored his warning, and an American judgment that the Russians would recognize that the President meant what he said. Yet one curious aftermath of the crisis is a rewriting of history, especially in Europe, that questions not merely whether it was obvious that President Kennedy meant what he explicitly stated in September, but doubts even that he had said it.

The situation is somewhat confused by the interminable wrangle over the distinction between "offensive" and "defensive" weapons. There is of course no sharp distinction between the two and there are many inter-connections. An aggressor can defend himself, limit the destruction wreaked against his own territory, among other subtler ways, by using surface-to-surface missiles or bombers to reduce his victim's retaliatory forces before they take off; and once his victim's retaliatory forces are launched on their way, he can use active and passive defences, such as surface-to-air missiles, jet fighters, and civil defence to reduce his victim's retaliation further. Moreover, the Cuban surface-to-air missiles and fighters themselves illustrate that active defences can be used to prevent or to impede surveillance and so help to cover the build-up of a force of surface-to-surface missiles and manned bombers. Even the direct use of fighter aircraft or short-range missiles with the help of torpedo boats would provide some minimal capability to hit American coastal targets. All of this ignores still subtler interconnections between the threats or the use of "offensive" or "defensive" weapons.

However, the distinction the President made between offensive and defensive weapons served the purpose of warning well enough, because he made very clear what weapons he had in mind as "offensive." On September 4 he said, "...the Soviets have provided the Cuban government with a number of anti-aircraft defence missiles with a slant range of 25 miles which are similar to early models of our Nike.... There is no evidence... of the presence of offensive ground-to-ground missiles; or of other significant offensive capability either in Cuban hands or under Soviet direction and guidance. Were it to be otherwise, the gravest issues would arise."

In other words the President drew a line with a broad and hairy brush between offensive and defensive weapons in general, but he clearly classed Russian medium and intermediate range surface-to-surface missiles in the offensive category. Emplacing them in Cuba would be strategic trespass. Moreover the Russians understood him. Their government authorized *Tass* to state on September 11 "...there is no need for the Soviet Union to shift its weapons...to any other country, for instance Cuba...the Soviet Union has rockets so powerful to carry...nuclear warheads that there is no need to search for sites for them beyond the boundaries of the Soviet Union...the Soviet Union has the capability from its own territory to render assistance to any peace-loving state and not only to Cuba."

The President knew that the message had been understood. He believed it would be respected. It was this last conviction, supported by Soviet reassurances, "both public and private," in September, that proved illusory in the following month. In President Kennedy's words,

> I don't think that we expected that he (Khrushchev) would put the missiles in Cuba, because it would have seemed such an imprudent action for him to take, as it was later proved. Now, he obviously must have thought that he could do it in secret and that the United States would accept it. So that he did not judge our intentions accurately.

The Americans assumed in short that the Russians understood that Americans are tolerant but cannot be pushed beyond a certain point, especially when that point has been clearly and publicly announced. But just how imprudent it was for the Russians to put missiles in Cuba depended on whether the Americans were willing to force a showdown. So the American esitmate that the Russians would not emplace the missiles depended on an American judgment about how the Russians thought Americans would act. Moreover, there is no doubt that President Kennedy's judgment of the American character was right. His own behaviour, with its brief explosion of anger at Gromyko's continuing deception, and the bitter repetition in the October 22 speech "That statement was false" was in a long tradition of sharp moral reactions at confidence betrayed. In more controlled form, it repeated the indignation of acting Secretary Polk and President Wilson at the decoded German message showing that while the German foreign minister had been talking peace he had plotted to encourage a Mexican attack on the United States. Or the fury of Secretary Hull and

President Roosevelt at the Japanese representatives Kurusu and Nomura at the time of Pearl Harbour.

On the other hand, to the Russians surely President Kennedy's response was an extraordinary over-reaction. Chairman Khrushchev had enunciated and withdrawn a succession of ultimata on Berlin beginning in 1958, and done so with distinct disappointment, but with comparative equanimity. He could hardly have understood either the enormous importance conferred by domestic party debate (with the Bay of Pigs disaster in the background) on the specific line the President had drawn between offensive and defensive weapons, or the great to-do over the deception. (Khrushchev's experience with cases in which Americans themselves had used deception might have suggested the accompanying sense of guilt and half-heartedness with which this is done. The American response to the shooting down of the U-2 piloted by Powers in 1960 forms an interesting cultural contrast with the indignant denial by the Soviet government in the United Nations of actions revealed by the detailed reconnaissance photos of the missiles in Cuba.) Each side in short tended to project its own psychology or certain stereotypes about the behaviour of the other. The Russians acted on the assumption that the Americans were so riven by domestic politics as to be unlikely to react in any decisive way; or that they would act like Russians.

In the period of withdrawing the missiles, once again, Americans tended to project American behaviour on to the Russians. Just as they had exaggerated the Russian estimate of risks and underestimated Russian daring, they now overestimated Russian reluctance to withdraw after a nice try. But here too Russian behaviour is very different from American. The prospect of humiliation was of enormous importance to President Kennedy. It did not have quite the same importance for Khrushchev. Serious students of Russian behaviour with such different approaches as George Kennan and Nathan Leites have long observed that "the Kremlin has no compunction about retreating in the face of superior force."[43] After the withdrawal, many journalists recalled Brest-Litovsk and Lenin's phrase about the good revolutionary being willing to crawl in the mud. But that recollection was much rarer in the actual week of quarantine and crisis. By December, 1962, Khrushchev himself was referring to Lenin's "sensible" and "temporary" concession. The Albanian dogmatists who criticized the withdrawal of missiles, he claimed, were sliding down Trotsky's path of unyielding infantilism at Brest. But the missile withdrawal was not even a temporary retreat, much less a capitulation. The concessions, Khrushchev said, were "mutual."[44]

Such cultural contrasts are of course a matter of degree; but nonetheless real. Ruth Benedict's *The Chrysanthemum and the Sword* offers a brilliant analysis of Japanese feelings toward retreat and humiliation—as far exceed-

---

[43] George Kennan, *American Diplomacy*, 1900–1950, p. 112. See also Nathan Leites, *Study of Bolshevism*, Chapter 19, and his recent "Kremlin Thoughts: Yielding, Provoking, Rebuffing, Retreating." RM 3618–ISA, the RAND Corporation (May 1963), pp. 24ff.

[44] Speech, December 12, 1962.

ing in depth and range American emotions on the subject. And there are limits to Bolshevik tolerance in withdrawal.

VI. INTERESTS AND INFLUENCE OF THE TWO PRINCIPALS AND THEIR ALLIES

This retrospect of the interests and policy alternatives open to the three powers in the crisis indicates the need for refining some of the questions with which we started. When we say that in the nuclear age force is no longer an instrument of policy, it is not clear whether this is description or exhortation. In fact a blockade, it was generally agreed in September, 1962, was an act of war. Attitudes and definitions changed in October. This is a delicate matter of semantics. The American interdiction of ships carrying arms to Cuba was called a "quarantine." Nonetheless it was an act of force. And threats of higher levels of violence were implicit at every stage in the developing crisis. The questions at issue directly affected Soviet, Cuban, and United States military power.

The availability of nuclear weapons to the great powers had a double aspect. The weapons imposed the need for great responsibility and careful, very conscious control over the limited encounters that took place. On the other hand, the use of lower levels of violence in such encounters is in a certain sense encouraged by the knowledge that a decision to escalate to nuclear weapons would be irrational and inappropriate for either of the participants and, for the prudent men in control, uncharacteristically irrational. And prudent antagonists can cooperate to insulate nuclear weapons from less prudent third parties. These encounters were rather clearly isolable from a decision to use nuclear weapons. Each of the nuclear powers took the time and had the information to see that the initiation of nuclear weapons would badly worsen its own position.

American nuclear power immobilized Russian nuclear power. And American local superiority in non-nuclear force together with a demonstrated willingness to use it discouraged further destabilizing moves. The familiar saying that overwhelming nuclear force simply disables its possessor from using any force at all is a rather shallow paradox. Nevertheless thermonuclear weapons clearly suit only the gravest purposes. And while small nations are less able to affect events than big ones, they do have an effect. There are serious limits to the control even a great nuclear power has over its non-nuclear allies. This applies more obviously to relations between the United States and its allies than it does to Russia's relations with its friends. Even allies whose defence and economy depend almost wholly on the United States are, as the headlines continually remind us, far from being its puppets. A variety of South Korean and South Vietnamese regimes in the last few years has made this point vivid. And the point is much more obvious for allies that are themselves great nations.

But in this crisis at any rate a small Communist power was the object of contention between its protector and its adversary and could not decisively affect the outcome. It had some capability for mischief, but even this was limited. Close and receding allies of the Soviet Union and the United States as well as the nonaligned countries could do little more than endorse or criticize after the fact. In the climactic encounter it was the United States and the Soviet Union who determined events.

The loneliness of the President's decision in such a crisis raises essential problems for allies, whose fates might be affected by it. They have an interest in sharing and influencing the decision. But also in seeing to it that the decision can be made—in avoiding paralysis. This is an essential dilemma of nuclear control. In some sense the problem is quite as acute from the standpoint of an American citizen as it is from that of a Briton, or an Italian, or a Frenchman, or a citizen of any of the NATO or OAS countries. In the five or six days in which the course of quarantine was selected, only an extremely small number of people (the President himself suggested a maximum of 15) had any share in the choice.

In spite of the very just allied, as well as domestic, concern, this is not the sort of problem that can be neatly "solved." It can be softened somewhat, and essentially the same methods can widen both allied and domestic participation. The crises themselves and the time for decision in crises are, we have suggested, likely to occupy a good deal longer interval than the magic 15 minutes frequently referred to when nuclear dangers are in mind. The small group concerned with the actual management of the crisis conceivably could then include a few high level allied political figures. It is notable that in the missile crisis, while allies were not notified of the American quarantine until the day before its public announcement, the decision itself undertook a very minimal use of force, leaving many decision points still open in the future conduct of the affair.

More important, one can prepare for a variety of contingencies in advance of crises; one can determine what might be done, if they occur. In fact, the quadripartite planning for Berlin at the very least strongly influenced President Kennedy and his immediate associates, predisposed them to the consideration of firm but carefully measured responses to any local action, and also made them more highly conscious of the worldwide repercussions inherent in many such "local" crises.

Unfortunately, however, acute perception of the importance of far off points in space tends to be highly localized in time—to be mostly limited, in fact to times of crisis.[45] The problem of sharing contingency planning is complicated by the fact that allies are notoriously ambivalent about

45 There was a strand of European opinion that seized on the Americans' firm response to Cuba as somehow a verification of the thesis that United States interests are also highly localized; it would act strongly in its own interests, when threatened close to home, but not in Europe, not, for example, in Berlin. We may leave aside the rather curious inference from the fact of positive reaction to a strong provocation close to home—to the conclusion that there would be no reaction to a more distant challenge. However, a careful scrutiny of the American response to Cuba would suggest that far from showing that the United States would not defend Berlin, the defence of Cuba from the very first revelation of the Soviet move was recognized to be a vital part of the defence of Berlin, and the fate of Berlin was prominent in the contingency planning.

distant troubles. Before the crisis itself, they are likely to feel that the remote problem is not very important from their point of view; they may believe either that the chances of disaster are small; or that the disaster will be local. They are almost sure to feel their resources are limited and they have troubles "of their own." Indeed America's troubles with Cuba tended to be deprecated by its allies as something of an American obsession. The United States on the other hand naturally often felt that its allies underestimated the depth and complexity of the threat of communism in Latin America, and its possible ultimate worldwide importance.

NATO collaboration in shaping policy for future crises is not easy for crises in the NATO treaty area. It is a good deal harder for any of the multiplicity of crises that, arising outside the NATO periphery, may ultimately be of concern to NATO. Nonetheless it seems that, for those allies that feel a concern, rather more contingency planning in common, formal or informal, bilateral or multilateral, could be done.

The interests of Latin American governments and people in the outcome of the missile crisis was most obvious. It was the first time that these countries had come directly in the shadow of a nuclear war. And the discovery of the missiles and their forced withdrawal in a dangerous crisis had a large emotional impact. While some of the concern was directed against the United States, on the whole Castro lost ground. By pulling Latin America into the centre of a confrontation between the two principal nuclear powers, he appeared to an increased number of Latin Americans to be dangerously irresponsible. Even Goulart's Brazil and Mexico, which had opposed OAS concert against Castro, backed the President's blockade; and there is no doubt that such effects lasted long beyond the crisis. The losses Castro suffered contrast with his exalted hopes before the crisis that Russian missiles in Cuba would fortify his prestige and influence in Latin America. But they do not show that his hopes were unfounded; just that he had gambled. Smaller countries may feel a great deal of ambivalence about the acquisition of nuclear weapons by their neighbours. So the mingled fear, pride, respect, and distrust inspired in Asia today by the first Chinese nuclear test. The main trouble with Castro's gamble from his standpoint was that it failed; at least for the time.

Finally a note of caution: it is easy to read too much into events, even those of outstanding importance. Once the crisis had passed, perhaps inevitably it was greeted as the herald of a new era—a testing and final stabilization of "the balance" of nuclear power between the Soviet Union and the United States, an essential elimination of the danger of nuclear war for the foreseeable future. Especially in Europe the notion seems widespread that the Cuban missile crisis represented a "turning point." But such an interpretation should be suspect in particular when advanced by those who before the missile crisis had felt the era of effortless stability had already arrived, and then during the crisis swung to the opposite extreme of panic in exaggerating the likelihood of war. In fact the "balance" is too vaguely defined, too complex, and too changeable for any such assurance. The hazards of change are political as well as technical and military. It would be a mistake to regard the Soviets' emplacement of missiles in Cuba as something like a crucial experiment deliberately conducted by the Russians and establishing for them definitely once and for all that the West is determined to resist any changes in the balance—however the "balance" is defined. Khrushchev himself quickly rejected Lord Home's hopeful declaration that the Russians, sobered by their recent experience in Cuba, might from that time revise their international role.

The Western show of determination in the missile crisis had its effects. Perhaps, as has been said, it made easier the conclusion of the test ban. Perhaps it contributed to the ultimate fall of Khrushchev. At least it provided both Khrushchev's foreign and domestic rivals with a sequence of two misdeeds to cite—"adventurism" followed by "capitulationism."[46] In spite of the ready vocabulary of abuse available to describe the sequence, such an apparently opportune advance followed by a prudent withdrawal in the face of superior force is entirely consistent with a Marxist canon of behaviour, which fixes no timetable for Communist expansion. The effects of the Western determination, however, in the long run are uncertain and are hardly likely to be definitive. It is most implausible to suppose that this one major Communist failure will foreclose all future significant attempts, should opportunities arise, to make further advance.

The world has changed then; but not completely. It is surely no simpler now than it was before. There are many possible dangers to the West other than a precisely timed world conspiracy of a perfectly unified, permanently hostile Communist camp. Some have to do with intense Communist rivalries and the great variety of "communisms" today. Even an abating hostility impels caution, so long as the change is uncertain, patchy, intermittent, and slow. The transformation of the whole world need hardly be at stake, only substantial parts of it. Castro is no Tito, nor a satellite, nor an immediate military threat, nor simply a minor nuisance, but a persistent source and model for insurgency and terror in the hemisphere.

Inevitably, one extreme reading of the missile crisis took it as proving that Communists in a showdown will always retreat, that we need only face them in the future with the alternative of nuclear disaster for them to abandon any use of force to transform the world. This simple view fortunately is not very influential. Yet, if it is dangerously implausible to suppose that a few future military confrontations are capable of having this happy result, it is at least equally implausible to hold that a single encounter has already had it.

46 Statement by the People's Government of China of September 1, 1963.

PART II

INTERNATIONAL

LAW

CHAPTER FIVE

INTERNATIONAL SYSTEMS
AND INTERNATIONAL LAW

Stanley Hoffmann

Harvard University

Stanley Hoffmann's far-ranging survey of the role of law in world politics elucidates the essential differences between international and domestic politics. By delimiting international systems, by outlining the basic functions of international law in stable and revolutionary periods, he suggests the manner in which legal norms and practices may contribute to world order in contrasting historical epochs. In tracing the pervasive changes in the status of international law, Hoffmann argues that from "the dialectic of the obsolete and the premature" has emerged some evidence of "a third way" based on the precarious elements of stability in the heterogeneous global milieu. The ambiguity of international law will remain its outstanding feature in the foreseeable future. The absence of common conceptions of legitimacy precludes a further extension of law into the intensive relations between political units, despite modifications in traditional conceptions of sovereignty.

Reprinted from *The International System,* Klaus Knorr and Sidney Verba, eds. Princeton: Princeton University Press, 1961, pp. 205–37. By permission.

The purpose of this essay is twofold. First, it proposes to undertake, in introductory form, one of the many tasks a historical sociology of international relations could perform: the comparative study of one of those relations which appear in almost any international system, i.e., international law.[1] Secondly, this essay will try to present the rudimentary outlines of a theory of international law which might be called sociological or functional.[2]

International law is one of the aspects of international politics which reflects most sharply the essential differences between domestic and world affairs. Many traditional distinctions tend to disappear, owing to an "international civil war" which projects what are primarily domestic institutions (such as parliaments and pressure groups) into world politics, and injects worldwide ideological clashes into domestic affairs. International law, like its Siamese twin and enemy, war, remains a crystallization of all that keeps world politics *sui generis*. If theory is to be primarily concerned with the distinctive features of systems rather than with the search for regularities, international law becomes a most useful approach to international politics.

This paper will examine the relations between international law and international systems, first in general terms, and subsequently in more concrete form, with evidence derived from history. Finally, in the light of such a historical presentation, I will examine briefly two of the main politico-legal problems raised by international law.

I

Most theories of domestic politics start from the ideal-type of 1) a community—i.e., an unconditional consensus on cooperation, a belief in a

[1] See some suggestions in my *Contemporary Theory in International Politics* (Englewood Cliffs, N.J.: Prentice-Hall, Inc., 1960), pp. 174ff.

[2] These adjectives are borrowed from Julius Stone, "Problems Confronting Sociological Enquiries Concerning International Law," *Recueil des Cours de l'Académie de Droit International*, Vol. 89 (1956), I, and Hans J. Morgenthau, *Dilemmas of Politics*, Chicago, 1958, ch. II, respectively. The only additional recent works which try to establish a political sociology of international law are Charles de Visscher's *Theory and Reality in Public International Law*, tr. by P. E. Corbett, Princeton, N.J., 1957; Percy E. Corbett's *Law in Diplomacy*, Princeton, N.J., 1959; B. Laundheer's "Contemporary Sociological Theories and International Law," *Recueil des Cours...*, Vol. 91 (1957), I; and, to some extent, John Herz's *International Politics in the Atomic Age*, New York, 1959, and Morton A. Kaplan's and Nicholas Katzenbach's "The Patterns of International Politics and of International Law," *American Political Science Review*, LIII (September 1959), pp. 693–712—the last two pieces being more concerned with politics than with law. The present essay, which supplements an earlier piece on "Quelques aspects du rôle du Droit International dans la politique étrangère des Etats" (Association Française de Science Politique, *La Politique étrangère et ses Fondements*, Paris, 1954, pp. 239–77), will itself be expanded into a volume on *International Law in World Politics*.

common good (however vague) and in the precedence of this common good over particular interests; and 2) an organization, the State, which has created this community or was established by it, and is endowed with the monopoly of the legitimate use of force. The theory of international politics must start from the ideal-type of a milieu in which 1) the behavior of the members ranges from, at best, that of partners in a society (who cooperate on a limited number of issues, rarely unconditionally, and give primary allegiance to themselves, not the society) to that of accomplices in chaos: the social group made up of the states is always on the verge of being a fiction; and 2) there is no monopoly of power, over and above that possessed by the members. Thus, whereas procedures for cooperation, for the creation and expression of consent, exist both in domestic and in world politics, the permanent possibility of free and legitimate recourse to violence remains the mark of international relations.

This simple and banal point of departure is of decisive importance both for the understanding of international law and for the delimitation of international systems.

a. Law is a body of rules for human conduct established for the ordering of a social group and enforceable by external power. Domestic law orders the national group by acting directly on the individual citizens and by regulating all the problems which are deemed to be of social importance; it is enforced by the power of the state, exerted directly on individuals. By contrast, international law suffers from three forms of precariousness. The first is its low degree of institutionalization. The second is its unique substance. In the domestic order, which regulates a great mass of individuals, law is an instrument of homogeneity. The international legal order regulates a small number of subjects. Consequently, its law is a law of differentiation, which vacillates from the Charybdis of universality at the cost of vagueness, to the Scylla of precision at the cost of heterogeneity. The scope of the subject matter is limited by the reluctance of the subjects to submit themselves to extensive regulations and by the inefficiency of premature regulations: hence the numerous gaps in the body of rules. The third weakness is the limited amount of solidity or authority in international law. I do not refer here to efficiency in Kelsen's meaning of the term, for it is true that most forms of international law are obeyed, but to the effect of the following factors: the obscurities or ambiguities which mar existing rules, since they are established by the subjects themselves; the fact, analyzed by de Visscher, that the greatest solidarities exist in matters which least affect the power and policies of the subjects and vice versa; the fact that, in Julius Stone's words, international law is the one legal order which provides for its own destruction by the mere force of its own subjects.[3]

b. An international system is a pattern of relations between the basic units of world politics, which is characterized by the scope of the objectives pursued by those units and of the tasks performed among them, as well as by the means used in order to achieve those goals and perform those tasks.

[3] *Legal Controls of International Conflict* (New York, 1954), p. 1.

This pattern is largely determined by the structure of the world, the nature of the forces which operate across or within the major units, and the capabilities, pattern of power, and political culture of those units.[4]

One of the main tasks of a historical sociology of international politics is the delimitation of such systems: where does one system begin or end, in space and in time? It is with the limits in time that I am concerned here. As Raymond Aron has observed, periodization is always both necessary and dangerous: the historian is free in his choice of criteria but should refrain from attributing to those he chose consequences which only empirical evidence could prove.[5] The criteria I would propose are what I would call the *stakes of conflict*. A new system emerges:

1. When there is a new answer to the question: what *are* the units in conflict?—i.e., when the basic structure of the world has changed (as in the passage from the city-state system to the Roman Empire; from the Empire to the medieval system; from the medieval hierarchy to the modern "horizontal" system of multiple sovereignties).

2. When there is a new answer to the question: what *can* the units do to one another in a conflict?—i.e., a basic change in the technology of conflict. Such a change may also bring about a transformation in the basic structure of the world: as John Herz has reminded us, the gunpowder revolution ushered in the era of the "impermeable" territorial state. Even within the same type of basic structure, a fundamental innovation in the technology of conflict changes the nature of the international system: the atomic revolution has rendered obsolete previous "multiple-sovereignty" systems because it meant the passage from a relative to an absolute power of destruction, and consequently the end of great-power "impermeability." An effective diffusion of nuclear power would mean another system still.

3. When within a single state of the technology of conflict there is a new answer to the question: what do the units *want* to do to one another? Here, we try to distinguish systems according to the scope of the units' purposes, and to the techniques the actors use in order to meet their objectives or to prevent their rivals from achieving theirs.

If we combine those sets of criteria, we come to a fundamental distinction between two types of systems: stable ones and revolutionary ones. A stable system is one in which the stakes of conflict are limited, because the relations between the actors are marked by moderation in scope and means. Whatever the world's basic structure and the state of the technology of conflict, the units act so as to limit the amount of harm they could inflict upon one another. In a revolutionary system, this moderation has disappeared. When one major actor's decision to discard it coincides with or brings about a

---

4 Such a definition corresponds to accepted definitions of domestic political systems, which are characterized also both by the scope of the ends of politics (the limited state *vs.* the totalitarian state, the welfare state *vs.* the free enterprise state) and by the methods of organizing power (constitutional relations between the branches of government, types of party system).

5 Raymond Aron, "Evidence and Inference in History," *Daedalus,* Vol. 87 (Fall 1958), pp. 11–39.

revolution in the technology of conflict, or a change in the basic structure of the world, or both, the system is particularly unstable.[6] In other words, a stable system is one in which the life or the essential values of the basic units are not constantly in question, and the main actors agree on the rules according to which the competition will take place; a revolutionary system is one in which the incompatibility of purposes rules out such an agreement.

For each kind of basic structure in the world, and each kind of technology of conflict, we may obtain the ideal-type of a stable system by asking what are the conditions from which moderation in scope and means is most likely to follow. Actual historical systems at times meet all those conditions, but often they do not; and they are, of course, marked by constant change in all their elements. Those changes 1) do not affect the system at all if they do not hurt or remove the essential conditions of stability; 2) merely weaken the system by making it operate in less than ideal conditions, if they do cripple some of those conditions but without destroying the moderation in scope and means; 3) ruin the system altogether if such deterioration, instead of leading to temporary disturbances, brings about a breakdown in moderation, a revolution in the technology of conflict, or in the basic structure of the world.

Whether a change which affects the essential conditions of stability damages the system decisively or not depends on the circumstances. A breakdown requires the collapse of a large number of such conditions. This can happen either 1) when one of the main actors decides to overthrow the system, and succeeds in removing so many of the conditions of stability that the system does indeed collapse—i.e., when this actor's move leads not simply to *any* kind of conflict, but to a revolutionary one; or 2) when a previous deterioration leads to a conflict which might not start as a revolutionary one, but becomes one because it develops into a decisive additional factor of disruption. In both cases, the end of a stable system is marked by a general war.[7]

In the world of multiple sovereignties before the invention of absolute

6 The *number* of violent conflicts does not intervene in these definitions. A stable period may be marked by frequent wars as long as they remain limited in objectives and methods. A revolutionary period may not necessarily be marked by all-out, general war, if the technology of conflict introduces a mutual interest in avoiding the total destruction such a war would entail; but as long as this restraint does not bring back moderation in the purposes and means of conflicts other than all-out war, the system remains largely a revolutionary one, although it disposes of an element of stability—a fragile element, given all the other circumstances.

7 Besides making the fundamental distinction *between* stable and revolutionary systems, we have to distinguish *among* stable and *among* revolutionary ones. Here our criteria should be, in addition to the basic structure of the world and the state of the technology of conflict: 1) in the case of stable systems, the kind of *means* used by the actors in their competition and cooperation: cf. below, the distinction between the stable system which preceded the French Revolution and the stable system which followed the Congress of Vienna; both were "balance of power" systems, but the latter was more institutionalized than the former; 2) in the case of revolutionary systems, the type of *objective* for which the conflicts take place (religious allegiance, form of government).

weapons, it was the balance-of-power system which brought stability into international politics: i.e., a pattern of relations among states which through shifting alliances and the use of various diplomatic techniques tends to limit the ambitions of the main actors, to preserve a relative equilibrium among them, and to reduce the amount of violence between them. The ideal conditions for such a system are as follows:

1. Conditions related to the structure of the world: a greater number of major states than two; a relative equilibrium of power among them; the existence of a frontier, a prerequisite of the kind of flexibility that a balancing system needs.

2. Conditions related to transnational forces: technological stability; a common outlook among the leaders of the major states, provided either by a similarity of regimes, or by a common attitude toward religion, or by similar beliefs about the purpose of the state. Such an outlook allows for horizontal ties as strong as, or stronger than, the political ties which attach those leaders to their domestic community; a common conception of legitimacy can thus develop.

3. A condition related to the domestic situation within the major actors: the existence of a political system in which the state exercises only limited control over its citizens' international loyalties and activities.

4. The outcome of these conditions is a system in which the objectives of the major actors remain limited to moderate increases in power or prestige, and in which many of the tasks which can be performed through the processes of world politics remain beyond the pale of those politics. The means used by the major units in their mutual relations are coalitions designed to prevent any single actor from disrupting stability, either by rewarding him for his cooperation or by punishing him for his misbehavior, without, however, making it impossible for him to cooperate again.

The ideal conditions for stability can be defined as *evenness* in the situation of the major units—just as a large degree of identity in the members of the state is necessary for the emergence of the general will. Conversely, the process of deterioration which leads to disturbances within the system and might provoke its breakdown beyond a certain point can be summed up as the reintroduction of unevenness or *heterogeneity*.[8] This process includes the appearance of the following conditions:

1. In the structure of the world: irrepressible ambitions of individual rulers,[9] ambitions kindled by a disparity in power between a major actor and its neighbors or other major units; the end of the frontier, which increases the likelihood of, and the stakes in, direct clashes between the major units.

2. In the forces which cut across those units: a technological revolution,

[8] See the little known but brilliant analysis by Panayis A. Papaligouras, *Théorie de la Société internationale* (Geneva, Graduate School of International Studies, 1941).

[9] They do not, by themselves, destroy the balancing system, but they make its operation uncertain and increase the likelihood of "in-system" wars, which may in turn destroy the system if other essential conditions for an ideal balance have also disappeared, or if the logic of war destroys previous limitations on the instruments of conflict.

which leads to instability when it produces a race; the destruction of transnational ties, either under the impact of domestic integration, which inevitably submits diplomacy to greater internal pressures, or because of an ideological explosion set off by a disparity of regimes or beliefs.

3. In the domestic situation of the major units: strong integrative trends leading to nationalism; the expansion of state control over the foreign activities of the citizens either for economic or for ideological purposes.

c. Let us turn now to the relation of international law to various international systems. International law can be studied as a product of international systems and as a repertory of normative theory about each one of them. On the one hand, it is shaped by all the elements which compose an international system:

1. It reflects the structure of the world. The nature of the actors determines whether the law of the system is the "law of coordination" made by territorial states, or the external public law of an empire, or whether it will disappear altogether as it did during much of the medieval period. The size of the diplomatic field determines the degree of universality of the legal order. The degree of unity of international law and the efficiency of a good deal of its provisions depend on the existence, duration, and seriousness of a relationship of major tension.

2. International law reflects the forces which cut across the units. Technology is of considerable importance: the intensity or density of legal relations between the actors depends largely on the state of the arts. The unity and authority of the legal order depend on the presence and number of transnational ideologies and conceptions of legitimacy.

3. The domestic situation of the major units is relevant here also. International law has always reflected the pattern of power and the political culture of the main actors.[10] The development of law by treaties and the reception of rules of international law within the various units depend on the provisions of constitutions and on the decisions of domestic courts.

4. Finally, international law reflects the relations among the units. It is shaped by the scope of those relations: the breadth and the nature of the subject-matter regulated by law vary according to the range and character of the goals which the units try to reach and of the tasks they try to perform. In particular, the rules of law often express the policies of the major units. Moreover, customs and treaties always both reflect the methods by which the units try to meet their objectives, and regulate at least some of the techniques used in the process.

On the other hand, if we turn from empirical systems to normative theory, we find in theories of international law a critical assessment of international systems from the viewpoint of world order. In any political system, order is achieved if the following three requirements are met: 1) security—i.e., dealing with the problem of conflict by assuring the survival and safety of the members of the system; 2) satisfaction—i.e., dealing with the problem of assent, and obtaining it through constraint or consent; 3) flexibility—

---

10 See Corbett, *op. cit.,* especially chs. 1–3.

i.e., dealing with the problem of change (which is crucial, since assent is never definitive or total), by establishing procedures capable of absorbing shocks and of channeling grievances. In a world divided into numerous units, order is always threatened. Legal theorists have constantly asked whether order was possible at all; if so, whether the system was capable of ensuring it; and if not, what kind of measures were necessary to obtain order. On the whole, in each period, there have been three types of reactions: the deniers, who question either the possibility or the desirability of a stable legal order; the utopians, who also question the effectiveness of the existing system but propose to substitute a radically different one; the adjusters, who try to show how and to what extent order can be established or preserved within the existing system. We learn a great deal about the nature and operation of a given international system if we study the range of disagreements among those three groups; the more stable the system, the narrower this range.

Since international law constitutes the formal part of whatever kind of order reigns and expresses the more lasting interests of the actors—their long- or middle-range strategy, rather than their daily tactics—the link between the solidity or authority of international law and the stability of the international system is both obvious and strong. The basic function of international law is to organize the coexistence of the various units: this presupposes that their existence is assured. In stable systems, it is possible to distinguish three kinds of international law.[11]

1. The law of the political framework—i.e., the network of agreements which define the conditions, and certain of the rules, of the political game among the states. By conditions, I refer to such provisions as the settlement of borders after wars, the main alignments expressed in treaties of alliance, the holding of periodic conferences among major powers; by rules, I refer to provisions which determine the mutual commitments of states, or the procedure for the settlement of major disputes.

2. The law of reciprocity, which defines the conditions and rules of interstate relations in areas which affect less vitally the power and policies of the states. This is the large zone in which states can be assumed to have a mutual and lasting interest in common rules: the zone of predictability, on which the competition of the actors in politically more sensitive areas rests and depends. We can distinguish two kinds of laws of reciprocity: first, the law of delimitation which defines the respective rights and privileges of states—in peacetime over such matters as diplomatic relations, territory, and people, in wartime over weapons, military objectives, non-combatants, etc.; second, the law of cooperation, which regulates joint interests, particularly in commerce.

3. The law of community, which deals with problems which can best be handled, not on the basis of a reciprocity of interests of states understood as separate and competing units, but on the basis of a community of action

---

11 See George Schwarzenberger, *Power Politics* (New York, 1951), ch. 13; and Hans J. Morgenthau, *op. cit.*, pp. 228–29.

independent from politics: problems of a technical or scientific nature for which borders are irrelevant.

This distinction is sound and legitimate in a stable period, for when the survival of the players is insured, a hierarchy of interests becomes possible. The law of the political framework deals the cards with which the players try to reach such objectives as greater power, or prestige, or the triumph of ideals; the law of reciprocity provides the underpinning of national security and defines those functions and attributes of the state which are not put at stake in the political contests. But in a revolutionary system, the distinction between these two kinds of law becomes extremely fuzzy; for when survival is not assured, the limits which the law of reciprocity sets to states' privileges or jurisdiction become obstacles to their quest for greater security and power, while cooperation over joint interests is replaced by conflict or competition which challenges previous rules. In such a system, the power and policies of states are directly involved in almost every aspect of international activity.[12] Thus, in a revolutionary system, the great bulk of international law partakes of the somewhat shaky authority of the law of the political framework.

The difference in the solidity of law in revolutionary and stable systems is reflected in the contrasting impact of political change on law. Changes which do not destroy a stable system have no lethal effect on the legal order, precisely because customs and agreements express, as I have put it, strategic rather than tactical interests. To be sure, the body of rules reflects such changes if they are of sufficient magnitude: in particular, the disappearance of some of the essential conditions for an ideal stable system has repercussions on the law of the political framework, which is the most sensitive to such tremors; it may also leave its mark on the law of reciprocity, because certain kinds of agreements become increasingly rare, or codification more troublesome, or difficulties appear in the discharge of treaties. However, the law of reciprocity may continue to develop even when the ideal conditions for stability are not present anymore (as was shown by the flowering of such law just before World War I), precisely because it reflects mutual interests which the fluctuations of politics do not impair so long as the stable system lasts. Also, while the essential moderation in the scope and means of international relations continues, the gaps and uncertainties of law do not become factors of disruption: in the areas which are not regulated or in which the rules are ambiguous, a purely political decision or interpretation by the states concerned will be needed, but, given the system, no destructive effects are likely to follow.

---

[12] Scholars may argue that important mutual interests still exist and that states have little to gain by turning the zone of predictability into a battlefield. The trouble is that what seems irrational to the scholar from the viewpoint of international society seems rational to the statesman from the viewpoint of his own national calculation, given the peculiar logic of such calculations in fiercely competitive situations. An "objective" common interest might not be perceived by the antagonists, and, even if it is, there remains an abyss between such understanding and a formal legal agreement which would sanction it. On these points, see Kenneth Waltz, *Man, the State, and War* (New York: 1959), pp. 192ff.

In a revolutionary system, however, gaps and ambiguities become wedges for destruction or subversion of the international order in the interest of any of the actors. The absence of any agreement on the rules of the game, the increase in the stakes of conflict, the reign of insecurity for the actors, mean that political changes will have the following impact on international law: 1) just as old theories and concepts outlive the system which justified them, old regulations which have become obsolete nevertheless continue to be considered valid (although they are less and less respected) because of the increasing difficulty in agreeing on new rules, or because the old ones serve the interests of some of the contending units; 2) new problems thrown up by political or technological change often remain unregulated, for the same reasons; 3) new regulations appear which constitute attempts to deal with some of the changes but turn out to be incompatible with the new system; and 4) since international systems change essentially through general wars, the collapse of previous laws of war is usually the first effect of the change on the legal order.

This conglomeration of ruin, gaps, and "dysfunctional" old or new rules denotes the major areas of friction and tensions in world politics during the lifetime of revolutionary systems and particularly in periods of passage from one system to another.

Thus, it is in balance-of-power systems that the authority of international law has been greatest: as Oppenheim has stated in his treatise, the existence of the balance is a condition of the flourishing of authoritative international law. However, this condition is at the same time a limitation.

1. Even when the balance functions under optimum conditions, the political framework may remain largely unregulated. We have to distinguish between systems in which the balance is more or less automatic or mechanical, and systems in which it is institutionalized to a greater degree—a distinction among stable systems based in particular on the law of the political framework (see n. 7).

2. Even when the balance functions under optimum conditions, it operates sometimes at the expense of law. In a system of "sovereign" states, the principles of equality and consent are essential to the legal order. But the daily practices of the balance may conflict with these norms: a preponderance of power often forces small or even isolated large states to assent to measures which go against their objectives or detract from the formal equality of all the units.

3. Among the many power configurations which characterize the relations of the major units in balancing systems, there is one which threatens the solidity of international law (especially that of the political framework) more permanently. When the optimum conditions are met, the most likely resulting combination is the "mechanism of imbalance"—a coalition of a majority of the main actors against an isolated would-be disrupter; but when those conditions are not all present, there may come into being an opposition of blocs of comparable strength, so that alignments stiffen instead of remaining flexible, with a tendency to shift. The authority and unity of international law may then be imperiled.

II

I will try now to support the preceding generalizations by examining briefly three concrete examples of relations between international systems and international law.

a. The first example, which I want to mention very briefly, is that of international law during the balance-of-power system which lasted from the Peace of Westphalia until the French Revolution.

The balance could operate effectively because the treaties of Westphalia had redistributed territory in such a way as to create a number of major states capable of neutralizing each other, and had also removed the poisonous element of religious conflict. Within the main units, mercantilism and absolutism weakened gradually. New transnational ties developed: the "corporate identity" of monarchs, diplomats, and officers across borders led to a consensus on the legitimacy of the balance, just as the community of European intellectuals produced a consensus on the values of the Enlightenment. The result, politically, was a mechanical balance, with frequent disturbances due either to the fact that a state could never be sure in advance whether or when others would try to stop it, or to individual ambitions. Hence numerous limited wars occurred: stylized wars of position which affected only rarely the civilian population.

Although there was little international law of the political framework, the law of reciprocity developed in a way which reflected both the moderation and the volatile character of a balancing system. On the one hand, in the area of trade, statesmen came to realize that law was the best technique for obtaining an increase in national wealth and power (as in past mercantilist practice), but with safety; the idea of a harmony of interests replaced the previous expectation of conflict, hence numerous measures to protect commerce at sea, especially in wartime. Neutrality became for the first time altogether possible, a good bargain, and a subject of legal regulation. On the other hand, the balance imposed limits to the development of law. The preservation of the system required, at the end of wars, practices which restored the equilibrium among the major powers at the expense of small states; those compensations proved that the norm of territorial integrity was efficient only as long as it was backed by force, and that it was subordinated to the operations of the balance. Also, there were gaps wherever rules would have restricted state power too sharply: maritime warfare remained anarchical, and no adequate procedure for the settlement of disputes developed, except for rare and delicate instances of arbitration.

The response of theory to these developments was most interesting. In the previous revolutionary system, a big gap had separated destroyers of the medieval dream of unity, like Machiavelli, creators of new dreams like Crucé or Sully, and the numerous would-be rescuers of the medieval theory, who reasserted the supremacy of natural law and the doctrine of just war, but secularized the former, hedged in the latter with qualifications, and came to recognize the existence of an international law created by the will of states. Now, in a system of increasing moderation, the gap narrowed. Even deniers of the efficiency of "covenants without the sword" showed that self-restraint might prevent a war of all against all. At the other pole, the Kantian utopia also reflected a new optimism: the problem of establishing order among the states was going to require essentially a change in the regimes but not the end of the division of the world into separate units, and it would be solved by the invisible hand of history. The theorists in the middle, still trying to save the idea of a legal community of mankind, gradually gave up natural law as its cement—a retreat which would have been taken as an invitation to and a confession of chaos in the preceding period, but which could now be accepted without anguish, for a positivistic emphasis on the fundamental rights of states as the foundation of order did not seem necessarily self-defeating any longer. The expectation of a harmony of interests had been fed by the system.

Its collapse was sudden and took the form of a swift chain reaction. 1) The decisive factor was the change in France's regime—a fact which shows that the study of international systems must extend to the analysis of the political ones they include. 2) The revolution, in turn, destroyed previous transnational links: the heterogeneity of regimes introduced an explosive element into Europe, and after a brief period of idealistic pacifism—a revulsion against the balance, that sport of kings—the revolutionaries, turning to Messianism, lit the fuse. 3) This attempt to destroy old regimes everywhere in turn removed another essential condition of the balance: nationalism in France led to the imposition of full government control on its citizens' acts and thoughts. 4) Next, the previous equilibrium among the major powers was destroyed by the French victories—an incentive to exploit unevenness even further. 5) Then, Napoleon's ambitions produced the first modern instance of total power politics, based on an ideological inspiration, and waged by total domestic and international means. 6) A further series of changes in the previous conditions of stability resulted: constant shifts in the map of Europe, a transformation of the domestic order of many of the actors, who moved away from feudal absolutism to defeat France's nationalism with its own weapons, the creation of two opposed ideological camps. Consequently, previous international law was thoroughly disrupted: the law of neutrality collapsed; wars of total mobilization, movement, and extermination of civilians replaced the ballet of limited wars. We have here the example of a system breaking down because of the deliberate attempt by one of its major actors to destroy it, and because of this actor's capacity to succeed for a while by exploiting the dynamism of revolution.

b. Let us examine now the international system of the nineteenth century, its fate, and its impact on international law. The defeat of the force which had destroyed the previous system—France—and the apparent collapse of French-inspired ideals seemed to make a return to stability possible. The victors of 1815 decided to restore a balancing system, for they saw in it the pattern which could best ensure such stability, by giving security to the main powers, providing the greatest amount of flexibility, and obtaining the assent of all, including France, on whom only a far tighter organization of her enemies than they were capable of maintaining could have imposed a punitive peace with any chance of success.

Some of the victors, however, wanted a new kind of balancing system;

what is interesting here is the discrepancy between intention and performance. Specifically, although England was willing to return to a mechanical balance, Austria and Russia wanted to extend the scope and means of world politics: whereas the eighteenth-century balance had excluded intervention in domestic affairs, Metternich and Alexander now wanted an organized balancing system which would include in its concept of legitimacy a formula for domestic order, and dispose of means of enforcement against the rise of liberal and nationalist forces. The international law of the political framework would have become an explicit and powerful instrument of the big powers' common policy of preserving the Vienna order, both in its international *and* in its internal aspects. But this was not to happen, for it soon appeared that a voluntary system of cooperation was too weak to control developments within nations which a previous balancing system had already been powerless to prevent. In other words, so extensive a community could not be created by superstructural means alone: the failure of the Holy Alliance proved that an effective new balancing system could be obtained only through a return to moderation in scope and means, not through an ambitious extension.

In the beginning, almost all the conditions for a successful balance were present. 1) The structure of the world was marked by a double hierarchy: first, there was a distinction between a civilized core and a frontier; secondly, within the core, there was a hierarchy between small and large states. No permanent relation of major tension emerged until after 1870. 2) In the core area, technology expanded but never to such a degree as to give to one major actor power of life and death over another. Despite the clash of political ideologies, supranational ties persisted: the dominant ideologies were themselves either supranational or favorable to the maintenance of bonds between national elites; the "Internationale" of diplomats allowed for a consensus on the rules of the game. 3) Although regimes were far from identical, the limited state developed everywhere. The conduct of foreign affairs could be divorced from domestic passions. Constitutionalism, marked by the legalization of public affairs and by the growth of the judicial apparatus, made notable advances. Liberalism led to a separation between state and society.

Consequently, the relations among states were once again characterized by moderation in scope and means. The moderation in scope was twofold. First, the number of tasks performed by the processes of world politics was limited to conflict and political accommodation. The failure of Metternich's hope meant that, within the core area, domestic developments were not a legitimate object of international politics: the "neutrality of alignment"[13] necessary to the effectiveness of the balance required neutrality toward regimes as well, which remained possible as long as internal revolutions made no attempt to disrupt the international system. The separation of state and society removed another vast zone from world politics—the field of private transnational activities, especially economic ones. Secondly, the objectives of the major units also remained moderate in scope: they sought

[13] See Kaplan and Katzenbach, *op. cit.*

limited increments of power and influence within the core area; they avoided on the whole the destruction of the actors' value systems or national existence in this area. As for moderation in means, it was shown by the return to limited wars, the practice of non-intervention within the core area, the multiplication of international conferences of all kinds.

In this system, international law—the law of the European core area—played all three of the roles described above, within the limits previously defined. The law of the political framework as the law of the Concert: as the instrument of the society of the major powers for the supervision of small states and the control of the individual ambitions of each member, it consecrated the power relations which developed for such purposes. Hence the prevalence of the legal techniques of neutralization and internationalization. They implied an agreement on common abstention from, or common action in, a given area or problem; they resulted from the consensus on moderation and cooperation rather than all-out isolated moves.[14] But since this law was a balancing technique, not a way of overcoming the balance, its development was hemmed in by the usual limitations. Many rules merely expressed the independence of states in such a system: for instance, the principle of unanimity in Concert meetings. Law was violated whenever the maintenance of the system required it—i.e., at both ends of Concert activities: the composition of the meetings violated the principle of equality, and the process of enforcement often twisted the independence, integrity, or free consent of small powers. Finally, there were major gaps in the law of the framework, as exemplified by the purely voluntary character of Concert meetings and by the total freedom to resort to war. Moreover, these limitations and violations became far more dangerous for world order during two periods: the 1860's, when the balance was too fluid—i.e., the mechanism of imbalance did not function, owing to the divisions or passivity of a majority of the big powers—and the last years before World War I, when the hardening of the blocs produced arteriosclerosis in the Concert.[15]

The law of reciprocity was a projection of the constitutional state into world affairs, a reflection of mutual interests, and a product of the balancing system, which curtailed states' objectives. The law of delimitation became firmly established. The law of cooperation progressed considerably in two areas: commerce, where the retreat from mercantilism opened a "depoliticized" zone for free trade and for the free establishment of aliens; the settlement of disputes, as states became willing to resort to judicial procedures in a variety of cases; either cases involving private citizens in the "depoliticized" area, or even cases which involved state interests directly, but which the actors found convenient to send to arbitration because the balance had made resort to force less profitable, or because the development of domestic legal institutions had given greater prestige to legal than to diplomatic mechanisms. But in all its branches the law of reciprocity suffered

---

14 For a more detailed analysis, see the author's *Organisations internationales et pouvoirs politiques des Etats* (Paris: Colin, 1954), part 1.

15 It was in 1871 that Russia denounced the Black Seas provisions of the Paris Treaty, in 1908 that Austria annexed Bosnia-Herzegovina.

from the same weakness as the law of the political framework. The different standards for the treatment of foreigners applied by the major states to "civilized" nations and to backward areas showed the limit of the norm of equality. The treatment of debtors by creditor nations proved that the law often identified right with might. "Depolitization" came to an end either whenever citizens ran into trouble abroad and appealed to their country of origin, or when a dispute fell within one of the numerous areas excluded by reservations in arbitration treaties. Spectacular failures at the Hague Conferences left many gaps in the laws of war and for the settlement of disputes. Again, these weaknesses became more severe when the Concert did not function well; at the end of the period, a return to protectionism, tariff wars, and the failure of the London Conference on maritime warfare were signs of deterioration.

The branch of the law of reciprocity which reflected best all the elements of the system was the law of war and neutrality. First, since war was a legitimate method of settlement of disputes, and law did not try to curtail the ends which sovereignty served but only to regulate the means which it used, war was entitled to a *status*: it received a legal framework, which distinguished sharply between peace and war (hence the need for a declaration at one end, a formal treaty at the other), and between international and civil strife. Within this framework, both the means and the various categories of war victims were regulated. Secondly, since total war practices were banned by the balance, and war had once again become a method of settlement of disputes but not a way of eliminating one's antagonist, war was considered to be merely a *moment*; it was a dispute between states, not between individuals: hence the customs and court decisions on the effect of war on treaties and, more importantly, the crucial distinction between the combatants and noncombatants in war, between the duties of the neutral state and those of neutral citizens. Furthermore, it was a political dispute, not an interruption of economic processes: hence the protection of the neutral trader, who was maintaining the continuity of these processes, and the inviolability of as much of the belligerents' private property as was possible, both at sea and in occupied territory.

The law of community expanded also through countless conferences, conventions, and even institutions; it regulated an increasing number of administrative and technical functions.

Consequently, the law of the nineteenth-century balancing system presented two sides. In matters which affected directly the power and the policies of the major states, law was the transcription of the balancing process in normative terms, the expression of a system in which each state submitted to law insofar as the rules were backed by the pressure of superior force. In other matters, law grew out of the restrictions to which power, in a liberal century, consented for the development of non-political forces of reciprocity and for the devaluation of borders. One result of this double role of law was a fairly effective system of world order. Security was achieved in the core area, especially for the major actors; lesser ones bought survival at the cost of supervision, and, often, partial sacrifices of sovereignty. The Concert tried to preserve flexibility by acting to legalize and harness revolutionary changes. Assent was never complete, but as long as the major powers preferred, or had no choice but to prefer, the maintenance of the system to the gains they might hope to reap by destroying it, this was enough.

Another result was a new rapprochement among the three groups of theorists who coexisted in this period. They agreed on three crucial points: first, the possibility of avoiding chaos; secondly, the basic character of the state as the foundation of world order (and the definition of the state in terms of will); thirdly—and paradoxically—the weaknesses of international law in the world as it was: an admission which, as in the previous stable period, could be made because of the general moderation of world politics. Even deniers such as Hegel believed in a European family or a "higher praetor" which would prevent the warring states from turning inevitable war into inexpiable hate. Even the visionaries no longer dreamed of supranational utopias: they thought that the world was moving toward a community of harmonious nation-states, thanks to free trade and public opinion. The positivists could deal with the previously avoided problem of the basis of legal obligation and come up with auto-limitation, *Vereinbarung,* or an indivisible community of interests, without feeling that these were circular answers. At the end of the previous period, the positivists, stressing the differences between international and municipal law, and the individual rights of the state, had sounded almost like the cynics. Now, on the contrary, it was the positivists and the visionaries who were close, as Walter Schiffer has shown.[16] Both groups saw a new world almost without power, and failed to realize that the retreat of power from certain spheres had been the result of a highly political balancing process—which was at its most rigid, and in its death throes, just when the theorists believed that the millennium was arriving.

The deterioration of the system had, once again, started with a change in the domestic order: but this time it was a change which occurred in most of the major units, and the deterioration was gradual, not sudden, and not deliberate. 1) The emergence of the modern nation-state weakened some of the essential conditions for an ideal balance: for in such a unit, the population is mobilized around national symbols, and the development of the machinery of the state reenforces internal integration at the expense of transnational ties: after 1870, the army's weight in domestic affairs increased everywhere, and pushed the nation toward imperialism. 2) Consequently, there came about a change in the structure of the world which almost obliterated the difference between disturbances within the system and destruction of the system: the end of the frontier. 3) The horizontal links between the major powers were progressively weakened by the rise of mass nationalism, the success of philosophies of conflict and of national or racial superiority, and the acts of nationalities' movements which sought allies among the major powers. The legitimacy of states which were not based on the national principle was being challenged: thus international legitimacy

16 *The Legal Community of Mankind* (New York, 1954).

concerned itself again with domestic affairs, and with this new dimension heterogeneity returned to the system. 4) As a result, the relations between states took on new and threatening aspects. The very frequency of disturbances, due to the uncertainty of the balance, created a climate of dissatisfaction in which small powers tried to escape from the control of bigger ones. The big states, also looking for an exit, could agree only on temporary adjustments which would not tie their hands for the future, but which in turn infuriated the small powers. In such a climate, the freezing of the balance after Bismarck's departure meant the end of "neutrality of alignment" and the replacement of the hierarchical system of the Concert with a vertical one, in which blocs composed of large *and* small states were facing each other. Hence a switch in means—the decline of the Concert, the return to arms races—and an increase in scope: the sphere of economic affairs became vital again for international politics. It was another change in means: the resort to general war, which dealt the death blow to the system: for the "technical surprise" of World War I, to use Aron's expression, destroyed all remaining restraints on means, and the logic of the war made the objectives of states once again incompatible and increasingly more universal.

c. Lastly I would like to discuss the relation of international law to world politics in the present revolutionary system.

The essential elements of the present system are as follows:

1. The structure of the world is characterized by one consolidation and two deep transformations. On the one hand, the diplomatic field, which had been gradually extended and unified by the previous system, embraces the whole world for the first time. On the other hand, two conflicting movements have destroyed the double hierarchy of the nineteenth century: bipolarity has replaced the multiplicity of major actors (and put an end to the mechanism of imbalance); the splintering of the former frontier into a large number of new units has obliterated the distinction between the core area and the rest.

2. A gigantic technological revolution has led to a race toward industrial power, and not been accompanied by the restoration of any universal transnational links. The diversity of regimes, "isolationist" reactions in many nations (especially the new ones) against the intrusion of foreign affairs into all spheres of life, the tendency of the major forms of regimes to project and promote themselves throughout the world have resulted both in the absence of any clear and extensive conception of international legitimacy, and in huge ideological rivalries. New transnational links have emerged as a consequence of the latter, but they are divisive, competitive, and often negative solidarities.

3. The spiritual and temporal control of the state on the citizens has increased everywhere. Just as the old territorial essence of sovereignty was becoming obsolete, the spreading ethics of nationalism and the universal practice of public welfare have given to sovereignty an incandescent "personal" core.

4. The outcome is a series of revolutionary changes in the scope and

means of world politics. Concerning the former, there is no longer any "depoliticized" zone of major importance. The collapse of empires has made the question of economic development, once dealt with by private investment or behind the walls of the empires, one of the biggest issues of world politics. Nor is there anymore a separation of domestic and international affairs: the logic of intervention, either to enforce some degree of conformity within one's own camp or to subvert the adversary's, has spread throughout the whole world and made the diffusion of political "ways of life" one of the tasks performed by world politics.[17] Consequently, the objectives of states have expanded in such a way that the full realization of the goals of one unit or bloc would often involve the physical or moral death of another actor or camp, and such goals include blueprints for domestic as well as for international order. As for means, they have never been as varied: "total diplomacy" ranges from highly institutionalized military alliances to economic warfare, from propaganda to a host of international organizations; quasi-Doomsday machines and traditional limited wars coexist with revolutionary guerrilla wars. There is one moderating force which makes this revolutionary system an original one: the possibility for one power alone to inflict unacceptable damage on its enemies, however numerous, makes a return to the principle of imbalance unlikely in case of a new multipolar system, but it also makes the actors hesitate far more to resort to violence than the dynamism of a revolutionary system would otherwise allow. Hence the appearance of a highly delicate and uncertain restraint.

Thus, by comparison with the pre-1914 system, the present one is marked both by extraordinary and continuing changes, and by great complexity.[18] Such changes and such complexity have had an enormous impact on international law; the European-made legal order of the past could not be stretched to the dimensions of the new system without major cracks.

Let us look first at the impact of the changes. It has been threefold. In the first place, huge chunks of the traditional body of rules have been destroyed. This destruction has four aspects.

1. Basic distinctions which translated into the legal order the restraints of the balancing system have lost any meaning or justification in the present one. The distinction between matters of domestic jurisdiction and matters regulated by international law has practically vanished, in a period when

---

17 Many of the difficulties of the UN operation in the Congo stem from the attempt to distinguish between the domestic and the international aspects of the crisis—an exercise in fiction.

18 We speak of a "loose bipolar system" in which "bloc actors" tend to become more important than unit actors—but at the same time the rate of obsolescence of strategies and the diffusion of nuclear power challenge such a view. Inversely, we refer to the fragmentation of the old frontier into multiple new sovereignties—but at the same time the necessities of the struggle against colonialism and for development might lead to the gradual emergence of "bloc actors" there. We discuss the atomic age but, as Herz has observed, many interstate relations are still in a pre-atomic phase. We have both a revolutionary system, and a tacit agreement on one rule of the game—the avoidance of total war.

the choice of a regime largely determines the international conduct of a state. The distinction between the civilized nations and the others is challenged by the new states' objections to many traditional rules (e.g., in regard to territorial waters or even about diplomatic representation). The distinction between private acts, for which the state is not responsible, and public acts has been destroyed by intervention or subversion by "private" groups manipulated by their governments, or by the growing importance of transactions which a large foreign or international "private" company concludes with a state. The distinction between war and peace has been replaced by what Philip Jessup has called situations of intermediacy: a period of irreconcilable oppositions, ideological clashes, *and* fear of total war could not but engender wars without declaration, armistices without peace, non-belligerency without war, and help for insurgents without recognition of belligerency.

2. Consequently, many of the traditional rules have been destroyed by massive violations. Numerous provisions on war and neutrality could not outlive the technological and political conditions of the nineteenth century; nor could the law which forbade states to help foreign insurgents or subversives. Similarly, many of the rules which governed territorial jurisdiction have vanished: instead of a fairly clear distinction among a number of separate zones and the sharp definition of the conditions in which state power could be exercised in each of them, there are now blurred, overlapping, and multiplying zones. The size of those on which states claim rights has augmented; the claims themselves have steadily expanded, even over the open seas, and often through unilateral moves. Traditional rules on the treatment of foreign property have been very generally disregarded. Those changes have been the reflection of all the transformations in the international system: the increase in the number of nations has often led the least viable or secure ones to demand the fullest amount of control over the biggest amount of space; the technological revolution has provoked a rush into air space; the decline of the old transnational consensus has affected the freedom of the seas; the modern welfare state, and the totalitarian regimes, have tried to grab resources wherever possible and to remove previously accepted restrictions on territorial sovereignty; the cold war has led to U-2 flights, to weapon tests in the ocean, and has added military overtones to the struggle about the breadth of the territorial seas; the anticolonial revolution has been one of the prime movers in this struggle and in the spread of expropriation; the Arab-Israeli conflict has had repercussions on canals and straits.

3. Many of the gaps in the body of rules have become opportunities for chaos. The silence of international law on the upper limits of air space may may lead to dangerous and conflicting claims. International law has little to say about most of the modern methods of propaganda, subversion, and intervention short of the actual use of force. Nor did it foresee that traditional privileges of domestic jurisdiction, such as the right of a state to grant its nationality, to regulate the conduct of aliens, to treat its own citizens as it sees fit, and to recognize new states or governments, would be

used as weapons in the struggle between the states. Here we find what is probably the best example of the different meaning for world order of gaps in stable and revolutionary systems. In the nineteenth century, recognition was deemed a privilege, not a duty, but no arbitrary consequences followed because, on the whole, very simple tests were applied: a double check of whether the state existed or whether the government was in control, and whether it accepted the existing framework of international law and politics. Since the latter was flexible enough, and contained no requirements about regimes or alignments, there were few instances of trouble. Today, the same privilege has become a nightmare, because of the collapse of the old consensus on international legitimacy—so that states use criteria of recognition which are tests of conformity to their own concept of legitimacy— and also because of the appearance of a new dimension of legitimacy: the nature of the regime or the way in which it came to power. This is as true in the case of the anticolonial conflict as it is in the cold war. Finally, international law has nothing to say about most of the new weapons which have appeared since 1914.

4. Some of the traditional rules which are still standing have become much more uncertain in their operation because of changes in the international system. Principles dealing with state immunities were established at a time when the state did not engage its "majesty" in trading or manufacturing activities; court reactions to those developments have been conflicting and subject to shifts. The validity of intervention at the request of a foreign government becomes dubious when there is a domestic contest about the legitimacy or legality of this government. Treaties reflect the forces of disintegration which have appeared in the world: the increase in the number of states has led either to the "individualization of rules" through reservations, or to the use of expressions as vague as, say, "genuine link" in the recent Geneva provision dealing with flags of convenience, or to conflicts between obligations accepted by the same nation in agreements which regulate similar matters but bind different groups of states. Domestic reactions against the increasing scope of treaties have brought about difficulties in ratification and moves such as the Bricker offensive. Clashes between new transnational solidarities explain the problem of the colonial clause. The intensity of interstate conflicts has made resort to the *rebus sic stantibus* argument more frequent than ever.

Thus, much of present international law, precisely because it reflects a dead system, is obsolete. But changes in the international system have had a second kind of effect on international law: some of the rules which are supposed to be valid today are premature. These are rules which express attempts at imposing a new scheme of world order which purported to draw the lesson from the ultimate failure of the balance-of-power system, but proved to be thoroughly unfit for the present revolutionary world. There were essentially two types of efforts.

1. On the one hand, there was an attempt to give to the law of the political framework a far bigger scope than in the past, by curbing states' sovereignty in matters as vital as the settlement of political disputes and

the resort to war. The conduct of states would have been subordinated to rules administered by international organization. The success of this effort *presupposed* a stable world which would not be racked by profound ideological splits, in which a basic homogeneity of regimes and beliefs existed, and in which the transnational forces of public opinion and "world parliamentarism" would keep disputes at a reasonably low pitch. The fundamental flaw of the formula was in the ambiguous nature of international organization: it is an "as if" international community, which leaves the basic character of the world system unchanged, and in which decisions are still made by the states. Consequently, its success depends entirely on the universe outside—i.e., on whether there is a system of basically satisfied, democratic units tied together by a common concept of legitimacy; if not, the organization itself has no power to bring about such a world. If such a happy world does not exist at the start, its indispensable establishment thus depends on the ability of the major powers to bring it to life—an ability which is totally missing. As a result, a new and dangerous gap has come to plague world order: the gap between the Charter provisions and practices on disputes (i.e., the power of the UN organs is limited to frequently ineffective recommendations), and the Charter's sweeping ban on the use of force: a gap which encourages states to devise highly refined techniques of offensive short of force, and drives those which are the victims of such tactics to disregard the ban.[19] The attempt to revert to a "just war" concept has proved to be impossible or absurd in a world of conflicting legitimacies.

2. The other type of effort was a direct projection, into the international sphere, of the legal relationships which exist between groups or individuals in a constitutional state. The resort to international jurisdiction for the settlement of many disputes, an international protection of human rights, the establishment of a criminal code thanks to which the punishment of warmakers would be the judicial side of a coin whose political side was the outlawry of war—all these measures reflected the utopia of a legal community of mankind, and they have suffered a fate even worse than the fictitious political community. International adjudication can be effective only when international relations are not fundamentally at variance with the conditions which exist within a liberal state: when there is a large zone of private activities uncontrolled by governments, when the objectives of states are not so incompatible as to rule out a joint resort to the judge. The prevalence of the desire to change the law over mere disagreements on interpretation and the opposition in the values of the major ideological camps have provoked a decline of the role of the World Court and a full-scale revolt against adjudication. Human rights are unlikely to receive adequate international protection at a time when the core of sovereignty is the link between the state and its subjects.

Out of the dialectic of the obsolete and the premature, contemporary

---

[19] See, for instance, the arguments of D. W. Bowett in *Self-defense in International Law* (New York, 1958), pp. 145ff., and Julius Stone in *Aggression and World Order,* (Berkeley, Calif., 1958), ch. 5. Contra, Joseph Kunz, "Sanctions in International Law," *American Journal of International Law,* LIV (April 1960), pp. 324–47.

international law has managed to show a third kind of effect of the changes in the international system; there are some pieces of evidence of a "third way" which is neither a return to the old system, nor a realization of the Wilsonian utopia, but the elaboration of rules which correspond to the few elements of stability in the present system. Although Charter provisions are used by all states as instruments for the enhancement of their own interests, procedures and institutions which correspond to the general desire to avoid total war have been developed by the UN. Although the competition of East and West for the allegiance of the "Third World" tends to become constantly more intense, it remains on the whole peaceful; consequently, an international law, and numerous international organs, of technical assistance and economic development have appeared: they correspond to the convergent interests of all three camps in channeling some of those measures through the procedures of an "universal actor." On the ruins of the nineteenth-century law of reciprocity, a few new conventions of delimitation and cooperation have been signed, dealing with the "humanitarian" side of war, or with the continental shelf, or with the joint exploitation of sea resources, or with the Antarctic.

This is not much. Some of those developments (e.g., the continental shelf) reflect a very traditional agreement on increasing, not curtailing, states' powers. The UN apparatus against the extension of conflicts remains an improvised one: contemporary internationalization of trouble spots, designed to avoid direct intervention by one of the superpowers, remains an *ad hoc* practice, despite efforts at turning it into a general rule, and East-West mutual interests in preventing nuclear war have expressed themselves in parallel unilateral measures but not in firm agreements. Only in the area of community—scientific research, health, communications—have the obstacles been few. Nevertheless, such developments suffice to make contemporary international law look like Janus: it has one face which announces chaos, and one which promises order.[20]

Not only does contemporary law thus bear the marks of all the changes in the international system: it reflects also the heterogeneity of the present system—indeed, of every element of this system; hence a permanent contradiction between such heterogeneity and the formal homogeneity of a legal system whose members are supposedly equal.

1. Contemporary law reflects the heterogeneity of the structure of the world. Although the nation-state is the basic unit and the common aspiration of men more than ever before, there is a major disparity between states which meet the traditional criteria of statehood—a population, a territory, a government—and those which are essentially governments still in search of their nation—governments which operate within explosively artificial borders.[21]

2. Present-day law reflects the asymmetry of domestic regimes: the dif-

---

[20] Similarly, during the period which preceded the peace of Westphalia, every legal development was ambiguous, for it destroyed the previous unity of the Civitas Christiana and the secular authority of the Church, but at the same time brought into shape the modern territorial state through a succession of wars.
[21] See Rupert Emerson, *From Empire to Nation* (Cambridge, Mass.: 1960), ch. 6.

ficulties met by various attempts at codification, or at regulating international trade, air communications, and raw materials, or at establishing
common standards of inspection for arms control have shown how much
the attitudes of a welfare state and a free enterprise state and, even more,
those of an industrialized and of an underdeveloped country differ in
international economic matters, or how radically a democracy's and a
totalitarian state's conceptions of secrecy diverge.

3. Contemporary law reflects the heterogeneity of the system with respect
to those forces which cut across the units. Technological unevenness has
left its mark: it is from the underprivileged states mainly that pressure has
come for a legal regulation of space problems; the opposition of nuclear
"haves" and "have-nots" has limited the effectiveness of international
cooperation for the peaceful uses of nuclear energy. As for ideological
asymmetry, even though Soviet international law appears to differ little in
its *rules* from Western law, there are most significant variations in the interpretation of, and the general attitude toward, law, which correspond to the
differences in the nature of the regimes;[22] in particular, there is a considerable difference in the attitude of each camp toward the use of force
within its sphere. Efforts at negotiating various agreements on human rights
have shown the incompatibility of the main competing conceptions of world
order on crucial issues.

4. Present-day law reflects numerous contradictions in the relations
between the units. In the first place, it shows traces of a basic clash which
affects the policy of every state: a clash between the determination to
increase its power, security, welfare, and prestige as much as possible by
its own means, and the dependence on others for those very purposes. Thus,
if we look at the principal source of law—treaties—we see that at the same
time as such agreements suffer from the weaknesses I have mentioned above,
their subject-matter has extended to objects never before regulated by
world law (i.e., labor, human rights, etc.), and numerous new subjects of
law (i.e., international organizations) have been created by agreements. If
we look at the military function of the states—the state as fortress—we see
that they try to ensure their security both by expanding their sovereignty as
far as they can (especially in the air) or by developing their own weapon
systems or armies, and also by participating in military alliances, which
involve a radical transformation of traditional territorial sovereignty. If we
look at the economic function of the states—the state as provider of welfare
—we see that they try to develop their own resources and to acquire additional ones wherever they can get them (for instance, under the sea), but
also that they have to join with others in order to promote the welfare of
their own citizens or to receive indispensable aid.

In the second place, international law reflects the complexity of states'
legal situations in the face of the main issues of contemporary world politics.
On the one hand, some of the provisions of the Geneva Conventions on
the law of the sea, most of the practices of expropriation, and UN stands

[22] For a recent discussion of those points, see the *Proceedings of the American
Society of International Law* (1959), pp. 21–45.

on the question of self-determination reflect the alignment over one such issue—a coalition of all those states interested in overthrowing the norms of the nineteenth-century system, against the *status quo* states of the West which are the heirs of this system. On the other hand, in the cold war, it is as if the world were composed of layers of states belonging to different ages of politics. On top, the two superpowers enjoy a large amount of independence (except from one another) and extensive advantages within their respective alliances (bases, status-of-forces agreements). Under this layer, there are those allies of the superpowers who are developing their own deterrent; they continue to depend on a superpower for their ultimate protection, but they are capable of bargaining hard before conceding privileges to it. Next we find other allies who tend to be in the position of more or less gilt-edged satellites (depending on the ideological camp to which they belong) : hence outbreaks of neutralism and of fear of war. Fourth, and last, we find all those states which have joined no military camp and live in a kind of fictitious nineteenth-century world of territorial sovereignty.

In the third place, law reflects the bizarre coexistence of revolutionary relations, exemplified by the dialectic of the obsolete and the premature, with elements of stability introduced by the "mutual dependence" characteristic of the balance of terror, just at the time when the role of the military in decision-making was becoming greater than ever, and weapons began to live a life of their own, almost distinct from events in the political universe.

The outcome of these and other contradictory impulses and situations is, once again, heterogeneity: the development of overlapping regional institutions and rules. They are evidence of partial integration; but they also show the fragmentation of the legal order which has accompanied the extension of the diplomatic field to the whole planet.

The reactions of theorists to those developments reflect both the heterogeneity of the legal order, and the impact of the changes of the international system on this order. On the one hand, there is little in common between totalitarian theories of law and non-totalitarian theories: we have here both conflict and asymmetry. The former are not scholarly discussions of the international system from the viewpoint of world order: they are instruments at the service of a state strategy. They are not normative examinations of the ideal order and of the gaps between the actual and the ideal: they are policy sciences showing how the actual should be used or abused in order to reach the ideal determined by official doctrine. On the other hand, within the non-totalitarian theories, changes in the international system have shattered the fragile rapprochement which had taken place previously between the main tendencies. Both of the nineteenth-century extremes have disappeared. It has become impossible to believe in a dialectic of clashing units with a happy ending, and in the vision of a world which moves inevitably toward law, order, and harmony. Even the middle group—positivism—has suffered severely from the marks that the free wills of states have left on world order. Gone is the common faith in the avoidance of chaos. Dead is the agreement on the indispensable character of the state as the basis of the system: theories today range from those that maintain this claim to those that make anguished pleas for world government. Vanished, also, is the agreement on the differences between international and domestic law: theories today range from those that still stress such differences to those that offer subtle, if unconvincing, demonstrations of the similarities.

It is characteristic of revolutionary systems that doctrines not only multiply but often pose as what they are not. Thus, today's deniers or cynics are either sorrowful (rather than gloating), or else disguised as "policy-oriented" theorists who dissolve rules and principles into a maze of processes, messages, and alternatives. Today's utopians are either straightforward adepts of world government, or outright natural-law revivalists, or natural-law thinkers in pseudo-sociological disguise, or "pure theorists of law" who derive normative order from empirical chaos by what I would call the parthenogenesis of law. In the middle, there are persistent, but troubled, positivists and sociologists of law who—as this author well knows—seem more adept at examining the weaknesses of law than at finding formulas which would conceal them, as positivism used to do, more adept at maintaining that it is absurd to separate the legal order from its political roots than at attempting to close the gap between the aspiration for order and the practices of chaos.

III

Let us now apply our findings about the role of international law in various systems to two of the more important theoretical issues of the discipline of international law: the foundation of obligation, and the meaning of sovereignty.

a. The basis of obligation is the same in every legal order: the consciousness, which prevails among the subjects of the legal order, of this order's need to realize a common end. Law is not obtained by deduction from a preexisting natural law or objective law à la Duguit; it is a creation toward an end. Thus, the purpose and the legal order cannot be separated, Kelsen's theory notwithstanding. The solidity or authority of a legal order depends on the nature and substance of the common end—which, finally, depends on the group: if the group shows a high degree of community of purpose, and is organized by central power, the binding force of the legal order will be great—not otherwise.

The feeble consciousness of a common end among multiple units, which allow no central power to impose its own vision or to promote theirs, weakens the binding force of international law permanently by comparison with domestic law. But there are variations in the degree to which such a common end exists in international politics, and consequently variations in the binding force of international law. First, we find variations in *level:* as we have seen, there are, in stable periods, three superimposed groups, with different common ends and, consequently, with an international law of varying binding force. The law of community is strongest because it rests on a common positive purpose. The law of reciprocity is relatively strong because it is the law of a limited partnership, whose members' common end is a set of mutual interests. The law of the political framework is weakest, for it is the law of a collection of actors engaged in a struggle, and whose common end is both limited to a narrow sphere—the rules of the game—and subordinated to the fluctuations of the balance of power.

Secondly, the binding force of international law is exposed to variations in *time*: it is not the same in stable and in revolutionary systems. The legal order of the nineteenth-century system was both modest and solid. It was modest, both because of the moderation in the scope and means of international relations and because the freedom of action of the units was curtailed by the operation of the balance rather than by law. It was efficient, because it was able, within these limits, both to serve as a restraint on the states and to consolidate their interdependence. Legal theories reflected both this modesty and confidence in the efficiency of the legal order. Contemporary law, on the contrary, has to serve a system in which the extension of international relations would seem to require a far wider range of common purposes, but in which heterogeneity has reduced this range drastically. Consequently, there is a divorce between the difficulties of practice and the delirium of theory; and practice is both highly ambitious and relatively inefficient. The increase in the scope of law's subject-matter demonstrates such ambition. But on vital issues, "society" is limited to a few identical or convergent interests, which are sometimes even too narrow or too flimsy to provide a firm basis for the development of any law. There is today no strong enough consciousness or representation of a common legal order of mankind.[23]

Finally, such binding force knows variations in *space*. Given the narrow range of common ends and the absence of worldwide central power, regional solidarities, institutions, and legal orders have appeared. They differ, first of all, in their political foundation—i.e., the structure of the group: the Soviet bloc is a "Roman" system in which the common ends are largely imposed by central power, whereas the Atlantic "community" is really a modern version of the limited partnership: the range of common ends is far from all-embracing and cooperation is far from unconditional, but today, owing to technological changes and the revolutionary character of world politics, such ends require a far greater degree of integration than in the past; the organizations of the European "Six" shape a somewhat less narrow or conditional society. These regional orders differ also in their degree of institutionalization, and in the subject-matter which they cover. The binding force of law in these systems depends on all those factors.

b. Another problem which should be treated in the light of a theory of

---

[23] The statesmen have images of world order which are mutually exclusive, and in which the highest power remains the state; the individual citizens have no way of breaking the statesmen's monopoly: the citizens' efforts at promoting their transnational common ends through law rarely succeed in transcending the borders of the state, which continues to fulfill most of their needs and to be seen as the best protection against outside tempests. Indeed, the development of contemporary law has occurred especially in those areas where individuals raised demands which the state could not satisfy alone: hence the law of international functions and economic integration, whose binding force seems quite strong.

the relations between international systems and international law is the problem of sovereignty. Few concepts are as obscure.[24]

Let us start with the classical definition given by the World Court in the Wimbledon case. Sovereignty means that the state "is subject to no other state and has full and exclusive powers within its jurisdiction without prejudice to the limits set by applicable law." Thus, sovereignty is the situation of the state which has no political superior over it, but is nevertheless bound by international law. Three consequences follow. First, the exercise of its sovereignty by a state—for instance, to sign agreements which may restrict its legal freedom of action—does not *exhaust,* and is indeed a demonstration of, its sovereignty. Secondly, the relations between sovereignty and international law are characterized by the principle of domestic jurisdiction: matters not regulated by the former fall within the latter. Thirdly, relations between states are marked by the principle of equality (whatever their size, all states are in the same situation: their only superior is international law), by the duty of non-intervention, and by the right of self-preservation.

The trouble with this set of definitions is that their neatness is an illusion. If we look at the relations between states, we see a broad gamut of situations in between the status of the mythical state-in-isolation which exercises all the privileges of sovereignty without any other limit than that of general international law, and the situation of a member state in a federation. There is in fact a hierarchy of legal statuses according to the amount of sovereignty whose exercise has been given away to, or restricted in favor of, other states or international agencies. The nature and range of this hierarchy vary with each international system. Thus, sovereignty, rather than a reservoir which can be only full or empty, is a divisible nexus of powers of which some may be kept, some limited, some lost. The point at which sovereignty can be assumed to have vanished is a matter of definition. Given such a hierarchy of situations, the equality of states is mythical. If we look next at the relations between states and international law, we find that the definitions are illusory because one of the two terms—international law—is a fuzzy one: the "limit" or "restraint" which such law imposes on states is both ambiguous and shifting. It is ambiguous because of the conditions of elaboration and enforcement of international law, which are the product of the states. It is shifting because the norms of international law vary from system to system.[25]

---

24 For a sharp analysis, see W. J. Rees, "The Theory of Sovereignty Restated," in Peter Laslett, ed., *Philosophy, Politics and Society* (New York, 1956).

25 The best combination of change over time and ambiguity is provided by the concept of domestic jurisdiction. On the one hand, the area regulated by international law has been drastically expanded in the present system. On the other hand, this increasing "legalization" of interstate relations could become an effective restraint on states only if there existed institutions capable of preventing states from extending the plea of domestic jurisdiction to issues where it does not apply—as well as institutions capable of preventing states from rejecting the plea in those cases where it is still justified. Instead, we find that states successfully invoke the argument even in areas clearly regulated by law (cf. the Interhandel dispute) and refuse to listen to it whenever a problem is of international concern, although it may not be regulated by law (cf. the attitude of the General Assembly of the UN).

Thus, the actual substance of sovereignty depends 1) on the international system and 2), in each system, on the position of a state on the ladder I have mentioned. In a stable system, such as the nineteenth century's, sovereignty is a fairly clear nexus of powers with sharp edges: the world appears as a juxtaposition of well-defined units, whose respective rights are neatly delimited, which allow few exceptions to the principle of full territorial jurisdiction, and which have few institutional links among them: cooperation is organized by diplomacy and by the market. In such a system, the limits of sovereignty are essentially set by general international law (customs and general treaties); the ladder is short: the basic distinctions are the double hierarchy I have described previously. In today's revolutionary system, sovereignty is infinitely more complex. First, diversity of legal statuses is extreme, owing to the multiple patterns of military, economic, and political cooperation which introduce various forms of inequality: hence the predominance of treaties over customs, and the prevalence of less-than-universal treaties. Secondly, the sum of powers of which sovereignty is composed as well as the limitations imposed by law are not only in constant flux: they are also increasing simultaneously, because of the intensity of international relations. The same paradox had marked the revolutionary system before Westphalia. Thus, the edges of sovereignty have become blurred. Although the basic legal unit remains the state, powers of action in the world are both widely scattered among states, blocs, and international organizations, and concentrated among the major industrial centers[26] or (in matters of life and death for the planet) the full nuclear powers.

After the dust has settled, a new stable system will probably be one in which a lasting redistribution of many state powers among international and regional actors will have been accomplished: for despite the very general aspiration (especially among the new nations) for a return to a world of sovereign states practicing non-intervention, the traditional substance of sovereignty is barely compatible with the political and technological conditions of the present world. However, we are bound to remain in the dust for quite a while: for a decline of military blocs in the missile age would not make the competition of East and West any less fierce; the emergence of new nations does not make their resentment of their former masters, their demands on the well-endowed states, and their own political uncertainties any less dangerous; the spread of nuclear power does not make the international system any less explosive. We are in the midst of a succession of revolutionary systems—not on the verge of a stable one— and the solidity of international law will continue to remain in doubt.

---

[26] On the impact of such concentration, see François Perroux, *La coexistence pacifique,* 3 vols. (Paris: Presses Universitaires de France, 1958).

CHAPTER SIX

REVOLUTIONARY NATIONS
AND THE QUALITY OF
INTERNATIONAL LEGAL ORDER

Richard A. Falk

Princeton University

The unsuitability of legal norms derived from relatively stable international systems for the contemporary system is a persistent theme in the writings of contemporary legal theorists. Richard A. Falk delineates the rivalries between status-quo and revolutionary nations that produce instability, distrust, and misunderstanding, and retard the growth of vertical and horizontal forms of international law. Subtle forms of coercion, difficult to regulate, mark state practice. The gap between rhetoric and conduct widens. Falk urges a "rethinking" of international law that would take into account other variables that together generate instability. The process of rethinking might help to diminish the destabilizing effects of revolutionary challenges to traditional norms.

Reprinted from *The Revolution in World Politics,* Morton A. Kaplan, ed. New York: John Wiley and Sons, 1962, pp. 301–31. By permission.

The tone of world politics today is being set by powerful revolutionary nations. A revolutionary nation is a state in which the government has sought or is seeking to reconstitute a national society in opposition to an established social order. Frequently, a revolutionary nation is the outcome of a successful revolutionary movement that has gained control of the governmental machinery by illegal means. Occasionally, as with Hitler's Germany, a revolutionary elite is voted into power by constitutional means. The Soviet Union is designated as the oldest existing revolutionary nation; Communist China, the United Arab Republic, and Cuba are others. The existence of these revolutionary nations is responsible for an extremely unstable pattern of international relations.

This essay examines the effect of this instability upon the current role of law in world affairs. There is a parallel need to study the international behavior or revolutionary nations during earlier historical periods.[1] For instance, one thinks of the liberal democratic revolutions that took place in France and the United States late in the eighteenth century. How did these revolutionary nations respond to the claims of the existing international legal order? Does the ideological character of the revolution control international participation in the post-revolutionary period? Or is the external conduct of the revolutionary nation primarily a consequence of the prevailing international political system? A historical study of the behavior of revolutionary nations would help us to distinguish between the unique and the repetitive aspects of the present world situation. It would, as well, increase our ability to isolate the variables that seem most responsible for the pattern of behavior chosen by the revolutionary nation. And finally, this improved knowledge might help us to formulate strategies to moderate the destabilizing impact of the newly emerging revolutionary nations.

The sequence of presentation in this study will be: first, a description of the manner in which international law is today conditioned by the dominance of revolutionary politics; second, the impact of this conditioning upon legal norms governing the use of coercion across national boundaries; third, an indication of the bearing of representative norms of international law upon the specific phenomenon of internal revolution.

It is evident that the international atmosphere is composed of many elements only one of which is law. Economic, social, psychological, military, and cultural factors all interact to generate stability or instability. Law is a relatively *dependent* variable, significantly useful in a stable social system, dramatically marginal in an unstable social system. By itself, legal technique cannot introduce stability. It is deceptive to rely upon international law as an independent variable. This explains why we should not isolate the

---

[1] The general idea of this paragraph was suggested to me by Professor Wesley L. Gould of Purdue University.

study of international law from concern with the broad social and political conditions prevailing in the world. International law can contribute to world order only in *conjunction with* other stabilizing forces.

I

A central aspect of the revolutionary spirit is a refusal to accept the limits of permissible behavior as developed by the established order, especially its legal limits. Law is identified with the status quo, and it is the status quo that is the target of revolutionary energy. Law thus bears a problematic relevance to the politics of revolution.[2]

Nevertheless, certain other extralegal factors give law, particularly international law, a potential importance for current world affairs. Law provides a convenient way for political rivals to specify limits of permissible behavior. If the consequence of unrestrained conflict is mutually destructive then it is rational to seek common limits that will prevent such unrestrained conflict from taking place. For instance, in the Korean War supply centers behind the Yalu and in Japan were both exempted from military attack.[3] The

---

[2] It is relevant to observe that the Draft Program of the Soviet Communist Party for the Twenty-Second Party Congress fails to make a single reference to international law in the course of an elaborate reformulation of Soviet foreign policy and aspiration. Even in the extended discussion of the relations between the Soviet Union and other members of the Communist bloc there is little tangible indication of a willingness to overcome national rivalries by the promotion of supranational political and legal integration. There is not even an expressed desire for regional institutions of an extent comparable to those developing in Western Europe. See full text of the Draft Program, *New York Times,* August 1, 1961, pp. 13–20. For negative accounts of the Soviet attitude toward international law see Marek S. Korowicz, *Introduction to International Law* (The Hague: M. Nijhoff, 1959), pp. 108–56; Leon Lipson, *Outer Space and International Law,* Rand Paper P-1434 (1959), pp. 12–17. For an affirmative account see Grigory I. Tunkin, "Co-Existence and International Law," *Recueil des Cours,* Academie de Droit International, Vol. 95 (1958).

[3] Throughout this essay it is important to take account of the particular character of the legal norm. The range of norms includes rules of the game and very specific provisions in international agreements. My preference is to extend the characterization "law" to any "norm" that appears to standardize international behavior. This acknowledges the decentralized character of the international system and emphasizes its deficient norm-producing procedures and institutions. The text example from the Korean War suffers from its specificity in time and place. We usually think of law as providing standards of more general application. Here again, however, the ad hoc nature of international regimes is part of the quality of contemporary world order. This feature of specificity serves to remind us of the primitive character of international law. However, it is important to use an inclusive image of law for international affairs so as to perceive all existing ordering possibilities. In contrast, a strict image of law, as developed by Austinian positivism, may usefully focus the task of the jurist in an orderly and advanced social system.

It is essential also to examine the manner in which cultural tradition bears upon normative behavior and expectation. For instance, the deeply embedded Asian experi-

development of nuclear weapons has made unrestrained conflict mutually destructive and the establishment of a legal regime mutually beneficial. There exists an urgent need to use suitable legal techniques to contain struggles for world power within safe boundaries. Thus, despite the existence of the revolutionary nations, international law is peculiarly relevant to contemporary politics because never before has it been so generally felt that means must be found to prevent the outbreak of major war between political rivals. The tension between the pressure for unrestraint generated by revolutionary energies and the pressure for restraint generated by the fear of nuclear war is central to an understanding of the contemporary relevance of international law.

This tension is made dangerously taut by the inability of the world community to legislate peaceful changes.[4] Oppressive elites in control of national societies yield only to coercion. The character of reactionary oppression is such that external aid is often needed by the internal protest movement if it is to succeed in its struggle for control of the national society. Two comments follow from this: First, internal social change in oppressive societies must come about by lawless coercion; the oppressive elite will otherwise tend to refuse the internal demands for social change, even when these demands have the support of the world community. The Union of South Africa is an instructive instance. Second, internal revolutionary situations can easily become the scenes of cold war conflict as a result of opposing Soviet and American interventions. Thus, internal social change can neither be achieved peacefully, nor can it be kept separate from the cold war. Traditional international law is ill-conditioned to control such political phenomena, since it is premised upon the irrelevance of internal coercion to the maintenance of world order. One way to emphasize the contemporary problem posed for international law by revolutionary nations is to insist upon the current fundamental relevance of internal coercion to international stability. The role of the United Nations in the Congo is, at least partly,[5] an acknowledgement of this relevance. Recognition of this

---

ence with relations of subordination and superordination influence their perception of what constitutes "law." It appears to inhibit commitment to a horizontal legal order—such as the international legal system—that lays stress upon considerations of reciprocity to restrain behavior within limits set by legal norms. This point derives from a comment on an earlier version of this study made by Professor John Lindbeck of Harvard University.

4 Perceptively foreshadowed in Herbert A. Smith, *The Crisis in the Law of Nations* (London: Stevens, 1947).

5 The United Nations initially was requested to send military assistance to the government of the Congo to permit it to repel "the present external aggression" charged to Belgium as a result of "the despatch to the Congo of metropolitan Belgian troops in violation of the Treaty of Friendship" between the two countries. However, it was evident that the Security Council responded to Lumumba's request primarily because, as it stated in its Resolution of July 22, 1960, "the complete restoration of law and order in the Republic of the Congo would effectively contribute to the maintenance of international peace and security." See generally E. M. Miller, "Legal Aspects of U.N. Action in the Congo," 55 *Amer. J. Int'l Law*, No. 1 (1961).

relevance leads to a repudiation of the traditional characterization of internal coercion as matter of domestic concern.[6]

These introductory comments seek to convey a sense of the texture of world affairs as it relates to the contemporary role of international law. Countless other correlative extralegal developments are important law-conditioning factors: the growing participation in world affairs of Afro-Asian countries, the development of economic and military regionalism, the growth of specialized and general supranational institutions, the ideological commitments in the current struggle for power, the impacts of shifting military strategies (the gradual replacement of bombers by missiles), the vitality and impatience of movements for national independence and social innovation in the newly developing portions of the world, and the bipolarization of the international political structure.

Revolutionary nations generate instability that challenges the role of international law. For one thing, a revolutionary nation is often evangelical in spirit, exemplary for nascent revolutionary movements in neighboring nations and interventionary in practice;[7] there is a strong tendency, hardened into an ideology of world revolution in Communist countries, to export the revolution to status-quo states[8] The new Draft Program of the Soviet Communist Party puts this explicitly when it accepts the "duty to support the sacred struggle of the oppressed people and their just anti-imperialist wars of liberation."[9] The revolutionary nations of Africa and the Middle

---

[6] Traditional international law, as developed before nuclear weapons, emphasized the territorial state as a sovereign minimum unit in world affairs. Territorial jurisdiction was absolute except for the duty to respect the rights of alien residents. Otherwise, international law exempted internal phenomena, even when it crossed the threshold of violence. This exemption was accelerated in the twentieth century by the gospel of self-determination given initial impetus by Woodrow Wilson. With nuclear weapons, the cold war political stability for the world rests progressively upon the control of internal violence. A sensitive study of the bearing of the new military technology upon the old political system is John H. Herz, *International Politics in the Atomic Age* (New York: Columbia University Press, 1959).

[7] Cuba exemplified this pattern by a series of futile interventions through Central America. The power used was so inadequate (a handful of men with an armful of light weapons) to the ends pursued (the overthrow of a well-organized government) that the revolutionary zeal of the Castro forces seemed like a bad comedy. For a brief description of these 1959 Cuban interventions see Richard P. Stebbins, *The United States in World Affairs 1959* (New York and London: Harpers, 1960), pp. 353–57.

[8] It is probably useful to point to phases in the post-revolutionary period. At first, the revolutionary government consolidates its internal position and seeks primarily to reconstitute its domestic society along the lines promised by the revolutionary program. External participation is marginal, limited to gestures of sympathy or token participation in foreign-protest movements. However, if the revolutionary government is successful and strong, then this emphasis is inverted. Internal policy becomes "conservative" (that is, conserving the character of the revolutionary society and moving slowly ahead along the same lines), while external policy becomes significantly interventionary. These comments refer to behavioral tendencies rather than to invariable patterns.

[9] *New York Times,* August 1, 1961, p. 16, Col. 4; see also W. W. Rostow, *"Guerrilla Warfare in the Underdeveloped Areas,"* Vol. 45, *Dept. State Bull.* (1958), pp. 233, 234.

East are eager to sponsor revolutions that aim to overthrow reactionary elites and replace them by revolutionary elites committed to radical internal social change. The missionary zeal of these revolutionary nations induces the status-quo nations to use their influence to resist the spread of the destabilizing gospel. The United States, as the dominant status-quo nation,[10] feels especially threatened by the revolutionary pressures generated by the Communist movement. It resists the spread of communism by recourse to every available means short of initiating a general war. This reflects the animosity that arises from ideological antagonisms between rival leaders in the cold war. It is partly also a competitive struggle for world domination. One effect is to compel the liberal democracies to support antidemocratic governments to resist a radical elite that has become identified with the Communist movement; United States relations with China since 1930 express fully this dilemma. It also leads the status-quo nations to sponsor counterrevolutionary internal movements. The rules of international law are today very ineffective to assure national governments their customary control over internal affairs.

Beyond this, the success of a revolution is often accompanied by a repudiation of those norms of international law which restrict the freedom of a state to shape its internal society. The revolutionary nation is usually committed to a program of rapid social change. This leads it to take control over internal capital and to relieve itself of external commitments, like bonded indebtedness. The Soviet Union, as a revolutionary nation, typified this pattern. It expropriated all property that it could reach without providing suitable compensation and repudiated the debts of predecessor Russian governments. One effect of widespread revolution is thus to weaken the legal support given to international investment. For, in addition to the actual losses incurred, investors tend to withdraw capital or avoid further commitments when the prospects for revolution grow strong. The security of American investment throughout Latin America is at least part of the explanation for our preoccupation with Castroism. The rules of international law were developed to support the interests of the capitalist nations of Western Europe during their expansionist phases of development. This is very vividly perceived by the revolutionary nations, especially those equipped with a coherent radical ideology. International law, in general, is viewed by orthodox Marxist thought as one way by which the bourgeoisie perpetuates its favored position in the world. This produces a basic disrespect for international law by the leadership of the revolutionary state.

---

[10] The designation of the United States as a status-quo nation has important disadvantages. It overlooks the support given by the United States for moderate change. The United States favors the gradual termination of colonial administration and a moderate program of internal social reform. Nevertheless, the United States is called a status-quo nation here to contrast its posture toward change with the indiscriminate radicalism of the Communist bloc. Of course, as the Hungarian uprising of 1956 so vividly revealed, the Soviet Union is hostile to adverse changes taking place within its own bloc. Thus, the contrast between "revolutionary" and "status-quo" is useful only when it makes reference to differing attitudes toward the pace of social change in underdeveloped countries.

Such disrespect is extended by the internal revolutionary experience. The revolutionary movement has necessarily flaunted the law to gain power and it has probably been subject to a variety of legal attempts by the former government to suppress its activities. Thus, "the law" tends to be identified with "the enemy" by the revolutionary elite.

In addition, the revolutionary nation is not sensitive to the dangers, even to itself, of external instability. In its early years it fails to perceive the advantages for its own internal development that would result from a reliable minimum world order. Red China continues to take a highly cavalier posture toward external instability.

These considerations lead one to be very skeptical about the impact of international law upon the conduct of revolutionary nations. However, a revolutionary nation, if it survives, comes to appreciate some of the advantages offered by an effective legal order. With the success of the revolution, a passionate insistence upon internal stability emerges to frustrate counterrevolutionary tendencies. This may lead to the moderation of interventionary external practices in tacit exchange for reciprocal deference to its own internal order. The Communist nations have always, in their formal participation in world affairs, emphasized the sanctity of the most conservative aspect of international law—that is, a broad, unrestricted doctrine of national sovereignty. The Soviet advocacy of an absolute position on sovereign immunity is an obvious matter of self-interest. State ownership combined with sovereign immunity would exempt socialist nations from legal duties in their commercial dealing in capitalist nations without depriving them of legal rights.

The experience of a successful revolutionary nation may in other ways lead it toward conservative participation in world affairs. It may regard war as a genuine danger to its future and seek to use law to reduce the risk. The Soviet Union often seems to be moving in this direction and is perhaps encouraged by its belief that there are safe ways to increase its relative position in the struggle with the West for world power; it is necessary to distinguish between conservative revolutionary nations (Soviet Union) and radical revolutionary nations (China). The radical revolutionary nation poses the most direct challenge to the maintenance of minimum legal order in international relations. The early experience of a revolutionary government tends to emphasize the negative tasks of eliminating the old order. But the experience of reconstituting the internal society along orderly lines makes the leadership dependent upon legal technique.[11] The revolutionary nation may be isolated in its early years of existence, but when it has consolidated its internal position, then it is likely to seek at least minimal external contacts. This leads to an appreciation for the convenience of legal standards to regulate routine contacts across national boundaries. The early hostility to international law tends to dissolve and is replaced by a rather

---

[11] See an analysis that suggests general tendencies of social systems to develop an orientation favorable to the application of legal rules, Roger Fisher, "Bringing Law To Bear on Governments," *Harvard Law Rev.* Vol. 74 (1961), pp. 1130–40; Roger Fisher, "Should We Veto the Troika?" *The New Republic,* August 21, 1961, pp. 11–14.

pragmatic attitude toward the rule of law. Soviet leadership has been particularly adept at improvising ad hoc invocations of international legal norms to promote its political policies. Thus, it stresses very much the doctrine of nonintervention in relation to Western efforts to transmit hostile propaganda to Eastern Europe[12] and behaves in a very interventionary manner in the dependent parts of the world, particularly in a non-European country controlled by a European imperialistic elite.

Revolutionary nations, then, are likely to be lawless and hostile to law in their early years of power. Later this attitude is likely to grow more flexible and is expressed by a pragmatic use of the legal norms provided by international law. Th nature of revolutionary ideology leads to a special burden upon the legal rules designed to preserve the independence of nations; interventionary policy generates counterintervention and creates conflict situations of high intensity. This is especially true when direct conflict is precluded by the obsolescence of recourse to war as a means of waging a struggle for world power. Status-quo nations, which today include the liberal democracies, also seem to regard international legal norms from a pragmatic angle that accords priority to cold war considerations. The significance of revolutionary nations then is to reduce the relevance of law to international politics for all national actors (including non-revolutionary nations).

The distinctive quality of international law as a legal system adds to the difficulty of achieving stability in a world community that includes revolutionary nations.[13] Compared with domestic legal orders, the formulation, interpretation, and implementation of legal norms is very decentralized in international society. The principal ordering device is reciprocity.[14] This requires communication and a basic confidence between leading national actors, since adherence to legal norms, except in marginal contacts, is voluntary. Fairness results from self-restraint. The incentive for conformity is supplied by the mutual advantages to all states that result from fair and reliable legal standards. Such a predominantly horizontal legal order, working effectively without a hierarchy of legal institutions or centralized organs for consistent enforcement, achieves fair and predictable legal behavior in stable societies;[15] this pattern is suggested by the legal order prevailing in numerous primitive societies.[16] It depends, however, on a com-

12 See the second Khrushchev Message to President Kennedy protesting United States intervention in April, 1961, in Cuba, "Mr. Khrushchev to President Kennedy" (unofficial translation of message dated April 22, 1961), reprinted in 44 *Dept. State Bull.* (1961), 664.

13 M. Kaplan and N. Katzenbach, *The Political Foundations of International Law* (New York: John Wiley and Sons, 1961), pp. 30–55.

14 See Myres McDougal, *Studies in World Public Order* (New Haven: Yale University Press, 1960).

15 This depiction is developed in some detail in Richard A. Falk, "International Jurisdiction: Horizontal and Vertical Conceptions of Legal Order," 32 *Temple Law Quarterly*, Vol. 32 No. 3 (1959) pp. 295–320.

16 See *e.g.,* Bronislaw Malinowski, *Crime and Custom in Savage Society* (New York: Harcourt, Brace and World, Inc., 1932). Max Gluckman, *The Judicial Process among the Barotze of Northern Rhodesia* (Manchester: Manchester University Press, 1955).

munity commitment to stability and to a common base of shared values. International law, as it emerged from the natural-law tradition of Western Europe, fulfilled this need so long as world affairs were dominated by Western European actors.[17] But with the significant world participation of non-Western European nations, the divergent cultural backgrounds placed burdens on the horizontal structures of international law; effective communication depends greatly upon the shared experience of a common culture. Distrust and misunderstanding of alien tradition is a universal phenomenon.

This basic tendency to destabilize the common base of understanding needed for a legal order that relies heavily on reciprocity has been accentuated by the emergence of powerful revolutionary actors. For the revolutionary energy is often directed against the restraints and standards that are urged by status-quo nations. The revolutionary nation emerges in a situation of internal instability often confronted by hostile status-quo nations. The status-quo nations fear infiltration and subversion by the revolutionary nation; the revolutionary nation fears counterrevolutionary or interventionary pressure by the status-quo nations. Thus, instability is introduced at the core of the international legal order, undermining the kind of trust needed for the communication that must accompany the reciprocal patterns of practice. Unless nations believe that there is a mutual desire for stability in their relations with one another, instability will result. The dominance of a reciprocal threat to national security induces leading nations to subordinate common standards of legal restraint to political and military goals. The U-2 incident and the April 1961 interventions in Cuba by the United States contrast with the rhetorical pleas of our statesmen for the rule of law in world affairs.[18] Thus, the presence of revolutionary nations generates a destabilizing response by status-quo nations thereby reducing the opportunities for horizontal legal order. And by the same circumstance, states are reluctant to transfer important legal authority to vertical, international institutions; the Connally Reservation instances extreme legal inhibition by the leading status-quo nation. With such diffidence exhibited by status-quo nations—the states responsible for the development of international law— it is hardly surprising that revolutionary nations are reluctant to participate at all in international judicial proceedings, and refuse, for example, to settle disputes in the World Court. For the instability occasioned by the rivalry between status-quo and revolutionary nations is even more detrimental to the growth of the vertical forms of international law than it is to the horizontal forms.

[17] Cf. C. Wilfred Jenks, *The Common Law of Mankind* (New York: Praeger, 1958), pp. 63–172; Filmer Stuart Cuckow, Northrop, *The Taming of Nations* (New York: Macmillan, 1952).

[18] For a collection of statements by important recent political figures in the United States ranging from Robert Taft to Adlai Stevenson agreeing on the urgency of extending the international rule of law see A.B.A., Special Committee on World Peace Through Law, *Compilation of Quotations* (1960); Cf. also William W. Bishop, "The International Rule of Law," 59 *Michigan Law Rev.* 553 (1961).

Another way to state this consequence of fundamental distrust is to emphasize the decentralized power of decision entrusted to nations in relation to norms of international law. A state has been allowed great discretion by international law to characterize its behavior in a self-serving manner. The notion of consent as the basis of international obligation and deference to sovereign prerogative is expressed with celebrated clarity in the *Lotus* case.[19] This decentralization does not mean that international law is a futile pretense, but it does mean that the effectiveness of the rule is dependent upon the mutual commitment of nations to minimal standards of legal order. So long as stability is *perceived* as mutually beneficial for all major states, the horizontality of international society is not a disadvantage. The capacity of states to attribute legality to their own contested conduct, without being forced to submit their description to third-party judgment, makes it very important to look at the social reality behind the norms and doctrines of international law. The meaning of the legal norm must be comprehended by an inquiry into the process by which it is translated into behavior.

Independent of the revolutionary situation, skepticism about the role of international law is generated by the refusal of contending states to commit themselves to a procedure that includes impartial characterization. Legal norms exist in complementary sets of opposed prescriptions, thus providing a national actor on every occasion with a lawful explanation of his conduct.[20] Centralizations of authority to characterize legal conduct often produce a more significant growth in international law than do the elaborate codifications of legal norms in law-making treaties like the Geneva Conventions on the Law of the Sea. In this regard the *Nottebohm*[21] and *Asylum*[22] cases have immense juridical importance. For in *Nottebohm* the World Court asserted a vertical test for nationality, rejecting the self-serving characterization made by Lichtenstein, and in the *Asylum* case, the majority judgment denied Colombia the right to determine unilaterally whether Haya de la Torre was entitled to diplomatic asylum. Acceptance of vertical characterization is essential to the growth of legal standards in a world composed of states that rarely trust one another. This constructive movement gains momentum as more nations can be made to feel that the risk of an unfavorable vertical characterization is more desirable than the disorder produced by two contradictory decentralized characterizations. Revolutionary nations in the early years of their existence are too jealous of their power, too distrustful of their adversary, too eager for unrestrained expansion to give important legal competence to international decision-makers.

Many discount the meaning of nonintervention pledges or renunciations of the use of force because the nations have not established an impartial

---

19 *S. S. Lotus, PCIJ.*, Ser. A, No. 10 (1927).
20 Cf. the excellent study by Myres S. McDougal and Florentino P. Feliciano, "Legal Regulation of Resort to International Coercion: Aggression and Self-Defense in Policy Perspective," 68 *Yale Law Journal* 1057 (1959) ; discussion of complementary prescriptions is clearly stated on pp. 1059–63.
21 Friedrich Nottebohm [*Lichtenstein v. Guatemala*] (1955), *I.C.J.* Rep. 4.
22 Colombia Peruvian Asylum Case (1950), *I.C.J.* Rep. 266.

procedure for determining when contested behavior falls within the prohibition of the legal rule. Legal rules, standing by themselves, do no more than frame diplomatic debate. The challenged nation invokes one group of legal norms to justify its conduct, and the complaining nation invokes the complementary set of legal norms. The United States condemns the Soviet Union for its "armed intervention" in the internal affairs of Hungary in 1956; the Soviet Union defends its conduct as a response to a request by the "legitimate" (Kadar) government for help in restoring internal order in a time of lawless civil strife. The invocation pattern is reversed if one examines reactions to the entry of American military forces into Lebanon in 1958. Impartial characterization of behavior is needed to assure the relevance of legal norms to patterns of conduct. Actors mutually committed to stability may be expected normally to restrain their conduct in accord with impartial characterizations.[23] It is common to find domestic courts, for instance, determining a controversy brought before it by deference to the national interests of another state. The doctrines of Act of State and sovereign immunity, as well as the solution of international choice of laws problems, reveal areas in which impartial legal standards of self-enforcement operate successfully because of the prevalent acceptance of the criteria of reciprocity. Expansions of this mode of legal order into central areas of contention such as, for instance, nonintervention is precluded by the revolutionary postulate. Political rivalry is given priority over legal moderation, especially where coercion is used by a bloc leader in the cold war to increase or preserve its relative power. The dominant political instability makes it impossible to render an impartial decision. Each rival views a determination adverse to its national interest as biased and is unlikely to entrust the power of decision to any third-party procedure that did not institutionalize its political ideology. The relative willingness of the United States to fight cold war issues within the United Nations is less attributable to its preference for the rule of law than it is to its political assurance of voting majorities on most controversial issues. In this respect even status-quo nations have not displayed a willingness to accept legal limits when vital national interests were involved. Political considerations in Kashmir quickly revealed the scope of India's commitment to the rule of law, and the Suez campaign in 1956 illustrated the willingness of even extreme status-quo nations to override the limits of law.

Despite the fact that complementary norms give nations a "legal" explanation for "illegal" conduct, the consensus of world sentiment tends

---

[23] It is well to observe that national actors have never operated in conditions of "normalcy" where vital matters were involved. Prior to our revolutionary age, the egoistic pursuit of national interest led states to refuse to accept comprehensive legal standards. For an excellent treatment of the earlier politicization of world affairs along these lines see Charles de Visscher, *Theory and Reality in Public International Law* (Princeton: Princeton University Press, 1957), pp. 71–129. Perhaps the advent of nuclear weapons during the European stage of world history might have produced an effective world legal order. A common cultural heritage might have overcome political differences in the face of the threat of mutual extermination.

to provide an independent judgment. This can result in conforming behavior to the legal norm if both superpowers happen to agree with the majority judgment; the effective response of the United Nations to the Suez invasion by France, England, and Israel provides a leading illustration. Even when the superpowers disagree, the vote in the General Assembly provides a weak form of objective characterization that has law-inducing consequences. The growing strength of world opinion, especially as expressed in the United Nations, gives to resolutions of censure the status of an inchoate sanction. It is relevant to compare the prominent ordering role played by ridicule in primitive societies. The Soviet Union has not been unmindful of its international prestige. The prospect of censure, with a resulting crystallization of world opinion, seems to influence, if not restrain, national actions; it acts as a marginal factor to discourage repetitions of Budapest, and it may yet spare Castro an invasion by the United States marines.

One hopes that the passage of time will transform the outlook of the revolutionary nations in the direction of the status-quo nations.[24] The process is cumulative, as when the status-quo nations perceive the waning of the revolutionary zeal they will, in turn, also rely more upon stabilities of law and less upon stabilities of force. The nuclear risks encourage both types of nations to hasten a willingness to strengthen legal order.

II

The effort of post-medieval Europe to restrict the right of a state to wage war to those instances in which it had "a just cause" ended in failure. Despite the moralizing rhetoric of the *bellum justum* doctrine, drawn by jurists from the corpus of natural law, it became evident that most nations were unwilling to adhere to legal limits when they had sufficient power to attain national goals by conquest. It was the wisdom of the nineteenth century to shift the emphasis from a delineation of the occasions when it was legitimate to wage war to a system of shifting alliances between the leading European states designed to make it impossible for a nation to mobilize superior force against its political rivals. Thus, stability was not a matter of enforcing rules restricting the use of force, but rather the control of force depended upon the existence of countervailing force. Political mechanisms of stability were more successful than the earlier attempt to establish stability by positing clear rules. Law thus became virtually irrelevant to the use of war to promote national interests, although law made

[24] A liberalization of the internal regime tends to encourage the pressure for external accommodation. Such a tendency is transformed by some into a presupposition; that is, legal arrangements with totalitarian nations are a trap for liberal democracies. Thus, we must not expect to develop a universal legal order until there has been decisive internal liberalization in the Communist states. This position is developed by Myres S. McDougal and Harold D. Lasswell in "The Identification and Appraisal of Diverse Systems of Public Order," *Studies in World Public Order* (New Haven: Yale University Press, 1960), pp. 3–10.

important contributions to the effort to restrict the scope of war by the doctrine of neutrality and to regularize the conduct of hostilities to eliminate superfluous horror. The decision to use force, however, was not subject to third-party characterization, and a state was in a position to legitimate recourse to war by giving its own explanation.

The First World War marked the end of the balance of power system. The destructivity of war in the twentieth century gave solemn urgency to the endeavor to control the use of force. The League of Nations was created to provide collective machinery for the determination of unlawful uses of force, thus internationalizing the characterization of war and aggregating the counter force of the world community. However, the unanimity principle, the nonparticipation of the United States, and the unwillingness of nations to act on behalf of world community interests made the League unable to cope with flagrantly aggressive recourses to force by Germany, Italy, and Japan. Widespread efforts were made to persuade nations to renounce the use of force in international relations, culminating in the solemn pledge of the Pact of Paris in 1928 to restrict recourse to force to situations of self-defense. One could question the seriousness of the legal commitment in view of the failure to provide definitions of aggressive war or self-defense and the absence of a mechanism for an impartial characterization of conduct alleged to be in violation of the pledge. With neither a standard nor an agency for third-party interpretation and enforcement, the legal commitment to renounce the aggressive use of force proved to be ineffectual, except possibly as sedation for status-quo nations. Legal rules, without the backing of available and sufficient force, seem unable to discourage recourse to international violence. This observation continues to pertain to the present world situation. The United Nations Charter restricts the lawful use of force to "the inherent right of individual or collective self-defense" in Article 51 and expresses in Article 2(4) a commitment by members to refrain from the use or threat of force in international relations. The prohibition of aggressive war was implicit in the Nuremberg Judgment and received the unanimous support of the General Assembly in a resolution adopting the Nuremberg Principles. Thus, recourse to unlawful war, if unsuccessful, might well result in criminal responsibility for the leaders of the defeated nation. But no serious progress has been made to outlaw war as a way to promote national interests. An authoritative definition of aggression is needed to establish a legal standard that could guide states and suggest the outer limits of permissible coercion. However, one notes with regret that the United Nations has failed in its attempts to formulate an acceptable definition of aggression;[25] instead reliance is placed upon an ad hoc political determination by the Security Council in the unlikely event of agreement among the permanent members or by a two-thirds vote of the General Assembly. Major states do not seem willing to entrust the

---

[25] See Quincy Wright, "The Prevention of Aggression," 50 *Amer. J. Int'l Law,* pp. 514, 517 (1956); Louis Sohn, "The Definition of Aggression," 45 *Virginia Law Rev.* (1959) 697.

determination of and control over recourses to force to a non-political commission operating with an advance definition and empowered to compel police action.[26] It is exceedingly problematic to rely upon the indubitable "norm" of international law proscribing aggressive war. For without an effective process for implementing the definition, could it be agreed upon, it is unlikely to govern the behavior of expanding states in their pursuit of national goals. The mere "norm" of international law positing a standard of behavior does not deserve the status of "law" unless it is accompanied by a process of implementation. However, it is not essential that the process be supplied by a central or supranational ("vertical") institution; it may bring about the desired behavioral results by decentralized or national ("horizontal") regularities. For instance, the modest success of the neutrality system in confining the scope of war was based upon the horizontal interplay of self-interested belligerent and neutral nations. Horizontal efforts to control aggressive war reveal more promise. Thus, cold war rivals are intimidated by the probable fulfillment of collective self-defense commitments and the fear of a retaliation that includes nuclear devastation. Such deterrent threats seem to have discouraged the cruder and more central exertions of coercion in the cold war; the Korean conflict is a special instance because the boundary crossed was not "international," and the United States had been publicly ambivalent about undertaking an advance commitment to defend South Korea. When border-crossing occurs outside the main context of the cold war, as in Suez in 1956, then the collective machinery of the United Nations increasingly provides effective community response.

Thus, the prohibition of aggressive war seems to be an effective contemporary legal doctrine if the concept of aggression is very crudely defined. However, subtle forms of coercion, even across borders, are not brought under legal control. The United Nations would not respond to the complaints by Israel of episodic Egyptian border-crossings for purposes of terrorizing inhabitants of Israeli territory; such coercive conduct fell short of "an armed attack," and Israel was not entitled to act in self-defense. The absence of control over subtle forms of coercion imposes an immense burden upon a nation that is expected to refrain from the use of "aggressive" force. It is on these grounds that Julius Stone defends the Sinai campaign in 1956.[27] The background threat of nuclear war is so overwhelming that the clear minimum standards of identifying coercion as border-crossing of sustained magnitude must be upheld, even though it may have been very unfair to expect Israel in 1956 to suffer continuing harassment at the hands of Egyptian terrorists.

The instabilities of the era, combining the expansive energies of the Communist bloc and the eruptive energies of the various Afro-Asian, Latin American revolutionary elites, have not been expressed in conventional war. Nuclear deterrence makes it highly irrational to promote national

---

26 Julius Stone, *Aggression and World Order* (Berkeley: University of California Press, 1958).

27 *Ibid.*, pp. 99–103.

interests by recourse to war. Thus, the legal norm is backed by political reality. However, the cost of "law enforcement" is exceedingly high, involving the immense outlay of resources needed to ensure a crippling second-strike capacity and the horrible risk of accidental war in one of its several forms.[28] It is characteristic of revolutionary politics to maintain order by a reliance upon terror, and it is this frightful condition that appears to be an integral aspect of the current situation. For the very presence of revolutionary impetus in the world particularly rigidifies the distrust of the status-quo nations, especially when the pendulum starts to swing against them, so as to make it impossible to transfer the struggle onto a level where the stakes are less ultimate. Consequently, legal arrangements to banish nuclear weapons and to give to an international organization the force needed to discourage non-nuclear "aggressive war" have small hope for significant adoption even though the dynamics of the actual conflict would remain unchanged. That is, the Communist bloc would continue to support internal revolutionary movements in the less developed parts of the world, and the Western nations would counter that support by helping the presently constituted governments. This is a crisis of confidence and imagination which must be overcome if law is to contribute its techniques to enable the conflict to be waged without endangering human survival. For the horizontal system of deterrence based upon a reasonable consensus as to the nature of "aggression" may break down if one side finds itself losing the cold war. The dysfunctional rigidity of the American response to Castro is an alarming sign of such a possibility. The accumulation of such signs may lead to the triggering of nuclear war and, thus, to a further fulfillment of Samson's last testament.

The tendency of revolutionary nations to export their ideological impetus rarely requires a direct use of force, much less recourse to a full-scale aggressive war. The expansion by the revolutionary nations is carried on by subtler forms of coercion than are entailed by the concept of "armed attack." In addition, the revolutionary spirit in the twentieth century is based upon an anti-imperialist ideology which stresses the urgency of radical internal social and economic changes. Despite the empire-building patterns of the Soviet Union, and now China, the revolutionary mission is primarily the sponsor of nationalist eruptions in the status-quo nations. Subordinate revolutionary energies in the Arab and African worlds stress racial unification on a political level; one supposes that Nasser and Nkrumah envision themselves as eventual heads of sprawling resurgent racial empires. The basic revolutionary appeal, however, is directed to the oppressed classes who are urged to seize control, redistribute wealth, and provide the state with a wide capital base that will support rapid industrial development.

Subtler forms of coercion, often called "indirect aggression," are difficult to regulate, partly because of the special status conferred upon nation-states by international law. The classical formulations of international law under-

---

[28] See John Phelps *et al.*, "Accidental War: Some Dangers in the 1960's" (Mershon National Security Program Research Paper, 1960).

score the dominance of states in world affairs. It is a historical fact that national governments consolidated internal power to permit effective participation in external ventures of discovery, settlement, and trade. This led to affirmations of the exclusivity of the authority of a state within its own borders and to marginal restrictions upon the capacity of a state to act in world affairs. Thus, there arose considerable doctrinal support for the independence of a state and the implied right of a national society to be free from external interference. Participation in world affairs was confined to the leading monarchies of Europe. Each sought to maximize its power at the expense of the others but had no particular impulse to interfere with the internal affairs of its rival. If conflict was unavoidable by balance of power calculations then war settled the issue—preferably fought on some colonial land far from the home country; war represented a conflict of professional armies and was not nearly so likely to require the total support of the internal population. However, the success of the American and French revolutions changed the character of world affairs. From the Congress of Vienna onward, the continental monarchies perceived the democratic objectives of revolutionary movements as a contagious disease to be stamped out wherever it appeared. Prussia, Russia, and Austria adopted a responsive interventionary policy in defense of the principle of legitimacy. Armed interventions restored monarchies in Naples, Piedmont, and Spain. For Spain, the avowal of intentions to recapture control over her revolting colonies led to the Monroe Doctrine in 1823, with its insistence that European nations refrain from intervention in the Western hemisphere. It is well known how the shield became a sword as the century progressed. Although Europe was kept out, the United States intervened to restore internal order or to protect American economic interests. The details of the story are no longer important, as a series of twentieth-century hemispheric agreements incorporated an absolute renunciation of the right of unilateral intervention in the internal affairs of a sovereign state.[29] However, the internal events in another state were not sealed off from international concern. The adoption of the principle of collective self-defense in Article 3 of the Inter-American Treaty of Reciprocal Assistance was supplemented by the Declaration of Solidarity at Caracas in 1954, with its condemnation of the interventionary character of the international Communist movement and an a priori commitment to view its appearance in any part of the hemisphere as "a threat to the sovereignty and political independence of the American states" that called for collective action. In effect, the formal claim was to revive the concept of protective intervention implicit in the experience of the Monroe Doctrine in order to set limits upon the expansionist tendencies of the Communist movement.

The development of American policy was influenced by events leading up to the Second World War that suggested political limits to the legal

---

[29] Comprehensive review found in Doris A. Graber, *Crisis Diplomacy* (Washington: Public Affairs Press, 1959); Aaron J. Thomas, Jr. and Ann Van Wynen Thomas, *Non-Intervention: The Law and Its Import in the Americas* (Dallas: Southern Methodist University Press, 1956).

commitment to nonintervention. The end of the First World War had led to strong sentiment, most dramatically attributed to Wilson, favoring policies of self-determination and nonintervention. The costly war was itself seen to be, in part, an outgrowth of colonial greed. The reaction led to a widespread endorsement of the right of a people to control their own political destiny. It was also felt that if noninterference prevailed, conflict could be localized. Gradually this induced the status-quo powers to give up interventionary practices and adhere to their pledges of nonintervention. Such a pattern of commitment was part of the atmosphere favorable to the aggressions of Nazi Germany. A combination of subversive intervention by Germany and nonintervention by other European nations facilitated the increases in national power won so easily by Hitler in the years leading up to the Second World War. The acme of nonintervention by the Western democracies took place during the Spanish Civil War and was paralleled by the full-scale intervention of the Fascist nations on the side of Franco and the Soviet Union on the Loyalist side. It became evident that intervention short of armed attack was an effective way to increase national power, at least assuring a friendly government. Furthermore, it was demonstrated that a potential aggressor becomes much more dangerous if it can consolidate its power by maximum use of interventionary tactics prior to recourse to war. The implication of nonintervention is to watch while a potential enemy grows strong through a series of successful interventions. When the occasion to resist arises for the "law-abiding" state, then it may be too late, or at least it is more arduous than it would have been at a stage when the aggressor was weaker. Certainly Hitler was more difficult to defeat because the liberal democracies did not regard his earlier manifestations of aggressiveness as an occasion for counteraction. Nonintervention is a system that brings stability only if all states powerful enough to intervene refrain from using their power. As soon as one state embarks on an interventionary policy then the legal standards used to measure the duties of nonintervention are a trap for status-quo nations and a shield for an aggressor nation. Thus, in the years leading up to the Second World War, nonintervention was deference to aggression rather than to self-determination. Hence, protective and preventive intervention may be essential to resist the pressure of expansion. This insight has been at the basis of United States policy in the cold war, accounting for American interventions in Iran, Guatemala, Lebanon, and now, abortively, Cuba and Laos.

Revolutionary internal action necessarily invites intervention[30] under modern circumstances. The dominant elite in control of the national government can often suppress a purely domestic revolutionary movement. However, the internal revolutionary group, especially if it is situated near

[30] It is useful to keep in mind the distinction between the *facts* of intervention and the *legal determination*. The process by which a factual pattern of interference is characterized as "intervention" is a significant aspect of the international system deserving of separate, detailed statement. One might experiment with the use of "interference" to describe the events and "intervention" to designate the actual or probable response of an authoritative decision-maker.

the periphery of Communist influence, can receive external help; such intervention transforms the domestic revolution into an arena for cold war conflict, subordinating the welfare of the inhabitants to the global struggle for power. This was the sad experience of Korea, Indochina, and Laos. Cold war rivalry can also be used by the successful nationalist revolution to obtain significant external economic aid to allow rapid internal capital development to take place. Nasser discovered this way to exploit the revolutionary situation of world affairs without endangering national independence. Castro, gaining control of a strategically situated nation, has tried the same tactics; but American property interests in Cuba, and the widespread fear that Castroism is a spreading cancer, led to intervention.[31] The United States acted to prevent the successful revolutionary leader from taking advantage of the cold war to achieve internal material gains.

The historical-political pattern of the revolutionary era conditions the legal norms prohibiting intervention in very comprehensive terms. Article 15 of the Charter of Bogota is typical of the broad doctrinal commitment to non-intervention:

> No State or group of States has the right to intervene, directly or indirectly for any reason whatsoever, in the internal or external affairs of any other State. The foregoing principle prohibits not only armed force, but also any other form of interference against the personality of the State or against its political, economic, and cultural elements.

The Draft Code of Offenses against the Peace and Security of Mankind even proposes individual criminal responsibility for promoting intervention in the political affairs of another country. But here, unlike with aggression, there is no horizontal implementation of the broad prohibitive legal commitment.[32] The superpowers do not think that an intervention will provoke a massive retaliation by their rival. In fact, the obsolescence of recourse to war shifts the international struggle for power into a series of interventionary settings. The United Arab Republic has found that intervention by hostile propaganda, subversion, and other means more subtle than so-called "dictatorial interference" in internal affairs is an economical and effective way to expand its influence across national boundaries by sponsoring internal revolutions in neighboring conservative countries. It is ordinarily true that intervention in Africa and Asia is a progressive force for social change unless it leads to an armed clash in the context of the cold war; it provides the oppressed peoples with an external lever or power that can often enable the revolution to overcome internal weakness. If the occasion for intervention is to prevent a defection by a cold war bloc member, then the danger of major nuclear conflict tends to discourage counter-inter-

---

31 For analysis of Cuban intervention see Richard A. Falk, "United States Participation in the Cuban Invasion and the Rule of Law," *Ohio State Law Jl* 546 (1961).
32 Domestic (horizontal) implementation of nonintervention policy is technically fulfilled by the provisions of the United States Neutrality Laws. See 22 USCA § § 441–65, No. 18 USCA § 960.

vention. This certainly seems to be evident for the United States intervention in Guatemala in 1954 and in Cuba in 1961, and for the Soviet intervention in Hungary in 1956.

Political factors take consistent precedence over legal considerations with regard to interventionary phenomena. The legal rules are quite clear, but the urgencies of revolutionary energy in the midst of the cold war rivalry give them little more than a rhetorical relevance. That is, especially the United States seeks to veil its interventionary practices by legalistic devices. Thus, the Eisenhower Doctrine stressed the consent of the constituted government to justify action taken to suppress internal revolutionary pressures, and President Kennedy emphasized the absence of direct military intervention to defend America's role in staging the 1961 counterrevolution against Castro. Such concern with legality is significant so far as it actually influences American decisions to resort to military intervention or to refrain from sending troops into a foreign country when the head of state has not requested their presence. In this sense the phenomena of intervention can be confined or enlarged by the broad relevance of reciprocity to the behavior of the leading actors in the cold war. Thus, the way the United States intervenes in Cuba may influence the way in which the Soviet Union intervenes in Laos. But from the viewpoint of the smaller status-quo nations in Latin America and elsewhere, reliance upon such legalistic factors does not disguise the defeat of the legal principle, and its embodied policy, that one state is not entitled to use its coercive influence to control the internal affairs of another state. For conformity to a technical interpretation of a norm matters far less than the fulfillment of the guiding policy of the rule by finding behavioral ways to unite power with prescriptive imperatives.

The Soviet Union has consistently abetted internal revolutions in the non-socialist parts of the world by following an openly interventionary policy.[33] In the context of colonialism, the principle of self-determination is given precedence over norms of nonintervention. But when a socialist country is the target of intervention, then the Soviet Union strongly stresses notions of domestic concern and noninterventionism. For instance, Premier Khrushchev's April 22, 1961, Message to President Kennedy on the American role in financing, training, and administering the rebel attack on Cuba relied heavily and piously upon the norm of international law proscribing intervention:

> What standards of law can be invoked to justify these interventions?...If such methods were to become predominant in the relations among states, there would be no place left for law. Its place would be taken by lawlessness and arbitrariness.

And later in his Message Khrushchev says:

> We are for the peaceful coexistence of all states and noninterference in the internal affairs of other countries....We consider that any interference by

---

[33] Premier Khrushchev publicly promised Soviet support for internal wars of liberation.

one state in the affairs of another, especially armed interference, is a violation of all international laws.[34]

It is accurate to attribute a schizophrenic quality to the American endorsement of noninterventionism. At the same time that we revive, like Lazarus, the Monroe Doctrine to justify intervention in Cuba, alleging our action to be in accord with the Caracas Declaration of Solidarity, we continue to celebrate Captive Nations Week each July by a unanimous Resolution of Congress despite its frankly interventionary tenor.[35] It is evident that the distinction between intervention and nonintervention is manipulated by the cold war leaders to justify their preferred political solution to a given situation. There is no adherence to a common standard, although Khrushchev's Message on Cuba emphasizes the destabilizing effect of the reciprocal acceptance by the Soviet Union of military security as a basis for intervention in states like Pakistan and Turkey that have American bases on the geographical border of Russia. This is an important consideration, as the degree of restraint in an unstable world is based more on reciprocal patterns of practice than it is upon abstract norms of legal control. Revolutionary nations, as their position grows strong, may shift from lawlessness to gradual patterns of reciprocal adherence to common standards. This may be one way to discern the transformation of a revolutionary nation into a status-quo nation.

The policy of nonintervention is closely allied to legal rules about territorial sovereignty, equality and independence of states, and domestic jurisdiction. The fundamental policy objective is to affirm the internal supremacy of the national government; however, generally, international law is not concerned with coercive *internal* movements, including revolutions, that threaten to overthrow the existing government. External states may give aid to the constituted government if the civil strife is characterized as "insurgency" but must remain neutral if it is regarded as "belligerency"; some regard the duty of noninterference to include a refusal to give the established government help regardless of the stage of civil strife. Despite contrary claims, no interventionary right ordinarily arises as a result of civil strife. Thus, under the Charter civil strife is a matter "essentially within domestic jurisdiction" unless it constitutes a threat to the peace. That is, the duty of the United Nations is to maintain *international*, not *internal* peace; but the expanding tendencies of civil strife under revolutionary world conditions very quickly transforms an internal war into an international conflict situation. This certainly accounts for the presence and the immense difficulty encountered by the United Nations in its effort to establish order in the Congo in 1960–61. The Congo conflict combines the cold war and the battle against colonialism with intense internal struggles for power. The factions are not susceptible, it has seemed, to reconciliation; the establishment of order requires the United Nations to make choices for and against the

---

34 *New York Times*, April 23, 1961.
35 Quincy Wright, "Subversive Intervention," 54 *Amer. J. Int'l Law*, No. 521 (1960), pp. 521–35.

contending factions, thereby identifying itself with one side in the global rivalry and alienating the opposed side. The United Nations has met this fate in the Congo operation, and yet it is not easy to conceive how else it might have acted to carry out its decision to intervene. The emergence of revolutionary nations—of the Left and of the Right—tends to subordinate actual implementation of centralized interventionary decisions to the urgencies of the cold war. This was curiously manifest in a recent study of intervention from the perspective of diplomatic history:

> Intervention is legal when it is used to protect vital national or international interests which are in imminent jeopardy and which cannot be protected by other means. When it is undertaken to safeguard lesser stakes, or when peril is not pressing, or when other means are available, or when it violates contractual obligation, intervention is illegal.[36]

In a decentralized legal order this makes law into an appeal to conscience; there are no criteria given whereby patterns of reciprocal behavior can establish reasonable limits to interventionary policy. This is a regressive approach to the relation between law and politics, as it confirms the primacy of political considerations. It is recommended that the motive for interference should not govern the legality of the interference unless it is carried out under mandate of the United Nations. The illegality of intervention is preferably viewed as a series of coordinates ranging from the manifest illegality of armed interference in internal affairs to the subtle legality of a prolonged withholding of recognition from a hostile government; as a second set of coordinates ranging from the illegality of unilateral interventions to the legality of world community intervention; and as a third set of coordinates that expresses the extent of coercive impact. Such a system of normative classification would help us to understand the legal quality of interventionary practice.

A second level of analysis could then relate a particular intervention to the dynamics of the revolutionary situation of the cold war. From such a perspective we can distinguish the Indian interventions in Kashmir and Hyderabad from the Soviet interventions in Czechoslovakia and Hungary and the American interventions in Guatemala and Cuba. In this connection it is useful to emphasize the spatial relation between the target state and the intervening cold war actor; compare for instance, the American response to the Chinese intervention in Tibet with the alleged Soviet intervention in Cuba on behalf of Castro. Part of the variation here is based upon the feasibility of counterintervention. We find, as well, a minimal stability that results from reciprocal deference by the leading cold war rivals to a region of acknowledged hegemony;[37] here it is useful to compare the verbal "counterintervention" with military counterintervention—for instance, United States–Soviet responses to Guatemala in 1954, Hungary in 1956, and Laos in 1961.

---

36 Graber, *op. cit.*, p. 361

37 See perceptive analyses, Georg Schwarzenberger, "Hegemonial Intervention," *The Year Book of World Affairs* (London: Stephens and Sons, 1955), pp. 236–65.

Thus, the interventionary policy of a revolutionary political era takes precedence over the norms of nonintervention present in international law. However, the aging of major revolutionary nations, the threat of war arising out of interventionary clashes, and the growth of regional and international institutions suggests that, possibly, legal claims will be given greater weight in the future. Certainly adequate norms and implementing processes relevant to nonintervention are a prerequisite of a successful shift from instability to stability in world politics.

III

The relevance of norms of international law to the specific phenomenon of an internal revolution is evident. The Communist governments of the Soviet Union and mainland China attained power by successfully staged revolutions. The main way in which the leading revolutionary nations seek to expand their influence, and this includes a non-Communist nation like the United Arab Republic, is to sponsor revolutionary movements in status-quo nations. Techniques of infiltration, subversion, and espionage have been perfected as instruments of indirect aggression without exposing the actor to the immense hazard of direct attack. The bearing of legal norms upon the phenomenon of revolution is a crucial aspect of the relation between a revolutionary nation and international law. The effort to export revolutions is, of course, prohibited by the norms of nonintervention; subversion, infiltration, and propaganda designed to foment a foreign revolution are maximum instances of an effort to influence the internal affairs of a sovereign state. In addition to this central notion of nonintervention, international law provides other norms which are more compatible with the interests of the revolutionary nation in instability. For instance, there is the positive legal duty to remain aloof from civil strife, thus legitimating the normal interest of revolutionary nations in denying external relief to the constituted government in its struggle to suppress the revolutionary movement. The nonintervention system of the liberal democracies contributed to the triumph of the Rightist revolution of Franco in Spain. Once a revolutionary government attains control of its national territory,. it frequently expropriates the private property and public assets of its predecessor government. The legal rules of Act of State and sovereign immunity in the domestic courts of foreign status-quo states tend to facilitate this process. Municipal courts may, however, seek to interfere with expropriation of property, especially if it is located outside the revolutionary nation. In fact, if a large portion of the assets of revolutionary nations are located in foreign status-quo nations, refusals to give effect to nationalization decrees can seriously interfere with the social program of the revolutionary nations. This is an indecisive area of law with many divergent decisions;[38] con-

---

[38] Decisions are interestingly represented in Milton Katz and Kingman Brewster, *International Transactions and Relations* (Brooklyn: Foundation Press, 1960), pp. 299–398.

148 RICHARD A. FALK

siderable disagreement among commentators exists as to the wisdom and effectiveness of using such invalidating legal norms as a weapon in the battle against revolutionary nations. Such partisan use of horizontal institutions of the world legal order (domestic courts) can undermine that portion of international law dependent upon reciprocity.

In addition, status-quo nations can withhold diplomatic recognition from and resist the admission to the United Nations of a revolutionary nation, thereby restricting its participation in world affairs. This politicizes the recognition process, making it depend upon the attitude of the status-quo nation to the revolutionary government, rather than making it depend upon the legal (objective) standard of factual control over land, territory, and institutions. Such politicization of legal norms enhances instability in international affairs and seems to have a dubious impact upon the target nation. American nonrecognition policy directed first at the Soviet Union, now at China, seems to be dubious politics, as well as weakening the appeal of our plea to other nations to adhere to the rule of law in world affairs. It also tends to legitimate resort to premature recognition by the revolutionary nations. The right to give political fugitives diplomatic asylum within the territory of a foreign state also has an obvious relation to revolutionary activity. Here again, however, the instability generated by the existence of revolutionary nations makes the institution of asylum also selectively valuable to status-quo nations. One thinks, for instance, of the grant of asylum to Cardinal Mindszenty by the United States.

This brief discussion intends only to illustrate how international law bears upon the specific phenomenon of internal revolution. The legal problems raised here are very diverse and complex. They generate controversial solutions and require fuller consideration to permit an adequate appreciation of the relevance of norms of international law to revolutionary activity.

CONCLUSION

The advent of revolutionary nations has accentuated the tendency of nations to pursue selfish ends by coercive means in world politics. Military strategy and latent internal instability in the newly developing portions of the world have shaped the patterns of coercion used by cold war rivals. Legal norms serve to restrain behavior only when they accord with a powerful nation's perception of its national security. Thus, the current relevance of legal norms to world affairs depends upon a careful comprehension of the bearing of social, economic, military, and political variables.

The dominance and pervasity of the cold war makes manifest the fact that the nations of the globe do not compose a world community. Divergent ideologies and cultures stress the absence of the kind of social cohesiveness propitious to the growth of law. The starkness of this social split is highlighted by the growing interdependence of nations. Nuclear testing, for instance, radiates a locus of concern far wider than the physical locus of action. Growing interdependence in a condition of intensifying hostility short of war is one way to summarize the contemporary crisis in world order. As the need for solutions grows more essential, the social basis for agreement continues to diminish to the vanishing point.

And yet we find a continued emphasis by our leaders upon the need to replace the reign of force by the rule of law. President Eisenhower put this very well at New Delhi in 1959: "The time has come for mankind to make the rule of law in international affairs as normal as it is now in domestic affairs." The sincerity of this sentiment makes especially ironic an emerging American pattern of departure from a law-oriented approach to world affairs. Such a departure has been highlighted by the U-2 incident, retention of the Connally Reservation, prolonged nonrecognition of Communist China, and intervention in the internal affairs of Castro's Cuba.

This distance between authoritative rhetoric and conduct is more than cynical opportunism by national leaders. It reflects the trap that seems to have been set for status-quo nations by the instabilities generated by the aggressive revolutionary nations. We are caught between the irreconcilable aspiration for a just international order and the necessity to meet force with force to assure our survival. The atmosphere is made particularly tense by the frightful dangers of nuclear conflagration. It is my feeling that this apparent crisis is partly a consequence of a failure of intellect and will. There appears to be a growing awareness that power politics is now more like Russian roulette than a game played for rational gain. But there is at the same time considerable official reticence to acknowledge the implications of this perception. Nevertheless I am led to hope, perhaps naively, that an awareness of the futility of a game will encourage its eventual abandonment.[39] If such an instrumental consensus can assert itself—called recently a "community of fear"—then the task of just ordering assigned to law is clear. But it will be a task that is less concerned with the formulation of "norms" and "doctrine" than with the implementation of rules in action by the development of strong procedures, processes, and institutions for making certain that the word becomes flesh. This desideratum suggests a whole direction for a contextual rethinking of the role of international law in world affairs.

[39] This line of thinking is somewhat suggested by Anatol Rapoport, *Fights, Games and Debates* (1960); and see H. S. Hughes, "The Strategy of Deterrence," *Commentary*, Vol. 31, No. 3 (1961), pp. 185–92.

CHAPTER SEVEN

UNITED STATES POLICY
AND THE CRISIS OF
INTERNATIONAL LAW

SOME REFLECTIONS ON THE STATE OF INTERNATIONAL LAW
IN "INTERNATIONAL COOPERATION YEAR"

Wolfgang Friedmann

Columbia University School of Law

The adaptation of international law to the political, economic, and social conflicts of the postwar decades has occurred at an uneven pace. Legal precepts purporting to regulate interstate conflict and civil strife are unclear. As a result, third parties are free to vindicate their interventions and counter-interventions in terms of international law and the U. N. Charter. These attempts at self-justification demand scholarly appraisal. As Wolfgang Friedmann insists, a high degree of national discretion in the use of force is not compatible with the present requirements of world order. In criticizing the interventionary policies of the U. S. in the Dominican Republic and Vietnam, he draws a distinction between arguments based on policy and legal claims that is applicable to other contemporary conflicts. Friedmann's warning that Charter principles should not be abandoned for short-term political gains is particularly noteworthy.

Reprinted from *American Journal of International Law* (October 1965), pp. 857–71. By permission.

If the twentieth anniversary of the United Nations, designated as "International Cooperation Year," had fallen in 1964 rather than 1965, a general assessment of the evolution of international law and organization since the end of World War II would have justified a measure of cautious confidence. Mankind was still very far from having organized itself against the danger of aggression. The danger of the proliferation of nuclear arms remained without effective control, apart from a partial nuclear test ban to which both the United States and the Soviet Union were parties. The world's largest state, Communist China, remained outside the United Nations and without diplomatic relations with the United States and a large number of other states. The United Nations remained without effective control in conflicts between major powers. The special agencies of the United Nations and other international welfare organizations still lacked, with few exceptions, the legal and executive power to cope with the many urgent problems of mankind. In the two most vital and dangerous areas: the conservation of resources, and the stemming of the explosive growth in the world's population, international organization was still embryonic or altogether lacking.

But these grave drawbacks and deficiencies were countered by many more hopeful and constructive developments. Since the end of the Korean War in 1952, many very explosive situations, including some direct confrontation between major powers, and most particularly, several direct encounters between the United States and the Soviet Union in Berlin and in the Cuban missile crisis, had not led to war, but to a limited measure of accommodation. The United Nations, despite the absence of Communist China and its continued lack of effective coercive power, remained very much in being and fulfilled at least two vital functions. One was its presence as the world's only universal forum before which all the Member states, big or small, felt compelled to vindicate their actions. The other was the gradual emergence of limited order forces, increasingly under the auspices of the General Assembly,[1] and able to prevent the escalation of conflict in

[1] Although the Security Council has been far from passive during the last decade—it discussed twenty-three issues between 1953 and 1965, as compared with five during the period 1948–1953, and thirteen during the period 1946–1948, most of these discussions did not lead to action. The Suez Canal intervention of the U.N. was exclusively under the authority of the General Assembly; the Congo Force was initially authorized by the Security Council but later on was carried on by General Assembly resolutions; the Cyprus operation was authorized by the Security Council. The latter thus recovered somewhat in recent years from the low level of its activities during the height of the cold war, but the General Assembly retained much of the initiative that it had assumed since the Uniting for Peace Resolution, and especially in the Suez Canal crisis. The—at least temporarily—successful intervention of the Security Council in the war between India and Pakistan (September, 1965) indicates a further resurgence of the Council, at any rate where the United States and the U.S.S.R. have parallel interests.

several dangerous situations: the renewed war between Egypt and Israel in connection with the Suez Canal crisis in 1956 (UNEF) ; the Congo disorders (ONUC) 1960–1961; the strife between Greeks and Turks in Cyprus, threatening to involve both Greece and Turkey as well (1964).

Above all, international law had proved able to meet the three major challenges of the postwar world, through the adaptation of the law of nations, as it had evolved under the almost exclusive leadership of the Western world, to new tasks and challenges.

The first of these was the accession of a large number of new states to the family of nations, overwhelmingly representing non-Western cultural systems, and thus testing the continued validity of a system built upon a Western-Christian culture.

The second was the importation into the law of nations—hitherto mainly concerned with the formalization of diplomatic relations and the delimitation of national sovereignties—of the problems of economic development, articulated by the new members of the family of nations as well as by many of the older ones. In the Geneva Conference on Trade and Development in 1964, the aspirations for economic development became the cement that bound 77 states, confronting a much smaller group of industrially developed states, virtually coextensive with the Atlantic group of nations— Western Europe and Northern America.

Third, international law was coping with the conflict of political and social ideologies which, in political terms, was expressed by the "cold war" conflict between the Communists and the Western world, and, in economic terms, by the differences and conflicts between socialist and non-socialist systems.

While each of these major challenges affected and modified long-established concepts and principles of international law, they did not destroy it. Indeed, they showed that the very weakness of international law— the absence of a definite constitutional system with legislative, executive, and judicial organs, and the looseness of many of its norms—facilitated the adaptation of its structure to the many new challenges of our time. The accession of many non-Western states—many of them deeply influenced by the religious and social traditions of Islam, Buddhism, or Hinduism—has produced some differences in the style of international techniques but few basic changes. For better or worse, and despite the undoubted diversity of their cultural traditions, the new states have behaved very much like the older states, pursuing their national interests to the maximum extent compatible with the acceptance of the rules of international law. The participation in international conflicts of recent years of states such as the United Arab Republic, Saudi Arabia, Pakistan, India, or Indonesia has shown few if any traces of methods or motivations significantly different from those of the older members of the family of nations.

The emergence of so many economically underdeveloped nations from subjection or poverty to the aspirations of twentieth-century statehood has had mainly constructive effects. It has produced a new type of structure of international organization of which the International Bank for Reconstruction and Development is the most important. Its business, and that of its affiliated agencies, is the organized redistribution of wealth, through joint organizations of which both donor and recipient countries are members. Again, the articulation of the conflicting interests between developed and developing countries is leading both to the expansion and the modification of many aspects of international law. International commodity agreements, international trade agreements between state trading and private trading states, the gradual modification of the principles and standards governing the protection of property interests in case of nationalization, the emergence of the principle of national control over natural resources, these and many other matters continue to be influenced by the confrontation between the interests of the developed and the developing nations. But this is essentially no different from the way in which international law has from time to time responded to the need to adjust conflicting interests between seafaring and landlocked states, between belligerents and neutrals, and many more.

Finally, International Cooperation Year 1964 could have registered an at least limited modification of the ideological conflict between the Communist and the Western world, through a tacit but nevertheless important acceptance of the need for coexistence as a basic interest of survival, and even of limited cooperation in matters of common concern. As the Soviet Union developed from a revolutionary and outcast society to a highly advanced modern state, it came to accept, though with considerable reservations, the major principles of coexistence between sovereign states. This was symbolized by her membership in the United Nations and a number of specialized agencies, by the conclusion of hundreds of treaties of all sorts, and more recently by the Nuclear Test-Ban Treaty, as well as by the tentative collaboration with the Western world in such matters as control over the Antarctic and sovereignty in outer space.

Thus, the most significant conclusion on the state of international law less than a year ago would have been that it had, since the end of the last World War, gone through a period of experimentation with new problems, unprecedented in all previous history. Horizontally, it had expanded from a small club of relatively homogeneous nations to a worldwide society comprising well over 100 nations of the most diverse size, cultural background, and economic evolution. It was in process of transition from the relatively closely knit society of economically advanced and private enterprise dominated states to a great variety of social and economic systems, ranging from complete state control over all major national and international economic activities to the loosely controlled private enterprise system of the United States. The evolution of the Soviet Union showed that certain minimum needs of international coexistence required the acceptance of certain basic rules of international conduct, while closer cooperation in matters of economic coordination, principles of social organization, or cultural collaboration required a closer identity of values, attainable only between states sharing such values and interests to a greater degree than the society of nations at large. Some of the most meaningful evolutions in the vertical extension of international law were occurring on a less than universal level, most notably in the European Community of six states. The most significant legal aspect of the evolution of these communities was the gradual and partial transfer of certain aspects of sovereignty from the national level to the supranational level.[2]

The need to preserve, on the one hand, some minimum rules of intercourse between all the nations of the world and, on the other hand, to absorb the increasing diversification and vertical extension of the fields of international collaboration in an expanding structure of international law has led to the growing articulation of two different types of international law: the law of coexistence and the law of co-operation.[3] The international law of coexistence incorporates the minimum principles and standards under which states representing a great variety of political, social and economic systems may preserve a minimum of ordered relations. The law of co-operation represents the many diverse attempts to promote, through permanent international organizations or through *ad hoc* schemes the common interests of mankind in what Röling has called the "international law of welfare." And much of this law has developed on a regional rather than a universal level. The United Nations, as the world's most nearly universal organization, became the principal organized expression of the interests and concerns shared by all nations.

THE CRISIS OF 1965

The increasing articulation of economic and social aspirations as a matter of international concern, on the one hand, and the astonishingly rapid absorption of a large number of new and, for the great majority, weak and unsettled states in the family of nations, postponed rather than solved two major problems which, by a bitter irony of history, have erupted in the International Cooperation Year of 1965. The proliferation of new states, and their admission, immediately upon the attainment of statehood, to the

---

2 One of the most abiding controversies in the theory of international law has been the question whether the alternative between national and international sovereignty is an absolute one, as is notably the thesis of Hans Kelsen. The present writer agrees with the view put, for example, by H. L. A. Hart in *The Concept of Law* (1961), that neither logic nor reality compels such absolute alternatives and that international law today may restrain sovereign states in some respects but leave them free to act in others. This may be an intermediate state, as illustrated by the present stage of evolution of the European Communities. Eventually, the Communities may have to grow into a federation, or relapse into a loose association of sovereign states, as is the purpose of de Gaulle's denunciation of the Rome Treaty (September, 1965). Meanwhile the coexistence of supranational aspects, as symbolized in particular by the permanent executives of the Communities and the European Court of Justice, and the national aspects, represented by the Council of Ministers, is a definite fact of contemporary international law.

3 See, for an elaboration of this theme, Friedmann, *The Changing Structure of International Law*, especially Ch. 6 (1964).

United Nations, increasingly accentuated the problem of discrepancy between power and responsibility. In the original conception and the hitherto unrevised text of the U.N. Charter,* this proliferation would have been mitigated by the predominance of the Security Council and the privileged position enjoyed within the Council by the permanent members. But this original concept died within a few years after the creation of the United Nations. As the Security Council became paralyzed through the conflict between the Soviet Union and the Western powers, and as the functions of the General Assembly, in which all members have one vote, increased to the point where some of its resolutions acquired executive or quasi-executive character, a revolution of the major powers was bound to occur sooner or later, as controls slipped more and more from their hands. It is this revolt which in this writer's opinion is the deeper cause of the crisis outwardly provoked by the resistance on the part of France and the Soviet Union to the International Court's assessment opinion. And at the same time, the fact that the overwhelming majority of the new states were weak, poor, and in a state of social turmoil, accentuated the social and civil war aspects of international conflict. The military, economic, and social weakness of most of these states has revived the power conflict between the world's major powers, competing for influence in the many turbulent and unsettled areas of the world, in terms of rival social ideologies, as well as of political and military power. And the principal antagonists in this struggle are today the United States and an increasingly powerful and articulate Communist China, rather than the Soviet Union, which is torn between its original revolutionary ideology and the needs for consolidation and coexistence within the framework of international law. Thus, the cold war which had become attenuated, as between the United States and the Soviet Union, through their mutual interest in a modicum of coexistence within the framework of international law, has acquired a new and sharper intensity. One of the antagonists, Communist China, does not even profess to be bound by the existing international order and can actually derive advantage from the fact that she is still excluded from the organized family of nations. This conflict is carried out by a variety of military, political, and economic means, ranging from open warfare to grants or interest-free loans, wherever there is social and political unrest, in Asia, Africa, or Latin America. And it is against this background that within the last few months the United States, traditionally the major defender of the existing system of international law and a champion of its peaceful evolution, has felt compelled to question two elementary foundations of the law of nations.

It has, through pronouncements of the President and some of his principal advisers, including the Legal Adviser of the Department of State, put in question—in deed, though not in words—the principle of "sovereign equality" of all states, big or small, powerful or weak; and it has chal-

---

* Editor's Note: The revised Charter now provides for an enlarged Security Council of 15 members and an enlarged Economic and Social Council of 27 members. Both these changes reflect the desire of member states to make these organs more representative of the U.N.'s altered membership.

lenged, or at least strongly qualified, the relevance of the distinction between international and civil war, on which international law is predicated, since it has traditionally made a sharp distinction between interstate conflict, on the one hand, and internal revolution, on the other. The latter, whether violent or peaceful, is a process of social change with which international law is generally unconcerned.

Neither of these challenges—one coinciding with an at least temporary paralysis of the United Nations—and the other shaking some of the foundations of the customary law of nations as well as of the Charter, was premeditated. They were responses to events, and both challenges are symptoms of much deeper problems. But in their combination, the two chains of events have accentuated a crisis in the law of nations which no international lawyer can afford to ignore or bypass. The following pages will attempt a brief and preliminary assessment of their significance and of the alternative policy choices now facing the nations and, in particular, the world's major powers.

In repudiating the *Certain Expenses* opinion of the International Court of Justice,[4] which, by a majority of nine votes to five, had held that the General Assembly had acted within its proper functions in compulsorily assessing all Members for their share in the expenses of the Congo (ONUC) and Gaza Strip (UNEF) operations, France and the Soviet Union—two of the four major powers in the Security Council—found themselves aligned against the two others, Britain and the United States. For different reasons, France and the U.S.S.R. were opposed not only to the extension of U.N. operations in general but also to the particular involvement of the United Nations in the Congo, a civil war with certain international aspects. On the other hand, Britain and the United States approved such operations, to which Britain has now promised a permanent contingent of its national forces, along with similar commitments made by Canada and a number of other smaller states. The United States also favored and had strongly supported the specific involvement and direction of the U.N. operation in the Congo. But under the surface, the true impact of the Franco-Soviet defiance is that it is a revolt against the increasing weight of a General Assembly more and more dominated by the smaller and poorer states, and in this respect the long-term, strategic policy of the United States may well tend in the same direction. When the United States in 1950 sponsored the "Uniting for Peace" resolution which purported to confer certain powers of "recommendation" for collective measures on the General Assembly in case of inability of the Security Council to act, it was still certain of a comfortable two-thirds majority of votes for any action strongly sponsored by the United States. But this situation has changed drastically. The Uniting for Peace Resolution has long ceased to be a major instrument of U. S. policy, while the Geneva Conference on Trade and Development has made it clear that a majority of the members of the United Nations will vote for economic obligations that would almost entirely burden the

4 [1962] I.C.J. Rep. 151.

industrially developed states and most particularly the United States. And as far as United Nations operations are concerned, it is increasingly likely that a combination of the smaller members, sometimes with the support of the Communist bloc, might authorize a United Nations operation to which both the United States and Britain would be strongly opposed. This would, for example, be almost certainly the case if the Assembly voted in favor of stronger economic or, perhaps, even military sanctions against the Union of South Africa. Despite the strong stand taken by the United States in favor of the implementation of the International Court's opinion, and despite the strong legal argument to be made in favor of such a posture, it is thus likely that a voluntary rather than a compulsory assessment of expenses for other than the minimum administrative tasks of the United Nations will coincide with the policy interests of the United States. Such a development will at least in part neutralize the power now enjoyed by a majority of non-Western and economically underdeveloped states in the General Assembly.[5]

But the crisis in the United Nations may go further. It is possible that it will never, or only very incompletely, recover from the suspension of a regular session of the General Assembly, and that what may be described as the "second life" of the United Nations may have come to an end. The characteristic aspect of the second phase was that, after the collapse of the Charter concept of a Security Council guided by the concert of the major powers and strengthened by the organization of permanent peace-keeping forces, the combination of a pivotal function of the Secretary General with a more active General Assembly gave the United Nations a general "watchdog" function in international conflicts, and the power to intervene actively, at least in certain conflicts, through ad hoc operations. A prolonged paralysis would inevitably lead to a more and more unrestrained use of national power in international conflict situations, and recent developments in Vietnam, Kashmir, and the Dominican Republic already provide some evidence for such a trend of affairs.

In assessing the possible impact of a continuing weakness of the United Nations on the prospects of peace and war, it should be borne in mind that the following types of conflicts have never come effectively within the purview of the United Nations:

First, direct conflicts between the major members of the United Nations. While the Charter applies in principle equally to all members, it subjects executive action against any of the permanent members to the veto power. In fact, the various conflicts between the United States and Soviet Union have been dealt with by direct confrontation or settlement. In the most important of the Berlin crises, the blockade of 1948, the United Nations did, however, provide an indispensable forum for the Jessup-Malik negotiations which prepared the subsequent settlement and lifting of the block-

---

[5] The above was written in July. As this article goes to press, the United States' abandonment of its insistence on payment of the assessed dues and of the threat to invoke Art. 19 in case of default, appears to confirm the trend outlined in the text.

ade. In the Hungarian crisis of 1956, the United States tacitly acknowledged that it could not effectively challenge the U.S.S.R. in its own sphere of power, and the United Nations had to confine itself to declamatory exhortations. The reverse happened in the Cuban missile crisis of October, 1962, where the United Nations was notified, but it was clear at all times that the question of peace or war would be decided between the United States and the U.S.S.R. by the latter's withdrawal, and that neither the United Nations nor the Organization of American States could effectively determine the outcome.

Second, while the Charter is in principle applicable to non-members (Articles 33, 35), it has not in effect been so applied where the non-member is a major power. In conflicts involving a minor non-member, the Charter has been invoked only where a major member of the United Nations actively seeks the endorsement of the United Nations. Both moral authority and factual power were weak with regard to the occupation of Tibet by Communist China, which had been denied representation in the United Nations for ten years. In the Korean War the United States, which was the major sponsor of, and supplied the principal power, other than South Korea, for action against North Korea, sought the authority of the United Nations. But it obtained the approval of the Security Council only because of a freak situation, since the Soviet Union at the time boycotted the meetings of the Council, and this was, by an arguable though far from compelling interpretation, held not to impair the "concurring" votes of all the permanent Members of the Council (Article 27). In the Vietnam conflict which, according to U. S. theory, is also a war between states not members of the United Nations, the United States, while claiming to act in conformity with the Charter (Article 51), has not sought the authority of the United Nations, except for a belated and general reference to the desirability of U.N. action by President Johnson in his Twentieth Anniversary speech in San Francisco.

Third, there are what one might call "open-ended" situations of conflict not clearly covered by the traditional distinctions between peace and war, aggression and defense. Such situations were characterized by Philip Jessup in 1954 as having an "intermediate status between peace and war."[6] This question is connected with the theoretical controversy whether international law is an "open" or a "closed" system.[7] But whether one's view is that all acts implying the application of force must be classified as either aggression or defense, or that the new situations of "intermediacy" must be incorporated into a growing and elastic system of international law, it would appear that the Cuban missile crisis presented an "intermediate" situation, and that the limited measures taken by the United States, in the form of

[6] "Should International Law Recognize an Intermediate Status between Peace and War," 48 *A.J.I.L.* (1954), p. 98.
[7] See, for a recent debate on this question, the conflicting views of the late Sir Hersch Lauterpacht, "Non Liquet and the Completeness of Law," *Symbolae Verzijl,* 196, at 205, and Professor Stone, "Non Liquet and the Function of Law in the International Community," 35 *Brit. Yr. Bk. Int. Law,* p. 145 *et seq.*

a quarantine and surveillance flights over Cuba in response to the massive transportation of men and missiles by the Soviet Union into Cuba, were a proportionate response to a definite threat falling short of aggression.[8]

Lastly, the mandate of the United Nations is uncertain in the case of civil war. In principle, civil war situations threatening international peace and security are within the purview of the Charter, and the United Nations did intervene in a civil war of such a character in the Congo operation. But this venture also showed the precariousness of this type of intervention, at least where it leads to action favoring the one or the other side in civil war. In this respect the Congo operation differs from the Cyprus operation, where the United Nations keeps the contending groups at arms' length but does not seek to impose a solution.

Granted the multiplicity and increasing importance of civil wars with international implications, the inability of the United Nations to control these situations is certainly a serious matter. But this state of affairs is implicit in the still very precarious organization of mankind. A large proportion of the world's states are subject to continuous upheavals and revolutions which, because of the renewed intensity of the political cold war between the communist powers and the West and the revolution in modern transportation often pose threats to peace.[9]

CIVIL WAR, INTERVENTION, AND U.S. POLICY

The combination of the vacuum created by the suspension of the United Nations and the steadily increasing importance of civil war in the international power conflict forms the background for the recent United States actions in Vietnam and in the Dominican Republic, and for their theoretical justification.

In the Vietnam situation the United States has sought, although not without some difficulty, to vindicate its military intervention in terms of international law and U.N. Charter. It has argued that: a) its military and logistic assistance was a response to a request by the Government of

8 To some extent, these new developments may be seen as an extension of "reprisals" and other limited measures falling short of war, which have formed part of customary international law and state practice for a long time. It should, however, be made clear that the United States' quarantine and other countermeasures, including a limited interference with the freedom of the seas, can be considered as legitimate only insofar as they were a response to a threat directed by the Soviet Union against the United States, and *not* interference with the right of Cuba as a sovereign state to buy arms and other supplies from whatever source it chooses, and to have such supplies transported on the open seas. This distinguishes the Cuban missile crisis from the Bay of Pigs situation of 1961, which was clearly an intervention in the internal affairs of another state.

9 The importance of the revolution in transportation may be illustrated by the fact that Queen Victoria once wished to send a gunboat to quell trouble in Bolivia but was dissuaded because Bolivia is landlocked. These inhibitions do not apply to the age of aircraft and missiles.

South Vietnam which, by international law, is entitled to ask for assistance from other governments; b) South Vietnam had been the object of an organized attack by North Vietnam, an attack to which, in accordance with Article 51 of the U.N. Charter, individual or collective self-defense is a legitimate response; c) the United States, in application of the right of "individual or collective" self-defense, acted on behalf of the organized community of nations in coming to the assistance of South Vietnam; and d) any interference with such activities of the United States by North Vietnam or another state was, therefore, an act of aggression. Each of these assumptions is challengeable, either in fact or in law. It may be conceded that North and South Vietnam are today de facto separate states, even though the Geneva Agreement of 1954 spoke of "two zones." It is more questionable whether the war in South Vietnam is essentially a civil or an international war, and, if it is now the latter, whether it has become so primarily as the result of North Vietnamese or U. S. intervention, the latter dating from its part in the postponement of nationwide elections in 1956, as provided for in the Geneva Agreement. It is furthermore questionable whether the decision of a foreign state to come to the assistance of a government makes any response to this assistance automatically an act of aggression against the state supplying it. But above all it is a matter of grave and fundamental doubt whether the widespread but always controversial view that in civil war situations only the government but not the rebels are entitled to ask for foreign assistance retains any justification under contemporary conditions. Neither the United States nor any other country has been consistent in the application of this doctrine—as is shown, for example, by the conflicting policies with regard to Vietnam, Guatemala (1954), and Cuba—nor is the turbulent condition of mankind, when numerous states are in a state of social turmoil, compatible with a doctrine of "legitimacy." The latter becomes an instrument to prevent social change, which is a vital aspect of national self-determination (Article 2(7), U.N. Charter).[10]

Be that as it may, it is clear that, in the absence of any international body such as the United Nations, a commission of inquiry, or an international judicial authority, the decision whether a particular conflict is essentially a phase of civil war or of foreign aggression, is one that cannot be objectively determined and therefore rests with the Powers directly concerned. This may be graced by the name of "decentralized decision making," but it is in fact a return to unmitigated national control over the use of force.[11] The degree of discretion is further heightened by the leeway which Communist theory has long accorded to intervention in wars

---

[10] See, for a more extended discussion of this question, Wright, *The Role of International Law in the Elimination of War* (1961), p. 61 and the same writer's "United States Intervention in the Lebanon," 53 *A.J.I.L.* (1959), p. 112, 121 *et seq.;* see further Friedmann, *The Changing Structure of International Law,* p. 264 *et seq.* (1964).

[11] *Cf.* R. Fisher, "Intervention: Three Problems of Policy and Law," in *Essays on Intervention,* 19–20.

of "national liberation," and by the counterpoint theory, now tentatively adopted by the United States, especially in the Dominican situation, that the involvement of Communists—even of a limited number—in an internal revolution, implies of necessity intervention by a foreign (Communist) power, and therefore justifies counterintervention. In effect, the distinction between civil and international war thus becomes a matter of national policy decision, and so does the use of force in such a conflict.

To justify its intervention in the disorders of the Dominican Republic in April, 1965, the United States went considerably further. There is respectable authority for the view that the original limited intervention to protect U. S. citizens from imminent danger, in a situation of anarchy, did not violate international law.[12] But the massive involvement of U. S. forces and the consequent occupation of the capital of a foreign "sovereign" state led to the already mentioned identification of Communist participating with an indirect form of foreign aggression. In his speech of May 2, 1965, President Johnson declared that the American nations could not and would not tolerate another Communist government in the Western Hemisphere. Even though this statement went far beyond the likely ambit of United States policy, its implication is that the United States, acting as an "American nation," reserves to itself the right: (a) to determine whether an internal revolution involves a degree of participation by Communists regarded as dangerous by the United States, and (b) to intervene by force in order to prevent such a possible outcome in the civil war. This implies possible intervention in the internal affairs of any one of twenty Latin American states. The possibility of such intervention is greatly increased by the fact that a majority of these states have gross discrepancies between the great wealth of a small minority and the abject poverty of the masses, and that almost any revolution against any of the various incumbent right-wing governments will have strong left-wing elements, which can easily be described as "Communist." The United States itself has recognized the importance and urgency of this social tension by the initiative it has taken in the establishment of the Alliance for Progress.

Not only does the recent intervention policy of the United States thus imperil the social objectives of the Alliance for Progress as well as the

---

12 The conditions under which a state may be entitled, as an aspect of self-defense, to intervene in another state, in order to protect its nationals from injury, were formulated by Professor Waldock in 1952 as follows: "There must be (1) an imminent threat of injury to nationals, (2) a failure or inability on the part of the territorial sovereign to protect them, and (3) measures of protection strictly confined to the object of protecting them against injury." ("The Regulation of the Use of Force by Individual States in International Law," 81 Hague Academy *Recueil des Cours* pp. 451, 467.) This was invoked, among other reasons, by the British Government in support of its armed intervention in Egypt during the Suez Canal crisis of 1956. Since, unlike in the Dominican Republic in April, 1965, there was no breakdown of organized government in Egypt nor any physical threat to foreign nationals, the United States had much greater legal justification for its original, limited intervention in protection of its nationals in the Dominican crisis than did Great Britain in the Suez crisis.

definite legal prescriptions of the U.N. Charter [Article 2(5), 2(7)] and of the O.A.S. Charter (Articles 15, 17); there is not even a limitation of such hegemonial claims to the Western Hemisphere. The latter "co-exists" with the "containment" doctrine, under which the United States claims to stand guard against Communist "aggression" or "subversion" anywhere in the world, even in parts which other empires may claim as their sphere of hegemony (e.g., China in Southeast Asia).

The U. S. intervention in the Dominican Republic was distinguished from previous interventions, e.g., in Lebanon (1958) or in South Vietnam, by the absence of any request from the incumbent government. It was thus much more clearly an infringement of national territorial and jurisdictional sovereignty. The world's most powerful state was, at least temporarily, occupying the capital of one of the smallest. Obviously this cannot be justified in the terms of the U.N. Charter, which is predicated on the principle of "sovereign equality." It could only be justified by eliminating the distinction between civil war and international war as having "largely lost its meaning." This is what President Johnson did in his speech at Baylor University in May, 1965. The President did not speak as an international lawyer, but shortly afterwards the Legal Adviser to the Department of State, in an address to the American Foreign Law Association of June 9, 1965, provided the following justification for the U. S. action:

> What I should like to suggest is that reliance on absolutes for judging and evaluating the events of our time is artificial, that black and white alone are inadequate to portray the actuality of a particular situation in world politics, and that fundamentalist views on the nature of international legal obligations are not very useful as a means to achieving practical and just solutions of difficult political, economic, and social problems....
>
> It does not seem to me that law and other human institutions should be treated as abstract imperatives which must be followed for the sake of obeisance to some supernatural power or for the sake of some supposed symmetry that is enjoined upon the human race by external forces. Rather, it seems to me that law and other institutions of society should be seen as deliberate and hopefully rational efforts to order the lives of human communities—from small to great—in such a way as to permit realization by all members of a community of the full range of whatever creative powers they may possess....
>
> ...The facts show that, had the United States withdrawn its forces from Santo Domingo after the evacuation of United States and other foreign civilians, the situation would have reverted to anarchy and bloodletting. Without our troops, the OAS would now have no foothold for constructive multilateral action and peacemaking efforts. Without our presence, it is quite possible the Dominican Republic could have been thrown into another 30 years of darkness.
>
> It will surprise no one here if I say that international law which cannot deal with facts such as these; and in a way that has some hope of setting a troubled nation on the path of peace and reconstruction, is not the kind of law I believe in....
>
> ...We recognized that, regardless of any fundamentalist view of inter-

national law, the situation then existing required us to take action to remove the threat and at the same time to avoid nuclear war. In the tradition of the common law we did not pursue some particular legal analysis or code, but instead sought a practical and satisfactory solution to a pressing problem.

What Mr. Meeker describes as a "fundamentalist" view is one of the major foundations both of the traditional system of international law and of the U.N. Charter, *i.e.*, the territorial and jurisdictional integrity of any state. And what he describes as "black and white" is a distinction between legal and illegal actions which is the very cornerstone of law.

It is not the purpose of this article to discuss the political merits of recent United States actions in a dangerous world situation. Nor is it relevant, in the context of a legal appraisal, to point out that the United States occupation of Santo Domingo will be a temporary one, unlike, for example, the occupation of Tibet by China. The Legal Adviser's argument is one of policy, not of law, and it seeks to justify what is patently, by standards of international law, an illegal action, in terms of the ultimate policy objectives of the United States. But by using the language of legal rather than of political justification, the argument comes unintentionally close to the attempts made by Nazi and Communist lawyers to justify the interventionist and aggressive actions of their respective governments in terms of a legal order of the future. Nazi lawyers spoke of *Völkerrecht- liche Grossraumordnung* (international legal order of wide spaces), and Communist jurists exempt wars of "national liberation" from the prohibition against intervention. Surely, the legal as well as the political style of the United States should remain unmistakably different from that of its totalitarian opponents.

There are close parallels between the arguments used to justify the Dominican intervention and the arguments used by the British Government to justify its occupation of the Suez Canal in retaliation against Nasser's nationalization decree, an action strongly condemned by the United States and successfully frustrated—on the joint initiative of the United States and the U.S.S.R.—by a resolution of the General Assembly. When Lord McNair, a former President of the International Court of Justice, in a House of Lords' debate, cast grave doubts on the legality of the use of force by the Government, the Lord Chancellor, Viscount Kilmuir, replied that he did "not want to get involved in theoretical arguments on international law."[13] Mr. Meeker's phrase that "law and other institutions of society should be seen as deliberate and hopefully rational efforts to order the lives of human communities..." has its counterpart in the Lord Chancellor's observation that "the United Nations...should take the view of international obligation which does not forget the duties of life." Such rhetoric undermines the claim of international law to be regarded as a legal system with definite rights and obligations.

A more constructive sequel to the Franco-British-Israeli intervention in Suez was the United Nations' constitution of the Emergency Force which

13 H. L. Deb., Vol. 199, Col. 718, Sept. 12, 1956.

provided a cover for the withdrawal of the intervening forces; but the United Nations was in a state of suspense at the time of the Dominican intervention, and the nearest parallel is the United States' attempt to constitute a standing O.A.S. force. But at this writing, the only supporters of this plan are Brazil and Paraguay, both right-wing military dictatorships. One major reason for the reluctance of the other 18 states is clearly their resentment at the unilateral action of the United States in defiance of definite provisions of the O.A.S. Charter (Articles 15, 17).

Surely, a better if negative service is rendered to international law by acknowledging a deliberate departure from the obligations imposed by it. In a debate held by the American Society of International Law on the legal aspects of the Cuban missile crisis,[14] Mr. Dean Acheson did not choose to defend the U. S. action in terms of international law, even though, as argued earlier, it was far more justifiable than the Dominican intervention. He said that "the survival of states is not a matter of law," although accepted legal principles "influenced the United States in choosing a course of action consistent with ethical restraint."

The real significance of the U. S. actions in Vietnam and the Dominican Republic—neither of them part of a long-term plan but graduated responses to increasingly complex and dangerous situations—is that the most powerful champion and defender of the existing international order against revolutionary ideologies may have come to the conclusion that it can no longer afford to abide by international law, that it must counter the imperial aspirations of the Soviet Union, and especially of Communist China, by similar means. A continuing paralysis of the United Nations would accentuate the intensity of the power struggle. In this process the tragic anomaly of a vastly increased number of "sovereign national states" in an age when modern technology and communications have made the national state obsolete, would be solved by the absorption of the great majority of the world's states as vassals or subjects in the few remaining empires. The inevitable advent of such a "Caesarean" stage was forecast after the end of the First World War by the German social philosopher, Oswald Spengler, in his then widely read book, *The Decline of the West.* After the Second World War, in 1948, the English writer, George Orwell, in his novel *1984* envisaged a world ominously apposite to our time. Three superstates named Oceania, Eurasia, and East Asia—in fact closely corresponding to the spheres of influence of the United States, the Soviet Union, and China —emerging from the atomic wars of the sixties (!)[15] have consolidated their empires, forming shifting alliances which would keep them constantly at war and above all maintain their populations in a state of discipline,

---

[14] 1963 *Proceedings,* American Society of International Law, p. 13.
[15] Such a division of imperial spheres would of course presuppose the defeat, by force or voluntary retreat, of present attempts to defend or expand positions outside the respective spheres of influence. The greatest sufferer in this would be the United States, which today maintains bases and forces in many parts of Asia. A new political sphere and possible source of big-power conflict has arisen in Africa, which was hardly a continental political force of significance in 1948.

oppression, and privation, but would stop short of any major disturbance of the existing divisions. In the year 1965 mankind is still far from the realization of this grim vision, but in the last year it has moved perceptibly nearer to it. The United Nations is the tentative and very imperfect beginning of an alternative to the obsolete system of some 120 national "sovereignties." It aims with severe qualifications at the gradual transfer of certain sovereign powers over war and peace from the nation-states to international authority. Built around it are a network of international welfare organizations concerned with economic development, social improvement and cooperation in numerous other matters. This is an attempt to overcome national sovereignty by functional collaboration rather than by constitutional blueprints. But all these attempts and their, in many ways, highly promising results will come to naught if the United Nations is paralyzed and the political and military tensions between the rival superpowers intensify. The abandonment of the principles of national integrity and of the distinction between civil and international war—both cardinal to the present structure of international law—is the legal corollary of imperial power struggle.

The events of the last year make it imperative for every student of international law to reexamine for himself, for his country, and for mankind the question of the reality and value of international law in the conduct of international affairs. Since the beginnings of modern international law, there has been a continuous struggle between obedience to the gradually widening rules of international law and the assertion of national policies in defiance of such rules. It was not starry-eyed idealism, but the realization of the catastrophic consequences of the unrestrained use of the prerogatives of national sovereignty, which led to the successive attempts of the League of Nations Covenant and the United Nations Charter to impose some restraints upon the use of force, and to lay the foundations for an international organization of mankind. The principal beneficiaries of such rules of restraint are the smaller states, which now form the majority of the family of nations. It is this writer's firm belief that the continued observance of the principles of the Charter, which leave the right of self-defense against armed attack unimpaired, is not only a question of moral rectitude but also a long-term policy interest of the country which is the leader of the Western alliance and has generally stood for the rights of small countries, at least in recent history. This does not in any way derogate from the paramount need to work actively for the modification and evolution of international law in response to the many challenges of a turbulent and changing society.[16] But if, in the considered judgment of this country's responsible policy-makers and of students of international affairs, international tensions have become too great to make the observance of inter-

---

16 The present writer has attempted to survey the principal challenges and structural changes in his *The Changing Structure of International Law* (1964); see also Jenks, *The Common Law of Mankind* (1958); Röling, *International Law in an Expanding World* (1960); Schwarzenberger, *The Frontiers of International Law* (1962).

national law compatible with elementary interests of survival, it will be better to acknowledge it, rather than to degrade the science and purposes of international law by special pleading. Nearly forty years ago the French writer, Julien Benda, in *La Trahison des Clercs,* castigated the intellectuals of the West for having in their overwhelming majority, betrayed their integrity for the abject glorification of nationalism and nationalist policies. A few years later, the Nazi period showed the calamitous consequences of such an intellectual—and political—surrender. Lawyers are, by virtue of their training, particularly well equipped to engage in "special pleading." Freedom is today threatened from many quarters. It has never survived the abandonment of intellectual independence.

CHAPTER EIGHT

CASE STUDY: THE "SATISFIED" AND "DISSATISFIED" STATES NEGOTIATE INTERNATIONAL LAW

Robert L. Friedheim

Purdue University

The case study of the two United Nations Conferences on the Law of the Sea brings the critical concerns of the "satisfied" and "dissatisfied" states into sharp focus. The conflict of interests between the "haves" and the "have-nots," the individual and collective strategies used by delegates, and the results of political attitudes toward international law are lucidly set forth in Friedheim's essay. While the poorer states displayed a predilection for vagueness, the established states chose to rely on experts and the validity of older norms. The reluctance of the satisfied states to accept the notion of the progressive development of international law and to concede the political ramifications of legal dicta widened the breach between the two groups of states and prevented completely successful agreements. Friedheim's conclusion that a change in attitude on the part of the satisfied might facilitate accommodation at international conferences is amply documented.

Reprinted from *World Politics* (October 1965), pp. 20–41. By permission.

Peace will be achieved, virtually all Western leaders say upon issuing a general statement on foreign policy, when all men learn to obey a common law. The achievement of world peace through world law is a popular solution to the problems of world politics of our times. However, creating a viable international law that all or even most states are willing to obey has proved difficult.

An examination of the two United Nations Conferences on the Law of the Sea held in Geneva in 1958 and 1960 will help illuminate some of the difficulties in creating a law to which there is common consent—and therefore in employing law as the road to peace.

This article will address itself—by an analysis of the content of the debates at Geneva—to the different attitudes that representatives of states and bloc groups brought to the negotiating table. Because the difference in attitudes was so sharp, the conferences proved to be less successful than hoped for by advocates of world law. Not only were participants split on the question of the substantive content of the law, but they also differed on the nature of the international system, present and future, and on the proper means of negotiating law in a United Nations-sponsored conference, which is itself a special political area with distinctive characteristics.

I

The first set of attitudes to be considered is that of those states at the Law of the Sea conferences who were dissatisfied with the legal status quo. They cannot all be labeled "new states," although most were. Although many were, not all were "revolutionary states" who felt compelled to "export their ideological impetus."[1] Nor can they be described as lacking an international law tradition, because the Latin American states, which are included in this category, are very much in that tradition. Rather, the common factor was that these states were "have-not" states, most of whom were located in the southern half of the world, and most of whom believed that their interests were not served by present concepts of international law. This is not an unusual position for those who consider themselves underdogs to take. However, the verbal vehemence with they expressed their revolt against the past trend of international law seemed to shock those participants in the conferences who were "satisfied" with international law. This antagonism resulted in a clash of wills on many important issues, with each

[1] Richard A. Falk, "Revolutionary Nations and the Quality of International Legal Order," in Morton A. Kaplan, ed., *The Revolution in World Politics* (New York: John Wiley and Sons, 1962), p. 323. (*Chapter 6 of this volume.*)

side seemingly incapable of understanding the attitudes and modes of operation of the other.

The "dissatisfied" were heavily represented at the Law of the Sea conferences. The core of this category was composed of states that in the United Nations General Assembly are associated with the Asian-African, Arab, and Latin American caucusing groups and the anti-colonial common-interest group.[2] These constituted fifty-four of the eighty-six states represented at the first conference, and fifty-six of the eighty-eight at the second. In addition, some of the members of the underdeveloped common-interest group who were not also members of the regional and anti-colonial groups felt discriminated against under present concepts of international law.[3]

The key attitude expressed by the dissatisfied states was a strong, conscious, and often expressed belief that the conference process was a *political* process. They clearly understood that their operations were to be guided by practices usually known collectively as parliamentary diplomacy. This meant bloc organization, bloc voting, bloc-sponsored proposals, bloc-sponsored candidates for the elective offices of the conferences, and bloc attempts to manipulate the rules of procedure. The groups of the dissatisfied were the most organized, evident, and self-conscious at the conferences. Mr. Ahmed Shukairi, chairman of the Saudi Arabian delegation, was very outspoken in referring to the Arab states "attending the conference...as a voting group."[4] Other instances of frank references to blocs are too numerous to list. The dissatisfied took advantage of their numbers by frequently sponsoring multinational proposals.[5]

Probably the major reason why the dissatisfied considered the conference process as political and why a considerable number of representatives reflecting this position demonstrated great parliamentary skill was the large

---

[2] Although the Soviet-bloc states are members of the anti-colonialist group, a full discussion of their conduct must be omitted for reasons of space. However, it should be pointed out that the Soviet-bloc states should not be classified as "dissatisfied." Although often allied with the dissatisfied, the Soviet bloc did not participate in the all-out assault on law *per se* so characteristic of the dissatisfied states. The positions adopted by the Soviet Union (and her satellites) at the conferences were typical of a conservative revolutionary state ambivalently trying to accomplish two ends—on the one hand, export of revolutionary principles and harassment of cold war enemies; on the other, a genuine attempt to negotiate commonly accepted legal principles in areas where important material interests would be protected if normative behavior could be enforced. For a discussion of conservative revolutionary states, see Falk, *op. cit.*, p. 315.

[3] The reader should not assume that the characteristics ascribed to a category of states created for purposes of analysis are wholly applicable to all states that generally fall into that category.

[4] United Nations Conference on the Law of the Sea, *Official Records*, Vol. III, First Committee (A/CONF. 13/39), 4th meeting, par. 30. Hereafter all citations from the records, documents, or reports of both UN Conferences on the Law of the Sea will be made with the official UN document number.

[5] See, for example, A/CONF. 13/C.5/L.6 (19 "dissatisfied" sponsors), A/CONF. 13/C.3/L.65, 66, 66/Rev. 1 (12 sponsors), A/CONF. 19/C.1/L.2/Rev. 1 (18 sponsors), A/CONF. 19/C.1/L.6 (16 sponsors), A/CONF. 19/L.9 (10 sponsors), among many others.

proportion of dissatisfied delegations which had as representatives men with recent General Assembly experience. Twenty of the dissatisfied states had at least one representative (five states had several) who was not only a "professional diplomat" but also—in Philip Jessup's phrase—a "professional parliamentarian."[6] Three other delegations had senior advisors who learned the art of parliamentary manœuver in the General Assembly.[7]

This is not to say that the dissatisfied controlled the conferences either by dominating a majority of the votes taken or by getting a majority of their proposals accepted. While the incidence of bloc voting was relatively high among the dissatisfied groups, so were the absence rates of members, which reduced the number of total votes the group cast. None of the dissatisfied except the underdeveloped group was among the groups that most frequently voted with the majority. But their evident, organized efforts constantly harassed their opponents and frequently forced them either to water down or to withdraw proposals opposed by the dissatisfied bloc. Even more important was the ability of the dissatisfied groups to mobilize their numbers to dominate voting on key proposals. While their general record for effectiveness was not good, they could point with satisfaction to several successful attempts to block passage of the various United States proposals for a six-mile territorial sea and a twelve-mile contiguous fishing zone, and to force elimination from a British proposal of a fifteen-mile limit on the use of straight baselines. They could also point to more positive victories, such as enlarging to twenty-four miles the baseline to be drawn from headland to headland in delimiting bays, forcing through an Indian proposal which gave the coastal state "sovereign" rather than exclusive rights over the continental shelf, and gaining majorities for several proposals sponsored jointly by Asian-African and Latin American states which increased the authority of the coastal states over fishing in waters off their coasts.

The satisfied states were annoyed by the political strategy used by the dissatisfied. But they were profoundly shocked by the dissatisfied's analogous assumption—that the *subject matter* to be dealt with in the conferences should also be political. The dissatisfied made frequent reference to the General Assembly resolution that allowed political factors to be considered in formulating the law of the sea: "[The conferences] should take into account not only the legal but also the technical, biological, economic, and political aspects of the problem."[8] These states early in the first conference made it evident that they understood this to mean carte blanche to fight for furthering what they conceived of as their own interests. While this

---

6 "International Negotiations Under Parliamentary Procedure," *Lectures on International Law and the United Nations* (Ann Arbor: University of Michigan Law School, 1957), p. 419.

7 These figures were compiled from the list of delegations to the Conferences on the Law of the Sea and to Sessions XII, XIII, XIV, AND XV of the General Assembly.

8 General Assembly Resolution 1105, XI Session, par. 2. For example, see A/CONF. 13/42, 19th meeting, par. 33.

motive was not uncharacteristic of most participating states and groups, the dissatisfied seemed more conscious of their interests and more outspoken in defending them.

A statement by the Vietnamese delegate, Mr. Buu-kinh, in a debate on the continental shelf, can scarcely be plainer: "His delegation would prefer to see the criterion of depth alone retained, particularly as the waters off its own shores were relatively shallow and did not reach a depth of 200 metres for more than 200 miles."[9] The Mexican delegate, Mr. Gomez Robledo, in discussing a Canadian proposal on reservations to any convention signed as a result of the conference, was equally candid: "Representatives wishing to permit reservations had been reproached for defending national interests; but they were attending the conference for that very purpose."[10] Or, as Mr. Caabasi of Libya flatly remarked about a United States proposal on the breadth of the territorial sea: "...His delegation had voted against the United States proposal because it contained provisions which were contrary to his country's interests."[11]

Since these dissatisfied states were so insistent and outspoken in asserting that the conference process was a political means of attaining their own national interest, they were no less definite in assigning to the states opposing them the same self-interested motives. For example, Dr. Alfonso Garcia Robles of Mexico, advocating a broad belt of territorial sea, ascribed to the narrow-seas advocates the motive of sheer self-interest. He ignored entirely any reference to traditional historic and legal doctrines of freedom of the seas: "It had been suggested that the states whose fleets carried almost all the world's maritime transport should be asked why they opposed the extension of the breadth of the territorial sea to twelve miles. He could not see what would be the point in putting such a question. Gidel had given the answer when he had stated that a dominant factor in the dispute was the inequality of sea power; the greater a state's sea power, the more it would tend to limit the breadth of its territorial sea, for it had no need to look to international law for means to exercise special powers over a broad zone of sea adjacent to its coasts. Unfortunately, the maritime powers, which were usually also fishing powers, were not confining themselves to exercising special powers in the areas of sea adjacent to their coasts, but were only too often attempting to exercise them in the territorial sea of other countries, too."[12]

Just as these states saw the conference process in terms of politics and their own interests, so they regarded international law. They saw it as a cloak, a set of ideas used to camouflage self-interest, the domination by the few of the many. Nothing could be more candid than these remarks by Dr. Jorge Castaneda of Mexico: "Rigid adherence to the traditional rules of international law could prove disastrous to all concerned, for the traditional rules on the regime of the sea had been created by the great Powers

[9] A/CONF. 13/42, 11th meeting, par. 14.
[10] A/CONF. 13/38, 9th plenary meeting, par. 34.
[11] Ibid., 14th plenary meeting, par. 66.
[12] A/CONF. 19/8, 10th meeting, par. 12.

for their own purposes before many major problems had arisen and before the birth of the new states which now formed the majority."[13]

The same theme was repeated again and again by delegates of many of the dissatisfied states. For example, Mr. Ba Han, or Burma: "...In the past international law had been a body of rules and usages adopted by powerful states. However, the international situation had changed and new sovereign independent states had emerged, keenly conscious of their liberty."[14] Mr. Ulloa Sotomayor, of Peru: "Rules of international law had sometimes been unilaterally created in the interests of great powers; it was therefore reasonable for certain rules of law to be initiated by small states in their legitimate interests.... It was inadmissible that a sort of colonialism of the high seas should be allowed in the name of freedom of the seas."[15] Mr. Diallo, of Guinea: "With regard to 'historic rights,'...the concept was nothing other than a manifestation of the right of the strongest and a vestige of colonialism, which [Guinea] would oppose in all its forms. To perpetuate those rights would be a grave injustice to the young states that were struggling not only for political but also for economic independence."[16]

This attitude was not exclusive to the more vociferously dissatisfied anti-colonial states, but also affected even friends and allies of the West. For example, Mr. Vu Van Mau of Vietnam observed that the purposes of the first United Nations Law of the Sea conference had been "...to single out from a mass of unilateral practices anarchically applied those which corresponded to rules of law, so that they could subsequently be adopted to the new needs of mankind and to the aspirations of emergent states."[17] And the Iranian delegate, Mr. Dara, said emphatically, "A great many delegations would not accept servitude to the large maritime powers which wished to fish in the waters of the other states."[18]

These views of the dissatisfied are, in effect, a denial of the entire history and body of international law. Several Latin American delegates did in fact deny that the great international law writers of the past had ever had anything more in mind than protecting the interests of the states or organizations to which they owed allegiance. As Mr. Melo Lecaros of Chile put it, "...The rise and development of the law of the sea had been prompted by one single factor: interest. Political or economic interest had always prevailed in defining the law of the sea through the centuries. Grotius had not argued for the freedom of the seas simply as an intellectual concept, but to defend the interests of the Dutch East India Company. Selden's sole aim in refuting Grotius had been to defend England's interests. Things had changed very greatly since that time. The rule of law had been extended, but it was impossible to overlook the fact that the reason for

---

13 A/CONF. 13/41, 13th meeting, par. 22.
14 A/CONF. 13/39, 4th meeting, par. 6.
15 *Ibid.*, 5th meeting, par. 13.
16 A/CONF. 19/8, 18th meeting, par. 6.
17 *Ibid.*, 3rd meeting, par. 6.
18 A/CONF. 13/38, 20th plenary meeting, par. 70.

the existence of law was interest. Law had been created by man for the use of man."[19] Mr. Llosa of Peru also felt it necessary to tilt against Hugo Grotius, the very "father of international law," who, he said, "...did not write a work on international law but a treatise to vindicate the claims of the Dutch East India Company, by whom he had been retained, to freedom of navigation and trade."[20] So international law had moved in the wrong direction from the outset!

The dissatisfied states were acutely aware of the factor of time in regard to international law. The new states among the group, those who often set its tone and behavioral pattern, were quite naturally very conscious of their own recent independence and separate national existence. They demanded that international law take them into account, and consider their interests and desires; they demanded participation and the right of consultation in formation of international law. Among innumerable statements of this attitude are the following two examples. Mr. Subardjo of the Philippines: "...The law of nations must take into account the fact that since the Second World War former dependencies and colonies in Asia and Africa had achieved the status of sovereign States."[21] And Mr. El Bakri of Sudan: "Those who had described the present conference as the third to codify the law of the sea, counting the Hague Codification Conference of 1930, had overlooked one of the major developments which had taken place since 1930, namely, the number of countries that had become independent and which, with their different outlook, had taken their rightful place in the international community. In considering the problem of the breadth of the territorial sea, full account must be taken of the changes in institutions and ideas that had supervened during the past thirty years, and the final solution would have to accord with the contemporary spirit of social and political progress."[22]

A close and perhaps necessary corollary of this extreme self-consciousness is that the new states and their allies did not recognize, and would not consider binding upon themselves, that law which was created before they became independent states. Expressions of this attitude at the conferences abound. Mr. Bocobo of the Philippines: "...The newer countries valued their freedom above all else and refused to accept certain rules of international law evolved before they had attained statehood."[23] Mr. Loutfi of the United Arab Republic: "...The majority of the new countries that had gained their independence since [the Hague Conference of 1930] had adopted a limit in excess of three miles. Their argument that the three-mile rule constituted a principle of international law was thus devoid of substance."[24] Mr. Ba Han of Burma "...could not accept the suggestion that abandonment of the three-mile rule was a concession. That alleged

19 A/CONF. 19/8, 14th meeting, par. 13–14.
20 A/CONF. 13/41, 23rd meeting, par. 11.
21 A/CONF. 13/39, 7th meeting, par. 1.
22 A/CONF. 19/8, 19th meeting, par. 14.
23 A/CONF. 13/39, 50th meeting, par. 1.
24 *Ibid.*, 21st meeting, par. 4.

rule had been established by others at a time when his own country, for one, was completely helpless under foreign rule."[25]

There was an impatience with, rather than a reverence for, age and tradition, a feeling that the old laws should be swept away or remolded so that the newer states could help create new laws for new conditions. In stating Afghanistan's position on the access of landlocked states to the sea, Mr. Tabibi remarked: "Besides, many of [the international instruments in question] were very old and an historic conference such as the present should replace them by others which would contribute to the development of international law, particularly since the signatories of the instruments relating to the rights of landlocked countries were mainly European countries."[26] Mr. Hekmert, explaining Iran's vote against a United States-proposed amendment to the International Law Commission draft, stated that he "...agreed with the arguments advanced against the proposed [amendments]. The International Law Commission, in whose proceedings he had taken part, had not forgotten the existence of the 1884 Conventions when it drew up articles 62 and 65. It had nevertheless felt that the provisions embodied in those articles were more in line with twentieth-century conditions. The group of Afro-Asian states now numbered more than thirty, whereas, in 1884 there had not been more than five or six independent states in that part of the world. In the days of the 1884 Convention international law had been largely a matter of concern to Western countries. It was important that it should now be applicable and accepted on a worldwide basis."[27]

The keynote, the driving force, of this attitude was the need for change. Change for these states replaced history and tradition as a commander of respect. Symbolic were the remarks of the Korean delegate, Mr. Kim: "Several representatives had stressed how useful the three-mile limit had been in the past—at a time when it had been consistent with prevailing conditions. But those conditions had changed, and the three-mile limit was no longer adequate. Korea... earnestly hoped the Conference would adopt a principle better adapted to the varying conditions obtaining in the different parts of the world."[28] Consistent with their enthusiasm for change, the dissatisfied states were fond of calling those who were satisfied with the main aspects of international law "conservatives," while their own group was labeled "progressive."

Their devotion to change in international law was based on political, economic, and, particularly, technological changes in world conditions: "Legal rules had to develop at the same pace as modern technology"; and "existing rules might no longer be practical because of changed conditions." But it is clear that such statements were only a rationalization for a more profound sentiment. Without being fully aware of it, the dissatisfied states had returned to an older concept: law equated with justice, and further,

25 A/CONF. 13/38, 14th plenary meeting, par. 51.
26 A/CONF. 13/43, 8th meeting, par. 32.
27 A/CONF. 13/40, 31st meeting, par. 24.
28 A/CONF. 13/39, 15th meeting, par. 14.

with justice defined in relation to themselves. The older foundations of international law, having been established before the independent existence of these states, when they were "completely helpless under foreign rule," without regard for their welfare, could not be regarded as just; and since the law was unjust, it must be changed. And change, in their view, was therefore a change for the better.

Justice to themselves was paramount, and it was elevated to the level of principle. But while they treated certain matters as principles, they rarely handled them in legal terms. They preferred to emphasize strictly political doctrines—coastal rights, wider areas of sea control—and to have these issues stated as vaguely as possible. In their practical, pragmatic, nonhistorical manner, they had no use for doctrine qua doctrine. Legal doctrine was for them political; they made no distinction in bargaining between legal matters and any other international problem. A speech by Mr. Quarshie of Ghana illustrates well the paradoxical concern for "principle" (justice) and disregard for law: "The African States, which had seen their continent divided among the great Powers without the consent of the populations concerned, found it difficult to understand the moral arguments now advanced against the division of the sea. That division was essentially a practical matter. The needs of shipping varied according to the region, and a 200-mile limit might be suitable in one place but unsuitable in another. Requirements also varied with time; for instance, the contiguous zone was now far more important than it had been in the past."[29]

The dissatisfied states, then, tended to use "doctrine" and "principle" not as bases for consistent legal philosophy, but, somewhat opportunistically, to attain their own political-economic ends, which they considered "justice." Frequently this resulted in absurd inconsistencies, but these states were not concerned with doctrinal purity—as U Mya Sein of Burma remarked characteristically, "There was an overemphasis on legal niceties."[30] A good example of this was the position the dissatisfied states took on the issue of sovereignty.

Of all the juridical concepts developed in the long history of international law, the most meaningful to the dissatisfied states was sovereignty.[31] They defined the concept very rigidly so that no external political unit, nor any obligation made, could deprive them of their sovereign rights as they defined and understood them. Sovereignty to them was a symbol of their independence. The dissatisfied were not, however, concerned with the development of a logical theory about the symbol, but rather with the preservation of the facts for which the symbol stood. They pressed ardently for sovereignty over the continental shelf, for control of fisheries off their shores as an extension of their sovereignty, and for a wider belt of territorial sea in which to exercise their sovereignty. These states were also adamant

29 A/CONF. 13/38, 21st plenary meeting, par. 21.
30 A/CONF. 13/42, 19th meeting, par. 33.
31 See the general debates of the Fourth Committee for views of the dissatisfied on sovereignty. A/CONF. 13/42, 1st meeting–29th meeting.

opponents of any scheme that conveyed to an international court or arbitral group compulsory jurisdiction over questions touching upon a state's sovereignty. They were concerned with the preservation of their own sovereignty even at the risk of impinging upon the sovereignty of other states. Afghanistan, Bolivia, Ghana, Indonesia, Laos, Nepal, Paraguay, Saudi Arabia, Tunisia, and the UAR (among nineteen sponsors), all ardent supporters of an absolute theory of state sovereignty, were able to introduce with no qualms a proposal that would give a landlocked state an absolute right of transit across the territory of a coastal state, thereby possibly impairing the sovereignty of the latter.[32] India, a leading advocate of sovereignty of the coastal state over its continental shelf, making no attempt to explain away the seeming inconsistency of her position, introduced a proposal that would prevent the "sovereign" coastal state from "building military bases or installations [on] the continental shelf."[33] Thus sovereignty was not treated as a juridical idea to be developed so that the same legal rules would be applicable to all states equally; it was, instead, appropriated by the dissatisfied as a means of maintaining tactical freedom. This was typical of their opportunistic use of legal doctrine and principles.

The significance of the dissatisfied states' wholly *political* attitude toward international law was that these nations were unable to differentiate between political and legal reality. They assumed, incorrectly, that political reality was identical with legal reality. These states, firm opponents of the three-mile territorial sea, assumed and pronounced it politically "dead and buried" when "two of its traditional champions had withdrawn their support."[34] However, while it is probably true that the three-mile limit is no longer politically viable—that is, there is very little chance of its being accepted by states that do not already adhere to it—it is not true that it is dead and buried in legal terms. As long as states that had traditionally held to the three-mile rule continue to affirm it, it will be the rule applied by them off their coasts and in their courts. Moreover as Mr. André Gros, representative of France, pointed out, it "was the only rule that did not need express recognition by the international community."[35]

The dissatisfied states also tended to assume that a resolution, sponsored by ten of them, establishing a twelve-mile fisheries zone was already part of international law, without any conference adoption. This presumption was based upon the willingness of opponents to consider the measure as a political possibility, a point for negotiation—that is, it was politically viable, but certainly not established international law.[36] On the other hand, at times the dissatisfied states were unwilling to recognize as international law that which had just been adopted by a majority of states. After a Swiss

---

[32] UN Doc. A/CONF. 13/C.5/L.6.
[33] UN Doc. A/CONF. 13/C.4/L.57.
[34] A/CONF. 13/39, 53rd meeting, par. 17. For other death pronouncements see *ibid.*, 54th meeting, par. 1 and 15; 55th meeting, par. 35; A/CONF. 19/8, 20th meeting, par. 26.
[35] A/CONF. 19/8, 20th meeting, par. 12.
[36] *Ibid.*, 12th plenary meeting, par. 24.

proposal on questions of landlocked countries had been adopted, the dissatisfied states, which had supported an unsuccessful nineteen-power proposal because it created new rights to overcome past injustices to land-locked states, claimed the contents of that defeated proposal to be "the existing rules of international law."[37] Thus, insistence upon the exclusively political nature of proposals which they wanted codified, led these states to a position in which communication with the more legally oriented nations was difficult and negotiation virtually impossible.

A few final characteristics of this attitude should be mentioned. The dissatisfied states displayed a typical "have-not" distrust of the expert. He was identified with the colonial powers, the West, and was therefore some-what feared and resented. Mr. Quarshie of Ghana expressed the psychologi-cal reaction of the underdeveloped states to Western technical expertise: "Ghana feared the exploitation of its fishing resources and threats to its security; it sought a solution which would guarantee it a maximum freedom from exploitation and threats. Its fears could not be allayed by exhibitions of technical knowledge or outright dismissal of its views. In consultation, the main point often lay less in the validity of the argument itself than in the reaction to that argument."[38] The Mexican delegate, Mr. Gomez Robledo, also expressed well the resentment of the learning and expertise of international law specialists of older, and especially of European, states: "...Although the Mexican delegation had the greatest respect for recog-nized experts in international law, it should be remembered that the Conference was not a university but an assembly of sovereign states. Furthermore, every country in the world could now inform itself as to the true meaning of sovereignty and no state had a monopoly of learning on the matter."[39]

Along with their fear of the expert went an unwillingness to commit themselves to legal details on the exercise of rights and duties under con-sideration at the conferences. Legal detail was viewed by them as a trap for the inexperienced or the unwary. In part, the reason that they preferred vaguely general statements to more exact definitions of legal rights and obligations was their lack of technical expertise. The dissatisfied states constantly feared that their agreement to a detailed proposal would create obligations for them that their negotiators could not perceive. Moreover, agreement on detailed solutions to problems in the law would have reduced their tactical mobility, which they did not wish to have happen. Relatively weak in power terms, they saw as their main protection from the physically powerful states both the ability to avoid being permanently obligated to perform required acts and the ability to perform acts not yet sanctioned by law. They preferred that legal rights and obligations be no more than moral imperatives—broad legal obligations that should be fulfilled but whose enforcement is backed only by the sense of obligation of the affected

[37] A/CONF. 13/43, 25th meeting, par. 40–43.
[38] A/CONF. 19/1, 25th meeting, par. 22.
[39] A/CONF. 13/38, 9th plenary meeting, par. 60.

state itself. Since their sense of obligation to the idea of law is weak, the law is weak. As a result of their preference for vagueness, many provisions sponsored by dissatisfied states embodied in the conventions, should they come into force, will present new ambiguities for states to continue to dispute.

II

Those states with an international law tradition manifested a behavioral pattern very different from that of the dissatisfied states. This group included all states represented that had a Western European political tradition—some twenty-three states in all. The core of the category was composed of the Western European, Benelux, European Community, and Scandinavian caucusing groups, and the NATO common-interest group. Usually voting with these groups were the "White Commonwealth" states, five European states not represented in the General Assembly, and Israel. In addition, the votes of five United States cold war allies—Japan, Pakistan, and the Republics of China, Korea, and Vietnam—could frequently be counted upon by the satisfied.

Although heavily outnumbered, the states in this category can be said statistically to have dominated the conferences. All the satisfied groups were able to command the votes of their members approximately eighty per cent of the time on substantive issues. They also had an outstanding record of voting with the majority on both substantive and procedural issues. With additional votes coming from the five non-UN-member European states and the five United States cold war allies, the satisfied voted with the majority on forty-three of sixty-six roll call votes on substantive issues, and on ten of twelve votes on procedural issues. Another significant index of the "success" of the satisfied was the high percentage of proposals made by its members that were adopted by the conferences. Eighteen states each proposed more than two per cent of the total number of amendments adopted. Of these states, fourteen were either in the satisfied category or were states such as Japan and Pakistan that ordinarily voted with the satisfied.

It should be noted, however, that statistics on the Law of the Sea conferences do not tell the whole story of the successes and failures of the satisfied. Although they controlled a majority of the votes taken, and proposed most of the amendments accepted, the satisfied failed to gain majorities for their proposals on *key issues* such as the breadth of the territorial sea and fishing rights in areas beyond the territorial sea. They failed here because they were unable to persuade the dissatisfied that the measures desired also guarded the interests of the dissatisfied. The failure can be laid in large part to the fact that the satisfied couched their arguments in terms of traditional law—which the dissatisfied did not recognize and would not accept—instead of in terms of more realistic political-economic bargaining. Although their political positions at the conferences were not uniform—ranging from flexibility on the part of the United States and the United Kingdom to extreme conservatism and legalism on the part of continental powers such as France and the Federal Republic of Germany —still they shared a common belief that international law exists, that it is fundamentally just, that it provides a hope for adjustment of interests as well as protection of interests. They showed clear agreement with the broad background of sea-law doctrine and its cornerstone, freedom of the seas. Many states showed great pride in their past roles as formulators of international law: the Dutch continually invoked Grotius and Bynkershoek; the Spanish, Vitoria; the French, their great international lawyers.

Naturally, the satisfied relied heavily upon technical experts to staff their delegations. Twenty satisfied states had one or more legal experts from their government legal departments, foreign offices, or leading universities as full representatives at the conferences. Eighteen of the satisfied also had as representatives men from their ministries of food, fisheries, transportation, navy, communications, and commerce. In addition, all of them brought to Geneva large delegations of advisers with legal or technical expertise. On the other hand, only five of the satisfied states—Australia, Canada, Greece, Italy, and Spain—had as representatives diplomats with recent experience in the political practices of the General Assembly.

Unfortunately the satisfied states' concept of law interfered with their understanding the process by which law must be negotiated in a contemporary international setting. They did not act as if they understood that the political process by which substantive questions are negotiated will itself help shape the results. In particular, many of the satisfied refused to admit that conferences with legal subjects on the agendas are political— that they provide forums in which agreements are forged by states when they believe that such agreements protect their mutual interests. Moreover, United Nations-sponsored conferences are legislative in nature. That is, they operate under the rules of parliamentary diplomacy, and decisions depend upon forming majorities. In such an arena, it is extremely difficult, and perhaps impossible, to create a majority that will vote for and be willing to be bound by what it believes to be an abstractly perfect legal or administrative formula. The satisfied tended to view the conferences as an opportunity to promulgate a legal code consistent with their international law doctrine. They viewed apprehensively the possibility that past law and the international law tradtion were only two factors among many that would be considered in creating conventions to which a majority of states could agree politically. Such conventions would add to mere codification an element of progressive development—that is, the creation of new rules of international law—which the satisfied delegates deplored.

The remarks of Swedish delegate, Mr. Sture Petren, illustrate precisely the reluctance of the satisfied to accept the notion of progressive development: "Mr. Petren...emphasized the difference between the 'progressive development' of international law and its 'codification.' In practice, the development of law and its codification could not easily be separated...."

Any conventions which might be drafted by the Conference, whether they related to the codification or the development of law, would therefore be of a mixed nature, containing both old rules of law and new ones. These two kinds of law had not at all the same legal effect. The old rules, if they were based on customary law, bound all mankind independently of the new conventions to be concluded, whereas the new rules, which would come into being only through the conventions, would bind only those states which signed and ratified those conventions. Other states would not be bound to recognize or observe them. The Swedish delegation therefore felt that the Conference should proceed with caution and should not depart too radically from existing law.''[40]

The satisfied delegates were not averse to using political tactics at the conference; in fact they were quite skilled at forming voting groups, making bloc proposals, lobbying, and manipulating the rules of procedure. All the while they were publicly deploring the very use of such tactics by others and implicitly apologizing for finding it necessary to use them themselves. One after another satisfied delegate took the floor to excoriate blocs and bloc voting. They felt issues should be handled as ideas "on their merits." Typical was a British appeal to de-emphasize national and bloc interests for "wider considerations."[41]

Another major blunder of the satisfied states was their failure to answer the charge of the dissatisfied that the former were interested in preserving the present law because it protected their own interests. It is true that their interests did coincide with their doctrinal views. Their key doctrine, freedom of the seas, while theoretically opening the seas to all, in practice can only be exploited by those who have existent navies and merchant fleets. The satisfied states are the biggest shippers, have the biggest surface fleets, have large, important trade and fishing interests. But the satisfied states could have answered this accusation in political and economic terms, and have declared that freedom of the seas is open-ended and in fact generous to small powers, since without it the powerful could physically control large areas of the sea.

Dumbfounded by the attack of the dissatisfied on what the satisfied regarded as a liberal concept, the latter fell back on rigid, legalistic defenses. At times this tactic was used politically simply to discourage change. But the evident dismay of many satisfied delegates indicated that they could not understand the need to answer this attack by different tactics and different language. All they could do was deplore the attack on the law of the sea. For example, Dr. Max Sorensen of Denmark felt that ". . . a trend which, over the past few decades, had weakened rather than strengthened the authority of the international law of the sea should be halted, and Denmark would cooperate wholeheartedly with other nations in restoring the authority of the law."[42]

40 A/CONF. 13/39, 6th meeting, par. 1–2; see also par. 24–25; 18th meeting, par. 10.
41 A/CONF. 13/39, 53rd meeting, par. 10.
42 *Ibid.*, 4th meeting, par. 10.

There were exceptions. Occasionally one of the less powerful states with an international law tradition such as New Zealand, Greece, Switzerland, Australia, or Sweden,[43] would defend the law of the sea not only as useful for the great seagoing powers, but also as valid for lesser and developing states. (Of course, these nations were themselves in the international law tradition, and law of the sea did serve their interests to some extent.) And, although they did not always act accordingly, both the United Kingdom and the United States occasionally recognized that explaining international law doctrine in traditional terms did not appeal to the newer dissatisfied states, but only contributed to their suspicion and fear of the West.[44]

But these were only exceptions; the rule was a rather inflexible legalism and refusal to answer the dissatisfied states' political attack against the norms of traditional international law. The satisfied states had come to the conference not to adjust interests but to argue law. They did so to the detriment and sometimes to the exclusion of political-economic questions. The Federal Republic of Germany, for example, refused to recognize that fishery conservation was a problem and therefore refused to sign the convention on that subject.[45] Germany also consistently doubted the validity of the idea of the continental shelf in international law. Most of the satisfied states shared this belief. There is of course a legal case for this position; that is, the concept of the continental shelf is not of ancient lineage and is not therefore part of customary international law. In that case, they insisted, their consent was necessary to bring the concept of the shelf under law binding on them. But when they reluctantly did accept the idea of the shelf, it seemed no compromise to the proponents of the shelf concept, since it had accumulated sixteen years of state practice by those states with an active interest in exploring or exploiting the shelf. By adopting a legally sound but extraordinarily conservative position, and then agreeing to no more than had been in practice for years, they gave their negotiating techniques an air of hollow unreality and empty legalism.

Too often delegates of satisfied states would not even concede any necessary relationship between law and politics. They saw law as an abstract perfectible entity, divorced from the compromises required by the politics of competing state interests. Consider the following remarks of Professor Paul de la Pradelle, the Monacan delegate: "... It was difficult to disentangle the law of the sea from the accretions imposed by national sovereignty. He hoped that one day the compromise formulas produced by the 'diplomacy of the sea' would give place to a true law of the sea, in harmony with the [United Nations] Charter."[46] Little wonder that the

---

43 *Ibid.*, 9th meeting, par. 10, 18; 16th meeting, par. 18; 17th meeting, par. 11; 44th meeting, par. 11, respectively.

44 A/CONF. 13/43, 21st meeting, par. 40. See also Loftus Becker, "Some Political Problems of the Legal Advisor," *Department of State Bulletin,* xxxviii (May 19, 1958), p. 835; and U.S., Senate, Committee on Foreign Relations, *Conventions on the Law of the Sea,* Hearings, 86th Cong., 2nd sess. (Washington, January 20, 1960), p. 5.

45 A/CONF. 13/38, 18th plenary meeting, par. 74–77.

46 A/CONF. 19/8, 23rd meeting, par. 17.

satisfied states were unable to cope with problems of negotiating legal sub-jects at a conference which was, after all, a political arena! Just as the political emphasis of the dissatisfied states led them to fear detail in drafting and to eschew expert opinion and technical arguments, so the legal emphasis of the satisfied states led them to a firm reliance on just such techniques. Because these primarily Western states had interests in many diverse aspects of activities dealing with the sea, and had the necessary legal and technical resources, they submitted a large number of very detailed proposals. One difficulty for these states as a group was that there were often numerous competing proposals from states with similar outlooks. One of the many examples of very detailed proposals is a Dutch revision of the International Law Commission Draft Article on the conti-nental shelf. The original paragraph 2 read: "Subject to the provisions of paragraphs 1 and 5 of this article, the coastal state is entitled to construct and maintain on the continental shelf installations necessary for the explora-tion and exploitation of its natural resources, and to establish safety zones at a reasonable distance around such installations and take in those zones measures necessary for their protection."[47]

This sentence was expanded by the Dutch to read: "Subject to the provisions of paragraphs 1 and 5 of this article and within the limits mentioned in article 68, the coastal state is entitled to construct and main-tain or operate installations and other devices in the said areas necessary for the exploration and exploitation of their natural resources. The said installations and other devices shall be surrounded by a safety zone of 50 metres radius prohibited for all vessels except exploration and exploitation craft. A group of such installations and devices shall be considered as one unit if the distances are less than half a nautical mile. Entrance into such units is forbidden for all ships of more than 1,000 registered tons, except exploration and exploitation craft. If such a unit is more than 10 nautical miles long, a fairway of one nautical mile wide shall be provided in the middle, and properly marked, without prejudice to paragraph 5. The area inside such units shall be a prohibited anchorage."[48] Like many other detailed proposals, the Dutch draft alienated several of the Netherlands' natural allies. In this case, the United Kingdom also proposed an amend-ment whose purpose was the same as the Dutch amendment, differing only in length and wording. The result was a quibble among states whose position was basically the same.

Submission of competing amendments to the same article, differing only in detail, was characteristic of the satisfied states at the conferences. Only infrequently would a legal specialist from one Western state agree that another's handling of details was technically correct and sufficiently com-prehensive to cover all contingencies. This often meant that states of similar outlook which submitted proposals differing only in detail would maintain their competing proposals into the voting stage, instead of uniting to back

47 UN Doc. A/3159.
48 UN Doc. A/CONF. 13/C.4/L.22.

one of the texts. As a result, it became difficult to get a detailed proposal adopted. When no agreement on details could be reached among these states, the committee or the conference adopted the most general proposal or the original International Law Commission text. While the desire of the legally sophisticated to write comprehensive codes is understandable, it would have been much more to the point to put greater effort into forming a consensus on basic issues. Without such a consensus, it is impossible to negotiate on details.

When the satisfied states tended to submit detailed proposals, their justifications and explanations for the proposals were of course complex legally and technically. These remarks were not, could not be, directed to the delegates from the dissatisfied states who most needed convincing. The dissatisfied delegates were never shown why certain proposals were not contrary to their interests and could indeed have been interpreted in the interest of all. Because the dissatisfied, suspicious of the satisfied states' position at the outset, were never sufficiently convinced by the arguments of the satisfied states' delegates, they tended automatically to oppose changes in the International Law Commission draft proposed by satisfied states. For example, it is difficult to see how a change requested by the United Kingdom in the definition of a pirate ship or aircraft should have been contrary to the interests of the dissatisfied. The International Law Commission draft had defined such craft by a clause of "intent"—that is, a craft was a pirate ship if "it is *intended* by the persons in dominant control to be used for the purposes of committing"[49] an act of piracy. The British desired to make the definition of fact; a pirate ship is one "which has been used to *commit* any acts of piracy."[50] Characteristically, another satisfied state, Italy, submitted another similar proposal.[51] Neither delegation clearly explained the legal difference between intent and act. Both proposals failed; the International Law Commission text was adopted.

The satisfied states placed reverent reliance upon expert opinion, particularly that of the great French expert on law of the sea, Gilbert Gidel, who was a delegate to the first conference. Great resentment was expressed by delegates of the satisfied states, the French in particular, when the dissatisfied states used a statement of Gidel's, taken out of context from a work written in 1934, to attack the three-mile limit: "La prétendue regle des trois milles a été la grande vaincue de la Conférence."[52] M. Gros, the chief French delegate, attacked the newer states for misquoting Gidel and mishandling expert opinion.[53] Furthermore, he informed them that, while expert opinion by its very nature is free of national or group bias, Gidel's opinion had the added authority of being practically synonymous with the

---

[49] UN Doc. A/3159 (italics added).
[50] UN Doc. A/CONF. 13/C.2/L.83 (italics added).
[51] UN Doc. A/CONF. 13/C.2/L.81.
[52] Gilbert Gidel, *Le Droit international public de la mer,* Vol. III, *La mer territorial et la zone contiguë* (Paris: 1934), p. 151.
[53] A/CONF. 13/39, 37th meeting, par. 16–20.

position of the French Government.[54] Ironically, and sadly for those states who revered the opinion of Professor Gidel and the experts, Gidel's proposed revision of the International Law Commission definition of the high seas, a masterpiece of drafting exactness, failed of adoption. This could not have eased the resentment felt at the "misuse and abuse" of expert opinion.

Another tendency of Western and international law-minded states was, not surprisingly for those legally oriented, to reargue decided cases in international law. In particular, the *Lotus Case* and the *Anglo-Norwegian Fisheries Case* were dissected by Western international lawyers at the first conference.[55] Politically, this was a waste of time. Legally, the differences between the respective positions were important, but no matter how the lawyers differed on the interpretation of the court's ruling, they and the states they represented felt bound by that ruling. The tendency to argue the legal niceties of the case often made them neglect the importance of convincing the dissatisfied of the basic validity of the court's ruling and its worthiness to be included in the draft articles on the law of the sea under negotiation.

III

From this article it may be concluded that the results achieved by the Conferences on the Law of the Sea, like those of any United Nations-sponsored international conference, were dictated by the willingness of the participating states to create essentially political agreements. States or groups of states which assume that a specialized subject matter such as international law should not be subject to the political rough-and-tumble associated with parliamentary diplomacy, but dealt with logically within the broad lines of its past development, are bound to be disappointed by results achieved in a conference.

Indeed, one conclusion that might be drawn from the study of attitudes of dissatisfied states at the Law of the Sea conferences is that future conferences would be useless for codifying and developing law because of the hostility of dissatisfied states toward international law, a remnant of their European and imperialist past. Their concern with sovereignty, their suspicion of legal details, their wholly political attitude—all make it unlikely that they will be willing to agree to universal norms. By characterizing international law as an institutionalization of the values of the "top dogs" of the European-centered past, the dissatisfied seemed to demonstrate that they could not conceive that states might value law for its normative quality. They could not acknowledge that states have in the past compromised in negotiating legal subjects in order to create a pattern of orderly relationships even though their interests might not be fully served

54 A/CONF. 13/42, 17th meeting, par. 36.
55 See, for example, A/CONF. 13/39, 5th meeting, par. 35; 9th meeting, par. 23; 17th meeting, par. 18; 28th meeting, par. 15.

by such norms, or even that order itself may be to the interest of a state. This attitude of the dissatisfied bodes ill for the possibility of creating universality in the law in our time. If, however, this is to be an end actively sought, international conferences, or some other United Nations-sponsored device, will probably be necessary to gain consent of the dissatisfied.[56] And if conferences are to be used for this purpose, it must be recognized, and not merely ruefully as Mr. Petren of Sweden did, that "progressive development" is guided by political considerations and that the results of a conference will be an undifferentiated mixture of "progressive development" and "codification." No purpose is served by deploring a "diplomacy of the sea" and distinguishing it from a true "law of the sea."

The course of attempting to achieve universality by means of conferences presents the satisfied with knotty problems. To avoid utter failure, the satisfied must alter their outlook on international law and on negotiating it.

The burden of responsibility for bringing conferences dealing with international law to successful conclusions rests with the states most devoted to international law. This does not mean that these states should make drastic changes in the law or sacrifice vital interests merely to foster agreement for agreement's sake. What is necessary is a recognition on the part of satisfied states that an international conference is a forum in which political negotiations must not be looked upon with distaste, and a determination on their part to find common interests, and to make real attempts to talk to other participants in terms which all understand. Such changes in attitude—if forthcoming—are no guarantee of success; indeed, they may only hasten failure by more clearly demonstrating the real reasons for disagreement. But a realistic appraisal of the conference process as a political process is the only approach which will make success even remotely possible.

---

[56] Alternative schemes, such as allowing the General Assembly to declare codes of customary law, or giving legislative power to an enlarged Security Council or to a special majority in the General Assembly, would not avoid those problems in negotiating that became obvious at the Law of the Sea conferences. Legal rules under these schemes would still have to be negotiated under parliamentary diplomacy. For these schemes see Jorge Castaneda, "The Underdeveloped Nations and the Development of International Law," *International Organization,* XV (Winter 1961), pp. 38–48; and Arthur N. Holcombe, "The Improvement of the International Law-Making Process," *Notre Dame Lawyer,* XXXVII, Symposium (1961), pp. 16–23.

PART III

INTERNATIONAL ORGANIZATION

CHAPTER NINE

DYNAMIC ENVIRONMENT
AND STATIC SYSTEM:
REVOLUTIONARY REGIMES
IN THE UNITED NATIONS

Ernst B. Haas

University of California, Berkeley

Ernst Haas' thorough discussion of U.N. political processes treats questions of continuing consequence in the study of international organization. His observations on the quality of "revolutionary" leadership retain validity even though political figures like Nkrumah and Sukarno have lost power. The national and international purposes of aggressive foreign policies are traced and the distinction between "legitimacy" and "authority" in the U.N. context is explored at length. Haas' judgments on the potential of the Organization for accommodation are cautious, but solidly based on the evidence of the U.N.'s first twenty years. Conflict-resolution is likely to remain ad hoc with few U.N. precedents that would introduce greater predictability into international affairs. A further disjunction between "dynamic environment" and "static system" could impede the Organization's work in the economic and social sphere, as well as in the field of peace and security.

Reprinted from *The Revolution in World Politics,* Morton A. Kaplan, ed. New York: John Wiley and Sons, 1962, pp. 267–309. By permission.

> So many worlds, so much to do,
> So little done, such things to be.

The words were written by Tennyson. Today they not only represent Kwame Nkrumah's *leitmotif*, but they seem to have become the theme of all contemporary revolutionary leaders. Many of us see, in the crest of violent and impatient doctrines which flood the scene, persuasive evidence of anxiety everywhere. Outcroppings of fear and hatred in politics are paired with distasteful self-awareness and self-loathing. Revolutionary politics and the politics of despair are often coupled in one syndrome. Political extremism and personal insecurity appear as inseparable twins. But to argue thus is to introduce a non-political consideration into the dissection of a decidedly political phenomenon.

No doubt the revolutionary leader violently rejects the present world, but the content of his dogma exudes self-confidence rather than self-fear—the assurance of security rather than the ambiguity of perpetual anxiety. The revolutionary leader is impelled by a vision which, despite its violence and destructiveness, is invariably geared to a utopia which is held to be attainable by rational political means, means which include the systematic dissemination of fear. Far from sharing the nihilism of the mere terrorist or the verbally precocious Beat, extremism in words and deeds is part of a political program, and politics implies structure, order, and formal relations—if only for playing out conflicts. The revolutionary leader does not want to abolish politics; his aim is the same as any other political leader: to fashion and maintain the kind of order which is consonant with his values. In what way, then, can the revolutionary leader and his state be distinguished from any state which participates in the life of the United Nations?

I

Revolutionary regimes, for our purposes, possess two central attributes. They are committed to the complete reordering of their own societies, to the creation of a new order or the restoration of an old order radically different from the present. Dogmatic modernism and fanatical nativism are equally acceptable as criteria. Furthermore, a revolutionary regime typically sees itself as struggling against some kind of international "conspiracy" or fighting a global "historic force"; this implies an external dimension in the revolution, since the regime must cooperate with kindred movements in other countries. A few examples will illustrate this combination.

In the words of two students of modern Africa, revolutionary leadership "being exclusivist...lives in a world of friends and enemies. Moreover it finds itself uneasy in negotiating on other than on its own terms." It seeks to "combine the skills and talents of a community and mobilize them for a wholesale assault on the problems that lie ahead." While this state of mind suggests a rigid ideological commitment, ideology is no more than the servant of task-oriented expediency.

> The immediate tasks of the day, whether to build a dam, change the tax structure, or modify the political arrangements in government, will be put in the context of ideological slogans as a form of communication, but opportunism is more compelling than ideology.[1]

At the same time, a peculiar variety of charismatic leadership is often associated with this type of regime. While its local cultural attributes may differ and while the institutionalization of revolutionary progress may attenuate its features, the Latin American admiration for a personalist *jefe* who is also a *mache* (male) is widely repeated, leader who

> ...is expected to show sexual prowess, zest for action, including verbal 'action,' daring, and, above all, absolute self-confidence.... In politics, a man is not commonly elected or acclaimed to office because he represents the social, economic, and political position of his followers, but because he embodies in his own personality those inner qualities that they feel in themselves and they would like to manifest, had they but the talent to do so, in their own actions.[2]

If Fidel Castro fits this bill, so do Kwame Nkrumah, Sukarno, Sékou Touré, and Gamal Abdul Nasser.

Perhaps the most direct way to spell out the external aspect of revolutionary leadership is to furnish an example of post-colonial statecraft which self-consciously eschews pan-Africanism. As Félix Houphouet-Boigny put it just one year before the Ivory Coast became independent:

> Why do we not demand independence? To answer this question I can only ask another: What is independence? Industrial and technical revolutions are making peoples more and more dependent on one another.... Indeed, the countries of Europe...are prepared to relinquish a part of their sovereignty. ...Why, if not to bring about, by association and mutual aid, a more fully elaborated form of civilization which is more advantageous for their peoples and which transcends a nationalism that is too cramped, too dogmatic, and by now out of date?[3]

[1] David E. Apter and Carl G. Rosberg, "Nationalism and Models of Political Change in Africa," The National Institute of Social and Behavioral Science, Symposia Studies Series No. 1 (Washington, D.C.: December 1959), pp. 8–9.

[2] John P. Gillin, "Some Aspects for Policy," in *Social Change in Latin America Today* (New York: Harper, 1960), p. 31.

[3] Félix Houphouet-Boigny, "Black Africa and the French Union," *Foreign Affairs* (July 1957), p. 594.

Note in contrast, Kwame Nkrumah's thoughts on revolutionary statecraft:

> My first advice to you who are struggling to be free is to aim for the attainment of the Political Kingdom—that is to say, the complete independence and self-determination of your territories. When you have achieved the Political Kingdom all else will follow. Only with the acquisition of political power—real power through the attainment of sovereign independence—will you be in a position to reshape your lives and destiny, only then will you be able to resolve the vexatious problems which harass our Continent.[4]

To what use should the Political Kingdom be put? It should consolidate freedom, create unity and community among African states, and finally, achieve the economic and social "reconstruction" of Africa by undoing the damage wrought by colonialism and tribalism. Pan-Africanism is an integral part of the program because only through African unity can the "African Personality" be called to life. Political boundaries and tribal divisions are the hallmarks of reaction; an African Personality able to demonstrate the black man's cultural equality with other races will arise only with their suppression. Cultural renaissance, economic progress, territorial revisionism, strong political leadership, and the Political Kingdom are one and inseparable.[5]

So much for the syndrome of factors making up the substance of the doctrine. They necessarily presuppose totalitarian national institutions, in embryo or in full bloom. In the Soviet case and in Cuba institutions are clearly flowering; in Ghana and Guinea the buds are shooting out. If Egypt, Indonesia, and Bolivia appear merely as one-party or no-party states, it is because their authoritarian way has not advanced to full totalitarianism for reasons associated with underdevelopment rather than from lack of intent.

But it is important *not* to equate revolutionary regimes with a number of closely related categories. Not every totalitarian state is also a revolutionary state, as shown by modern Spain, Portugal, and Yugoslavia. Policies of imperialism may well be pursued in the modern world without being linked to an intention to transform society. Thus, Egypt followed a pan-Arab course, often interpreted as simple Egyptian imperialism, under

[4] Speech by the Prime Minister of Ghana at the Opening Session, December 8, 1958, All-African People's Conference, Accra. The same point was made by the Tunisian delegate to the first Conference of Independent African States, Accra, April 22, 1958.

[5] *Ibid.*, for this train of thought. See also the similar remarks of Sékou Touré as reported in *Afro-Asian Bulletin*, Monthly Journal of the Permanent Secretariat of Afro-Asian Solidarity (Cairo: October-November, 1959), p. 6. The argument that "national" independence of single ex-colonial territories whose boundaries were fixed by Europeans is meaningless as long as any colonial situations survive is common to pan-African thought in English-speaking West Africa and the Cameroons. See George Padmore, *A Guide to Pan-African Socialism*. The same doctrine is expressed unblushingly in the Constitution of the Convention People's Party. See K. Nkrumah, *Ghana* (New York: Thomas Nelson and Sons, 1957), pp. 289-90.

Farouk as well as under Nasser.[6] But this does not make the pre-1952 oligarchical regime a revolutionary one. Nor is every nationalist regime specifically revolutionary. Indian or Burmese nationalism is not revolutionary because it has no articulate external referents. But Ghana's nationalism is identifiable as revolutionary because of the pan-African strain; Indonesia's is equally so because it holds

> ...that God Almighty created the map of the world in such a fashion that even a child can tell that the British Isles are one entity...and that a child can see that the Indonesian Archipelago is a single entity, stretching between the Pacific and Indian oceans and the Asian and Australian continents, from the north tip of Sumatra to Papua.[7]

A further refinement in the application of this defintion of revolutionary status is imperative. Having linked contemporary revolutionary pressures with totalitarian political institutions, we automatically exclude from our purview such international revisionist dogmas as may be associated with oriental despotisms, mercantilist imperialisms, and early capitalist assertions. This is *not* to argue, as some contemporary commentators do, that revolutionary conduct in our era is purely a non-Western and anti-Western phenomenon which ought to be linked to cultural differences between the Western creators of international law and its Asian challengers. After all, the impetus underlying such attacks on the international status quo as were hurled from Moscow and Berlin during the thirties can hardly be shrugged off as "non-Western." The international politics and legal doctrines of sixteenth-century Spain, the seventeenth-century Dutch republic, and the fledgling American republic showed definite evidence of a "new" state's impatience with certain aspects of the status quo and resulted in the advocacy of international legal norms which were regarded as "revolutionary" in the context of their times. However, they are not "revolutionary" for our purposes because the element of drastic *internal* revolutionary zeal was lacking in the case of three examples adduced: There was no overwhelming commitment to remake Spanish, Dutch, or American society, and the refinements of totalitarian control remained to be invented.

Soviet behavior offers a still finer point. While the Soviet Union is clearly a revolutionary state whose foreign policy fits the requirements of our purpose, it does not follow that every Soviet move is part of a "necessary" and "planned" revolutionary behavior pattern. One careful study, for instance, casts doubt on the "inevitable" character of the Communist coup in Czechoslovakia.[8] We are, therefore, concerned with the attitudes and

---

6 See Farouk's use of the Arab League and of the caliphate in Elie Kedourie "Pan-Arabism and British Policy," in W. Laqueur, ed., *The Middle East in Transition* (New York: Praeger, 1958), pp. 102–103. On Nasser's pan-Arab nationalism see Jean Vigneau, "The Ideology of the Egyptian Revolution," in *ibid.*, pp. 136–38.

7 Quoted in R. Emerson, "Paradoxes of Asian Nationalism," *Far Eastern Quarterly,* Vol. 13, No. 2 (February 1954), p. 132.

8 Morton A. Kaplan, *The Communist Coup in Czechoslovakia,* (Princeton: Center of International Studies, January 1960).

poses, the demands and expectations, the style and doctrines, of totally revolutionary regimes rather than with every detail of their foreign policy moves.

Our concern can be pinpointed in another way. If we ask what type of political *system* constrains and limits a policy of self-assertion abroad, because the enunciation of such a course encounters well-entrenched domestic opposition or runs afoul of domestic weakness and disorganization, we come across a number of types which cannot be revolutionary in our sense. To use the typology of Edward Shils, political democracies, traditional and traditionalistic oligarchies do not fit;[9] modernizing oligarchies may, and totalitarian oligarchies, as well as tutelary democracies, most certainly do. The picture becomes clearer if we ask what type of domestic policy requires a foreign policy of self-assertion; or, under what circumstances a domestic policy aiming at the creation of a new society becomes revolutionary in the outside world as well? Put in these terms, we arrive at two varieties of revolutionary regimes, without having to commit ourselves to a specific typology of systems.

A revolutionary elite which is commited to a doctrine of historical struggle represents the first variety. It includes, of course, the major countries of the Communist bloc. The foreign policies of China and the Soviet Union may be interpreted merely as the international application of the inevitable rise to power of the proletariat through the establishment of socialism and eventually communism, first in certain countries and finally everywhere. While this implies neither commitment to the notion that war is inevitable nor to the proposition that all Soviet-bloc moves are part of a "Communist conspiracy," it does locate the Communist bloc within a revolutionary syndrome based on class struggle. In it, the security and survival of Communist states is the minimal, but only the minimal, motive of a foreign policy organizationally and doctrinally linked to drastic domestic change. In the mind of Fidel Castro, this class struggle is "nationalized" in the sense that underdeveloped countries living at the mercy of monopoly imperialism become the equivalent of the proletariat. The international class struggle now is identical with the struggle for freedom and progress on the part of all underdeveloped countries.[10] Agrarian reform in Cuba, for example, is held out as an internationally valid example of inevitable revolutionary transformation. It is hardly surprising, therefore, that Cuba had identified herself publicly with Egypt, Guinea, and Ghana.

Africa, however, offers a different example of thinking along lines of an international revolutionary struggle. As our examples of pan-Africa doctrines

9 As cited in G. A. Almond and J. S. Coleman, eds., *The Politics of the Developing Areas* (Princeton: Princeton University Press, 1960), pp. 52–55.

10 For Castro's views see the revealing marathon speech delivered to the United Nations General Assembly, September 26, 1960. A similar doctrine was developed as early as 1918 by Sultan Galiev. See A. Bennigsen, "Sultan Galiev," in Laqueur, *op. cit.*, pp. 398ff. Peronista nationalism and policy often used the same arguments and conformed to similar social pressures. See John J. Johnson, *Political Change in Latin America* (Stanford: Stanford University Press, 1958), Chap. 6.

have shown, the creation of the African Personality ranks high among the goals of the revolutionary leaders. Class is here replaced by race. The fight against the racism of the imperialists includes the new self-assertion of "the African," suspicious, if not impatient, of all white institutions and practices. The salvation of Africa becomes the redemption of the black man, with the practical international consequence of giving a reverse racist character to the foreign policy of Ghana and Guinea. To sum up: the Soviet Union, Cuba, Ghana, and Guinea represent a variety of revolutionary leadership in which international policy follows from a "historical struggle" doctrine which is initially and predominantly applied to the domestic plans of these nations.

No similar central theme is present in the variety of revolutionary leadership displayed by contemporary Indonesia, Egypt, Bolivia, and perhaps Iraq or Morocco. To be sure, the internal reformist emphasis is present here too, but it is by no means simply or dialectically translated into foreign policy. Instead, the linkage occurs through the strains and tensions set up by the dissociation between modernizing and traditional political structures and policies, by the vagaries of the so-called non-Western political process. At the simplest level of explanation, self-assertion and even aggressive attitudes on foreign policy are related to the familiar scapegoat, or displacement, device.

> When the *raison d'être* of nationalism—the attainment of political independence—has no longer existed, leaders have endeavored in various ways to perpetuate nationalism as an active and unifying force: by demanding a positive role for their new state in world affairs, by creating new external enemies or threats, and by dramatizing the vision of a new society through monumental public works and other such symbols.[11]

Opposition groups have found it easiest to challenge authoritarian-reformist governments by merging their specific grievances with a global appeal for drastic external and internal change, a challenge the government leaders then tend to take up by making equally sweeping demands.

But aggressive foreign policy attitudes in these countries may well serve a more fundamental functional role than scapegoating. The achievement of independence often causes rifts in the national movement. In Indonesia, segments of the urbanized Indonesian bourgeoisie, in alliance with segments of the nobility, had no interest in turning the political revolution into a social upheaval. Hence, they try to divert the continuing revolutionary fervor into external channels, whether directed at the Chinese or the

---

[11] James S. Coleman, in Almond and Coleman, *op. cit.*, p. 554. See the similar points made by Lucian W. Pye, "The Non-Western Political Process," *The Journal of Politics,* Vol. 29 (1958), pp. 473, 480. For the identification of such tensions in an African setting involving the danger of disintegration on the part of a pyramidal social structure, merging notions of legitimacy, kinship, religion, land ownership, and chieftaincy (Ashanti), see David E. Apter, "The Role of Traditionalism in the Political Modernization of Ghana and Uganda," *World Politics,* Vol. 13, No. 1 (October 1960).

Europeans. At the same time, as rural discontent grows and the demand for further socio-economic reform continues, the fight for change is seen by rural leaders as a continuation of the struggle for political freedom, especially if the obvious "monopolist-imperialist" targets are also foreign corporations, aid-missions, plantation owners, and the like. The struggle for industrialization thus acquires a xenophobic quality despite, or perhaps because of, its dependence on the foreigner. No wonder that the Indonesian Army was able to use the West Irian issue as a device to channel and direct mass discontent in the direction of seizing control over Dutch property.[12] In addition, xenophobic nationalism has the functional role of taking the place of traditional religion. It is suggestive that in Indonesia the Panja Sila are often put forward as a secular-universal reformist creed and that Indonesians tend to invoke the hallowed principles of Bandung far more frequently as an international doctrine than do other Asian nations.[13] Much the same applies in contemporary Bolivia, in which the dispossessed urban middle class and the ascendant Indian peasantry vie with each other in aggressive anti-American sentiments, with the Indians seeking to maximize an only partly successful economic upheaval and the middle class anxious to undo it.

Nor is scapegoating a complete explanation of Nasser's self-assertive foreign policy. The policy is clearly revolutionary since it claims a "civilizing mission" for Egypt in Black Africa and is committed to pan-Arabism. It is linked to domestic reform in Nasser's explicit recognition that the social and the political revolutions are proceeding simultaneously and that it is the duty of the army to advance both.[14] But it appears that this doctrinal commitment was put to the test of policy in 1955, when the domestic revolution ran into difficulties. It then acquired substance in what appears as a self-conscious effort to divert public attention from domestic failure. But it is also true that the turn to foreign adventure coincided with restlessness in the army, with the ambitious Aswan Dam project and with the announcement, in 1957, of the plan to create a "socialist, democratic, and cooperative society, free from political, social, and economic exploitation."[15] A reinvigoration of the program to remake Egyptian society under the tutelary auspices of the National Union and the Army would imply an intensification of the tensions common to non-Western contexts. A glorious role in international affairs would thus serve the same function as in Indonesia.

12 This thesis is developed by W. F. Wertheim, *Indonesian Society in Transition* (The Hague: W. Van Hoeve, 1959), pp. 327–34.
13 See Guy J. Pauker, "Indonesian Images of their National Self," Rand Corporation Report No. P-1452-RC (August 1, 1958).
14 Gamal Abdul Nasser, *Egypt's Liberation: The Philosophy of the Revolution* (Washington, D.C.: Public Affairs Press, 1955), pp. 43–44, 69–71, 84–85, 110–14. Anwar El. Sadat, *Revolt on the Nile* (London: Wingate, 1957). And especially, Morroe Berger, *Military Elite and Social Change: Egypt since Napoleon* (Princeton: Center of International Studies, February 1, 1960).
15 Keith Wheelock, *Nasser's New Egypt* (New York: Praeger, 1960), pp. 51, 69–70, 134.

To sum up again: Certain revolutionary regimes are compelled by the tension and crisis-ridden nature of their internal reform programs, suffering from the hiatus between modernizing and traditional political processes, to turn to foreign poses of self-assertion. The changes they thus come to demand in the international scene are every bit as revolutionary as their domestic aims, and often dovetail neatly with those advanced by revolutionary regimes impelled by doctrines of class and race.

So far we have concerned ourselves only with the substance of policy pursued by revolutionary regimes. But shoe-thumping, name-calling, unbearably long harangues by bearded heroes dressed in green fatigues, uncompromising language, appeals to some universal brotherhood—whether of the black, the downtrodden, or the victims of various conspiracies—are aspects of style rather than of policy. Because of the danger of confusing substance with style, and the possibility that unconventionality of style is not necessarily and always perfectly correlated with an inherently aggressive policy, an effort will now be made to isolate certain recurring stylistic aspects in the international behavior of revolutionary regimes.

It is a commonplace that the more rationally oriented among revolutionary regimes, that is, Communist regimes, rigorously subordinate means to the achievement of postulated ends. Hence, conventional and perverse styles of behavior alternate freely, depending on the immediate definition of ends. In the case of Fascist regimes the case is otherwise. Here the means themselves reflect certain end values, such as the glorification of violence. Hence, their international style is less flexible than the Communists' and more consistently at odds with the canons of "bourgeois" diplomacy. All revolutionary regimes share an affinity for "dual" diplomacy: the simultaneous conduct of their foreign policy through the medium of conventional channels, with their rules and decorum, and through various non-official channels. The search for allies among "the people," "the peace partisans," or "the freedom fighters" among the citizens of enemy states leads to the widespread use of revolutionary political parties and movements, front organizations, and other "progressive" elements as carriers of the revolutionary regime's policy. Since these non-official allies can be mobilized and disbanded at will, can be made to dovetail with conventional gambits, or can be de-emphasized completely, they are aspects of revolutionary style rather than inherent attributes of doctrine or policy.[16]

Revolutionary style thrives on apocalyptic language, immoderate threats, and manufactured international crises. But it would be a mistake to dismiss these manifestations as evidences of infantilism or of irresponsibility. Like the practice of scapegoating, such techniques may well possess a functional role in the political processes of non-Western countries. The scarcity of

---

[16] This judgment is not accepted by all observers. Michael Lindsay, for example, found that the Chinese Communists see no contradiction in professed allegiance to the *Panch Shila* and the simultaneous commitment to intervention in other countries through the medium of national liberation movements. If Lindsay is correct, the dualistic commitment is not a matter of style, but of doctrine. See his "China and Her Neighbors," in *The Challenge of Communist China,* (Proceedings of a Conference held at the University of Minnesota, April 4 and 5, 1960), pp. 21–22.

stable, representative, and functionally specific interest groups and of well-organized political parties aggregating their demands, results in national policies being divorced from any sort of structured upward flow of communication. National leaders tend to act in isolation from popular concerns simply because they do not always know what important segments of the public may wish, and consequently feel compelled to appeal in vague and total terms to an undifferentiated public. At the same time, the very absence of specific policy impulses from below enables the leadership to take more clearly defined positions in the international than in the domestic field. To the extent that such positions, couched in the most undiplomatic terms of a Nasser, a Sukarno, and a Castro, reflect an apocalyptic vision, they may be aimed at unifying their own divided societies while staking out a claim for it in the United Nations.[17]

Immoderate style tends to carry with it an impatience for traditional, legal, as well as diplomatic, techniques. Modes of dealing with international conflict by peaceful means frequently imply the open or tacit acceptance of certain principles of law. Revolutionary leaders are always impelled, at least initially, to deny the legitimacy of aspects of international law, in the evolution of which they had no part but which hinder their aims. The practical reasons for this attitude are obvious. It may be suggested, however, that the very qualities of charismatic leadership which are a recurring feature in revolutionary regimes are connected with this impatience. In many non-Western countries the advent of the urban-industrial society implies the erosion of the uprooted villager's reliance on the rural *patrón,* or the tribal chief. In the unfamiliar urban environment he turns to a demagogic national leader as a substitute, identifies with him, relies on him, supports him unthinkingly.[18] The leader, thus supported, feels free to indulge his freedom of manœuver so as to make claims upon and embarrass foreign countries, and to indulge his charismatic role by denying the validity of international law and diplomatic protocol.

Clearly, the nationalism of revolutionary countries is always integral in character. It brooks no qualifications, no nuances, and no considerations which would destroy the image, however unreal upon inspection, of an organically unified people yearning for "justice." Integral nationalism is as much a part of the revolutionary international style as neutralism is a minimal foreign policy attitude. Certainly, as Robert A. Scalapino has demonstrated, a rational basis for neutralism can be found in the realities of contemporary world politics; there is no doubt that it also represents a curious mixture of ambivalence, distrust, and disinterested tolerance for the competing Western doctrines of Marxism and liberal democracy.[19] But a neutralist pose also serves the functional role of confident self-assertion

---

17 This point is developed in detail in Pye, *op cit.,* pp. 480, 482, 484, and in Almond and Coleman, *op. cit.,* p. 150 ff.

18 In the case of Brazil, this relationship is developed with respect to Vargas by Charles Wagley, in *Social Change in Latin America Today, op. cit.,* p. 220 ff. A similar point is made by David Apter in his *The Gold Coast in Transition.*

19 Robert A. Scalapino, " 'Neutralism' in Asia," *American Political Science Review,* Vol. 68, No. 1 (March 1954).

for the impatient and emergent charismatic leader in legitimating his own arrival upon the world scene and effectively juxtaposing himself to the "vested interests"—barricaded behind power politics and traditional international law—of the older successful nations.[20] The new regimes, whether in Africa, Latin America, or Asia, represent the advent to power of social groupings not conspicuously successful in terms of wealth and prestige as long as the countries in question were under Western rule of influence. There is no reason now to expect the new classes to display any great respect or affection for Western policy or its international tradition. The very eclecticism offered by a neutralist pose is a much more convincing way of demonstrating self-confidence.

Having thus pinpointed the characteristics of revolutionary regimes, in domestic politics, in substantive foreign policy, and in international style, we must put this force into the context of institutionalized world politics— the United Nations. And we must ask ourselves whether the success and multiplication of such regimes makes doubtful the survival of the kind of international system represented by it.

II

In assessing the responsiveness of revolutionary leaders to influences emanating from the international scene, we must posit the characteristics of the central international institution, the United Nations. In doing this, care must be taken to avoid the analytical extremes of assuming a completely structured and fully deterministic UN "system" or of complete freedom of the will for national actors to fashion a cooperative international commonwealth. Abstraction from reality is certainly a necessity, but the system we abstract must remain faithful to what we know to be true in the conduct of the actors. Hence, the recurring patterns and the structured relationships of UN life must be thrown into relief without reification, without sinning on the side of determinism to the extent of not being able to accommodate the organizational evolution, which is no "instability," we know to have taken place. The "system" must permit the "free will" of the national actors to impinge on the totality of relations while retaining the necessarily deterministic properties of any system.

Hence, the category called the "loose bipolar system," made popular by

---

20 On this point, the particular form of "active neutralism" sponsored by Egypt should be kept in mind. As distinguished from the Indian prototype, this attitude frankly equates the advancing of pan-Arab interests with the organization of a neutralist bloc which would manoeuver permanently between the two military camps and thereby compel them to inaction, without expecting necessarily to dismantle them or to eliminate the cold war, though this eventuality would be welcomed. Since the United States has the reputation of opposing pan-Arab aims, with the Soviet Union at least neutral on this point, "active neutralism" in practice is bound to work itself out in a pro-Soviet direction.

Morton Kaplan, cannot be used as our point of reference. We sacrifice aesthetic neatness by not using this type of system and no claim for an equally cleanly structured approach can be advanced.[21] The desire to remain close to the data saddles us with a more ragged scheme which does not assume as regularly applicable to the UN the systemic rules abstracted by Kaplan. Furthermore, the kind of "systems" approach, here used deliberately, avoids the unnecessary and misleading "balance" and "structure" hypotheses offered by some social psychologists.[22]

But it is equally easy to sin on the side of free will. Some of the ablest commentators on the UN interpret the world organization as an attempt at international institutionalization of Western parliamentary deliberation based "upon the conviction of the reality of freedom of man in the social universe."[23] International organizations are held to fall squarely into the liberal-thought pattern, in the sense that they presuppose sufficient freedom of the will for statesmen to alter the international environment by means of rational discussion, negotiation, and voting. Since the institutions of most of the founding states are held to conform to this view of things, the UN could be expected to reflect these influences and thereby gradually "civilize" international politics, if not reform the national political processes of new states. Gradually, a concept of "universal public interest" will come to inform UN deliberations.[24] It is unfortunate for this approach that we already possess convincing evidence from the mouths of Western statesmen that the UN has come under the anti-parliamentary influences of the non-Western world, as the membership has grown more universal; the changing environment has influenced the system more than the liberal school is able to concede and it makes little sense to speak of the UN as a "Western system."[25] A universal public interest could be demonstrated only if members of the UN consistently practiced the kind of "wise statesmanship" which

[21] Morton A. Kaplan, *System and Process in International Politics* (New York: John Wiley and Sons, 1957), pp. 36–43, 56–64, 83–85, 117–20.

[22] For an example of a nonsensical systems approach to international relations, derived in simplistic fashion from Freudian theory, see Frank Harary, "A Structural Analysis of the Situation in the Middle East in 1956," *Journal of Conflict Resolution,* Vol. 5, No. 2 (June 1961).

[23] Inis L. Claude, *Swords Into Plowshares,* 2nd ed. (New York: Random House, 1959), p. 15. This work is the most incisive in treating the United Nations from this vantage point, as well as the most judicious.

[24] This idea is developed in some detail by Arthur N. Holcombe, "The United Nations and American Foreign Policy," University of Illinois *Bulletin* (October 1957). See also the reports of the Commission to Study the Organization of Peace for specific proposals for strengthening the UN in line with this conceptual commitment.

[25] See the blunt statement on this score by P. H. Spaak, "The Experiment of Collective Security," Carnegie Endowment for International Peace, *Perspectives on Peace, 1910–1960* (New York: Praeger, 1960), p. 85. Further evidence for increasing disappointment with the liberal-parliamentary aspect of the UN can be found in the Carnegie Endowment's series *National Studies on International Organization,* notably the volumes on Belgium, Australia, Canada, Sweden, and Britain. George Modelski treats the UN as a "western universal system" in *The Communist International System* (Princeton: Center of International Studies, December 1, 1960).

Arnold Wolfers advocated in his reconciliation between determinism and free will, his prescription for following the minimal national interest of self-preservation in such a way as to retain a maximum fidelity to universal values.[26] In the absence of such a demonstration, recourse to the liberal yardstick would saddle us with an approach too hortatory and too effervescent to yield more than disappointment.

Comparative historical-sociological analysis, as in Stanley Hoffmann's study of the Concert of Europe, the League of Nations, and the United Nations comes close to an appropriate system. Assessments are made on the basis of typologies of conflict situations correlated with the characteristics of the states which were prominent participants. And the conclusion:

> With respect to relations among the Big Powers, the record of the three organizations is this: when solidarity existed the organizations were unnecessary. When it did not exist, they were powerless. The remedy cannot be found in the formal association of these states, whose nature makes a real association impossible. In relations among the Great Powers, decisive for the maintenance of world peace, international organizations stand exposed to perpetual defeat.[27]

Although Hoffmann grants that in disputes among a minor power not allied with a great power, the methods of collective security have worked and, although he credits the League with advancing a concept of international legitimacy in compelling discussion of national aggressive designs, no fundamental change in international relations should be attributed to these trends. My own interpretation of history differs in that it does not assume the category of "great power" to possess the same implications at all times. Put another way, the application of trend analysis to international *systems* requires equal, if not more, attention to the various *environments* in which they operate. Patterned relationships between demands and policies in international systems compel attention to the source of the demands. These remain rooted in the national aims of member states, but, as the advent of revolutionary regimes makes plain, these aims constantly change to produce a variety of environments. Hence, historical conclusions making no allowance for shifting environmental influences are not convincing.

Therefore, the United Nations must be described as a multi-phase system, whose characteristics and evolutionary potential must be specified in terms of the changing environment in which it operates. Environments, in turn, are made up of the totality of policies, aims, expectations, fears, hopes, and hatreds funneled into the institutional structure and its political processes, the "system" proper. If the policies of the United Nations can be demonstrated to change the environment, including the part contributed by the revolutionary regimes, perhaps systemic growth at the expense of the

26 Arnold Wolfers and Laurence Martin, eds., *The Anglo-American Tradition in Foreign Affairs* (New Haven: Yale University Press, 1956), pp. xxvi–xxvii.

27 Stanley Hoffmann, *Organisations Internationales et Pouvoirs Politiques des États* (Paris: Armand Colin, 1954), p. 412.

member units can be established. It is important here to distinguish between a "static" system and a "dynamic" one. In a static system the actors channel policies and demands through it and .use it as a medium of communication as well as a forum for resolving some conflicts, but they do not necessarily increase the powers and functions of the system in so doing. No growth then takes place. In a dynamic setting, however, some of these efforts carry with them an accretion of new functions and powers for the system, implying the kind of growth we wish to examine in connection with the demands provided by revolutionary regimes.[28]

The variety of demands contributed by member states can be easily grouped along the recurrent lines of discussion which prevail in the UN. They entail 1) collective security, including both enforcement and pacific settlement functions; 2) peaceful change, including the substantive aspects of such areas as the dissolution of colonial empires and disarmament, and the procedural concern with perfecting mediatory and arbitral methods; 3) economic development, technical assistance, and world economic policy; 4) the definition and implementation of human rights. General, as well as highly specific, issues arise in each meeting of UN bodies under each of these headings. But the manner of resolving the issues differs in each phase of the UN system, and no issue has so far even been settled in principle and in perpetuity.

Why is this the case? Formal as well as informal resolutions of issues always take place on the basis of bloc politics; member states never yield a position in its entirety and usually compromise their differences—at various levels of meaningfulness—by a mixture of negotiation and voting. But issues are rarely discussed with sole reference to the category in which a functionally specific analysis would place them. Foreign policy being a web of interlocking aims, the totality of state objectives is fed into the UN system, resulting in a pattern of decisions featuring interfunctional as well as interbloc compromise. The character of the environment seems to determine the nature of this compromise, and the environment is unstable with reference to the predominance of this or that aim. A further environmental instability is introduced by the enlargement of the membership and the resultant quantitative change in the relations among the blocs.

During the first phase of the UN system (1945–47), the honeymoon period among the Great Powers prevented these strains from impinging on one another. Collective security was the dominant concern and it hinged around skirmishing in the Security Council, and at times it looked as if the Churchillian notion of the postwar status quo might achieve institutionalization by virtue of the UN. But the real onset of the cold war proved this suspicion wrong, and by 1948 the second phase of the system got under way, characterized by the dominance of the United States and its successful enlisting of the UN on its behalf.

---

[28] For the distinction between static and dynamic system see Kenneth E. Boulding, "Organization and Conflict," *Journal of Conflict Resolution,* Vol. 1 (1957), pp. 122–23.

202

ERNST B. HAAS

During the second phase, the dominant *motif* was the identification of collective security with the military-political aims of the Western bloc, successfully asserted in Korea and in the Uniting for Peace Resolution. Demands for a world economic policy and far more ambitious economic aid measures than actively championed by the West were put forward by Afro-Asian and Latin American states but were not implemented in full. Discussion of human rights was initiated and championed by the West so long as it fitted in with cold war policy, though non-Western blocs advanced demands in this area for quite different reasons. Peaceful change was demanded in a variety of anti-colonial claims but found implementation only in the case of the former Italian colonies. While the Soviet bloc placed itself in a non-bargaining position by completely disputing the legitimacy of all UN discussion and steps not in line with Soviet policy, the Western bloc dominated the system by successfully obtaining the support of the Latin American and part of the Afro-Asian blocs on collective security issues and "paying" for this by occasional concessions in the economic and colonial fields.

By 1954 the second phase came to its end with important changes in the environment. The number of Afro-Asian members increased, especially after 1955. The European members of the Western bloc grew disenchanted with a policy of collective security which seemed too close to general warfare. The colonial and human rights issues were linked ever more closely in the demands of the Latin American and Afro-Asian blocs, and the crescendo of economic demands rose as the American security policy grew more and more dependent on general support. And most importantly, Joseph Stalin died. With his demise the role of the Soviet Union in international organizations underwent such an important—if tactical—change as to destroy the environment of the second phase.

Since that time, the third phase has prevailed, involving institutionalized inter-regional and interfunctional bargaining in a setting in which the colonial and human rights issues have furnished the dominant *motif*, and the practice of collective security has been increasingly subordinated to it in terms of the kind of support forthcoming for Western bloc demands. Peaceful change, of sorts, has prevailed along with intensified international economic development efforts, in the relatively amicable way in which colonial empires have dissolved under UN prodding. Neutralism has come into its own, quantitatively, and the "balancing" pattern of collective security holds sway, featuring conciliation rather than enforcement.

Shortly, however, a fourth phase will arise. Functionally, it will be marked by the end of the colonial issue as a dominant theme. The human rights issue well may be eliminated from the demands of the very Afro-Asian and Latin American states which have featured it in connection with their anti-colonial campaign and may re-acquire value for Western nations freed from a variety of skeletons in their closets. Economic demands will increase, and collective security aims by the West will have to be paid for exclusively in this area now. Further, if the alliance between the Soviet and certain underdeveloped nations continues, the Soviet bloc may funnel its particular variety of collective security into the UN, and may be expected to pay for it in economic aid. Whatever the precise outline of the pattern of inter-functional and interbloc politics may be, a behavior pattern discerned for the revolutionary regimes during the second and third phases cannot a priori be expected to continue with the sharp change in the environment introduced by the end of colonialism.

The UN system is hyperdependent on its environment. Precedents set in one phase, therefore, do not necessarily predetermine action in the next. Unless a great deal of "internalization" of "rules" can be demonstrated, the very multiphase character of the system militates against substantial growth. All issues are resolved ad hoc, stable alliances among interests cannot develop, compromises and related communication patterns among participants can generate no fixed institutional characteristics. Even the "non-resolution consequences" of UN activity display no cumulative pat-tern.[29] Substituting debate and voting for fighting, in the sense of using the UN as a litmus paper for determining the strength of the opponent, wanes with the change in functional preoccupation. While communication among members may narrow differences in the perception of reality, in one phase, the process may have to start all over in the next. There is evidence that the United States has "learned" the lesson of Korea in no longer expecting the kind of collective-security operation which it mounted in 1950 and is now seeking security through balancing; but there is less evidence that Nasser and Nkrumah have learned the same thing.[30]

How can we assess the impact of a multiphase system on its environment? Granting the variation in demands and the changes in the political process which convert them into United Nations policy, how do we relate the policy pattern to the environment to determine whether the United Nations is having any kind of influence? One way of assessing the impact is merely to study the behavior pattern of the member states, specifically the revolu-tionary states. Do they respond to UN resolutions? To what kind of resolu-tions, in what functional contexts? In other words, does the *authority* of the UN system increase as determined by the fidelity of its revolutionary members in carrying out resolutions? Does the *legitimacy* of the system increase as revolutionary states invoke the Charter and past resolutions to link these with an increase in the institutional power and autonomy of the organization?

Another way of obtaining answers is to study the system itself rather than the effects on the conduct of its members. Here it would be tempting to profit from general organization theory, if this discipline were not so dependent on hierarchical models with firm boundaries and predisposed toward identifying rationality with functionally oriented behavior. In terms of such standards the UN system is not an "organization" at all. "The prevalence of bargaining," say March and Simon, "is a symptom *either*

---

[29] Chadwick F. Alger, "Non-Resolution Consequences of the United Nations and Their Effect on International Conflict," *ibid.*, Vol. 5, No. 2 (June 1961).

[30] For such evidence see Arnold Wolfers, ed., *Alliance Policy in the Cold War* (Baltimore: Johns Hopkins Press, 1959).

that goals are not operational or that they are not shared."[31] In the case of UN decision making, they are neither one nor the other; operational goals are not rationally contrasted in policy making, there is no hierarchy, and problem solving does not predominate as a technique of deciding issues. This has been true in all phases of the system, which would come close to being identified as almost entirely dysfunctional in its behavior. Yet the system has survived, and if membership, finance, and scope of operations are the yardsticks of evaluation, even prospered. Hence, formal organization theory is unlikely to yield answers to our question.

In fact, it must be stressed that in a different focus the UN is a successful, if phase-ridden and politics-dominated, international institution. It has served to channel aspects of national foreign policy never before submitted to any collective scrutiny. It has tamed and civilized national policies by serving as an approximation to an institutionalized process of interest politics, and thereby containing the interests. If the Western political process be conceived, not as dispassionate debate, capped by voting and subject to judicial review, but as the articulate defense of rival group interests in permanent confrontation and subject to cumulative compromises, the UN process is not so very different. The study of policies during the various phases of the system could thus become a study of the methods used to achieve various types of compromises. Systemic development or growth could be evaluated by the role of the organization itself, as distinguished from components contributed by the environment, in advancing compromises.

We already possess a good deal of evidence permitting such evaluations for the period 1945–55.[32] It permits the conclusion that the system did *not* increase the *legitimacy* it enjoys in the eyes of its members. Demands for UN action and invocation of its Charter were *not* accompanied by cumulative claims for a greater autonomous institutional role for the system. This was true for revolutionary as well as nonrevolutionary states. However, the *authority* of the system *did* increase for all types of member states, in the sense that many of them increasingly heeded resolutions and decisions addressed to them.[33] In fact, authority tended to increase as many of the member states grew more and more dissatisfied with the style of debate and the quality of the decisions. Growing dissatisfaction, then, did not engender loss of authority. Whether a similar picture obtains more in recent years and whether it will be true in the next phase of the UN's life remains to be investigated.

Clearly, then, an effort must be made to assess changes produced on the environment, as reflected in the policies and attitudes of member states.

---

[31] James G. March and Herbert A. Simon, *Organizations* (New York: John Wiley and Sons, 1958), p. 196 (italics in original).
[32] See the seven-volume study of the Brookings Institution, published between 1956 and 1958, as well as the twenty-odd volumes which make up the study of the Carnegie Endowment for International Peace, previously cited.
[33] This argument is developed in detail in E. B. Haas, "The Comparative Study of the United Nations," *World Politics,* Vol. 12, No. 2 (January 1960).

But an effort must also be made to specify possible systemic changes after 1955; and the attitudes of revolutionary states with reference to accretions of autonomous UN powers is here a particularly sensitive yardstick. Relationships developed in resolving conflicts peacefully also furnish a useful index at the level of the system itself. They may hinge around the degree to which member states have internalized the purposes and procedures used to resolve one conflict, and are then prepared to apply them to new ones. Since this would vary with the importance attached to the conflict, with the satisfaction derived from the solution, the adequacy of the attendant communications network, and the number of roles served by the relationship, different patterns most likely can be found during various phases. An overall increase in involvement, irrespective of phase and type of state involved would provide excellent evidence of systemic growth.[34] But Robert North, the author of this approach, also cautions that the extent to which a member state relies on the notion of the external and internal "enemy" to resolve or channel domestic conflict, is likely to determine his responsiveness to the international modes of resolving conflicts. Dependence on "enemies" is a typical feature of revolutionary regimes; but would this imply declining responsiveness to the peaceful solution of conflicts in the next phase of the UN's life? It should be remembered that the history of the League of Nations and of the nineteenth-century Concert of Europe indicates that revolutionary regimes are insensitive to the pressures of the international environment in their preoccupation with domestic change. In contrast to conservative and status-quo oriented regimes, external regulative mechanisms were not accepted in the value systems of revolutionary elites and therefore had to be imposed by the use or the threat of force.

Dag Hammerskjold once described the UN as an "institutional system of coexistence" which might evolve toward a federative social system with its own public law if it is entrusted with new tasks which it alone can carry out, and if new environmental challenges are met by growing autonomy and delegated power, including the revitalization of portions of the Charter which have not yet been used.[35] One way of testing the evolutionary strength of the UN is to apply these yardsticks of development to the portion of the environment contributed by revolutionary regimes. If they prove responsive to the system's stimulus, growth is likely. The alternatives might be stated thus:

1. Successful institutionalization of interest politics will enhance the authority of the UN system and transform the environment by toning down the international aspects of the revolutionary behavior of certain member states. A growth in legitimacy would also follow.

2. The growing number and extreme demands of revolutionary member

---

[34] Robert G. North, Howard E. Koch, Jr., and Dina A. Zinnes, "The Integrative Functions of Conflict," *Journal of Conflict Resolution,* Vol. 4, No. 3, (September 1960), p. 366.

[35] Dag Hammerskjold, "Towards a Constitutional Order," in *Perspectives on Peace, op. cit.,* pp. 66–75.

states will substantially change the system during its next phase and perhaps destroy it.

3. New functional relationships will have the result of transforming the environment in toning down aspects of revolutionary behavior without concurrently contributing to the authority and legitimacy of the system itself.

III

Revolutionary states were exposed to the influence of international organization since 1919. If the revolutionary state simply withdraws from the system when national aims are in danger of being blunted by its rule, the problem of the system's transforming the environment can be simply dismissed. This, indeed, is what occurred in the League of Nations in relation to Japan, Italy, and Germany. Each pursued aims inconsistent with the rules of the system, and upon being stigmatized—however ineffectually— simply pursued the same aims outside the system. Withdrawal barely caused any soul-searching; the ideology and style of the revolutionary leadership in question was inconsistent with "international cooperation" in any case because of its insistence on national strength and self-sufficiency. The League's impact on the revolutionary environment was nil.

The same is true of the Soviet Union even though its role in the League was far more complex. Dallin interprets the Soviet role in Geneva as a species of popular front diplomacy designed to dovetail with the concomitant anti-Fascist work of the Comintern and aimed at maximizing Soviet security. While it certainly involved no doctrinal commitment to the rules of the Covenant, Soviet participation had the incidental consequence of seeking to strengthen the universal system. Not only did Moscow carry out the sanctions voted against Italy and Paraguay, but it actually sought to strengthen the legal powers of the League in the field of enforcement.[36] When contrasted with the earlier sweeping Russian denunciations of the League as "an alliance of world bandits against the proletariat," the Soviets then, as now, seemed to demonstrate a fine appreciation of systemic possibilities in *one* set of environmental circumstances. But the events of 1939 demonstrate that no internalization of rules was involved.

Since 1945 the international environment has undergone such drastic changes that a more functionally complex analysis is required to do it justice. The field of collective security will be examined first as a source of revolutionary initiatives, including the enforcement as well as the pacific settlement aspects.

---

[36] Alexander Dallin, *The Soviet View of the United Nations* (Cambridge: MIT Center for International Studies, August 1959), pp. 10–12, 18–19. Elliott Goodman, *The Soviet Design for a World State* (New York: Columbia University Press, 1960), pp. 383–85. Kathryn Davis, *The Soviets at Geneva* (Geneva: Librairie Kundig, 1934), p. 21.

Neutralism, not a specific revolutionary content, is responsible for the policy expectations regarding collective security put forth by Indonesia, Egypt, and Ghana. The monarchist regime in Egypt entertained great expectations of UN mediatory and armed help in its struggles with Britain and Israel, until it realized that the Great Power balance in the Security Council would give its policy little solace. At that point it turned to neutralism even before the advent of the Nasser regime and denounced UN collective security as "unjust power politics."[37] Whenever the East-West conflict dominates, these regimes seek to conciliate Moscow and Washington, and failing in this, abstain from endorsing any kind of collective action. Indonesia and Egypt gave no assistance to UN forces in Korea, opposed the crossing of the 38th parallel, and abstained on votes concerned with alleged atrocities by UN forces in Korea. Both abstained in the vote on the Assembly's critical report on Hungary, even though Indonesia had supported the creation of the Special Commission on Hungary. "The problem we have to solve here now," said the Indonesian delegate, "is how to diminish and if possible how to dissipate the distrust that exists among the opposing parties." But Indonesia was active in persuading Syria and Turkey not to press their differences to a vote in the Assembly in 1957. In cold war disputes, collective security implies exclusive dedication to conciliation by uncommitted powers and abstinence from any enforcement or investigatory action which would favor one side or the other. In disputes involving the colonial issue, however, energetic action is advocated, provided it can be carried out in such a way as to exclude the East-West conflict. The full panoply of UN techniques is then to be thrown into the fray, including troops and neutralization agreements negotiated under the auspices of the General Assembly, as indicated by Ghana's role in the settlement of the Lebanese-Jordanian crisis of 1958. The prejudice against armed action or energetic peaceful settlement, in short, does not apply to the type of dispute which concerns revolutionary nations most intimately.[38]

Soviet policy in the UN conforms more closely to specifically revolutionary

[37] *Egypt and the United Nations*, Report of a Study Group Set up by the Egyptian Society of International Law (New York: Manhattan Publishing Company, 1957). However, the passage to "active" or "positive" neutralism was an innovation of the military regime. While no doubt produced by the internal needs for status and prestige of Nasser, both in Egypt and in the Arab world, this concept implies an enhanced role for the UN in collective security and in disarmament negotiations as a means to prevent superpower summitry and to institutionalize the balancing role of uncommitted nations. Possible relationships between African neutralism and anomic conceptions of authority in new nations are explored by Francis X. Sutton, "Authority and Authoritarianism in the New Africa," *Journal of International Affairs,* Vol. 15, No. 1 (1961).

[38] Jan F. Triska and Howard E. Koch, "The Asian-African Nations and International Organization," *The Review of Politics,* Vol. 21, No. 2 (April 1959), pp. 450–51. Sydney D. Bailey, *The General Assembly* (New York: Praeger, 1960), p. 155. Consulate of Indonesia (San Francisco), *Indonesia's Voting Record in the United Nations.* Kwame Nkrumah, "African Prospect," *Foreign Affairs,* Vol. 37, No. 1 (October 1958), pp. 49–50.

expectations. In the early years of the UN the Soviet regime still regarded the Charter and its rules as legitimating the postwar status quo of Big Power dominance, institutionalized through a concert in which each major power wielded a veto, and collective security was to be practiced at the expense of smaller powers. Even though the Soviet Union took a very conservative position with respect to the powers of the UN and the absolute sway of the principle of national sovereignty, it relaxed these opinions in practice to permit the peaceful solution of the Corfu Channel and Iranian disputes in such a manner as to strengthen the authority of UN organs. The system seemed to assert itself even over revolutionary members.

This trend was reversed with the announcement in 1948 of the "two camps" doctrine. No concessions to systemic authority were permitted in the Greek, Korean, Berlin, and satellite peace-treaty cases. The UN became a holding operation in which the Soviets sought merely to protect the position of the "socialist camp" by blocking American action and by propaganda attacks, buttressed with constitutional arguments opposing majority decision making, functional expansion, and neutrality in administration. But the exceptions are vital: Whenever the interests of the Soviet Union happened to converge with those of the West (as in Palestine, Kashmir, Indonesia), the ad hoc concert produced by the international environment resulted in UN mediatory and enforcement action in which the Soviets ignored their own opposition to third-party intercession, commissions of investigation, Secretariat participation, and teams of military observers. But the outbreak of the Korean War proves that this pragmatic attitude of the Soviet Union involved no acceptance of the intrinsic legitimacy of the norms of the Charter.[39]

There are those who insist that the more recent active participation of the post-Stalinist Soviet leadership in the UN marks merely a tactical shift and no change in ultimate objectives: Weakness forced Stalin into an isolationist position toward the universal system, while strength and self-confidence propel Khrushchev into using the UN as a vehicle for actively advancing revolutionary aims.[40] While this may be true, it is not of direct importance to the problem of assessing a systemic impact on the environment; an upgrading of the UN in Soviet policy may bring with it unexpected consequences which must be accepted even by a revolutionary leadership if more basic Soviet aims are to be advanced. In any case, the settlement of the Korean crisis demonstrated for the first time Soviet responsiveness to the balancing efforts of the uncommitted Afro-Asian bloc, to be followed soon by the scrapping of the "two camps" theory. By granting the existence of an uncommitted bloc, a "zone of peace" was now interposed between East and West which had to be wooed in nonaggressive ways in

39 On this period see Alexander W. Rudzinski, "The Influence of the United Nations on Soviet Policy," *International Organization*, Vol. 5, No. 2 (May 1951), and Rupert Emerson and Inis L. Claude, "The Soviet Union and the United Nations," *ibid.*, Vol. 6, No. 1 (February 1952). Subsequent events have done nothing to change the validity of these interpretations .
40 Especially, Goodman, *op. cit.*, pp. 128–52.

order to assure the demise of capitalism without setting off nuclear war. In the process the UN was found useful for the propagation of the doctrine of competitive peaceful coexistence. In instances of outright challenge to the Soviet bloc, as in Hungary, the Stalinist tactics are revived; but in all other situations the new assessment has produced a thoroughly expediential attitude with respect to collective security in which balancing operations, involving conciliation, armed forces recruited from neutrals, and the intercession of the Secretary-General, are tolerated, even if not lauded. Korovin aptly summed up the current attitude with its invocation of the Charter on behalf of the new Soviet world view:

> ...the constant growth of Soviet economic and defensive might, of the moral authority of the USSR, of the merger of the entire socialist camp on the basis of proletarian internationalism and its growing strength, the support of its international policy by the partisans of peace throughout the world vividly testify to the fact that the realization of the democratic principles of the UN Charter becomes increasingly the unanimous demand of all peaceloving humanity.[41]

It is in this vein that the invocation of UN principles by the revolutionary government of Cuba must be understood. Its appeals to the Security Council and the General Assembly are devices of the cold war, to equate the policies of the United States with colonialism, and to rally the "democratic principles of the UN Charter" to the side of socialist and anti-colonial revolt. Although the revolutionary government of Bolivia has supported the Western conception of collective security, the growing link between Havana and Moscow has been accompanied by a Cuban attitude toward collective security which is identical with the Soviet position. The change in the international environment, which was ratified by the package deal on admission to UN membership in 1955, has been a source of self-confidence to the Communist bloc, inducing it to use UN institutions as a means for exacting recognition from the West of the legitimacy of the new status quo. In disputes not immediately invested with the aura of the cold war, at least this change in the environment has facilitated continuation of balancing as a mode of maintaining collective security, at the expense of concerted Big Power action and of permissive enforcement by one of them.

Policy aims in the context of collective security test the capacity of the UN system to deal with violent challenges to its norms. More commonly, however, demands for a change in international relations correspond to national policies falling short of recourse to war. Another test of the system's capacity, then, lies in its ability to facilitate peaceful change, especially the drastic demands put forward by revolutionary member states. Peaceful change, as distinguished from collective security, is any successful adjustment

41 Quoted in Dallin, *op. cit.*, p. 43. My interpretation owes much to Dallin's analysis of the post-1955 period. Dallin offers convincing evidence that the Soviet leadership made a reasoned decision in 1955 to profit from the tripolarization of power in the UN to upgrade the organization as a vehicle of national policy.

in the international status quo brought about before a specific "dispute" involving force or the threat of it arises; this adjustment is always made at the expense of certain reluctant member states and is due to pressure organized through the medium of parliamentary diplomacy.[42] Peaceful change so defined does not imply the complete absence of violence; it merely covers situations in which no formal interstate hostilities take place, but in which the bone of contention does arouse competing state postures.

The contrast between Suez and the Congo provides an example. In the Suez case, previously unsuccessful efforts to change the status quo non-violently (Nasser's unwillingness to satisfy France on Algeria and Britain on the continued neutrality of the Canal) resulted in an act of war, followed by pacific settlement and threatened enforcement measures voted and implemented by the General Assembly, thus restoring the *status quo ante bellum* by means of a balancing operation. The Congo, on the other hand, is an example of "preventive diplomacy," in which the UN, acting through the Secretary-General, sought to anticipate interstate rivalry by insulating the troublespot, and in so doing, "peacefully changing" the bubbling cauldron into a gently seething potion.[43]

This definition of peaceful change corresponds to the actual experience of international organizations and thus conflicts with generally held legal conceptions. It takes for granted that there is no international judicial order which can induce major political change by legal techniques. As Brierly put it:

> When a state claims...something which is not its legal right, something even which it knows it can have only by an alteration of the legal position, it is useless to suggest that it should submit the determination of its claim to legal decision. It knows beforehand that the answer of the law will be adverse; and that answer is precisely what it claims to have altered.[44]

Nor does it assume the existence of an international legislative order which might give substance to Article 14 of the UN Charter. Legislating territorial change would imply the willingness of the drafters of the Charter to forego the very status quo they wished to institutionalize in writing the norms. Only when the territorial change corresponds to a new generally held consensus, or when it follows from a previous decision by the large powers to wash their hands of an unresolvable issue not vital to them, can the UN successfully perform a legislative task. This happened only in the case of the Italian colonies.[45]

---

[42] I follow the definition of parliamentary diplomacy invented by Dean Rusk and applied by Philip C. Jessup in "Parliamentary Diplomacy: An Examination of the Legal Quality of the Rules of Procedure of Organs of the United Nations," *Recueil des Cours,* Vol. 89 (Leyden: Académie de Droit International, 1956).

[43] The difference is well developed by Inis L. Claude, "The United Nations and the Use of Force," *International Conciliation,* No. 532 (March 1961), p. 383.

[44] As quoted in Lincoln Bloomfield, "Law, Politics and International Disputes," *ibid.,* No. 516 (January 1958), p. 284.

[45] For interesting information concerning the lack of success of attempted UN

So defined, the most conspicuously successful area of peaceful change has been the disengagement of the Western powers from colonial responsibilities. The shrinking number of trust territories, the ever more intense examination by the General Assembly of colonial policy in other dependent areas, the instituting of colonial reform by Britain, France, Holland, the United States, and New Zealand in anticipation of UN criticism are a matter of record. Belgium and Portugal, less responsive in the past to parliamentary diplomacy, are now being subjected to its possibilities. In general, all Afro-Asian and Soviet-bloc and most Latin American countries have made up the UN majorities providing the necessary pressure, whether the regimes were revolutionary or not. Yet it is instructive to single out certain countries and the Congo crisis in order to discover whether anti-colonial demands emanating from revolutionary regimes were exceptionally extreme.

The Soviets have taken the most extreme position in consistently putting forward measures aiming at immediate independence for all dependent territories and blaming the Western powers for failing to cooperate. They have used the debates of the Trusteeship Council for this purpose alone; they justify their acceptance of the principle of trusteeship only because it "contributes to the struggle of the colonial peoples for freedom," and continue to stand "for the revolutionary method of solving the national-colonial question."[46] The African and Asian revolutionary regimes sympathize, as do Cuba and Mexico, but they are willing to tone down specific resolutions on concrete issues to permit gradualist compromises. Nkrumah is candid about his disregard for the legitimacy of the boundaries of UN trust territories when these stand in the way of pan-African aims. He and other revolutionary African leaders not only invoke the principles of the Charter in support of specific demands for ejecting European influence but play them down when it comes to future programs. For the coming years they stress sealing off the African continent and creating a regional system of pacific settlement, nonintervention and economic development.[47] In the

---

legislative change in the peaceful reunification of Korea prior to 1950, see Leon Gordenker, *The United Nations and the Peaceful Unification of Korea* (The Hague: Martinus Nijhoff, 1959). The same conclusion could be drawn from efforts "legislatively" to solve the Palestine issue prior to the outbreak of hostilities, since the resolution recommending partition was never implemented in its official form. But it should be noted that unwillingness to agree to peaceful change is not the exclusive privilege of revolutionary regimes. The Egyptian monarchy initiated the policy of closing the Suez Canal to Israel-bound ships. See Leo Gross, "Passage through the Suez Canal of Israel-Bound Cargo and Israel Ships," *American Journal of International Law,* Vol. 51, No. 3 (July 1957).

46 B. M. Shurshalov, as quoted in Dallin, *op. cit.,* p. 60.

47 K. Nkrumah, *Ghana* (New York: Thomas Nelson, 1957), pp. 258 and 261. See also Nkrumah's speech and the final *Declaration* of the Conference of Independent African States, Accra, April 22, 1958, especially Resolutions 1 and 5. All revolutionary regimes sought to influence the plebiscite in British Cameroons so as to result in union with a radical independent Cameroons rather than with a moderate Nigeria. They also favored the attainment of independence by French Cameroons under such conditions as to strengthen the outlawed opposition groups.

meantime they argue in favor of strengthening all conceivable agencies of the UN system which might bring closer the day when colonies will cease to exist: the constant use of UN-supervised plebiscites, UN inspections of progress toward independence, more UN follow-up on petitions, strengthening the Committee on Non-Self-Governing Territories, and requiring more and more detailed reports from the colonial powers under Article 73e of the Charter. Interestingly enough, this integrative aspect of the anti-colonial demands is supported by the Soviet Union, which otherwise opposes the creation of new UN institutions. It also has more support from Bolivia, Mexico, and Cuba than from traditional Latin American regimes.

The history of the Congo imbroglio, however, demonstrates the selectivity observed by revolutionary regimes in seeking to obtain satisfaction for national policy through UN action. The extreme of unilateralism is represented by the Soviet bloc. The Communist nations supported UN intervention, as long as such action unambiguously opposed Belgium and seemed to aid Lumumba. Soviet opposition to UN operations, which culminated in the attacks on the person and the institution of the Secretary-General, did not formally arise until the balance had shifted to Kasavubu. But approval of the early UN action had never precluded unilateral Soviet assistance to Congo factions. After the death of Lumumba, Moscow considered the Stanleyville regime of Antoine Gizenga as the only legitimate Congo government, even though the Leopoldville delegation had been seated in New York; drastic action against Belgium, the autonomous Katanga regime, and the Mobutu "mercenaries" were demanded. The failure of the UN to adopt sufficiently stringent resolutions was met by a Soviet refusal to participate in the financing of the Congo Operation. At the end of the fifteenth Session of the General Assembly, the Soviet bloc, alone among the revolutionary regimes, opposed the creation of the second Conciliation Commission, which, unlike the first, was to include European and American representatives; the Soviets also opposed the prompt convening of the Congo Parliament under UN protection and the UN-aided interfactional negotiations leading to a shoring up of the Kasavubu government.

Of the other revolutionary regimes, only Cuba and Guinea supported the Soviet extreme at all times. But up to March, 1961, Ghana, Mali, Indonesia, Morocco, and the United Arab Republic had taken the same qualified position in favor of UN intervention: They went along with it as long at it seemed to serve the pan-African end of creating a united Congo under Lumumbist rule and opposed it when the balance swung to the Kasavubu forces. At that point these leaders withdrew their contingents from the Congo or resigned from the first Conciliation Commission, thus demonstrating their displeasure with the policy of the Secretary-General. The United Arab Republic gave unilateral support to Gizenga, and Ghana openly intrigued against Mobutu.

Second thoughts seemed to arise among these governments when Hammerskjold continued to take an uncompromising position in favor of following a patient policy of supporting whatever regime in the Congo seemed to offer the greatest promise of unifying the country in such a manner as to exclude cold war rivalries. Despite its threats, Ghana never withdrew its sizeable forces and the United Arab Republic sought to act as a conciliator (together with Ceylon) in the Security Council debate between the United States and the Soviet Union. As the fifteenth Session drew to its close, all the non-Communist revolutionary regimes went along with the creation of the second Conciliation Commission—which they no longer control—and thus separated themselves publicly from Soviet Congo policy.[48] The peculiar international role played by Guinea, Mali, Ghana, and the United Arab Republic in the deliberations of the UN concerning the Congo and the three Cameroons suggests that the utilization of these potentially integrative techniques remained, at first, rigidly subordinated to the achievement of pan-African goals.[49] But when the dangers of such a course became apparent, they supported the continuation of the UN effort even when hopes for achieving the maximal program had to be abandoned.

Disarmament negotiations exemplify attempts at peacefully changing a serious international irritant which have so far been unsuccessful. Most of the recent substantive negotiations have been carried on outside the UN framework, with General Assembly debate merely creating a "moral climate" and concentrating on procedural aspects. The superpowers them-selves have sharply narrowed the areas of difference between them, but this must be attributed to the nature and perception of warfare, rather than to any specific systemic impulse which can be credited to the UN.[50] On the procedural question of whether the Soviet or the Western proposals for various disarmament commissions should be followed, the bulk of the revolutionary states has sided with the Soviet Union or abstained. Bolivia, however, regularly supports the United States; Mexico seeks to mediate and the Cuban position shifted in 1960 from unswerving support for the

---

[48] This summary is based on the debates concerning the following resolutions: S/4369, S/4383, S/4386, S/4404, S/4426, S/4425, S/4453, S/4494, S/4519, S/4523, S/4525, A/L.292/rev 1, A/L.294, A/L.293, A/L.319 Rev 2, A/L.322 Rev 1, S/4578, S/4579, A/L.331 Rev 1, A/L.332, S/4625, S/4741, S/4733 Rev 1, S/4740. I have also drawn heavily on the Secretary-General's statement of December 7, 1960, embodying his comments on docs. S/4573 and S/4571.

[49] See Immanuel Wallerstein, "Pan-Africanism as Protest," in *The Revolution in World Politics*, ed. Morton A. Kaplan, for the explanation of how territorial pan-American goals fit into the revolutionary ideology of negritude and independent national modernization. However, the "conservative" new states of the Brazzaville grouping, though not uniformly in sympathy with pan-African principles, followed a course in the UN's handling of the Congo which was every bit as expediential in motivation as was the attitude of the "revolutionary" Casablanca grouping. When UN intervention seemed to protect a confederal solution to the Congo crisis they praised the organiza-tion; when, however, the intent of the intervention seemed to be the shoring up of Lumumba, the Brazzaville nations denounced UN action as interference with national sovereignty. See the excellent analysis by Robert C. Good, "Congo Crisis: The Role of the New States," *Neutralism* (Washington, D.C.: Washington Center of Foreign Policy Research, 1961), pp. 1–46.

[50] For a thoughtful analysis of the growth of agreement, see Philip E. Jacob, "The Disarmament Consensus," *International Organization,* Vol. 14, No. 2 (Spring 1960). My summary of UN discussions is based on General Assembly disarmament debates since 1955.

West to equally fervid alignment with Moscow. All revolutionary states greeted Khrushchev's general disarmament plan with favor, whereas in previous years they had studiously avoided taking sides on the merits of rival proposals and had merely prodded the superpowers to continue negotiating, though Ghana, Morocco, Mali, and the United Arab Republic moderated their stance by stressing the mediation of uncommitted nations. Again, on the matter of suspending nuclear tests, in general, and preventing the French from going ahead with their plans, in particular, most revolutionary states espoused the extreme disarmament position also taken by the Soviet Union. To the extent that disarmament negotiations are at all influenced by the process of parliamentary diplomacy, the pressure of the revolutionary countries bolsters any proposal which looks promising even if the inspection provisions do not meet with Washington's approval. An eventual softening of the Western position on this point is likely, without implying an accretion of new powers of inspection and supervision to the UN.

The UN may gain nothing from disarmament, and it will soon lose the field of action represented by the dissolution of colonial empires. What areas for potential peaceful change through the medium of parliamentary diplomacy remain which may prevent the system from losing its scope? Controls in outer space, supervision of space exploration, sovereignty over the moon, or at least, the preparation of legal rules for national space activity are obvious examples, even though little progress has been made so far. The preparation of an international investment code and a multipartite system for protecting foreign property in newly independent territories come to mind. The permanent neutralization and administration of inclement but vital territories, such as Antarctica, is such an activity. Whenever a common sense of danger or uncertainty inhibits national action, the systemic ground rules of UN diplomacy are given the environmental scope for introducing change. Science and technology are more likely to furnish the stimulus in the future than are national self-determination and boundary disputes.[51]

Multilateral action for technical assistance and economic development comes closest to meeting rigorous criteria for a general UN "consensus," as constituting a recognized "universal interest." It has not always been so. Prior to the period of Afro-Asian ascendancy in the UN, the economic development issue had split the membership into three blocs; but by 1955 a cumulative train of events had been unleashed which resulted in ever growing accretions of institutional and financial authority in UN hands. Expansion of the system's task was due to the fact that the Western-developed nations gave in, up to a point, to the demands of the under-

---

[51] Examples for fields of action offering opportunities for peaceful change by quasi-legislative action are given in C. Wilfred Jenks, *The Common Law of Mankind* (London: Stevens, 1958), Chaps. 7, 8, and 9. Commission to Study the Organization of Peace, *Developing the United Nations*, 13th Report (January 1961), pp. 35–40. Lincoln Bloomfield, *The United Nations and U.S. Foreign Policy* (Boston: Little, Brown, 1960), pp. 157–86.

developed nations and that the Soviet bloc dropped its absolute condemnation of UN assistance.

Yet, with the exception of changing Soviet policy, little can be demonstrated about specific concerns of revolutionary regimes in policy aims relating to economic development. All underdeveloped member states stood for a maximum of multilateral aid, free from strings, and dispensed by international agencies which would be dominated by their votes. Revolutionary, as well as traditional, oligarchies, socialist and conservative regimes, called for the Expanded Program of Technical Assistance, SUNFED, the International Finance Corporation, and the Special Fund. Indeed, the striking feature is the willingness of revolutionary regimes to give up certain cherished aims in the process of finding compromises acceptable to the developed nations.[52]

Mexico, despite its intense nationalist suspicion of foreign capital, strongly supported IFC. The same is true of Egypt, Indonesia, and Bolivia. These revolutionary nations took the initiative in proposing the creation of the Special Fund and expressed their willingness to subordinate themselves to a strong managing director and a qualified majority voting formula in the Governing Council.[53]

Soviet conduct is more complex. Until 1954 the policy of the Soviet Union in UN economic agencies was entirely negative: It blamed underdevelopment on imperialism and opposed multilateral aid as a camouflaged device for perpetuating colonial dependence, insisting instead on the wholesale application of socialist techniques; Soviet speeches and resolutions were confined to attacking Western economic moves, especially the strategic embargo, and to making propaganda charges. Stalin's death changed all this. With the offer of Soviet contributions to EPTA came the recognition of the propriety of multilateral aid. Suggestions for the creation of a new universal trade organization were made, while some of the satellites offered to join GATT. Soviet participation in the work of the economic commissions for Europe and for Asia and the Far East grew cooperative, so much so that the Soviet Union offered to contribute to the Mekong River Project. Consistent with this change, Moscow then proceeded to support the creation of SUNFED, IFC, and the Special Fund. In procedural and administrative disputes with the Technical Assistance Board and the Secretariat over the degree of bilateralism to be permitted in the distribution of the Soviet contributions to these agencies, the Soviet position was invariably

---

[52] Benjamin Higgins and Guy Pauker, "Economic Aspects of the Asian-African Conference and its Aftermath," *Ekonomi dan Keuanqan Indonesia* (Nos. 5–6, 1955), pp. 16–17. Oscar Lewis, "Mexico Since Cardenas," in *Social Change in Latin America Today*, pp. 306–307. B. E. Matecki, "Establishment of the International Finance Corporation: A Case Study," *International Organization*, Vol. 10, No. 2 (May 1956). Robert E. Elder and Forrest D. Murden, "Economic Cooperation: Special United Nations Fund for Economic Development" (New York: Woodrow Wilson Foundation, 1954).

[53] See the revealing case study on SUNFED and the Special Fund in John G. Hadwen and Johan Kaufmann, *How United Nations Decisions Are Made* (Leyden: A. W. Sythoff, 1960), pp. 85–122.

overruled—and yet the Soviet Union continued to participate on a modest scale. Bilateral aid is also offered by the Soviets within the confines of UN discussions and some commentators suspect that it is the long-range policy of Moscow to manœuver the UN aid effort into a universal bilateralist scheme. But in failing to achieve this, the Soviets as well as other revolutionary regimes have so far accommodated themselves to the evolving rules of the UN system.[54]

Aspirations concerning economic development are common to all types of regimes and even revolutionary governments will swallow aspects of international control in this realm which would otherwise be an anathema. Hence, it is instructive to contrast the policy aims of revolutionary regimes in the field of the international protection of human rights with economic development. The Soviet Union, prior to 1953, strongly supported all general declarations and specific legal texts affirming and defining human rights, especially the rights to national self-determination and protection of natural resources against alien control. But it equally strongly opposed all efforts to provide even a minimal UN machinery for enforcing these rights or reporting on their implementation. A subtle change crept into this position after 1953: Soviet delegates proved quite willing to approve the creation of commissions of inquiry to probe into situations damaging to the West but continued to oppose these when they were to deal with allegations relating to the Soviet bloc. The mellowing of opposition to UN institutional competence in the human rights field went hand in hand with some disagreement among Soviet jurists as to the degree of jurisdiction international judicial bodies might enjoy over national sovereignty. At the same time the Soviet Union consented to participation in several efforts by the International Labor Organization to probe the existence of trade union rights in Russia.[55]

Other revolutionary nations show little evidence of an increasing willingness to submit to UN jurisdiction. To be sure, they all espouse the Universal Declaration of Human Rights and have supported the drafting of some of the most far-reaching clauses of the two Covenants. Yet the emphasis is uniformly not on civil and political rights of individuals, but on the collective right of national self-determination, in its political and economic

[54] Dallin, *op. cit.*, p. 63. Alvin Z. Rubinstein, "Soviet Policy Toward Underdeveloped Areas in the Economic and Social Council," *International Organization,* Vol. 9, No. 2 (May 1955); "Soviet Policy in ECAFE: A Case Study of Soviet Behavior in International Economic Organizations," *ibid.*, Vol. 12, No. 4 (Autumn 1958). R. L. Allen, "United Nations Technical Assistance: Soviet and East European Participation," *ibid.*, Vol. 11, No. 4 (Autumn 1957). Harold K. Jacobson, "The Soviet Union, the UN and World Trade," *Western Political Quarterly,* Vol. 11, No. 3 (September 1958).

[55] E. R. Goodman, "The Cry of National Liberation: Recent Attitudes Toward National Self-Determination," *International Organization,* Vol. 14, No. 1 (Winter 1960). J. A. Armstrong, "The Soviet Attitude Toward UNESCO," *ibid.*, Vol. 8, No. 2 (May 1954). Dallin, *op. cit.*, pp. 45–47. Dallin and Armstrong suggest that the post-1953 Soviet interest in human rights and international intellectual contacts is connected with the Soviet hope of turning all UN agencies into a pro-Communist front organization.

aspects. The African states use the Declaration to legitimize *national* freedom but ignore its provisions when it comes to the rights of *tribal* groups. Universal rights are invoked against present colonialism but untrammeled national sovereignty or regional cohesion is held out for future developments. UN commissions are created to inquire into the colonial aspect, but the revolutionary states vote against the establishment of commissions to define terms carefully, to investigate conditions of national development, or to protect tribal populations living within metropolitan territories. The very intensification of the attachment to nonintervention implies a hardening of opposition among revolutionary nations to international supervision of private and group rights, while the economic and social programs of these regimes make respect for such rights a matter of considerable doubt. When, in 1959, the General Assembly voted to condemn the Peking regime for a violation of the Universal Declaration of Human Rights in Tibet, the bulk of the revolutionary states abstained; the Soviet Union voted "no"; Indonesia opposed the inclusion of the item on the agenda; but Bolivia, Mexico, and Cuba voted in the affirmative.[56] While policy expectations of the UN system correspond to permanent national aims in the field of economic development, they merely mirror a temporary concern in the area of human rights, thus being only an aspect of the current phase in the history of the system.

This survey of the policy aims of revolutionary states has demonstrated only that their demands are neither rigid nor uniform, that they respond to the give-and-take of parliamentary diplomacy, and that many of their aspirations do not differ from those of conservative regimes. Therefore, the emergence of new common interests in the realms of outer space and in the prevention of limited wars among uncommitted states may yet give the UN new tasks in the next phase of its life, which may facilitate a balancing process involving different functions and different balancers than in the current phase.

IV

The present phase in the life of the UN system, which began in 1955, is earmarked by an interregional and interfunctional balancing process. The policies of the system were produced as a result of continuous compromises among regional blocs which differ in internal cohesion with respect to specific UN functions. Functional differentiation, in turn, explains how

[56] See the resolutions of the All-African People's Conference, Accra, *op. cit.*, for the contrast between domestic exclusiveness and UN legitimacy for anti-colonialism alone. A similar case for Latin America is made by Martin Travis, "The Political and Social Basis for the Latin American Doctrine of Nonintervention," *Proceedings of the American Society of International Law,* Vol. 53 (1959). The Tibetan case is discussed in Bailey, *op. cit.*, p. 248ff. The fact that a number of Western democracies and Latin American oligarchical regimes with minority and human rights problems also abstained suggests that many members were unwilling to set a precedent.

the mediating role can be assumed by varying balancers and how stalemates can be avoided by shifting majorities. In some situations the mediating role is played so well and national aims are so interrelated that significant policy measures can be produced by almost unanimous votes. Compromises involve not only concessions by one bloc to another, but also feature bargaining on the basis of concessions among functions: increasing economic assistance and support for decolonization efforts are demanded in return for support on questions relating to collective security and peaceful change. Typical policies of the current phase, then, have included the cumulative creation of new UN economic aid institutions and procedures, a growing commitment to peaceful decolonization, and the protection of human rights in Africa and Asia, as well as institutionalized balancing through conciliation, police forces, and Secretariat intercession in crises involving an immediate threat to peace.

Policy aims contributed by revolutionary regimes in this pattern were examined above. While the imperatives of symmetry would be neatly satisfied if all the non-Communist revolutionary regimes were to be grouped as "balancing" states, this is obviously not the situation. If the Western bloc represents the "thesis" of the status quo and the Soviets the "antithesis" of change, revolutionary regimes may be found on both dialectical extremes as well as in the neutralist "synthesizing" force. We must now assess the impact of the system's policies on the revolutionary environment, but we must let the chips fall where they belong. Our question is simply: Has the balancing process resulted in a change in the demands and expectations of revolutionary states so as to demonstrate responsiveness to the system? If so, a revolutionary environment clearly need not destroy an institutionally static system based on imperfectly internalized norms.

Soviet conduct in relation to the collective security issue illustrates this conclusion. It is impossible to demonstrate that the basic Soviet policy of advancing a gradual world revolution toward an international socialist and Communist society has been abandoned; therefore, the UN has not influenced the substance of Moscow's policy aims. On the contrary, a careful study of Soviet attitudes toward international relations and systems makes clear that a policy of peaceful but competitive coexistence, conceived as a means of combat, has always been favored at least by some of Russia's leaders. Soviet participation in a variety of international systems, some of them hostile to Soviet aims, was always considered feasible in an international environment felt to be transitional on the road to socialist internationalism.[57]

Membership in the UN system, however, has definitely influeaned the tactical manner in which the Soviet Union participates in world affairs. All the early pronouncements concerning the sacrosanct nature of national

---

[57] Julian Towster, "The Dogma of Communist Victory," *Current History* (November 1959). For a collection of statements supporting this conclusion see also *Khrushchev on the Shifting Balance of World Forces,* U.S. Senate, 86th Congress, 1st Session, Doc. No. 57 (September 1959).

sovereignty, big power unanimity, and the dominance of the Security Council have been downgraded during the current phase of UN life. Despite Soviet hostility to international police and enforcement measures, the Soviet delegate merely abstained on votes creating such forces for Suez and the Congo; even though the veto is still cherished, little effort was made to protest the Security Council's brushing aside of the double veto cast in the Laotian crisis of 1959; when it suited the Soviet purpose, the delegation was quite willing to make use of the General Assembly and the Secretariat; finally, whenever the immediate military security of the Soviet bloc itself was not at stake, the Soviet Union seemed eager to mobilize the UN for collective security operations.[58]

There has been no internalization of norms. The quality of Soviet UN diplomacy has become more sophisticated and self-reliant; its style of participation, far from being defensive, is now self-confident. To that extent, the rigid rejection of institutional evolution has been abandoned and a tactical responsiveness to systemic forces is now evident. But this has been true of a period when the peaceful coexistence phase of Soviet thought happens to coincide with the decolonization phase of the UN. Certainly, a responsiveness to systemic influences is suggested by the continued membership of the Soviet Union in the UN even during the height of the phase of American dominance, though Zhdanov and his supporters seem to have advocated withdrawal.[59] Reciprocal converging interests with the West and with the uncommitted nations have clearly been experienced, thus explaining the continued stability of the system during the current phase. But the evaporation of the convergences may also imply a passing of the phase. As long as systemic rules have not been internalized, but merely "learned" for short-range tactical purposes, the revolutionary environment remains as volatile as before.

Ghana, Indonesia, and Morocco have shown themselves to be far more responsive to systemic influences on matters connected with peace and security. Even Egypt has complied with the bulk of the UN decisions connected with the liquidation of the Suez crisis, though not without hard bargaining and at little cost to itself. They have appreciated that collective security operations conducted by balancing states can stop local wars and confine the East-West conflict. Again, we cannot claim that long-range objectives have been abandoned, but short-range responsiveness to systemic pressure is pronounced enough to promise its outliving the current phase.

The difference in responsiveness between Communist and non-Communist revolutionary regimes is equally patent in activities relating to peaceful

---

[58] On Laos see Leo Gross in *American Journal of International Law*, Vol. 53, No. 1 (January 1960), pp. 118–30. The other examples are discussed in Dallin, *op. cit.*, pp. 49–51, 84, 90–94, 99–100. But it should be noted that the Soviet Union refused to contribute to the maintenance of these forces. Other revolutionary regimes declining to support UNEF include Bolivia, Cuba, Iraq, Mexico, and Egypt. All the other African and Asian revolutionary regimes have faithfully paid their contributions. Details in Bailey, *op. cit.*, p. 216ff.

[59] Dallin, *op. cit.*, pp. 33–38.

change. Soviet policy has been unflinching in opposing all formal procedural steps for strengthening the executive, legislative, or judicial competence of the UN in providing centralized, third-party dominated solutions. Verbal demands for UN measures in South Africa or Spain have not been accompanied with institutional suggestions. Operations in the Congo were denounced as soon as they turned against the Soviet-sponsored regime. UN activities in the realms of disarmament, outer space, and other "frontier" areas of possibly converging interests were never supported unless the Soviet substantive position was also accepted. In short, there has been no increasing responsiveness to the possibilities of peaceful change offered by the UN system.

Other revolutionary regimes have been perfectly willing to respond to and initiate measures of peaceful change in problem areas in which they had as yet no direct interest. With respect to disarmament and UN controls in space roadblocks, international agreement came from the nations with an established interest or policy, but not from Asia, Africa, or Latin America. But it should be noted that much less responsiveness was in evidence in the efforts of the International Atomic Energy Agency to establish rules for inspecting the utilization by revolutionary regimes of fissile materials. Here, after all, is an area in which even underdeveloped nations have already acquired a rudimentary vested interst. If systemic expansion through peaceful change is to take place in these frontier fields, the current phase must be exploited before a changed international environment will make task expansion impossible here too.

Decolonization, it would appear at first blush, is the prime field of peaceful change commanding the responsiveness of revolutionary regimes. This is an accurate impression insofar as they invoke the phrases of the Charter and of the Universal Declaration of Human Rights to dislodge the colonial powers and to make use of international debate and supervision to implement the provisions of the trusteeship system. But the manipulative inspiration of this attitude stands revealed in the limelight of the Congo crisis, leading to the conclusion that the dominance of instrumental motives has led to no internalization of systemic rules. Ghana, for example, joined the other African revolutionary regimes in threatening, at the Casablanca Conference, to take "appropriate action" unilaterally unless the UN supported the Lumumbist forces. Nkrumah softened this position later to the extent of seeking to channel the same demands through the UN Operation, provided the Congo were made an all-African responsibility, with the independent African states acting as the "agent" of the UN, much as the United States did in Korea.[60] This still implied a reduction in the powers of the Secretary-General and an indirect endorsement of the Soviet position with respect to supporting the Gizenga regime. Far from acting

---

[60] On the Casablanca Conference see Conference of Heads of African States, Casablanca, January 3–7, 1961, "Declaration Concerning the Situation in the Congo." Also Kwame Nkrumah, speech at General Assembly session, March 7, 1961. When the Osagyefo took the oath of office as President of Ghana, he swore "that the union of Africa should be striven for by every lawful means and, when attained, should be faithfully preserved..." *External Affairs* (September 1960), p. 221.

as neutral balancers, the Casablanca powers made themselves the mouthpiece, under "African" auspices, of the Soviet extreme position; Liberia, Tunisia, and Ceylon—none of them revolutionary nations—acted as the classical balancers. If the search for an African Personality persuaded Guinea, Ghana, Mali, and Morocco to subordinate the processes of the world organization to their specific aims, Ghana at least did not carry its regional focus to the extreme of withdrawing its forces from the Congo. Nasser's United Arab Republic, however, did precisely that, while undertaking unilateral assistance to Gizenga. Egyptian support for UN operations aiming at peaceful change was strictly calculated on the basis of its convergence with Cairo's policy of penetrating Africa. Nasser was far less inclined to assume a balancing role in the Congo, as compared to Nkrumah, and has shown no interest in maximizing the peaceful-change capacity of the UN. The policy of revolutionary Egypt in relation to international institutions is as inconsistently imperialistic as its general foreign policy.[61]

Clearly, not all revolutionary regimes are equally unresponsive to the possibilities of institutionalized peaceful change procedures. Few of them approach the extreme of the Soviet Union, as even Indonesia might accept a temporary trusteeship status for West Irian. But, as we can demonstrate no change in national policy, responsiveness is an ad hoc phenomenon which has not predictably stabilized the environment.

While expediential considerations have imposed a certain amount of responsiveness upon most revolutionary regimes in the realms of collective security and peaceful change, the impact of the UN is much more striking when we deal with economic development. There the very conditions of the revolutionary environment, when impinging upon one another in the context of multifunctional demands, have produced a massive systemic response in which almost all member states have acquiesced, even the Soviet bloc. The impropriety of indefinitely and irrevocably opposing demands for dealing with the revolution of rising expectations has been recognized by all types of nations at the UN, with the result that parliamentary diplomacy has here produced a genuine new consensus, with an expanded organizational task. To judge by the policy of Bolivia, Egypt, and Indonesia, new nations find it much easier to respond to "capitalistic" development concepts when advanced by international agencies than under other auspices, and consequently tone down earlier policy aims in the field of development. The impact on the Soviet Union, though less marked, is still considerable if we keep in mind the unqualified insistence on "socialism" as recently as 1953.

If we are to believe speeches and conference declarations, the devotion to the universal protection of human rights felt by revolutionary regimes is much greater than such devotion elsewhere. The context in which such sentiments are expressed was explored above; here responsiveness and internalization of the procedures and values involved are under scrutiny. The Soviet Union has flatly asserted that the rights envisaged in the

---

[61] My assessment of UAR foreign policy objectives and their "inconsistent imperialism," is based on Wheelock, *op. cit.*, especially pp. 223–57, 270–82.

Covenants exist already on its territory so that no special enforcement machinery is necessary. Guinea's Constitution endorses the Universal Declaration by name and enumerates, as binding on herself, the rights there defined. Apparently, this example is followed only by those African territories which owe their status to UN action, but not by Ghana, Mali, or Morocco.[62] Dedication to the UN as the instrument for effectively enforcing human rights cannot be assumed any more than devotion to institutionalized processes of peaceful change controlled by third parties. Mere repetition of verbal sincerity has had no discernible impact on the environment.

As far as the international style of revolutionary regimes is concerned, the balancing politics of the UN's third phase can hardly be credited with having toned down manifestations of truculence and impatience. The fifteenth Session of the General Assembly would seem to represent a high point in overt instances of revolutionary style. But to view the systemic impact on style purely in terms of parliamentary behavior is to miss another possible pattern of responsiveness to institutionalized diplomacy, the attitude toward international law as a means of peaceful change.[63] Assuming, at least for the sake of argument, that the Western powers—as the representatives of the international status quo—took the provisions of the Charter with respect to legal means of peacefully changing the norms of the international system literally in 1945, it is easy to demonstrate that certain key revolutionary regimes did not. Communist unwillingness so submit to any kind of UN judicial process is well known, an attitude shared quite obviously by Nasser.[64]

But just as the Western powers, in their inability to mobilize the law consistently in support of the old status quo, have displayed a more and more instrumental attitude toward UN judicial institutions, the doctrinal opposition of revolutionary regimes to this aspect of the system has weakened.[65] This is especially true of the Soviets. The sharp contrast

[62] For details see Egon Schwelb, "The Influence of the Universal Declaration of Human Rights on International and National Law," *Proceedings...*, *op. cit.*, pp. 223–28. Court decisions citing the Declaration were handed down in West Germany, Belgium, Italy, United States, and the Philippines.

[63] Attitudes toward international law are deliberately treated as aspects of "style" rather than as a rubric of peaceful change because of the predominantly verbal role of UN legal discussion. Thus far, at any rate, judicial considerations have figured more as an aspect of propaganda inputs than as a constituent of an institutionalized pattern of outputs.

[64] Nasser, when asked why he did not wait until 1956 for the natural expiration of the 1936 treaty on the Suez Canal, maintained: "We are quite aware that this treaty wouldn't just expire. The British would take it before some international tribunal and obtain permission for prolonging it. We smaller nations haven't much confidence in these tribunals, which we know full well to be nothing more than courts run by and for the big nations." J. and S. Lacouture, *Egypt in Transition* (London: Methuen, 1958), p. 459.

[65] The limited role of the International Court of Justice is reviewed and explained by Shabtai Rosenne, *The International Court of Justice* (New York: Central Book Company, 1957) and Max Sorensen, "The International Court of Justice: Its Role in Contemporary International Relations," *International Organization*, Vol. 14, No. 2 (Spring 1960).

between Communist and Western attitudes toward international law, which is so often pointed out, applies only if we compare *Soviet practice* with *Western doctrine,* a facile and meaningless juxtaposition. If Soviet practice is compared with that of the West, the differences are much less pronounced. The "law habit" of the West—in international relations—is not much better developed than the Soviets': Both sides observe and violate their treaty and customary obligations when it suits their policy purposes. More striking still, when we examine lower-level legal habits with reference to very specific fields, rather than focus on central points of legal doctrine, the Soviet practice has increasingly approached that of most states in the last decade.[66]

Differences are narrowed further if we compare *Soviet doctrine* with *Western practice.* The early Soviet insistence on the role of treaties as the sole source of international obligations has given way to an instrumentally motivated recognition of custom and general principles of law as sometimes useful, just as the West has increasing turned to treaties: By now both postures have met somewhere between these extremes. Western legal doctrine is increasingly moving in the direction of a less absolute and more instrumentally oriented view of the origin and purpose of norms.[67] And as William Welch has shown in an admirable survey of Soviet legal doctrine concerning the position of regional arrangements, these are viewed essentially as the West interprets its military pacts: Both postures are explicable easily on the basis of the search for immediate military security and the desire to manipulate the rules of the UN Charter so as to sanctify one's own treaties and castigate the opponent's. In the process, the arguments have become very much alike.[68] To the extent, then, that revolutionary and status-quo powers have turned to the UN to legitimate their national policies, they have responded to the systemic forces they invoke by relaxing their earlier legal styles.

Observations of the impact of the system on the revolutionary environment and assessments of changes in revolutionary style do not exhaust the analytic means at our disposal for determining whether the universal system is mastering its impatient members or whether they are destroying the system. The evidence is uneven with respect to the moderation of revolu-

[66] On this point see the articles by Oliver J. Lissitzyn and John N. Hazard, in *Proceedings...*, *op. cit.*

[67] On the evolution of Soviet thought on the sources of international law, see Jan F. Triska and Robert M. Slusser, "Treaties and Other Sources of Order in International Relations: The Soviet View," *American Journal of International Law,* Vol. 52, No. 4 (October 1958), especially pp. 724–26. An Egyptian lawyer has argued that the revolutionary regime in Cairo has abandoned the doctrine of the two *dars* in Islamic legal thought, including the concept of the *jihad,* and thus reapproached a universal law which recognizes an identity of norms governing the relations among Muslims and non-Muslims. Saba Habachy, in *Proceedings...*, *op. cit.,* p. 61. The Western position on the reorientation of international law is prominently represented by Myres McDougal and his associates.

[68] William Welch, "Soviet Commitments to Collective Action," in A. Wolfers, ed., *Alliance Policy in the Cold War* (Baltimore: Johns Hopkins, 1959).

tionary demands, and it may be doubted that the rapprochement of legal styles is of permanent significance. But if we can establish that the system itself has grown in the legitimacy it enjoys in the eyes of its members and in the authority it exercises over them, then the inconsistent impact of UN decisions on member state expectations is not a fatal blow to the survival of the organization.

We may conclude that the system proper has increased in importance at the expense of the states which make up the environment, if cumulative institutional decisions continue to be regarded as "legitimate" even by revolutionary regimes. The criterion of legitimacy is the regular invocation of UN Charter principles in advocacy and debate by those holding out for more UN action as well as by those who seek to block such action (the balancer and the aggressor both invoke the Charter regularly), *plus* the demonstrated willingness to expand the UN's task in order to implement the Charter principles put forward. What is especially significant here, of course, is the willingness of states to support eventually new organizational tasks which they had initially opposed. "Authority," by contrast, implies no acceptance of the rightness of specific organizational action. The "authority" of the system might be said to increase if member states carry out decisions even if they did not advocate them, if they continue to oppose them in principle, and if they do not link the continued exercise of the task to the invocation of Charter principles.

The growth in legitimacy enjoyed by the UN should be observable in the utterances of prominent statesmen associated with the Afro-Asian Solidarity Conference, a grouping particularly useful for the study of revolutionary leadership since it tends to serve as an international front organization for the United Arab Republic as well as for the Communist bloc. Indeed there seems to have been a considerable amount of tugging between Cairo and Moscow as to who should manipulate the Conference.[69] Typical causes which the Conference espouses, apart from a general condemnation of "imperialism" and "colonialism" in terms which conform to the Communist line, include the banning of nuclear weapons testing in Africa, complete disarmament, the Stockholm World Peace Council, the Japanese drive against the United States Security Treaty, the return of Okinawa to Japan, the elimination of all foreign military bases everywhere, Castro's Cuba, and the complete rejection of any Western influence whatsoever in recently "liberated" countries, including economic and military ties voluntarily accepted by the new governments. Indeed, the Conference shows a marked consistency in serving as the mouthpiece of the most extreme anti-Western strands of opinions to be found in Africa and Asia: the UPC in the Cameroons as opposed to the Ahidjo government, the FLN in Algeria, the opposition parties in Somalia against the Somali Youth League government, Lumumba against Kasavubu, etc.[70]

---

69 Wheelock, *op. cit.*, pp. 266–68.
70 For a complete survey of such causes see *Afro-Asian Bulletin,* Vol. 2, Nos. 11–12 (September–October, 1960).

Legitimacy appears to receive a strong prop when the demands of states and of independence movements invoke the phraseology of the Charter in connection with the drive against colonialism. To be sure, such invocations are heard ad nauseam when they are useful in supporting the argument for independence. But the Charter principles are held to be violated unless "freedom" conforms to the international revolutionary mystique:

> A nation cannot attain real independence if there are foreign troops stationed in its independent territory and if it is a member of an organization controlled by an imperialist State if it joins military pacts within imperialist power. [sic][71]

Therefore, the legitimacy of the UN operation in the Congo was vehemently denied when it appeared that the "unlawful activity of Mr. Hammerskjold" [sic] proved unsuccessful in bolstering Lumumba.[72] On the occasion of the fifteenth anniversary of the UN, the Conference Secretariat again "hails all the efforts aiming at the application of the principles of the Charter, such as for example, those of the neutralist and Afro-Asian countries," but also noted that "the enchantment vanished. The cases are in fact very rare when the UN served the cause of peace and the liberty of peoples."[73] One African spokesman flatly asserted that whenever the pan-African variety of nationalism fails to win endorsement in New York, the American imperialists succeed in subverting the organization and its Secretary-General. He also argued that multilateral economic aid under UN auspices is to be resisted in such circumstances because "this would only help in perpetuating economic neo-colonialism [sic]."[74] Yet is should be noted that the Conference Secretary-General, Youssef El Sebai, urged that:

> ...because of the pressing need for the United Nations in the present circumstances, Afro-Asian peoples are determined to see that the World Organization does not collapse. It is our duty to consolidate it by every possible means, and to endeavour to enable it to play its great role in world affairs, uninfluenced by pressure or intimidation, for the sole benefit of all peoples of the world, for justice and for peace.[75]

Clearly, the failure to achieve full endorsement for revolutionary objectives in New York is reflected in a continued overt denial of legitimacy. But the ambivalence of El Sebai's statement and the support Ghana still gives the UN in the Congo warrant the conclusion that eventual legitimacy may still develop either because the UN is a useful Soviet front in some future crisis, or because it still offers the safest way out of a dangerous situation. But it should be noted that the second part of the criterion of legitimacy,

---

[71] *Ibid.*, p. 32.
[72] *Ibid.*, p. 60.
[73] *Ibid.*, p. 61.
[74] Osende Afana, "Consolidating Afro-Asian Solidarity," *ibid.*, p. 7.
[75] Youssef El Sebai, "Afro-Asian Solidarity Marches On," *ibid.*, pp. 4–5.

consent to an expanded UN task, has been lacking as far as the Soviet bloc and several African revolutionary regimes are concerned.

Some precision is needed at this point. The two criteria of legitimacy have clearly been satisfied in the case of the expanded UN task in economic development. Charter invocation, equally clearly, has not been accompanied by task expansion with respect to collective security, human rights, and most aspects of peaceful change. Decolonization, however, has conferred increasing legitimacy on the UN even if the reservations explicit in the activities of the Afro-Asian Solidarity Conference are borne in mind. Plebiscites have been held and their results implemented; Trusteeship Council and General Assembly injunctions concerning steps for achieving self-government and independence have been carried out; groups and individuals persecuted by the colonial administrations have achieved respectability and even power as a result of UN intervention. While the Soviet Union, Cuba, Guinea, and Mali have denied the UN full legitimacy over the Congo, they have acquiesced in it with respect to other colonial episodes, thus altering an earlier, more intransigent position. But even if decolonization has conferred increasing legitimacy on the world organization, the passing of the colonial phase makes it doubtful that this acquisition will be readily transferred to new tasks.

Growth in authority, rather than in legitimacy, is the most striking aspect of UN history in its current phase—even at the expense of certain revolutionary regimes. This growth is demonstrable by observing the accretions of certain UN institutions and the implementation of their decisions by revolutionary member nations in the face of declared indifference or opposition, following the adoption of appropriate resolutions in the Security Council or the General Assembly.

Even though a general consensus embracing almost the entire membership has developed with respect to the increased institutional role of the UN system in economic development, the revolutionary states had been among those who were most anxious to retain a maximum of national freedom of action in the preparation and execution of development projects. The Soviet Union, in fact, had made a fetish of the need for absolute national autonomy in economic planning. Notwithstanding these commitments of principle, the evolution of UN techniques shows a growth of power on the part of international officials and a willingness of revolutionary regimes to carry out their proposals. The Special Fund exercises much more detailed supervision over national development projects enjoying UN support than did the Technical Assistance Board in earlier years, and the TAB is now adopting more stringent measures. The recommendations of survey teams and inspectors dispatched by the International Bank for Reconstruction and Development are readily implemented by borrowing nations, despite the "Wall Street connections" of that institution. Bolivia has agreed to comply with the drastic deflationary "recommendations" of the International Monetary Fund as a price for receiving further loans in the face of strong domestic resentment. The mediating role of the Bank, when sweetened with appropriate financial sugar, has been a significant one in resolving such crises as restitution to the Universal Suez Canal Company and development of the Indus River Basin. The most capitalistic of aid-giving institutions receives cooperation from revolutionary (but non-Communist) nations when systematic economic development is at stake.[76] A similar conclusion is made possible by the experience of the rapidly growing system of UN Resident Representatives in aid-receiving countries, an institution not initially proposed by the underdeveloped nations. Almost fifty such officials now reside in member states receiving technical assistance, proposing and channelling projects, coordinating and supervising their execution. On their impact, one UN official writes:

> It is an administrative maxim that power should equal responsibility. The role of resident representative violates the precept; its responsibilities are endless, its powers nil. The resident representative knows that in whatever direction he looks—at the [Technical Assistance] Board, the participating organizations, the government, or the experts—he can order no one. For the essence of the post is that the person holding it achieves results not by commanding and ordering, but by persuasion and giving good counsel.[77]

Obviously, the actual influence of these officials varies from country to country. But since, increasingly, the flow of new grants, loans, experts, and fellowships depends in no small measure on the confidential reports submitted by the resident representatives to authorities at UN headquarters and to specialized agencies, their counsel on the spot is unlikely to be disregarded. Guinea was anxious to receive assistance in this form and turned to the Soviet bloc only when the UN was unprepared to meet hurried requests; Bolivia accommodated itself to it despite a nationalist revolution.[78]

[76] On Egypt's relations with the TAB and specialized agency programs see Walter R. Sharp, "The United Nations System in Egypt," *International Organization,* Vol. 10, No. 2 (May 1956). On the Special Fund see Hadwen and Kaufmann, *op. cit.,* and UN Special Fund, Doc. SF 1 (January 1, 1959). On the Bank see Eugene Black, "The Indus: Moral for Nations," New York *Times* Magazine (December 11, 1960), p. 51. Wheelock, *op. cit.,* pp. 190–97. Conditions imposed by the IMF in Bolivia were widely disregarded in 1957–58, but a new IMF effort in 1960 was apparently accompanied by firm assurances on the part of the Bolivian regime. The Left Wing of the MNR continued to oppose cooperation with the IMF and equated UN "imperialism" with that of the International Cooperation Administration. For details see, Robert J. Alexander, *The Bolivian National Revolution* (New Brunswick: Rutgers University Press, 1958), Chap. 13. Richard W. Patch, "Bolivia: Decision or Debacle," *American Universities Field Staff,* Latin America (Bolivia) RWP-3-'59 (April 18, 1959).
[77] C. Hart Schaaf, "The Role of Resident Representatives of the UN Technical Assistance Board," *International Organization,* Vol. 14, No. 4 (Autumn 1960), p. 556.
[78] See Alexander, *op. cit.,* pp. 245–46. Carter Goodrich, *The Economic Transformation of Bolivia* (Ithaca: Cornell University Press, 1955). Albert Lepawsky, "The Bolivian Operation," *International Conciliation,* No. 479 (March 1952). This, of course, is not to deny that many governments—though not necessarily revolutionary ones—disregard the advice tendered by technical assistance personnel and that resident representatives vary a good deal in the measure of their influence in propor-

Undoubtedly the most convincing item in an argument stressing the growth of UN authority is the development of the office of the Secretary-General. Compared to the ineffectual groping for autonomous influence displayed by Trygve Lie, Dag Hammerskjold had some right to claim that his stand on actual or emerging conflicts "to the extent that such stands can be firmly based on the Charter and its principles...thus express what may be called the *independent judgment of the Organization.*"[79] The Secretary-General, thus, can speak and act as if he, rather than the member states, represents the system *if* he is able to practice "quiet diplomacy" and enjoy the support of governments as a truly independent agent. It these conditions are not met, admitted Hammerskjold, "he must be prepared to see his future value as a negotiator endangered or even lost. In the latter case, he ought, naturally, to resign from his post."[80] To what extent, then, has this claim to a new autonomous status withstood the test of international politics?

One aspect of the Secretary-General's quiet diplomacy has unfolded in efforts to warn, and encourage, the major powers with respect to disarmament negotiations, test bans, and protection against surprise attack. This, of course, implies direct intervention in a cold war issue, and the results are common knowledge. Although this type of effort has contributed little to strengthening the authority of the system, another type of quiet diplomacy has prevailed in Hammerskjold's attempts to maintain peace in regions at the periphery of the cold war. In fact, the major justification advanced for intervening in Arab-Israeli crises, in Suez, the Congo, and Laos has been the exclusion of these trouble spots from the cold war. In these cases the Secretary-General undertook personal mediation, appointed UN personnel to take charge of specific jobs, such as establishing and supervising cease-fire agreements and clearing the Suez Canal, or created a "UN presence" in the person of delegates to watch and report on implementations of earlier agreements. Success was rarely complete. Israeli-Arab tensions flared up despite mediation and the Laotian crisis was not stabilized; it is too early to predict the attainment of the economic and military objectives of the Congo Operation. Yet, quiet diplomacy did, apparently, succeed in liquidating the Suez Crisis and in stabilizing the

---

tion to their own personalities. While some, in effect, act as key advisers on economic development plans to governments, others are content to play a modest "clearing house" role. For a wealth of information on the degree of control exercised on behalf of the UN system by field personnel and headquarters review procedure, see Walter R. Sharp, *Field Administration in the United Nations System* (New York: Praeger, 1961), especially pp. 376–401, 406–17, 449–63, 494–503. On the discreet controls exercised by international financial institutions see Henry Bloch, "The Fiscal Advisory Functions of United Nations Technical Assistance," *International Organization* (Spring 1957). International Bank for Reconstruction and Development, *The World Bank: Policies and Operations* (Washington, D.C., 1957). R. G. A. Jackson, *The Case for an International Development Authority* (Syracuse: Syracuse University Press, 1959).

[79] Address in Copenhagen, UN Doc. SG/812 (May 1, 1959), p. 9 (Italics mine.)
[80] *Ibid.*

relations between the United Arab Republic on the one hand and Jordan and Lebanon on the other. What is the explanation for the differences in impact?[81]

Quiet diplomacy, far from being separable from parliamentary diplomacy, functions best as an arm of some consensus, however limited temporally or functionally among the member governments. This consensus must include the major revolutionary regimes, if only because most of the tensions have arisen in their areas of the world.[82] In the Arab-Israeli and Laotian crises this condition was not met, since mediation was not preceded by unambiguous Security Council and General Assembly resolutions and ad hoc meetings of the mind. But in the Suez Canal crisis, the General Assembly did furnish the Secretary-General with explicit authorization born from the process of parliamentary diplomacy, and in the resolution of the Lebanese-Jordanian civil war of 1958 the governments again welcomed a balancing operation which would free the area from the danger of American, Soviet, and Egyptian armed action. In all these situations the Soviet Union and the UAR, as the major revolutionary regimes concerned, deferred to UN authority even though they did not welcome or advocate it. Whether the same principle is established by the example of the Congo Operation is still uncertain. To be sure, a consensus produced by parliamentary diplomacy accompanied the actions of the Secretary-General in recruiting and deploying armed forces and in running the Congo economy; but the consensus proved to be ephemeral and had to be bolstered by repeated threats on the part of Hammerskjold to tender his resignation. While the endorsement given to the Secretary-General's authority in the Congo in the resolution of April 15, 1961, was a sweeping one, the revolutionary regimes did not join in it.[83] In the Suez Crisis, the General Assembly created an Advisory Committee on the UN Emergency Force which functioned peacefully, without voting, in backing up the Secretary-General.[84] In the Congo crisis, the Advisory Committee created for similar purposes led to

[81] The major instances in which the Secretary-General intervened are enumerated, but not evaluated and analyzed, in Bailey, *op. cit.*, pp. 22–25.

[82] The success of the Beck-Friis Mission in mediating the border dispute between Thailand and Cambodia is an exception. It was a very minor affair which remained outside the policy aims of all other member states.

[83] Conclusions were drawn from the debate and vote on the 17-power resolution A/L.340 and Adds. 1–4, Add. 3/Corr. 1, as well as draft amendments A/L.348 and A/L.342. The overall tenor of the resolution was to "balance" various Congo factions while strengthening the authority of the Secretary-General and of UN conciliation in stabilizing the broadened Leopoldville regime. It was sponsored by nonrevolutionary Afro-Asian states. The unsuccessful amendments seeking to limit the UN role were introduced by Guinea. On the final vote, the Soviet bloc and some of the French Community African states voted in opposition; all the other revolutionary regimes (except Bolivia) abstained. *United Nations Review*, Vol. 8, No. 5 (May 1961), pp. 35–37.

[84] Details on the Committee in Bailey, *op. cit.*, p. 25. A judicious evaluation of the independent role of the Secretary-General and of ways of reducing the impact of some kind of "troika" system on the Secretariat can be found in Michel Virally, "Vers Une Réforme du Secrétariat des Nations Unies?," *International Organization*, Vol. 15, No. 2 (Spring 1961).

a less harmonious existence. The success of the Secretary-General in asserting the authority of the system depends on the mobilization of a majority of members states—including the revolutionary governments—in favor of a balancing operation for the maintenance of peace. It remains linked to the environment and has not yet attained the force of an autonomous agency superimposed over it.

However subtle its manifestations and inconsistent its public assertions, there has been an increase in systemic authority during the third phase of the UN's life. But this increase has not been accompanied by an equal growth in the acceptance as right and proper of these manifestations; there has been no parallel growth in the system's legitimacy. Member states, and especially the revolutionary regimes among them, acquiesce very reluctantly in the assertions of systemic autonomy. They do so only because policy aims of primary importance to them cannot be satisfied in any other way without grave danger to their hopes for peace, independence, and economic modernization. But their acquiescence is thus generated by the environment and is not yet based on an internalization of systemic rules. As long as this is the case, the current phase determines behavior patterns. With a shift in national policy and a reorientation of national expectations, the current environmental phase will come to an end, and with it the newly triumphant authority of the system may pass into history. *Systemic growth at the expense of a fluid environment demands concurrent growth of authority and legitimacy. With one but without the other the survival of a stable system into the next phase of its life is all that can be expected.*

This, as yet non-existent, unity of authority and legitimacy can also be regarded as the global *consensus* which must inhere in any system which is supreme over its environment. It is at this level that those who speak of an international public interest can make a conceptually meaningful contribution. The objective existence of such an "interest," some basic values and associated policies experienced in common by the membership, could be demonstrated if there were a reliable substantive consensus in the organization. To be sure, each phase in the system's history exhibited substantive areas of agreement among and within many of the blocs: But a shift in environment caused this substantive agreement to be dissipated. A pervasive substantive consensus, an agreement on an interest of mankind transcending short periods of almost accidental convergences of national demands, has emerged neither with respect to the imperative of preserving peace, nor with reference to peaceful and orderly changes in troublesome conditions, nor yet on the issue of exalting and protecting the individual as a subject of international law. But substantive consensus, so defined, has come about with reference to meeting the revolution of rising expectations. Furthermore, it is extremely unlikely that this would have happened without the political pressures and avenues of accommodation opened up by the UN system. And so the Marxist, as well as the liberal, who fashions policy on the basis of some kind of economic determination has come into his own in the machinery of international organizations. His efforts, not those of the direct advocate of peace, order, and human rights, have carried the day in fashioning a genuine international interest.[85]

But there is also a procedural dimension to consensus, the dimension held basic to the life of democratic systems. If procedural uniformities transcending the phases of the UN's history can be isolated, systemic growth could again be demonstrated to have occurred. The role of majoritarian as against unanimous voting, provided whatever trend exist outlives a given phase, would furnish an indicator here. Thus we find that voting in the Security Council has in effect been gradually emancipated from dependence on an absolute unanimity rule on substantive matters, and that this development has not been obliterated by changes in national policy. The admission that abstention by a permanent member does not constitute a veto originated in the early "honeymoon" phase of the system; but it has survived. More striking still, the "consensus" procedure of issuing directives or recommendations without formal vote and the liberalization of the rules regarding the participation of the Secretary-General in Council meetings evolved during the Western-dominated second phase; not only did the Soviet Union acquiesce, but the procedure has been carried over into the third phase in situations not requiring a new basic decision of the Security Council.

Yet no such conclusion can be stated for the General Assembly. The rules of procedure are notoriously permissive and presiding officers are very inconsistent in holding member governments to them. Permanent agreement has not emerged as to whether votes on certain questions involving decolonization demand a simple or a two-thirds majority; the First Committee makes all its decisions on a two-thirds vote even though some of the issues before it could be considered as "unimportant" under the Charter and the Rules of Procedure. No discernible evolution seems to have occurred.[86] And so consensus remains as changeable as the environment which it might stabilize.

---

[85] Francis Canavan, S.J., in "The Levels of Consensus," unpublished paper read at the American Political Science Association Convention, September 8–10, 1960, argued that "consensus" in a democratic society can never mean more than pragmatic, mundane, task-oriented agreement that certain governmental functions of a non-controversial character should be carried out. While he also suggests that this kind of consensus is probably inadequate to legitimate the activities of a strong welfare state, his formulation goes a long way toward accurately identifying the international consensus.

[86] I do not mean to suggest, in my analysis of voting rules, that "voting" should be considered as *the* supreme integrative device which explains consensus in the sense of telling us why minorities submit to majorities. Demonstrably, consensus comes about in certain situations without voting and may fare better if voting is avoided. But the history of decision-making on certain issues in the UN also suggests that cumulative votes do create a new consensus, though this consensus does *not* carry over to other functional contexts. I would argue as a general proposition, however, that voting is an integral constituent of the process of parliamentary diplomacy—which is basic to UN decision-making—and that an evolution of voting rules is a meaningful indicator of systemic development.

V

Let us assume that within the next two or three years the current phase of interregional and interfunctional balancing will come to an end—at least in its present form. This occur because the policy aims uniting the Afro-Asians will begin to diverge as the colonial issue ceases to be relevant. Even now the internal cohesion of the Afro-Asian caucusing groups, like that of the Latin American caucus, is among the weakest of any of the Assembly groups.[87] The elimination of the colonial issues will probably imply the further splitting of both groups, which will remain united only on questions of economic development. As concerns human rights, the revolutionary states in all regions will factor themselves out from status-quo powers in opposing an expansion of the systemic task. Hence, it will become much more difficult for the Western and Soviet blocs to attract uncommitted and underdeveloped nations to their respective positions on collective security because the fields in which concessions can be offered will shrink in scope. Under these circumstances it is difficult to predict whether the Latin American and Afro-Asian nations will unite on the issue of mediating in the cold war, or will begin to choose sides in the conflict to a greater extent than heretofore.

In any case, if the current phase, with its great opportunities for bargaining, has been unable to transform the UN system into an organization in which institutionalized-interest politics brings about increasing consensus, authority, and legitimacy, a future phase which reduces the scope for bargaining is unlikely to succeed. Hence, we cannot predict that the system will increasingly control that portion of the environment which is due to the aims of revolutionary regimes. But the opposite conclusion, that the revolutionary environment will destroy the system, is equally unlikely. Legitimate authority, if we argue on the analogy of administrative behavior in democratic states, *follows* the successful coordination of separate group and institutional efforts achieved by means of continuous bargaining, which results in a revolution of attitudes—a "breakthrough." In the UN we have merely had compromises based on quantitative bargaining and rigid insistence on concessions of equal value, with a failure to yield "integration" in the sense of the visualization by the parties of new alternatives for common action in which no state "gives up" anything.[88] But we have had continuous bargaining in which the revolutionary states have fully participated. There is no reason for thinking that even an environment offering fewer opportunities for the exchange of concessions will eliminate the incentives for retaining such stability as the system now possesses. And if the UN task does expand to the "new frontier" of space and science, the level of

---

[87] See Table 1.
[88] The distinction between accommodation based on "compromise" and "integration" is elaborated in North, Koch, and Zinnes, *op. cit.*, pp. 370–73. They, in turn, draw heavily on the definitions of Lasswell, Mary Follett, and Chester Barnard.

negotiation which results in integration may yet be achieved during the next phase.

We thus arrive at the conclusion that revolutionary regimes may be deterred into truculent inactivity by their participation in the United Nations, but not thereby be socialized into the gentle arts of accommodation, leading to ever higher planes of universal progress under the benevolent aegis of the hundred-odd flags displayed at the East River. "We tend to identify peace, stability, and the quiescence of conflict with notions like trust, good faith, and mutual respect," wrote T. C. Schelling.

> To the extent that this point of view actually encourages trust and respect it is good. But where trust and good faith do not exist and cannot be made to by our acting as though they did, we may wish to solicit advice from the underworld, or from ancient despotisms, on how to make agreements work when trust and good faith are lacking and there is no legal recourse for breach of contract. The ancients exchanged hostages, drank wine from the same glass to demonstrate the absence of poison, met in public places to inhibit the massacre of one by the other, and even deliberately exchanged spies to facilitate transmittal of authentic information.[89]

If we add that participation in the politics of the UN acts as a channel for the transmission of blackmail threats, even if it be multilateral and multifunctional blackmail, the civilizing impact of the United Nations system on the revolutionary component of its environment will have been established. The environment is changed even if the system itself sustains no growth in task and receives no shining new mantle of legitimate authority.

This relationship bears a marked—if grim—resemblance to the notion of "mutual recognition" of the limit on violence in the theory of limited war. The Yalu River was so perceived by the belligerents, but

> ...not as something that we and the Chinese recognized unilaterally and simultaneously.... We recognized that they recognized it, they recognized that we recognized it, we recognized that they recognized that we recognized it, and so on.... In that sense, limits and precedents and traditions of this kind have an authority that is not exactly granted to them voluntarily by the participants in a conflict; they acquire a magnetism or focal power of their own.[90]

Likewise, in United Nations bodies, debates and votes, without directly and self-consciously motivating those who debate and vote to behave differently than they rationally wish to do, deter them just the same.

---

[89] T. C. Schelling, *The Strategy of Conflict* (Cambridge: Harvard University Press, 1961), p. 20.
[90] T. C. Schelling, "Toward a General Theory of Conflict Applicable to International Relations," *Midwest Journal of Political Science,* Vol. 4, No. 2, pp. 136–37.

TABLE 1   COHESION OF REGIONAL CAUCUS GROUPS IN THE UNITED
NATIONS GENERAL ASSEMBLY, 1945-1958

COHESION OF MEMBER STATE

CAUCUS	BEFORE CREATION OF CAUCUS %			AFTER CREATION OF CAUCUS %			DURING THE WHOLE PERIOD %*		
	Iden-tical	*Soli-darity*	*Divided*	*Iden-tical*	*Soli-darity*	*Divided*	*Iden-tical*	*Soli-darity*	*Divided*
African **	—	—	—	46.7	33.3	20.0			
Western European	65.0	23.8	11.2	82.4	11.0	6.6			
Asian-African	11.4	36.4	53.9	34.4	42.2	23.4			
Benelux							77.5	17.0	5.5
Scandinavian							68.3	23.9	7.8
Commonwealth							13.0	27.7	59.3
Arab							63.4	27.2	9.4
Latin American							28.8	33.2	38.0
Soviet							96.0	3.9	0.1

Source: Thomas Hovet, Jr., *Bloc Politics in the United Nations* (Cambridge: MIT, Center for International Studies, 1958), pp. 64–65, 86, 98, 111, 121–122, 131, 155, 172, 187.
* The caucusing groups listed for "the whole period" were formed before or at the time of the first meeting of the General Assembly.
** The African Caucus had functioned for only two sessions at the time these computations were made, thus precluding firm conclusions. Prior to the formation of the Caucus there were not enough African member states to create a meaningful statistical pattern.
Hovet's study is based on the counting of an "adjusted gross" number of roll call votes. For the meaning of this device, see Hovet, pp. 239 ff. On an "identical" vote the frequency of members voting the same way, not considering abstentions, is counted; on a "solidarity" vote, the frequency of members of a caucusing group abstaining rather than voting against their colleagues is determined; a "divided" vote covers the situations of direct opposition among members of a group.

CHAPTER TEN

TRENDS IN
INTERNATIONAL PEACEKEEPING

Oran R. Young
Princeton University

The principles and purposes of the United Nations indicate that the framers of the Charter regarded accommodation and conflict-resolution as important tasks for the Organization. As Oran R. Young observes, in recent years several patterns of international peacekeeping have evolved in response to demands placed on the Organization by the political setting in which it functions. These patterns have often vied with one another and despite the dominance of "the Hammarskjold approach," there are indications that new assumptions may be needed, as the superpowers become less willing to entrust peacekeeping or peace-making responsibilities to smaller states or the U.N. personnel. Young's succinct appraisal of the Organization's executive capacities and pluralistic trends in world and U.N. politics leads to the conclusion that greater effectiveness for the U.N. in superpower crises or conflicts is possible. The dimensions of a "facilitative role" for the U.N. in future confrontations are imaginatively advanced in an essay that deserves wide reading and comment.

Reprinted from *Research Monograph No. 22*. Center of International Studies, Princeton University January 1966. By permission.

Recent analyses of international peacekeeping operations are marked by a disturbing lack of imagination and a tendency toward repetitious rigidity. Most thinking in the area of peacekeeping is now structured heavily and rather inflexibly by a set of concepts, principles, and practices stemming from the Hammarskjold administration at the United Nations. Variations on the resultant approach[1] to international peacekeeping are still relevant to a number of situations in which the United Nations is likely to become involved in the future. But trends both in the international system and in the United Nations itself are now affecting actual patterns of peacekeeping in ways that have reached the level of significance.

As a consequence, the peacekeeping picture is becoming more diffuse and complex. The United Nations continues to become involved in a variety of situations that have at least some bearing on peacekeeping, but classifying the resultant activities under the heading of a single approach is increasingly difficult. The original Hammarskjold approach itself has come to encompass a broadened range of distinguishable activities. And there are growing indications that several distinct approaches to peacekeeping are now developing simultaneously at the United Nations. Although there are some fuzziness and interpenetration, it seems possible to make some meaningful distinctions among the approaches.

I. THE HAMMARSKJOLD APPROACH:
PEACEKEEPING DESPITE THE COLD WAR

The pattern of international peacekeeping that developed in the mid-fifties out of the lull following the disappintments of the Korean situation is by now becoming familiar. The designers of this pattern were impressed above all both by the desirability of keeping the United Nations out of the currents of East-West controversies and by the growth of opportunities for constructive peacekeeping operations in third-world situations. As Hammarskjold himself expressed it some years ago, "Conflicts arising within the non-committed areas offer opportunities for solutions which avoid an aggravation of big power differences and can remain uninfluenced by them." In this connection the peacekeeping operations of the United Nations "must aim at keeping newly arising conflicts outside the sphere of bloc differences. Further, in the case of conflicts on the margin of, or inside, the sphere of bloc differences, the United Nations should seek to

---

[1] The term "approach" is used throughout this essay to signify an integrated set of concepts, principles, and practices concerning international peacekeeping. It is not meant to carry with it the formal implications of a theory or a model.

bring such conflicts out of this sphere through solutions aiming in the first instance at their strict localization."[2]

This orientation led to the evolution of the concepts of preventive diplomacy that focus on using the United Nations to restrict the instrusion of the great powers into conflicts in the third world. As I. L. Claude puts it, "Preventive diplomacy involves the use of the Organization for politically impartial intervention into a troubled area peripheral to the cold war, for purposes of forestalling the competitive intrusion of the major cold war antagonists. . . . This development is rooted in the cold war and the arms race, the thermonuclear revolution and mutual deterrence, and the increasing prominence in the United Nations of the new states."[3]

The list of problems amenable to United Nations activities under the Hammarskjold approach includes local difficulties arising between small powers not aligned with either East or West, internal disruptions stemming from the processes of liquidating colonialism, post-colonial crises, conflicts arising at the periphery of the cold war which can be isolated from involvement of the core powers, and, according to Hammarskjold at least, certain disputes within the cold war vortex which can be fished out and localized.

Operations within this framework are broadly describable as "peace-keeping by consent." In contrast with some of the Charter provisions and earlier approaches to peacekeeping, the Hammarskjold approach focuses on noncoercive and facilitative activities rather than on checking aggression or on collective enforcement. Secretary-General U Thant captures this point well in the statement that "there has been a tacit transition from the concept of collective security set out in Chapter VII of the UN Charter, to a more realistic idea of peacekeeping. The idea that conventional military methods—or, to put it bluntly, war—can be used by or on behalf of the United Nations to counter aggression and secure the peace, seems now to be rather impractical."[4]

As a result, the Hammarskjold approach postulates no need to label aggressors or to assign blame. Peacekeeping activities are set in motion with the consent of at least the state or states on whose territory the United Nations "presence" is to be located. And the emphasis tends generally to be on what might loosely be called "executive actions," aimed at terminating the crisis, as contrasted with enforcement actions of the collective security type. This is not to say that substantial pressures for compliance cannot be mustered under the Hammarskjold approach in various informal ways; they have been so mustered on a number of occasions. Examples such as the pressures placed on Egypt and Israel in connection with UNEF in 1956, on both the central government and the Katangese authorities at

---

[2] "Introduction to the Annual Report, 1959–1960," in *Dag Hammarskjold: Servant of the Peace*, Wilder Foote, ed. (New York: Harper, n. d.), pp. 302–303.

[3] "Implications and Questions for the Future," *International Organization*, Vol. XIX, No. 3 (Summer 1965), p. 840.

[4] "Address at Harvard University, 13 June 1963," *United Nations Review*, (July 1963).

various stages of the Congo operation, and on the Netherlands in connection with the West Irian settlement in 1962 attest to this. What *is* true, however, is that the approach de-emphasizes the older notions of collective security and enforcement action. The basic objectives underlying this approach to peacekeeping focus on the attempt to underwrite minimal international stability and support peaceful change outside the East-West axis rather than to regulate breaches of the peace or quell acts of aggression.

The Hammarskjold approach encompasses a very flexible and many-faceted conception of international peacekeeping. It has gradually grown to include a number of central ideas and concepts that have remained fairly stable over time. These concepts include the following focal points: filling vacuums in existing systems designed to maintain international peace and security; quiet diplomacy; the diplomacy of conciliation; brushfire operations; insulation of crises from great power involvement; and the localization of conflict. This foundation has been used to support a wide variety of specific activities at the operational level. Relevant operations since the mid-fifties include police forces, observer groups, supervision teams, United Nations "presences," mediators, personal representatives of the Secretary-General, technical assistance aimed at increasing political stability, and temporary executive authorities. Moreover, there is every reason to suppose that this general approach to peacekeeping will be able to supply the conceptual foundation for a wide variety of specific activities in future crisis situations.

Like any approach to international peacekeeping, this one contains a number of central assumptions. Above all, it calls upon the great powers to acquiesce in a decidedly secondary role in making policy for any given peacekeeping operation, as well as to accept partial exclusion from the field of operations as far as political objectives are concerned.[5] Under this assumption, the fundamental conceptualization of peacekeeping under this approach suggests that its employment depends upon a willingness of the great powers to forego at least some opportunities to manipulate specific conflicts for cold war purposes. At the same time, however, the approach rests upon the readiness of at least some of the great powers to provide various resources (such as transportation) and to help with the financing of operations. A second assumption requires that concrete operations under this approach be accepted by at least some of the participants in a dispute or crisis. It does not sanction or even conceptualize the use of force to set up an operation on the territory of any sovereign state.

A third assumption deals with the fact that successful operations under this approach to peacekeeping depend upon the availability of sound and energetic executive leadership at the United Nations. In fact, the nature of the relevant operations expands the influence of the Secretary-General and Secretariat as contrasted with that of the policy organs. Though this

5 On this point consult, *inter alia*, Brian Urquhart, "United Nations Peace Forces and the Changing United Nations," *International Organization,* Vol. XVII, No. 2 (Spring 1963), pp. 338–54.

executive role was largely unforeseen in 1945, it has since become crucial to many peacekeeping operations. As Andrew Boyd puts it, "The unexpected executive role of the Secretariat has developed mainly because the Assembly, the Council, or other organs demanded it. They, in turn, found they had to. The Council's approach to a decision can often be quite as halting as the Assembly's, even when there is no use of a veto. The Assembly has hardly ever succeeded in forming small committees capable of handling urgent business. Both bodies soon began to lean on the Secretary-General, and later got the habit of virtually asking him to work out a problem himself."[6]

Finally, the Hammarskjold approach assumes that the physical resources for any given operation will be forthcoming and that financial arrangements for at least the initiation of activities can be worked out.

The acid test of any approach to peacekeeping comes in the practice of it. And the fact that the Hammarskjold approach, in its various forms, has been applied in a substantial number of cases since the mid-fifties indicates that it has passed the test of practice with greater success than have other doctrines of United Nations peacekeeping. Outstanding applications conducted by Hammarskjold himself include the Peking formula of 1954–1955, the Emergency Force in Suez, the observer group in the Lebanon in 1958, the United Nations presence in Jordan established in the fall of 1958, the Beck-Friis mission to Thailand and Cambodia, the sending of the Secretary-General's personal representative to Laos in 1959, and the early phases of the Congo operation.

Moreover, much to the surprise of skeptical observers, the death of Hammarskjold did not lead to the demise of this approach to peacekeeping. U Thant has adapted and applied the approach vigorously in such cases as the later phases of the Congo operation, the establishment of the temporary executive authority for West Irian, the observer mission in the Yemen, the United Nations Force in Cyprus, and the fact-finding mission sent to the Dominican Republic in 1965. Recent years have witnessed some reductions in the scope of mandates given to the Secretary-General; moves on the part of the Security Council to retain greater control over concrete operations; attempts by the Secretary-General to exercise politically significant independent initiatives; and serious financial difficulties. Nevertheless, the core concepts of the Hammarskjold approach are still clearly visible in a number of the more recent peacekeeping operations.

The success of specific applications of the approach are hotly debated from time to time, but there is little disagreement on the proposition that the Hammarskjold approach to peacekeeping has a number of successes to its credit. Perhaps the single most important set of complaints about these peacekeeping operations stems from the fact that, as Leland Goodrich says, "the measure of success that the UN has achieved to date in discouraging and controlling the use of armed force has not been accompanied by equal success in bringing about accommodation of the conflicting interests and

6 "The UN at Twenty," *The Economist* (April 3, 1965), p. 44.

demands that are the source of tension."[7] There is an important difference between terminating a crisis and finding a solution to an underlying conflict, and the Secretary-General has addressed himself to this problem on several recent occasions. Nevertheless, the approach has in a number of cases acquired a reputation for keeping the peace in the sense of controlling or reducing open hostilities. And the existence of a substantial body of practice attached to it is undoubtedly one of the major reasons why it has become established as the dominant doctrine of United Nations peacekeeping today.

There is, in addition, good reason to suppose that this approach to peacekeeping will continue to be relevant to a number of international disputes and conflicts in the future. Many areas of the third world are either now in a condition of turbulence or are likely soon to become scenes of upheaval and disturbance. The United Nations has already gained relevant (and presumably applicable) experience in dealing with such upheavals in cases such as the Congo, the Yemen, Cyprus, and the Dominican Republic. The rubric of post-colonial crises, which covers disturbances in states that have recently become independent but have not yet become viable and well-defined national communities, is likely to be especially important in providing opportunities for international peacekeeping. Moreover, it is a safe prediction that there will be no lack of confrontations between various states in the third world in the years to come. In terms of United Nations experience, illustrations of this category of problems would include many of the Middle Eastern problems, the Thai-Cambodian disputes, and the Malaysia-Indonesia confrontation.

The current attitudes of the various nation-states tend to favor the utilization of preventive diplomacy in various future situations, even though Claude is no doubt voicing a proper note of caution in saying that "its future possibility remains uncertain."[8] The great powers are growing more aware of the dangers of becoming too closely involved in local wars and of the importance, in at least some cases, of minimizing the possibilities of escalation of local conflicts to broad-scale and destructive confrontations. Moreover, these powers are also becoming increasingly chary of lengthy involvements in messy, local conflicts which, though they may be unlikely to escalate to large-scale warfare, do not promise outstanding gains even in the event of success. For these reasons, it is by no means impossible to imagine a variety of situations in which the great powers might be willing to give their blessing to United Nations activities aimed at regulating local violence while they themselves remain on the sidelines. Future disturbances in Africa and the Middle East are likely to be particularly important from this point of view. At the same time, many of the smaller states are coming to accept United Nations operations as natural and appropriate. As Julius Nyerere put it several years ago, "When there is a dangerous flare-up in

---

7 "The Maintenance of International Peace and Security," *International Organization*, Vol. XIX, No. 3 (Summer 1965), p. 442.

8 *Op. cit.*, p. 842.

the world, or a fear of a local power vacuum, many of the nation-states now think in terms of calling for international action. . . . In other words, an attitude of mind is being built up among the peoples of the world which accepts—and will finally favor international political action."[9] Though it would be wrong to make too much of these points, the growth of favorable attitudes and expectations is likely to play an important part in encouraging United Nations peacekeeping efforts in future crises and conflicts.

Finally, the executive capacity of the United Nations has shown a very considerable ability to survive the ups and downs imposed on it by international politics and to remain a source of active leadership in the United Nations. It may well be that the present structure of international politics generates a substantial role for an office of this kind[10] even though this structure may destroy the usefulness of any particular Secretary-General from time to time. The top leadership of the Organization may, therefore, be expendable. But expendability of this kind is not uncommon in national political systems, and it may not be a bad thing in the hands of a leader who takes the attitude that "it follows that the powers and possibilities of the Secretary-General must be husbanded so that they can be used to the best possible advantage in the common interest of all nations. I have no intention of using them for any other purpose, nor yet of failing to use them to the full if I believe the situation demands it."[11]

For all these reasons, then, it seems a safe bet to assume that the Hammarskjold approach will remain a relevant doctrine of international peacekeeping and that it will continue to provide the principal conceptual framework for a certain number of United Nations operations in the future.

II. THE RE-EMERGENCE OF THE GREAT POWERS:
SOME CHARTER CONCEPTS REVISITED

As the introduction to this paper suggested, recent years have witnessed a growing diversity in the peacekeeping operations of the United Nations. An initial tendency to blur certain distinctions and concepts is evidently resolving itself into a situation characterized by the coexistence of several patterns of international peacekeeping. In the last two years, in particular, there have been some developments at the United Nations which suggest that the Hammarskjold approach is losing its exclusive dominance in the field of peacekeeping and that in certain situations the Great Powers may be reemerging as the guardians of international peace and security. This trend can be approached both negatively, through the discussion of prob-

---

[9] "The Courage of Reconciliation," in Andrew W. Cordier and Wilder Foote, eds., *The Quest for Peace* (New York: Columbia University Press, 1965), p. 24.

[10] On this point consult, among others, Nyerere, in *op. cit.*, p. 23.

[11] U Thant, "Statement by U Thant read at Queen's University, Kingston, Ontario, May 22, 1965," *UN Monthly Chronicle,* Vol. II, No. 6 (June 1965), p. 104.

lems that have arisen for the Hammarskjold approach, and positively, through an analysis of several new forms that have begun to emerge in recent peacekeeping ventures.

To begin on the negative side, several of the assumptions of the Hammarskjold approach are being brought into question—at least for certain purposes and in certain contexts. There is a sense in which this approach emphasizes a "neutralist" orientation toward international peacekeeping. It looks toward "a neutralizing function, to be exercised as far as possible by states whose uncommittedness in the cold war is matched by a commitment to making the United Nations an effective stabilizer of international relations in the era of the cold war."[12] And it is true that the development of this approach has corresponded with the rapid increase in numbers and influence of the middle and smaller states at the United Nations in recent years. For many purposes, the Organization has become an instrument of the smaller states, and the great powers have acquiesced in this to a substantial degree both as an alternative to control of the United Nations by the opposing side in the cold war and as a consequence of the tendency of the superpowers to cancel each other's influence on many issues, leaving a vacuum for the lesser powers to fill.

Recently, however, there have been signs that the assumption of great power acquiescence in playing a secondary role in peacekeeping operations will no longer hold true in a number of cases. This is not because the superpowers are stepping up their struggle in the third world and are therefore no longer willing to accept the insulation of many crises and disputes from the cold war. On the contrary, there is growing evidence to suggest that the superpowers are becoming more and more aware of their common, or at least their overlapping, interests in regulating coercive interactions in the international system in various situations.[13] As a result, they are no longer willing, in all cases, to occupy a back seat in the field of peacekeeping and to trust in the capabilities of other actors at the United Nations in this area.

The upswing in effective Security Council supervision of activities in the field of peace and security since 1963 deserves close consideration in this context. There is good reason to suppose that this development is more than a simple sign that the Council is finally beginning to heed the call of Hammarskjold for more explicit directions in the delegation of responsibility by the Council to the Secretary-General. In fact, an analysis of peacekeeping operations since Thant's assumption of the Secretary-Generalship suggests that the policy-making organs of the Organization have tended to be more hesitant to delegate effective responsibility for peacekeeping

---

12 Claude, *op. cit.*, p. 840.

13 There is an important difference between common and overlapping interests. Common interests exist in cases where the parties want similar outcomes for similar reasons. Overlapping interests occur in cases where the parties desire a similar outcome but for different reasons. While the existence of important common interests between the superpowers is debatable, there is little doubt that they have important overlapping interests.

operations to the Secretary-General than they were in the Hammarskjold
era. There was the episode in June 1963 when the Council, led by the
Soviet Union, reined in Thant's attempt to expand the scope of his executive
initiative in the establishment of the observer mission for the Yemen.[14]
And in this case as well as in the important case of Cyprus, the Security
Council has exercised its control by authorizing operations for only three
or six months at a time and requiring an affirmative vote by the Council
to extend the operations. Moreover, cases during 1965, such as the
Dominican Republic and the observer operation for India and Pakistan
(UNIPOM), in which the Council requested the Secretary-General to
undertake various actions on its behalf, indicate an interest on the part of
the Council in retaining more control than it had at the height of the
Hammarskjold era.

This discussion leads directly to a further problem that now faces the
Hammarskjold approach in at least some cases: the decreasing certainty
that extensive executive leadership will be available for future peacekeeping
operations. As mentioned above, the Secretary-General has shown remarkable survival capacities in recent years. But there are several points to
emphasize here concerning the availability of executive leadership. First,
the recent tendency of the Security Council toward caution in delegating
authority has led to a situation in which Thant, in conducting peacekeeping
operations, relies more and more on the implied powers of the Secretary-
General.[15] Important examples include his political initiatives in terminating
the secession of Katanga; his attempt to establish the Yemen mission
without specific Council authorization; his activities in directing the mediation operation in Cyprus; and his initiatives in directing and coordinating
the pressures that led to the West Irian settlement and the establishment
of the United Nations Temporary Executive Authority. Although this
procedure has led to some notable successes, it has also made the long-
term position of the Secretary-General more precarious since there is no
assurance that similar executive leadership will be tolerated in future
crisis situations.

Second, the attacks on Hammarskjold and on the office of the Secretary-
General in the early sixties have left their mark. The office has survived
far better than many would have believed possible at the time, and in many
ways Thant's renewal of the executive capacities of the Organization has
been remarkable. But the experience of these attacks and the sure knowledge
that they could be renewed in the future have led to a certain caution in
many circles concerning the deep involvement of the Secretary-General in
extensive peacekeeping operations.[16] In short, some of the same political

[14] On this point, see Washington Center of Foreign Policy Research, *The Future
Character and Role of Peace Observation Arrangements Under the United Nations,*
December 1964, Appendix III, pp. 490–522.

[15] For a discussion of these powers consult C. H. Alexandrowicz, "The Secretary-
General of the United Nations," *International and Comparative Law Quarterly,*
Vol. XI, 1962, pp. 1109–30.

[16] Recent indications of Soviet unhappiness with some of Thant's initiatives only
add substance to this caution as far as future cases are concerned.

influences that have sometimes tended to paralyze the policy organs of the United Nations cannot help but have a restraining influence on the freedom of the Secretary-General.

The Hammarskjold approach has also been affected by the recent controversy over the financing of peacekeeping operations, and especially by the outcome of this controversy. The lack of sound financing has already had serious effects on United Nations peacekeeping activities. The Congo force (ONUC) was withdrawn with disruptive consequences because of a lack of funds. The Secretary-General has repeatedly enumerated the restrictions placed on the Cyprus force by the weakness of its financing. And the necessity of employing ad hoc and piecemeal financing arrangements for future operations cannot but limit the launching of future peacekeeping operations.

Although direct United Nations financing and Assembly authority in this field are not clear prerequisites for the success of the Hammarskjold approach, the ability substantially to separate an operation from the immediate influence of the great powers is of considerable importance. Paradoxically, however, while the financing crisis initially took the form of a Soviet-American dispute over the desirability of assessed financing for past operations under the Hammarskjold approach, there is a sense in which the crisis ended with both superpowers agreeing that they themselves should have a greater hand in future peacekeeping operations and that a tighter rein should, in the future, be placed on the institutional independence of the Organization in the peacekeeping sphere. The Soviet Union "won" on the issue of financing past operations since the United States did most of the giving in to resolve the impasse.[17] The August 31, 1965, report of the Special Committee on Peace-Keeping Operations[18] announced the following terms on which the Twentieth Session of the Assembly would proceed: 1) the Assembly would resume operations as if nothing had happened; 2) the applicability of Article 19 would simply not be raised; and 3) the members would consider making voluntary contributions at some subsequent date to offset the peacekeeping debts.

In some ways more important, however, are those consequences of the confrontation affecting the clarification of policy on the financing of future peacekeeping operations. The key result in this sense is the tacit agreement of the two superpowers that they should not be forced to pay for any operation which they want to "opt out of" and that the position of the Security Council should be strengthened in matters concerning peacekeeping. The United States has even managed quietly to drop its proposal for a weighted committee of the Assembly to deal with financing arrangements. Thus another of the assumptions of the Hammarskjold approach

[17] For an excellent review of the step-by-step developments in the crisis see Meg Greenfield, "The Lost Session at the U. N.," *The Reporter* (May 6, 1965), pp. 14–20.
[18] The Special Committee was set up on February 18, 1965, by General Assembly Resolution 2006 (XIX). It made two reports to the Assembly, on June 15 and on August 31, 1965.

has been hedged about with restrictions though it would not be correct to say that it has been invalidated in any sense.

At the same time, it does not seem accurate to argue that these recent trends represent nothing more than a limiting move in the direction of circumscribing the presently dominant approach to international peacekeeping. The Secretary-General, for example, seems to be overpessimistic when he says, "The first five months of this year have witnessed developments which have tended to undermine the position of the United Nations as the primary agency for maintaining international peace and security. We are witnessing today a definite reversal of the slow progress the United Nations has made toward world stability and world peace. A further drift in this direction, if not arrested in time, will mark the close of a chapter of great expectations and the heralding of a new chapter in which the world Organization will provide merely a debating forum, and nothing else."[19] In fact, rather than being destructive, the trends under discussion have manifested themselves especially in several recent efforts in the field of peacekeeping in which the United Nations *has* played an important role. And it is probably not overstating the case to argue that there are here, in incipient form, a number of the ingredients of an additional approach to international peacekeeping emphasizing the role of the great powers and bearing at least some resemblance to concepts that stem from the original Charter arrangements. The key cases on which these comments are based include the Cyprus situation which the Security Council took up early in 1964; the activities of the United Nations during the renewed Indian-Pakistani hostilities of September 1965; and the actions of the Council concerning Rhodesia in late 1965.

The Security Council debated the Cyprus situation during February 1964 but was unable to agree on a peacekeeping operation for some time. On March 4, 1964, however, the Council voted unanimously to establish a police force for Cyprus (UNFICYP) and to authorize the Secretary-General to appoint a mediator.[20] Since then there have been several interesting developments in this case which affect the present discussion. To begin with, by far the largest contingent in the force is supplied by a great power, Great Britain. For the first time in recent years, therefore, the operating rule that a United Nations force should contain no contingents from the great powers has been set aside. In addition, the Council has kept a tighter rein on this operation than it did on those from Suez to the Congo. The initial authorization was for three months and extensions have been for either three or six months. (All of the votes for extensions, however, have been carried unanimously.) The Soviet Union has been accused of various obstructive activities in Cyprus—including making arms deliveries and abetting some of Makarios's plans—but it has always voted in support of UNFICYP, and its declaratory position to the effect that

[19] Thant, "Statement read at Queen's University," p. 102.
[20] The relevant document is Security Council Resolution 186 (1964).

any Cyprus solution must take into account the interests of both communities is impeccable.[21]

The Indian-Pakistani case is even more striking in its relation to the approach to peacekeeping under discussion here. Above all, on this issue the superpowers cooperated actively in the Council in putting through a series of strong resolutions. Whether this cooperation was explicit or tacit is difficult to say, but it is clear that the Soviet Union and the United States had at least strongly overlapping interests in pushing for a termination of the open hostilities. Nikolai Fedorenko, permanent delegate of the Soviet Union, spoke strongly in favor of action by the Security Council as well as casting affirmative votes on the resolutions.[22] Moreover, Premier Kosygin sent messages to Premier Shastri and President Ayub on September 14, 1965, expressing the concern of the Soviet Union and offering good offices.[23] On the American side, Arthur Goldberg, who was serving as president of the Council for the month of September, took a very active role in pushing for United Nations action in the situation.

As a result, the Security Council passed four resolutions (on September 4, 6, 20, and 27) concerning the Indian-Pakistani hostilities.[24] Perhaps the most interesting thing about these resolutions is the strength of the language employed. Despite the objections of India and Pakistan the last two in particular used language based upon Article 40 of the Charter. In Resolution 211 of September 20, for example, [the Security Council] "demands that a cease-fire should take effect on Wednesday, 22 September 1965, at 0700 hours GMT and calls upon both Governments to issue orders for a cease-fire at that moment and a subsequent withdrawal of all armed personnel back to the positions held by them before 5 August 1965."[25] A similar statement appeared in the resolution of September 27. This represents the first unequivocal resort to the language of Chapter VII of the Charter since the fighting in Palestine in 1948. In addition, the Council authorized the recruitment and operation of a United Nations India-Pakistan Observer Mission (UNIPOM) to supervise the implementation of the cease-fire. This case especially shows the superpowers in a role of guardians of the peace which is strikingly reminiscent of the concepts discussed at San Francisco in 1945.

The Council's response to Rhodesia's unilateral declaration of independence offers a study of trends in the area of peacekeeping and of the fluidity

---

[21] For an example, see the statement of Platon D. Morozov, delegate of the Soviet Union, in the Security Council in August 1965, *UN Monthly Chronicle*, Vol. II, No. 8 (August-September 1965), p. 8.

[22] See Fedorenko's statements in the Council on September 18, 1965, *UN Monthly Chronicle*, Vol. II, No. 9 (October 1965), pp. 18–19.

[23] *Ibid.*, p. 12.

[24] *Ibid.*, pp. 7, 10–11, 20, and 22.

[25] This is the first operative paragraph of Security Council Resolution 211 (1965). For a discussion of the Article 40 language see *UN Monthly Chronicle*, Vol. II, No. 9 (October 1965), pp. 16–20.

of positions in the United Nations. On May 6, 1965, the Council passed a resolution calling for the prevention of a unilateral declaration of independence (UDI) on which Britain, the United States, and the Soviet Union abstained.[26] Britain abstained because it considered the matter an internal affair; the United States supported the principle of the resolution but abstained to show cohesion with Britain, and the Soviet Union abstained in protest at the *weakness* of the resolution. Following the actual declaration of Rhodesian independence on November 11, the Council passed two resolutions, one on November 12 and the other on November 20, by votes of 10–0–1 with only France abstaining.[27] The first resolution condemned UDI and called on the members of the United Nations not to recognize an independent Rhodesia. In somewhat stronger terms, the key sections of the resolution of November 20 call on the United Kingdom to quell, by force if necessary, the rebellion of the Smith government and on the member states to participate in economic sanctions against Rhodesia, including an embargo on oil and petroleum products.[28] This resolution does not actually use the language of Chapter VII of the Charter but it comes very close to it. In fact, a linguistic manipulation was necessary to prevent a clearcut finding of the existence of a threat to the peace under Article 39.[29]

Security Council activities in this case came more and more to resolve themselves into a case of African pressures to muster stronger actions aimed at overthrowing the Smith regime—pressures supported by the Soviet Union, on one side, with a reluctant United Kingdom on the other side. The former group pushed for United Nations operations based on the language of Chapter VII, while the United Kingdom threatened to veto any resolution that so much as found the existence of a threat to the peace under Article 39. Under these circumstances, the United States tended to assume a position in the middle. But it is important to notice that, in the Security Council at least, the United States inclined toward the side demanding action and attempted to prod the British into accepting a stronger position that they would have subsequently been willing to enforce.

There are several ways in which these developments suggest a partial resurrection of earlier views of United Nations peacekeeping. The evidence cited above indicates that the Security Council is showing signs of increasing its utilization of the "primary" responsibility for the maintenance of international peace and security assigned to it in Article 24 of the Charter. And at least in some cases, the great powers, and especially the superpowers, seem to be developing a real interest in reverting to a pattern of taking an active hand in peacekeeping activities rather than simply acquiescing in

---

[26] This was Security Council Resolution 202 (1965). See *UN Monthly Chronicle,* Vol. II, No. 6 (June 1965), p. 20.

[27] The French abstained on the grounds that the matter is an internal political problem for the United Kingdom and is therefore a case in which United Nations action is not relevant.

[28] For the text of the resolution see the New York *Times,* November 21, 1965, Section I, p. 2.

[29] *Ibid.,* cols. 3–4, for a discussion of this point.

them. The Soviet Union, in its memorandum of July 10, 1964, and in its subsequent statements, has been particularly keen on this position. The Soviets have even called for the revival of the Military Staff Committee, and the drafting of the agreements called for by Article 43 of the Charter.[30] The United States, on the other hand, has restricted itself to a somewhat more moderate shift of position. But as a result especially of its experiences with the financing conflict, it has begun to deemphasize its "Uniting for Peace" posture and to push for more active Security Council control over many of the peacekeeping operations of the Organization.

Moreover, the developments of the Indian-Pakistani case, in particular, suggest a willingness on the part of the Great Powers at least to contemplate the application of serious coercive as well as noncoercive pressures in the name of international peace. The reversion to the language and concepts of Chapter VII of the Charter is particularly interesting in this connection. As a corollary to this Great Power willingness, it may be reasonable to suppose that the great emphasis in recent years on peacekeeping by consent and on the restrictive operating rules of the Hammarskjold approach is likely to be reduced in certain cases. In short, the trappings of peacekeeping operations designed to play down the role of the great powers will become less important as a function of the ability of these powers (and especially the superpowers) to coordinate on active programs of peacekeeping in the Security Council.

The importance of these trends should not, however, be exaggerated. It is difficult to see any conclusive reason why an either/or choice should develop between activities of this kind and those called for under the Hammarskjold approach. This essay suggests that the United Nations is moving toward a situation characterized by the development and interplay of several peacekeeping patterns existing simultaneously. The two patterns under immediate discussion are likely to coexist for some time and there may even be specific peacekeeping operations in which elements of the two are joined together. The unfolding of United Nations operations in the Cyprus case suggests that this is a live option. In addition, there are some substantial reasons to believe that there are serious barriers to the full-scale re-emergence of an approach to peacekeeping dominated by the great powers which will prevent it from becoming, in its turn, the dominant doctrine of United Nations peacekeeping.

The sources of this last judgment lie both in the unfolding patterns of international politics and in the politics of the United Nations itself. Though it may not be unreasonable to discuss at least an embryonic détente in Soviet-American relations, this development has not yet reached the stage at which it seems safe to argue that there will be a sufficient continuity of interests between the superpowers to make a full-blown approach to peacekeeping of this type possible in the near future. Occasional collabora-

---

[30] For a good example see Fedorenko's remarks in the Special Committee on Peace-Keeping Operations in May 1965 as reported in *UN Monthly Chronicle,* Vol. II, No. 6 (June 1965), p. 50.

tion in utilizing the Security Council is not only plausible but highly likely. The current loose discussion of détente, however, tends often to obscure the fact that there remain very substantial divergences of interest and orientation between the superpowers. In terms of cases with actual or potential relevance for United Nations peacekeeping, Soviet-American disagreements are well illustrated by situations such as the problems of the Congo (Leopoldville), the confrontation between Malaysia and Indonesia, the Vietnam war, and the 1965 difficulties in the Dominican Republic. For this reason, an on-again-off-again pattern of collaboration on peacekeeping issues is far more likely than a full-scale approach dominated by the superpowers.

At the same time, current trends toward increasing pluralism in international politics and toward a diffusion of usable or effective power in the international system[31] cast doubt on the ability of the superpowers to operate such an approach to peacekeeping in many potential situations even if they themselves should be able to reach operational agreement. It is highly likely that the declining relative influence of the superpowers in the system will increase their common, or at least overlapping, interests in developing a pattern of peacekeeping characterized by superpower dominance. But such an approach incorporates an assumption that the superpowers will continue to wield a sufficient preponderance of usable power in the system to make Security Council resolutions influential and, if necessary, to uphold them against armed opposition. It is, however, debatable whether, at the moment and in some cases, the superpowers can meet the requirements of this assumption, and, judged by these requirements, the future does not look bright. The Indian-Pakistani conflict of 1965 points up, among other things, the difficulties the superpowers face in attempting to bring recalcitrant smaller powers into line. If the two sides had not agreed to a ceasefire, it would have been difficult, though not impossible, for the superpowers to develop further techniques of applying pressure which were both acceptable to themselves and not insupportable liabilities in the arenas of international politics. The recent Rhodesian episode only emphasizes this point. Though sanctions may be effective in the long run, it is extremely difficult for the powers to bring direct coercive pressure to bear on the Rhodesian regime. This situation is made even more difficult for the superpowers by the fact that the United Kingdom claims primary authority in the area and would undoubtedly resist any direct superpower attempts at intervention even if they took place in a coordinated fashion.

Developments of a political nature have occurred in the United Nations itself which are likely to act as brakes on the growth of an approach to international peacekeeping dominated by the great powers. The growing impact of the principle of universality, which has led to the large influxes of new members in recent years, is changing the political complexion of

---

[31] For a lengthy discussion of these trends consult my *The Intermediaries: Third Parties in International Crises* (Princeton: Princeton University Press, 1967), Chapter 9.

the Organization. And this trend, in conjunction with the tendency of the great powers to allow themselves to be placed in a secondary role in many of the more dynamic and constructive processes of political interaction at the United Nations, has generated in the Organization new patterns of political power and influence. There is a sense in which the United Nations has indeed become a stronghold of the smaller powers and the middle powers. The smaller states especially are now the principal recipients of the economic and social benefits produced by the Organization. And the middle powers have played an important role in providing the force contingents as well as a good deal of the political backing for many of the peacekeeping operations set up under the Hammarskjold approach.

As a consequence, the political patterns of the United Nations have changed very substantially in recent years. New blocs and coalitions have arisen within the Organization; issues that are of greater significance in the North-South dialogue than in East-West relations have come increasingly to the fore; and a number of new norms and modes of operation have achieved central importance in the operating code of the United Nations. Though the superpowers are still extremely influential, they cannot simply announce either by declaration or by actions that they have decided to resume the reins of authority in the field of peacekeeping and expect the remainder of the membership to fall into line behind them. Aside from the obvious fact that many of the lesser powers have important vested interests in retaining their allegiance to at least substantial portions of the Hammarskjold approach, there are significant institutional problems in shifting from one mode of operation to another. The established pattern of peacekeeping is hardly likely to go under entirely, even if the trends under discussion in this section become more pronounced in the near future. A more likely development would be the rise of a kind of dual structure within the United Nations to accommodate these two approaches to peacekeeping.

There are, in addition, several more institutional matters within the United Nations which are likely to hamper the development of an approach to international peacekeeping focusing on the role of the superpowers. First, it appears that there will be overwhelming pressures to keep the General Assembly open as an alternative to the Security Council for the initiation of peacekeeping tasks. The Afro-Asians and the Latin Americans have come out strongly on this issue and the United States has publicly committed itself to support their position. In addition, the impact of this situation is heightened by the existence of a sharp Soviet-American disagreement on Council-Assembly relations. The Soviets would invest the Council with virtually all the relevant authority on peacekeeping issues. As Fedorenko put it in May 1965, "The competence of the Security Council include[s] the taking of decisions on all questions dealing with the creation of United Nations armed forces, the determination of their tasks, the membership and number of such forces, the command of the operations, the structure of the command, the length of the force's stay in the area of operations, and the financing of the expenses involved."[32] With the exception of some partially supportive statements from the French delegation,[33] however, the Soviets are virtually isolated in taking such an extreme position.

The United States, for its part, is moving away from its "Uniting for Peace" orientation and toward renewed interest in utilizing the Security Council.[34] Nevertheless, it is thoroughly committed to a view of the Assembly as an important safety valve and a policy of keeping "an emergency line to the Assembly" open.[35] Moreover, the extreme nature of the Soviet position will make it difficult for the United States and the Soviet Union to coordinate on a policy of reducing the role of the Assembly, at least in the near future. The Assembly is therefore likely to remain a factor in the area of peace and security. If nothing else, this situation will provide the lesser powers with a legitimate framework in which to authorize tasks compatible with the procedures of the Hammarskjold approach in the event that it should become impossible to do so in the Council. This will more likely hold true if various disputes are raised at the United Nations in such a way as to give the Assembly original jurisdiction over certain specific cases.

The retention of the capabilities of the General Assembly in the peace-keeping area will provide a safety valve in the event that the Security Council is again effectively paralyzed. This raises an additional institutional factor with far-reaching political implications. The Council will be expanded to fifteen members at the beginning of 1966. While this expansion may not generate any serious difficulties in conducting peacekeeping operations, it is impossible to predict its consequences with any precision. Perhaps more important are various indications of increasing difficulty in at least some situations in mustering the acceptance of the five permanent members of the Council even when the superpowers themselves find that they are in agreement. There are, for example, a number of potential situations in which a French veto would be quite plausible. And the United Kingdom can also be placed in a position where it would use its veto to stop a United Nations action, as was demonstrated by the negotiations preceding the November 20, 1965, resolution on Rhodesia.[36]

The most important potential problem in Council operations, however,

---

[32] *UN Monthly Chronicle,* Vol. II, No. 6 (June 1965), p. 50. See also Green-field, *op. cit.,* for an account of the Soviet position.

[33] The French have recently attempted to hedge on some of these questions. They want greater control for the Security Council but they tend to leave some outs for Assembly activity. For an example see the statements of Roger Seydoux in the Special Committee on Peace-Keeping Operations in May 1965, *UN Monthly Chronicle,* Vol. II, No. 6 (June 1965), pp. 48–49.

[34] Greenfield, *op. cit.,* p. 18; and Dean Rusk, "The First Twenty-five Years of the United Nations: San Francisco to the 1970's," in Cordier and Foote, *op. cit.,* pp. 67–81.

[35] The quotation is from Greenfield, p. 20. See also United States Mission to the United Nations, *Press Release No. 4586* (June 15, 1965), for a strong statement of the American position on this issue.

[36] See the New York *Times,* November 21, 1965, Section I, p. 2, cols. 3–4.

concerns Communist China. On November 17, 1965, the latest motion to admit China to membership was defeated, although the vote of 47–47–20 was far more favorable to China than past votes have been. In addition, the Chinese might refuse to accept membership, at least at first. It is likely, however, that China will be seated in the United Nations within, at most, a few more years. And it is not difficult to imagine cases in which the presence of the Communist Chinese in the Security Council could disrupt peacekeeping activities that the Soviet Union and the United States were able to agree upon and toward which they were prepared to coordinate their policies, even in support of action under Chapter VII of the Charter. For all these reasons, the superpowers may be unable to continue to operate through the Security Council in moving toward new concepts of international peacekeeping. It is even possible to imagine situations in which the superpowers themselves might actually initiate a return to the Assembly in order to avoid the paralysis of the Council. At this point, the whole cycle of ups and downs in the field of international peacekeeping would begin again.

III. THE UNITED NATIONS
AND SUPERPOWER CRISES

The preceding discussion suggests that the future of international peacekeeping is presently uncertain, though not necessarily insubstantial. The international system is now in a period of rapid and extensive change, and this means that the opportunities for United Nations operations in the field of peacekeeping are also likely to shift and change. This essay argues, in fact, that a situation is arising in which a variety of peacekeeping arrangements may be relevant from time to time and that the era of a single dominant approach is passing. This last section touches on an additional peacekeeping role involving the United Nations—one that may well become more relevant in the next few years if present trends in international politics continue.

For a long time it has been argued as part of the reigning doctrine that the United Nations cannot intervene successfully in great power conflicts and crises.[37] In undertaking such activities, the Organization would, according to this view, only expose itself to serious risks and might well suffer a reduction in its ability to handle other problems. This seems to be the principal point of Hammarskjold statement that "within its constitution and structure, it is extremely difficult for the United Nations to exercise an influence on problems which are clearly and definitely within the orbit of present conflicts between power blocs. . . . It is in such cases. . . practically impossible for the Secretary-General to operate effectively with the means

---

[37] The doctrinal basis of this position is, in fact, embedded in the Charter of the United Nations.

put at his disposal, short of risking seriously to impair the usefulness of his office for the Organization in all other cases for which the services of the United Nations Secretariat are needed."[38] This view is almost certainly still accurate if intervention is taken to mean the initiation of collective measures and enforcement actions within the meaning of Chapter VII of the Charter.

It is becoming more and more apparent, however, that in East-West crises the United Nations might in the future undertake with some real success another type of intervention. This type calls for a third party to act as a catalyst in enabling the participants in a conflict or crisis to escape the rigidities of their bargaining relationship in order to realize their common or overlapping interests. As U Thant suggested in his address at Johns Hopkins, "There are various...issues like Berlin on which it may become imperative to reach solutions on the basis of compromise and the principle of give-and-take on both sides. In all these situations the United Nations is available to the major powers, as it is to all its members, as a channel of friendly contact and informal discussion, and not merely a forum for public debate."[39] Rather than attempting to coerce the protagonists, the third-party intervenor aims at helping the parties to help themselves.

Relations between the superpowers are of a clearly competitive-cooperative nature at the present time. Somewhat loose discussion of a Soviet-American détente should not be allowed to obscure the fact that the two nations are still sharply at odds with one another in a variety of ways.[40] In particular, divergences between the two in basic philosophy, governmental structures, sociopolitical priorities, straightforward national interest calculations, and accumulated distrust are substantial. At the same time, however, it is probable that the cooperative side of the balance will become stronger as time passes. The advance of common and overlapping interests between the superpowers is traceable in both general and specific terms. Basically, the revolution in military science and technology has generated a situation in which the mutual fear of destruction is great, and awareness of the dangers of a nuclear environment is growing. In addition, the two powers are coming to share the overlapping interests of "have" nations in a world of "have-nots"[41] and to realize that they are both beginning to occupy conservative positions in the overall power structure of the international system. This situation is now manifesting itself sharply in the worries of the superpowers about the challenges of several lesser but rising

[38] "Introduction to the Annual Report, 1959–1960," p. 302.

[39] "Address at Johns Hopkins University, 2 December 1962," *United Nations Review* (January 1963), p. 57.

[40] A well-balanced statement on Soviet-American relations appears in Albert Wohlstetter, "Technology, Prediction, and Disorder," in Richard Rosecrance, ed., *The Dispersion of Nuclear Weapons* (New York: Columbia University Press, 1964).

[41] While there are, of course, important asymmetries between the United States and the Soviet Union in terms of material wealth, the two countries are decidedly on the same side of the fence in any comparison with the bulk of the underdeveloped states.

powers such as China and France. More specifically, the United States and the Soviet Union now manifest a variety of overlapping as well as divergent interests dealing with such matters as the stabilization of strategic weapons systems, the development of tacit rules of the game to govern their relations, the dangers posed by the possible escalation of various local conflicts to higher levels, and the problems posed by political imbalances in such areas as the Indian subcontinent and the Chinese periphery.

There are, however, good reasons to suppose that severe crises involving the superpowers will continue to occur from time to time. This is likely to be so even if the two states continue to move in directions that will increase their interests, in overall terms, in avoiding serious confrontations. Above all, specific political problems and points of conflict are likely to arise in such a way as to embroil the superpowers and to complicate their relations with each other. Important recent cases would include Berlin, Cuba, and, most recently, Vietnam. Moreover, there are several "dilemma" mechanisms built into the interactions of the two states which will tend to generate crises from time to time unless the competitive side of the relationship should somehow rapidly disintegrate; and this is highly unlikely. To begin with, there is a series of problems related to the underlying aspects of the military confrontation and compounded by the existence of a nuclear environment. The notion of the balance of terror encompasses a number of problems, including 1) the classic mechanisms of the security dilemma, which lead to military instability through a mutual pursit of absolute security; 2) the present superiority of offensive over defensive capabilities, which leads to the incentive to strike first in warfare and to the problems of preemption; 3) the dangers that a local confrontation will escalate to a large-scale conflict through an upward spiral of commitments; and 4) the problems posed by the perceived necessity of raising alert statuses and by the possibilities of inadvertent actions during periods of heightened tension. In addition, the military balance is made more uncertain and less stable by the dynamics of developments in military technology and by the prospects of perceived asymmetries in technology.

At the same time, the international dealings of the superpowers are often based on the processes of "strategic" bargaining[42] which contain their own difficulties and crisis-generating potential. Ignorance, ambiguities, and misunderstandings concerning the nature of a particular bargaining context are not uncommon. And this type of interaction tends to generate a rather strong and influential emotional field. Above all, however, "strategic" bargaining, by its very nature, is apt to engender a series of difficulties stemming from the mutual utilization of various bargaining tactics. In this connection, the uses and problems of commitments, threats, distortions, dissimulation, and manipulation are particularly important. For all these reasons, it is quite possible for the superpowers to find themselves in a

---

[42] "Strategic" bargaining refers to a situation in which one or both sides attempt to alter the relative bargaining strengths, at least temporarily, through the use of various bargaining tactics.

conflict or crisis situation in which it is extremely difficult for them to realize their common or overlapping interests in terminating the situation short of large-scale violence.

It is at this point that a facilitative role for a third party with little ability to mobilize coercive pressures arises. There are several ways in which a third party may be able to help the protagonists out of the "dilemmas" of a crisis confrontation.[43] In brief, the wide range of possible roles for a third party can be broken into the following general categories: conciliatory and mediatory actions, positive and independent actions, and service activities. In the first case, the third party would actually enter the bargaining arena, converting it into a three-cornered process in order to influence the interaction. Relevant activities would include persuasion, the enunciation of views and positions, the elaboration of proposals and initiatives, interpretation of confused situations, and participation in formal negotiations. The second category mentioned above encompasses actions that leave the two-sided bargaining process intact but aim at influencing it from the outside. Included here are certain communications roles, data-collection activities, and various types of physical interposition. The final category refers to difficulties that sometimes arise because the protagonists feel that they cannot make moves toward an accommodation without losing bargaining strength or because there is no machinery for implementing a paper agreement. In such cases, a third party can sometimes service the interaction usefully by facilitating indirect communications; providing verification, inspection, or monitoring arrangements; supervising the implementation of various conditions; or even establishing semi-arbitral arrangements that have the virtue of acting as "face savers."

The central proposition of this section is, therefore, that the United Nations may be able to play a useful third-party role in future crises involving the superpowers. In particular, it seems likely that the Secretary-General and the Secretariat of the Organization may be able to function successfully in such a role. There are several reasons for concentrating attention on the Secretary-General in this context. First, many of the roles a third party might undertake are primarily executive in nature, and there is good reason to suppose that the office of the Secretary-General will remain the principal source of executive strength in the United Nations system in the near future. In fact, the policy organs are often so unwieldy and sluggish that they simply cannot begin to undertake many of the more delicate and informal activities under discussion. In addition, the Secretary-General, as the principal permanent representative of the United Nations, represents continuity and has a greater capacity to act with some dispatch than have the policy organs. And he is in a superior position to command the physical resources of the Organization both during a crisis itself and during pre-crisis periods when various kinds of planning and training are important. Beyond this, the Secretary-General and Secretariat are better prepared in terms of various specific resource requirements to play third-

---

[43] See my *Third Party Intervention,* Chapter 3, for further details.

party roles than are other organs. Such resources include impartiality, independence, salience, and available personnel.[44] There are certainly inadequacies in the Secretary-General's resources as compared with those that might be ideal for a third party. The point here, however, is that the Secretary-General tends to be better off in these terms than other potential third parties.

Relevant United Nations experience in this connection is very limited, but it is worth noting that the Organization has not stood idly by during the most direct superpower crises of the postwar period. Perhaps the most relevant cases of this period are the Berlin crisis of 1948–1949, the second Berlin confrontation which came to a head in 1961, and the Cuban missile crisis of 1962. In each of these situations, the United Nations and especially the Secretary-General have played at least a small role.

Speaking of the first Berlin crisis, Stephen Schwebel points out that "the sum of the Secretary-General's effort, all in all, together with that of the Security Council and the Assembly President, while it did not resolve the Berlin crisis, is generally conceded to have eased it."[45] And Trygve Lie, after an extensive discussion of United Nations activities during the crisis, summarizes as follows:

> The role of the United Nations was not discreditable. The United Nations applied nearly all the devices at its disposal to a problem the solution of which, in any event, rested essentially with the party which had created it: the Kremlin. The Security Council, the General Assembly, and the Secretariat; mediation, fact-finding, expertise; public airing and private negotiation—all these weapons of modern diplomatic method were enlisted. The electric tension that the Berlin blockade generated between two non-negotiating worlds was very great. Had there been no United Nations, it might have been so great that the electricity would have shot across the gap, setting both sides afire.[46]

It is necessary to make a discount for Lie's somewhat crusading spirit and for his insistence on politicizing issues in a partisan fashion. This statement does, however, suggest that the United Nations was an active and not altogether uninfluential participant in the situation.

The Organization seems to have taken a relatively small part in the second Berlin confrontation which began in November 1958 with Khrushchev's ultimatum and reached its height in the dual confrontations of August and October. This was a period when the Hammarskjold approach, which tends to de-emphasize United Nations roles in East-West conflicts,

[44] For some interesting material bearing on these points consult Sydney Bailey, "The Troika and the Future of the United Nations," *International Conciliation* No. 538, 1962; and Eric Stein, "Mr. Hammarskjold, the Charter Law and the Future Role of the United Nations Secretary-General," *American Journal of International Law*, Vol. 56, No. 1 (January 1962), pp. 9–32.

[45] *The Secretary-General of the United Nations* (Cambridge: Harvard University Press, 1952), p. 144.

[46] *In the Cause of Peace* (New York: Macmillan, 1954), p. 218.

was very dominant at headquarters in New York. And during the 1961 confrontations, the Organization was first caught up in the tensest period of the Congo operation and then in its own internal crisis precipitated by the death of Hammerskjold on September 18, 1961. Despite all this, however, Joseph Lash relates in his biography of Hammarskjold that "in the tensest moments of the Berlin crisis, Francis Wilcox, the Assistant Secretary of State for International Organization Affairs, commented: 'I have more confidence with [Hammarskjold] there, realizing that you can turn to him when the chips are down. As time goes on it is quite possible the occupying powers in Berlin will find a role for him to play.' "[47] And there are clear indications that Hammarskjold himself had thought before his death of various possibilities for a United Nations role in Berlin.[48]

The role of the United Nations in the Cuban missile crisis of 1962, more than any other single case, supports the proposition that the Organization may be able to intervene constructively in various future crises involving the superpowers. With particular reference to the role of the Secretary-General, Henry Patcher suggests that

> ...the Secretary-General served as a moderator and letter carrier, as a conveyor of rumors, assumptions, and gestures—a role someone must assume in international relations. If U Thant or an office of the Secretary-General had not existed, it would have been necessary for the powers to invent them. Both parties found it practical to channel suggestions and semi-official communications through their United Nations ambassadors and to initiate preliminary contacts in discussions with the Secretary-General. Every time the U.S. and the USSR were not talking to each other, they could talk separately to the Secretary-General.[49]

In addition, the Secretary-General himself has provided several interesting descriptions of his activities during the Cuban crisis. In his annual report for 1962–1963 he stated,

> The Cuban crisis, which erupted rather suddenly in October 1962, provided the United Nations with the opportunity to help avert what appeared to be impending disaster. A large number of Member States not directly involved in the crisis consulted with me on the need for action to ward off a confrontation of the two major nuclear powers which seemed inevitable, and I was encouraged to take the initiative in making certain proposals which had the immediate effect of tending to ease the situation. As a result of the high sense of responsibility and statesmanship demonstrated by the leaders of the powers directly concerned, as well as the assistance which the United Nations was able to give, the danger of a major conflagration was averted. The United Nations also provided, both through the Security Council and the Secretariat, an opportunity for dialogues amongst the interested parties.[50]

[47] *Dag Hammarskjold* (Garden City: Doubleday, 1961), p. 168.
[48] For an interesting indication, see Hammarskjold, address at Copenhagen, May 1959, in Foote, *op. cit.* pp. 200–206.
[49] *Collision Course* (New York: Praeger, 1963), pp. 95–96.
[50] U Thant, "Introduction to the Annual Report, 1962–1963," *General Assembly Official Records,* 18th Session, Supplement No. 1A, p. 1.

And he used even more unrestrained language in an interview during the early part of 1963 in saying that "the role played by the United Nations in the Caribbean crisis is the most recent and perhaps the best example of the usefulness of the world organization when a confrontation of major powers is looming. . . . The debate in the United Nations and the intervention which I felt necessary to undertake are generally recognized as having contributed to reduce the crisis at its critical point."[51]

Interestingly, President Kennedy's Report to Congress on United States participation in the United Nations during 1962 takes up the Cuban crisis at some length and concludes that the role of the United Nations was of great importance in a number of respects.[52] While the Soviets have said very little about this point, it is of real significance that the United States at least took a rather enthusiastic view of the third-party activities of the Organization in the Cuban case.

The actual record of the United Nations, therefore, appears to be somewhat at variance with the proposition that the Organization cannot intervene constructively in superpower conflicts and problems. And finally, the fact that the superpowers seem to demonstrate a growing awareness of the dangers of the nuclear environment and of the desirability of terminating confrontations before destructive exchanges take place suggests that the third-party role may be a live one for the United Nations in future crises involving the superpowers.

This essay is a plea for efforts to reduce doctrinal lag in the analysis of international peacekeeping rather than an argument in favor of any particular type of peacekeeping operations. In fact, the thesis of the essay is that the present situation generates a horizontal spread of relevant peacekeeping arrangements as opposed to a sequence in which one dominant approach follows another in temporal succession. The general problem of doctrinal lag is almost universal in dealing with current and unfolding developments. But it is important to combat this lag and to minimize its influence on analysis.

51 U Thant, "Interview with the Secretary-General," *United Nations Review* (January 1964), p. 5.
52 *U.S. Participation in the U.N.,* Report by the President to the Congress, 1962.

CHAPTER ELEVEN

WORLD ORDER AND
THE NATION-STATE—A
REGIONAL APPROACH

Lord Gladwyn

Lord Gladwyn's extensive diplomatic experience in bilateral and multilateral relations is revealed in his consideration of regional institutions as modes of accommodation and conflict-resolution. He is not encouraged by prevailing tendencies in Africa, Asia, the Middle East, and Latin America, but is somewhat more optimistic about supranational or federative possibilities in Western Europe. His impressions are a useful counterweight to academic speculations in which regionalism is often accorded preferential status divorced from political reality.

Reprinted from *Daedalus* (Spring 1966), pp. 694–703. By permission.

There is no doubt that the nation-state is still the only unit in international relations which has any real political, as opposed to economic, significance. By this I mean that no conventional alliance, from NATO downwards, can speak on all ocasions with one voice, still less organizations like the Afro-Asian group, the Organization of American States, the Arab League or even (now) the EEC. Since World War II, the number of nation-states has greatly increased—there are now one hundred and seventeen members of the United Nations with a possible twenty or thirty to come—and many of those recently created are even more conscious of their so-called "independence" that the more historical ones. Nowhere since 1945 has the absolute sovereignty of the nation-state been questioned, still less restricted, save only in two areas, Eastern and Western Europe. In Eastern Europe, as a result of Soviet occupation, the various nation-states were subjected to a form of centralized control exercised by the Communist Party in Moscow; in Western Europe between 1950 and 1965 some of the nation-states came together voluntarily in an effort to achieve a supranational entity. This was largely due to the experiences of a war in which all of them had been at some stage totally defeated. In the East, however, it now looks as if the nations concerned are recovering a good deal of their independence, if not of their central sovereignty, while in the West the whole idea of a supranational entity has now been challenged by the open and declared hostility of the present French government to any such notion.

Elsewhere in the world it must be admitted that efforts to achieve federations or their equivalents among the so-called "emergent" nations have all failed. For instance, the United Arab Republic is now united only in name. The Arab League exists only as a sort of discussion forum. The proposed association of Kenya, Tanzania, and Uganda has not materialized. It is questionable whether the Federation of Nigeria will survive. The Federation of Rhodesia has already collapsed. There is little hope that the unification of the Maghreb in North Africa will be achieved. Unfortunately, little progress has been made in South America toward any real association of the various states under the auspices of the Organization of American States. Further afield, the prospect of a united India as a continuation of the old Raj broke down in 1946. Even the newly formed Federation of Malaysia has already partially collapsed, and that in South Arabia is encountering the most grievous difficulties. In North America it is true that Canada and the United States may be coming closer together in a general way, though even here we are faced with a rise of nationalist feeling in the Province of Quebec.

Must we then assume that any attempt to limit the complete independence of the nation-state, which varies in size from the 600 million of China to the 200 thousand of the Maldive Islands, is the only possible basis for the construction of the new world order, and that all efforts to produce a more rational, indeed a less dangerous, international structure are inevitably doomed? But first let us try to define the nation-state in its international significance.

Perhaps we can say that it is a collection of people, usually though by no means always consanguineous and monoglot, accustomed to being governed from one center, who regard themselves as possessing virtues and qualities that must at all costs be preserved, and who are not disposed to allow their collective power to be shared with any other nation. It will be observed that any collection of people who wanted to run their own affairs would come under this definition, including quite a number which would like to be nation-states if they could; but in practice we must say that any such collection is a nation-state only if it is generally recognized as independent and capable of membership in the United Nations. It then becomes an entity whose defense against aggression is in principle assured. (China is, of course, so recognized as a state; it is only the representative character of the government that is disputed.)

Clearly such a nation-state can be merged in another state either by its own desire or (if the United Nations does not function) by some act of force. Wales, or Ireland before the rebellion, or even to some extent Scotland, are examples of amalgamation by force. Other potential nation-states, such as Bavaria, are now part of a German whole. The Kingdom of Savoy and other Italian states were eventually merged in the Kingdom of Italy. If historical precedent is any guide, it is quite possible that some existing nation-states may in the future be merged in larger entities, perhaps by extreme economic pressure, perhaps even by war. It is equally possible that some existing nation-states may break up, perhaps especially those that are in effect the remains of empires, containing as it were "submerged" nations that are racially and linguistically distinct. But, with the emergence of some world order based on the United Nations, actual suppression of a nation-state except by its own volition, or as a result of internal disruption, is becoming increasingly difficult. Even the smallest states can now depend to some degree on a collective guarantee against aggression.

Naturally, since the beginning 450 years ago of this strange system, which nevertheless did not prevent an extraordinary cultural period, countless learned men and even some statesmen produced schemes to end a suicidal and dangerous anarchy. None had the slightest effect. The League of Nations, between the two wars, was the one which came nearest to curbing the nation-state, but even that collapsed because of its evident inability to control in any way the actions of its members, not only Italy and Japan, but even to some extent the U.S.S.R. After World War II, it is now evident that the United Nations, in default of some major political settlement between East and West, is in much the same position. Anarchy prevails in the world. The nation-state's freedom of action is limited only by its power. Worse than that, it is often enabled to pursue what it imagines to be its own individual interests at the expense of its neighbors because of an inability of the larger powers to impose their will, owing to the necessity of preserving the only existing guarantee of peace, namely, the nuclear Balance of Terror. Tension therefore is only too likely to accumulate, and one day there will be a war of some kind, which may well spread, even if we manage, through sheer fright, to avoid a general nuclear explosion.

It is of course evident that sovereign nation-states can and do enter into alliances and indeed into international associations under which they agree to abide by common rules, drawn up in the interests of the group as a whole. There is thus in effect often some temporary restriction on their complete freedom of action. But in all such alliances or organizations it is possible for a nation-state to resign in the last resort, and, therefore, there is no ultimate obligation to have regard for any decision taken in common if such a decision is not deemed to be in accordance with the interests of the nation-state concerned. And, as most of them like being independent, there is now less compulsion or desire to merge with some group than there was at the end of World War II. This tendency applies even to the United Nations itself, from which one large state has resigned already. The United Nations, it is true, has power to overrule the declared will of a nation-state, though this applies only to the majority of the international community and not to the five permanent members of the Security Council. However, it is true that if these five members are in agreement it is possible now to put legal sanctions behind any action taken against any nation-state which may be thought to be acting against the interests of the world generally. The only instance, since the war, of nation-states voluntarily taking the enormous jump from total independence into some kind of supranational ‘entity occurred when six European countries ratified the Treaty of Rome, but it is by no means certain as yet that this Treaty will still apply when there is no further means of escaping from its evident supranational implications.

It might consequently be supposed that, except for some slight control exercised in theory by the World Organization, the chances are that the various nation-states of the world will continue to have complete freedom of action and will join one alliance or another, as it seems in their interest. If world peace is maintained at all, in such circumstances, it will have to be on the basis of some constantly changing world balance, in which there will necessarily be a strong element of instability. It may even be argued that the very balance of terror between the superpowers, or giants, of the modern world in itself encourages the dissolution of alliances and therefore actually encourages the tendency of the nation-states to insist on complete independence. Regrettable though this may be, it is a fact that the authority of the superpowers can only with difficulty be exercised over allies who do not accept the ideas of the most powerful section of their own group and prefer to take an independent line. If the balance rests on the impossibility of either the one superpower or the other committing an act of aggression against any member of the opposing side, then it is clear that there is no danger for any of the smaller powers since *ex hypothesi* their own leader cannot exercise more than a certain pressure on them if he does not want them actually to desert and go over to the other side. This is clearly a position which can be and is exploited, though it is rather difficult to see what a rebellious ally can gain from the operation except psychological satisfaction.

Finally, if one considers the arguments in favor of retaining the nation-state, there is that of "plus ça change plus c'est la même chose." If indeed we succeed in merging various nation-states, especially in Europe, where their existence has given rise to so many and so great disasters in the past, what is there to prevent the new potential superpower from behaving as irrationally as any other nation-state and thus increasing rather than diminishing world tension and the risk of nuclear war? It can indeed be pleaded in refutation of this that a united Europe would not have those national ambitions which characterize a divided one, and, further, that if a world balance resulted from unification there would be that much less possibility of some European dictator emerging. But all these are legitimate arguments which must be answered by those who believe in the gradual tempering of international anarchy by the building up of an effective and lasting world authority.

Nevertheless the case against the maintenance of the nation-state in its historical integrity, and certainly against the disruptive, nationalistic tendencies now at work in that cradle of war, which is Western Europe, is very strong. We must, of course, consider the integrating influence of the industrial system of the latter part of our century. Whatever the arguments in favor of the maintenance of the nation-state, it is, economically speaking, becoming increasingly difficult for the latter to preserve its complete independence unless it is very large or (paradoxically) very primitive. The great "automated" factories of our age require huge "home markets" if they are to sell their goods at a profit. In the long run the maintenance of tariff barriers around medium-sized states can produce only unemployment and economic distress. But if customs unions are formed then more and more "integration" become inevitable. The nation-states concerned may try to resist this process; but the only choice in front of them, assuming the process of industrialization continues, is between union among themselves or absorption by one of the existing superstates.

Should they choose union the way is now less difficult than it was. For it is no longer a straight choice between hegemony, conquest, or federation. The new techniques of the Treaty of Rome have clearly demonstrated their efficacy and their suitability for the ancient historical nation-state which is in nowise prepared to lose its integrity or its "personality." Within the framework of the Commission, the Council, and the European Parliament there is scope for the continuation of genuine national identities and thus for the constitution of a supranational entity in which the dreaded "loss of sovereignty" would come, as it were, unawares. It is only the atavistic urge which stands in the way of such a development, and it is doubtful if even that can stand in its way very long. As soon as the embodiment of past glories is removed from the scene, the real forces of the future will take over; and though these may be "communistic" (in the sense of directed economies) it seems likely that they will at least not be nationalistic. France, it is true, has the ability to build herself up into a self-sufficient neutralist state if she so desires; but, if no other Western European state follows her example, what then? Would she really be prepared to be a Soviet satellite forever?

The position therefore is that even if the EEC of the Six achieves political unity—which it cannot in practice do on a non-supranational basis because the Germans will not accept the hegemony of France—the two giants will continue to glare at each other over the Elbe and the position will remain unstable. If nationalism prevails and the EEC breaks up, the position will be much the same, except that it will be even more unstable than under the first hypothesis. Only if Britain joins will it be possible to create a situation which in the long run may enable the Americans and the Russians to disentangle themselves from the Continent by agreement and to prepare for the peaceful reunification of Germany, perhaps at first in the sense of an association of the various Germans within a larger demo-cratic and politically inoffensive whole. After this has been done relations with Eastern Europe could be gradually improved, though no doubt the West will continue to look primarily toward Washington and the East toward Moscow. In a real sense there is a community of interest between the United States and Western Europe. But it is possible to imagine the emergence of a Europe which will gradually acquire an individuality of its own, and which could, not from the nuclear (because that would be absurd even if it were possible) but from every other point of view, be something equivalent to Russia and America. And I maintain that this would be the best of all possible stabilizing factors.

It seems thus on the whole probable that the present bipolar world balance itself will be slowly transformed by the emergence of a regional *bloc* in Western Europe. If it is not, and if the nation-state endures, then the chances of World War III would probably be considerably greater, and it would in any case be difficult to conceive of any advance toward the achievement of a world order involving some reduction of international tension. Nationalism may indeed represent the "live forces" making for change, and in a non-nuclear world there is no doubt that constant and violent struggles between nations would gradually produce a synthesis of some kind. But modern weapons are so horrifying that to a large extent this logic is no longer applicable; and if it does not apply, then what are the alternatives before us? Are we really to eliminate reason in our concept of the development of human events? Assuming that reason does prevail and that some sort of regional bloc does emerge in Western Europe (which is the only district in which the nation-state may be to any noticeable extent modified in present conditions), what consequences would flow from the point of view of the construction of an eventual world authority?

Clearly the general situation would be substantially altered by the crea-tion of another "pole." The bipolar world that has virtually existed from 1945 until now has already been changed to some degree by increasing restiveness on the part of the superpowers' allies on both sides of the Iron

Curtain and by the explosion of the first Chinese nuclear device. The formation of a political community in Western Europe (which might eventually
embrace some Eastern European states as well) would create a new world
balance, even if Europe did not attempt to become a nuclear power on a
scale emulating Russia and America. For it is clear that once a united
Europe has been achieved by peaceful means the whole international situation changes. If the two superpowers no longer confront each other on the
line of the Elbe, they will be free to indulge in common policies toward
the third world, and notably, of course, toward China. Thus a "climate
of peace" may gradually be established in the Northern Hemisphere, and
the eventual admission of China to the U.N. might facilitate some long-term
peaceful solution of the difficulties of that great country, for it is indeed
hard to see how the Chinese could in such circumstances successfully
pursue any territorial claims they may have on the Soviet Union. We ought
therefore to arrive at a situation in which North America, associated perhaps
with Australasia and enjoying friendly relations with a united Western
Europe, would find herself in a world embracing also some equivalent power
in Russia and eventually even in China, which themselves would, no doubt,
have close relations with the Middle East and Southeast Asia respectively.
There would thus be three nuclear poles (or five, in the unlikely event that
Europe and Japan would begin large-scale production of nuclear weapons)
but not more than five in the sense of great regional politico-economic *blocs*.
Naturally, if Japan ever made common cause with China that would alter
the entire world balance for the worse, but it does not look, at the moment,
as if there is any chance of such a development during the next twenty or
thirty years.

Can we then conceive of any further politico-economic entities of the
same sort of importance? Clearly there is another potential one—the Indian
subcontinent. But as far as can be seen at present, it looks as if India and
Pakistan—or rather the Hindus and the Muslims—will be unable during
the next years or so to settle their differences; nor is it even certain that
India will not break up into her component parts during this period. Still,
it cannot be denied that there is a certain chance, if not of the Indian
subcontinent, at any rate of India becoming a world power during the
period contemplated; and it is not to be excluded that if it does so it will
possess some kind of nuclear capability, though probably not of the first
order and hardly on a level with that of Europe or (conceivably) of Japan.

Elsewhere in the world there seems little prospect of many positive supranational entities emerging out of the welter of nation-states which now
exists. In the Middle East it is true that there is a common Muslim sentiment that extends from Casablanca across North Africa (if the heretic
Shias are included) to the frontier of the Pakistani-Indian border, and
within this area there is the more limited Arab League. It is not to be
denied that there is a possibility that the Arab League, which, after all,
rests to some extent on a common language, will become more united during
the next twenty years or so; at the moment, however, the rivalries between
its component parts are so great that this seems on the whole to be unlikely.

The other three world "regions" are clearly Southeast Asia, South America, and Africa south of the Sahara. Here also everything suggests that no definite supranational entity will emerge. There is indeed talk of some "Malayan" coming together which would include Indonesia, Malaysia, and the Philippines; but the structure of such a huge conglomeration is clearly not present and could hardly be built up in the time available. There may indeed be some vague political association which, it is to be hoped, would come more under Western than under Eastern influence. In the north of the region all the countries have been at one stage in history under the domination of China or, alternatively, of India. The hope would surely be that, exposed to the pressure of surrounding great powers, these states could eventually work out some scheme for friendly association with the one great power or the other. If the whole area is to avoid becoming a battlefield, this clearly will have to be done.

In Latin America much would seem to depend on whether the United States can come to terms with the revolutionary regimes which will probably come into power in some of the countries during the next twenty years. If it does, it should be possible to achieve greater cohesion between some of them than has proved possible up to now. If the Organization of American States continues—as is devoutly to be hoped—this could also be used for encouraging greater unity. Here again, it seems unlikely that anything equivalent to an international entity will emerge either in the whole of Latin America or in parts of it. Perhaps the most unlikely ground for the emergence of any new region is Africa south of the Sahara, where the tendency probably would be toward a disruption of the present "nation-states" (which are really colonial artifacts) and a reversion to tribalism of some kind, which will result in new nations emerging over a period of time.

Assuming that things work out more or less along the lines suggested, it will thus be seen that a world balance replacing the present "bipolar" system will have to be achieved through some world authority in which the United States, the Soviet Union, China, and probably Japan, and (we must hope) a European Community will be sitting as the permanent members, with perhaps one representative chosen from the still separate nation-states of the Arab world, the Indian subcontinent, Southeast Asia, South America, and Africa south of the Sahara sitting with them. Such a world authority ought after a period of time to be able to act on some basis of majority rule. It would of course be a world *authority* and not a world *government*, since clearly the idea of direct elections to a world parliament would be inconceivable at any rate before the end of this century.

All this is only the vaguest of outlines, but provided we do succeed in setting up some supranational authority in Europe it seems to be at least possible that this is the general way in which the world is going to evolve. The emergence of a supranational authority in Europe might serve as an example which would encourage other areas less disposed toward a general supranational conception to look upon it more favorably. In any case, the great advantage of regionalism is that international disputes can be solved to a large extent regionally, and that the problems confronting a world authority would simply be those concerning any clash of interest between the superpowers or the organized "regions" concerned. It could be in such circumstances that there would no longer be any real need for the General Assembly of the United Nations, though clearly it will be desirable to maintain and to reactivate the International Court. Even if this should be considered an ideal dream, what is the alternative conception for the establishment of a world order and the construction of a real political basis for enduring peace? As I have suggested above, the principle of each for himself and the devil take the hindmost might well have worked after World War II, as indeed it worked after the Napoleonic Wars, were it not for nuclear weapons, which in themselves make any such principle a simple recipe for suicide. I can only hope that the general idea of regionalism will be examined by experts with greater academic qualifications than my own, but in the meantime we must all advance toward the unification of Europe and the eventual construction of some Atlantic society.

CHAPTER TWELVE

CASE STUDY:
THE CONGO IN WORLD
POLITICS—AN APPRAISAL

Linda B. Miller

Harvard University

Major influences in world politics, especially the cold war and decolonization, are dramatically reflected in the case study of the Congo's civil strife. For five years events in the Congo surprised, shocked, and dismayed observers. As a global and regional concern, the African state's turmoil required revision of prior ideas of legitimacy, self-determination, nationalism, and tribalism. The challenges to the U.N.'s capabilities as an instrument of peaceful change and harmonization of competitive interests were unprecedented. The effects of the Organization's "overextension" in the Congo are still apparent in the Security Council, the General Assembly, and the Secretariat. The subsequent refusal of member states to place heavy responsibilities on the U.N. in circumstances of civil strife and the insistence that the disputing parties themselves bear the burden of political settlements are evidence of the Congo's permanent legacy to the Organization.

By what processes and with what consequences may a decolonization issue become a matter of regional and global interest? An appraisal of the Congo disorders from 1960–1965 suggests provocative answers to this question. The sheer complexity of unfolding events influenced the responses of Congolese political figures, African, Belgian, American, Soviet, and United Nations officials. In turn, the attitudes and actions of local and outside parties shaped the violent and subviolent conflicts that challenged continental and world order for half a decade.

It is instructive to consider the sequential development of diversified national interests in the Congo from the perspective of the United Nations, since the new state's internal strife became a *world* concern immediately, as distinct from an African or Eurafrican one. The Congo's future is of residual importance for the general international society, despite ONUC's termination in June, 1964, and the increased involvement of European and African states on bilateral and regional levels.

I

The internationalization of the Congo's post-independence disturbances occurred swiftly.[1] The Kasavubu-Lumumba government appealed directly to the United States President for military assistance in the wake of tribal violence in Leopoldville and Luluabourg and the uprising of Congolese soldiers against their Belgian officers in early July, 1960. Ernest Lefever attributes the American decision to urge U.N. action rather than a bilateral intervention to three related motives: the desire to achieve stability without alienating other African states, the desire to avoid a major military commitment on the African continent, and the desire to strengthen the peacekeeping capability of the U.N.[2] Whatever the relative weight observers should attach to each of these reasons, American authorities did prepare the way for United Nations involvement, for active international participation in an internal disorder.

U.N. Secretariat officials were familiar with some of the serious problems Congolese leaders faced in effecting the transition from colonial to indige-

1 For detailed discussions of pre-independence politics in the Congo, see Colin Legum, *Congo Disaster* (Baltimore: Penguin, 1960); Alan Merriam, *Congo: Background of Conflict* (Evanston: Northwestern University Press, 1961); Fernand Van Langenhove, *The Congo and Problems of Decolonization* (Brussels: Institute Royal des Relations Internationales, 1960).

2 Ernest Lefever, "The U.N. as a Foreign Policy Instrument: The Congo Crisis," *Foreign Policy in the Sixties: The Issues and the Instruments,* Roger Hilsman and Robert C. Good, eds. (Baltimore: Johns Hopkins Press, 1965), pp. 141–57.

nous rule. Prior to independence, Ralph Bunche and Congolese officials had discussed the possibility of U.N. military assistance in retraining the *Force Publique*. Through responsibilities placed upon him by the Council and Assembly and his own diplomatic initiatives in UNEF, UNOGIL, and other instances, Hammarskjold had enhanced his own personal prestige among delegates as well as the power of the office he held. Therefore it was natural that member states should look to the Secretariat, specifically to Hammarskjold, for guidance on the suitable course for the Organization to pursue when, on July 13, Congolese authorities appealed directly to the Secretary-General for U.N. military aid. It was also natural that when the Security Council decided to undertake collective action in response to the severe breakdown of law and order in the new state, Hammarskjold should be entrusted with executive responsibilities.

The July 11 announcement of the secession of Katanga Province by its President, Moise Tshombe, dramatized the inadequacies of the Belgian-drafted *Loi Fondamentale* and the fragile basis of support for the Leopoldville coalition regime of Lumumba and Kasavubu. The Government's cable to Hammarskjold on July 12 had charged Belgium with responsibility for the secession, calling it a "conspiracy" and "a disguised perpetuation of the colonialist regime."[3] The Kasavubu-Lumumba telegram to the Secretary-General emphasized the "illegal" Belgian actions in violation of the Treaty of Friendship concluded just prior to independence. Hammarskjold convened the Council to consider the new government's request for U.N. military assistance. He later explained his first use of Article 99 in terms emphasizing the need for prompt U.N. action:

> ...the breakdown of law and order created a situation which through its consequences had imposed a threat to peace and security justifying United Nations intervention...whether or not it was also held that the U.N. faced a conflict between two parties was, under the circumstances, in my view, legally not essential for the justification of the action.[4]

Anxious to avoid having the Congo difficulties drawn into cold war politics, Hammarskjold played down aspects that might have supported the Russian-inspired drive to apply enforcement measures under Articles 41 or 42 against Belgium.

In his remarks to the Council prior to the adoption of the first resolution on the Congo, the Secretary-General stressed that he would be guided by principles developed in the UNEF operation. In keeping with the pacific procedures employed in the establishment of U.N. military forces in the Suez crisis, the proposed Congo force would consist of troop contingents drawn from small and "middle" states with the permanent members of the Security Council excluded from participation. The disorders in the Congo at the time of the first resolution had not taken on the character of

---

3 U.N. Doc. S/4382, July 13, 1960, p. 2.
4 U.N. Doc. S/4389, July 18, 1960, p. 2.

full-scale civil war; on the basis of the information available, the Security Council supported Hammarskjold's proposals. Clearly, the Western powers were not prepared to call for "enforcement" action against Belgium and neither superpower wished to see forces of the other positioned in the unstable African country.

In its first resolution on the Congo, the Council "called upon" Belgium to withdraw its troops from the Congo but did not cite Articles 39 or 40 explicitly. The order of priorities the Secretary-General emphasized in his remarks to the Council was incorporated in the resolution of July 14 sponsored by Tunisia:[5] Belgian withdrawal from the Congo's territory and dispatch of military assistance to the Central Government to "enable national security forces to meet their tasks."[6] The resolution, empowering the Secretary-General, rather than member states, to "take steps" to render the distressed government aid, revealed the assumptions of members and the Secretary-General that a temporary security force of moderate proportions would suffice to restore order in the Congo after the withdrawal of Belgian troops. Behind the resolution lay additional assumptions: that the Belgian government would withdraw its forces as soon as the U.N. Force could become operational that the Congo's civilian administration (with U.N. assistance) could exercise its direction over the mutinous army, and that the Congolese authorities could work out their own constitutional arrangements for Katanga and other dissident provinces. No member state attempted to place cost or time limitations on the proposed Force; indeed the use of the term "United Nations Force" was specifically excluded from the first resolution.

The initial recruitment and dispatch of the new Force was accomplished smoothly. By July 31, 1960, ONUC, consisting of 11,155 troops from seven African nations and one European country, was deployed in all Congo provinces except Katanga. What Hammarskjold described as the "biggest single effort under United Nations colors organized and directed by the U.N. itself"[7] had begun its controversial existence.

Definition of ONUC's functions and powers proceeded in Council debates prior to the Council's second and third resolutions of July 22 and August 9. The July 22 resolution, adopted unanimously, called upon Belgium to "implement speedily" the withdrawal of its troops.[8] The August 9 resolution called upon Belgium to withdraw its troops from Katanga and authorized the entry of ONUC into the rebel province.[9] The Council upheld Hammarskjold's interpretations of the prior July resolutions: The U.N. could neither interfere in the Central Government's relation to Katanga nor could it undertake military operations against the secessionist province. In keeping with UNEF principles, Hammarskjold had

5 The U.S., the U.S.S.R., Argentina, Ceylon, Ecuador, Poland, Italy, and Tunisia voted for the resolution; China, Britain, and France abstained.
6 Security Council Resolution S/4387, July 14, 1960.
7 U.N. Doc. S/P.V. 877, July 20, 1960, p. 8.
8 Security Council Resolution S/4405, July 22, 1960.
9 Security Council Resolution S/4424, August 9, 1960. France and Italy abstained.

insisted from the beginning of the U.N.'s concern with the Congo that the new Force would not become a party to internal conflicts. The Organization's operation in the Congo as set forth in the first three Council resolutions was thus conceived as fulfilling the essentially negative task of preventing escalation by 1) securing the withdrawal of Belgian troops, 2) restoring law and order, and 3) ensuring respect for the territorial integrity and political independence of the Congo. The reactions of the U.N.'s officialdom to the political confusion in the Congo following the breakdown of law and order and the establishment of ONUC indicated that constitutional issues would be handled as a separate problem to be solved by the Congolese themselves.

II

Whatever the apparent relevance of UNEF for ONUC in the recruitment of men and matériel, it became clear in the summer and autumn of 1960 that the vacuum left by the flight of Belgian civilian personnel coupled with Katanga's secession and the tendency of each Congolese leader to solicit aid from foreign powers useful to his own political ends confronted the U.N. with a wholly different situation from that of Suez in 1956. As Ruth Russell has remarked, the effectiveness of U.N. peacekeeping operations "is in almost mathematical proportion to the degree of political accord that underlies them"[10] The minimal consensus that had made ONUC a reality in July began to shift in August and September, 1960, as it would in other critical moments of ONUC's history. Continuing disorder in the Congo challenged the principles and assumptions underlying ONUC's initiation and administration, principles and assumptions drawn from the Organization's previous experiences in Suez and Lebanon.

As the superpowers' national interests in the Congo became clarified, the fluid positions of the major powers that permitted passage of the July and August Council resolutions hardened. Soviet support for Lumumba during disorders in Kasai and American support for Kasavubu as the more moderate figure of the Leopoldville group were mirrored in Council debate.[11] Thus in August, the Soviet Union and Poland, expressing satisfaction with the idea of a nonintervention policy, maintained that the conflict between Leopoldville and Katanga could not be considered an internal disorder in view of Belgian support for Tshombe, hence the nonintervention posture suitable for the U.N. in internal matters should not apply. At this stage of the U.N.'s involvement in the Congo, both superpowers were willing to approve or reaffirm ambiguous measures so long as they could be re-evaluated in the clearer light of national policy considerations when problems of implementation arose. Clearly, no major power regarded ONUC as a substitute for its own diplomacy.

[10] Quoted in The New York *Times,* July 5, 1964.
[11] American endorsement secured the seating of Kasavubu's representatives in the Assembly on November 22, 1960, over Soviet and African protests.

Yet by September, 1960, as the largest economic and military factor in the Congo, ONUC had become a stake in the conflicts between the leaders in Leopoldville, Stanleyville, and Elizabethville. At the same time, working relations between U.N. field personnel and Congolese de facto and de jure authorities steadily deteriorated. U.N. field representatives were unable to repair the unsatisfactory relations obtaining with first the Kasavubu-Lumumba government and later with the Mobutu incumbents. Cordier's decision to close the radio station and the airport on September 5 at the height of the Kasavubu-Lumumba controversy showed that every act or omission of ONUC or its civilian personnel could affect relations between factional leaders throughout the Congo and their foreign backers, as well as relations between U.N. representatives and local officials. Cordier's replacement, Dayal, an experienced negotiator who had served in Lebanon, withheld recognition from Mobutu's commissioners and chose to deal with second-level officers. The ensuing friction, culminating in Dayal's recall in the spring of 1961, threatened to poison feelings between U.N. administrators and Congolese leaders. Thus nonintervention as a philosophical position had little operational value in the Congo itself, where, as Dayal observed, "almost every significant measure taken by ONUC in the impartial fulfillment of its mandate had been interpreted by one faction or another as being directed against itself."[12]

There were several ways in which dissatisfied members could express annoyance with Hammarskjold's management of ONUC. States could vote against U.N. resolutions, they could withhold funds for the Force, they could vilify the executive and administrative officials connected with ONUC, and they could sabotage field missions by means of their proxies on the scene, by withdrawing or threatening to withdraw troop contingents or logistical support. These methods were employed frequently by various states from September 1960 to February 1961.

In September, 1960, the failure of Council members to approve American and Soviet draft resolutions and a compromise resolution sponsored by Tunisia and Ceylon led to a convening of the Assembly in emergency session under the Uniting for Peace Resolution. The divergent views recorded in the Council were echoed in the Assembly. Nevertheless, a resolution sponsored by seventeen Afro-Asian states was adopted without negative votes on September 20.[13] The resolution, supporting Hammarskjold's actions, was notable for its inclusion of a request that all states direct aid to the Congo through U.N. channels, and its appeal to all Congolese groups to resolve their internal conflicts "with the assistance, as appropriate, of Asian and African representatives appointed by the Advisory Committee on the Congo, in consultation with the Secretary-General, for the purpose of conciliation."[14]

In the months between September 20 and February 21, 1961, neither the Council nor the Assembly was able to agree on additional resolutions

---

12 U.N. Doc. S/4557, November 2, 1960.
13 General Assembly Resolution 1474 Rev. 1 (ES-IV), September 20, 1960.
14 *Ibid.*, para. 3. For further discussion of the role of the Advisory Committee, see the author's *World Order and Local Disorder: The United Nations and Internal Conflicts* (Princeton: Princeton University Press, 1967), Chapter 3.

on the Congo disorders, despite the fact that events in the field made it clear that the guiding principles of the operation were inconsistent with each other and with the nature of the disorders the U.N. field personnel were attempting to ease. Questions arose requiring further clarification of ONUC's mandate: Could ONUC, under the rubric of "military assistance" to the Central Government, interpose itself between the disorganized ANC and the civilian population? Should the Force protect all Congolese leaders regardless of their relationship to the Leopoldville authorities? How far should ONUC's protection extend? Could action be taken against the Central Government if it violated the status of forces agreement or informal agreements negotiated by field personnel in order to give effect to Council resolutions? Could ONUC remain aloof from internal conflicts and still promote respect for the Congo's territorial integrity and political independence in the face of Katanga's continued secession? By February, 1961, it was evident that reconciliation of Congolese factions along lines set forth in conflicting aspects of the August 9 and September 20 resolutions had failed. Field officials had demonstrated the unworkability of nonintervention as a guiding precept: "in practice every day they were taking decisions implying the use of U.N. forces in ways capable of influencing the internal affairs and the political future of the Congo, nor was it possible for them to do otherwise."[15]

Thus ONUC reached a turning point. The situation in the field—the continued constitutional crisis, secession, and indiscipline of the ANC—indicated that temporary interposition on the UNEF model was inadequate to the task the U.N. faced in the Congo. Other assumptions at the root of the Council's decision to organize the Force required revision. The Assembly's September resolution had vindicated Hammarskjold's actions, but by February the unsavory circumstances surrounding Lumumba's death had aroused additional criticism from Soviet and Africa leaders. Important choices had to be faced if the mission were to remain in the Congo. For, it had become obvious that:

> The promotion of law and order in a setting of domestic factionalism is not compatible with the idea of neutrality and impartiality. It requires that a choice be made among competing prescriptions for law and order and competing candidates for the order-giving function.[16]

The Council could withdraw the Force from the Congo, leaving the country prey to externally abetted civil war, a more dangerous condition than July's domestic anarchy; or the Council could agree to go beyond the interposition concept by allowing ONUC more initiative in the promotion of a political settlement and in the use of force vis-à-vis principal disputants. The Council also could consider a change in the executive direction of

[15] Conor Cruise O'Brien, *To Katanga and Back* (New York: Simon and Schuster, Inc., 1962), p. 60.

[16] Inis Claude, "The United Nations and the Use of Force," *International Conciliation*, No. 532 (March 1961), p. 379.

the ONUC. Guinea, Morocco, and the UAR had withdrawn contingents from ONUC, and others had announced plans to follow suit. Entangled in a web of political, logistical, and economic problems, ONUC faced its gravest threat—civil war and complete breakdown of law and order— when its numbers were seriously depleted.

III

In the Security Council debate prior to adoption of the February resolution, the Soviet Union extended its attack on Hammarskjold's direction of ONUC. Other states, again rejecting Russian suggestions that the U.N. apply sanctions under Article 41 against Belgium, and that the Council set a one-month time limit for ONUC's termination, nevertheless were disturbed by Hammarskjold's "too narrow legality" in the interpretation of Council and Assembly directives. The Secretary-General insisted that a new mandate was needed, that the Council "cannot shirk its responsibilities by expecting from the Secretariat action on which it is not prepared to take decisions itself."[17] Replying to Soviet criticism of his handling of Lumumba's capture, Hammarskjold argued:

> The United Nations had neither the power nor the right to liberate Mr. Lumumba from his captors by force—I say the United Nations because to my knowledge not even this Council or the General Assembly could have such a right, much less did it exist for the U.N. representatives in the Congo under this mandate.[18]

Other interested parties agreed that ONUC's mandate should be reviewed, though there were apparent differences of opinion as to which "prescription for order" in the Congo should be followed, if indeed such a prescription could be found. American and Soviet disagreement over the U.N.'s policies in the Congo could be expected, but splits between the various African states were to prove equally harmful to efforts to resolve the Congo's difficulties. The cleavage between the Brazzaville and Casablanca groups of African states stemmed from their different attitudes toward Tshombe. For the former French colonies, Tshombe seemed to be the most stable element in the turbulent political scene and could be regarded as a bulwark against Communist intrusion into Africa. These states were critical of ONUC, for they feared that the Force might set a dangerous precedent if military action were used to crush the Katangese President. In Andrew Boyd's opinion:

> Many Afro-Asians were, I think, cautious about creating precedents for U.N. action in domestic conflict cases. In the various discussions about U.N. forces

---

[17] Security Council, *Official Records,* Sixteenth Year, 935th Meeting (February 15, 1961), para. 35.
[18] *Ibid.,* para. 10.

there had always been a marked Afro-Asian caution, arising, one supposes, basically from fear of "neo-imperialist" use of the U.N. in weak newly-independent states. The Communist countries share, even foster this attitude of caution.[19]

The Brazzaville group itself split later at the sixteenth Session of the Assembly. As regards ONUC in early 1961, the Casablanca states, a loose grouping of African nations led by Ghana and Guinea, were more sympathetic to Soviet attitudes. Advocating the opposite of a cautious attitude toward Tshombe, Nkrumah pressed for strong action to eliminate the rebel leader. He feared that a successful revolt of a Congolese province from the Central Government might lead to U.N. sanctification of African separatist movements that could engulf his own one-party state.[20] As early as September, 1960, Nkrumah had warned that the U.N.'s nonintervention posture in the Congo conflict would prove disastrous:

> The United Nations need not go to the assistance of any country which invites its intervention but once it does so, it owes an obligation to the government and the people of that country not to interfere in such a way as to prevent the legitimate government which invited it to enter the country from fulfilling its mandate. In other words, it is impossible for the U.N. at one and the same time to preserve law and order and to be neutral between the legal authorities and the lawbreakers. That is, unfortunately, exactly what the U.N. has attempted to do in the Congo and that is the cause of all the present difficulties and disagreements.[21]

Having secured independence and self-determination for their countries, Nkrumah and Touré were determined to consolidate a favorable political and territorial status quo in Africa. The Congo conflict threatened to undermine the basis for stability on the African continent, they stressed.

The diplomatic isolation that was to mark Soviet conduct during ONUC's four years had taken form by February, 1961. As the U.S. had become committed to the fortunes of Kasavubu and the series of Leopoldville functionaries, the Soviet Union groped for a proxy figure popular enough to challenge the American-backed Central Government. Lumumba's downfall narrowed the choice to Antoine Gizenga, whose lack of popular support impaired Russian strategy in the Congo. Within the U.N., the Soviet delegate dubbed Tshombe Belgium's "lackey" and attempted to portray Khrushchev as the personal guardian of all new states against the colonial powers. Quick to denounce American domination of ONUC, the Russians developed a conspiracy theory to explain Belgian involvement in Katanga. The Soviets were irked that no Russian delegate or official was party to the inner workings of the Secretariat's Congo club, which consisted of a Nigerian, an Englishman, an Indian, and three Americans. But the

[19] Andrew Boyd, quoted in O'Brien, *op. cit.*, p. 89.
[20] See John Spencer, "Africa at the U.N.," *International Organization*, XVI (Spring 1962), p. 375ff.
[21] General Assembly, *Official Records*, Fifteenth Session, 869th Plenary Meeting, September 23, 1960, p. 62, para. 17.

Soviets had no success in winning acceptance for their troika proposals or other plans that would have altered the executive direction of the Force. Significantly, the Russians, in maligning the Congo operation, did not counter it with massive unilateral aid which might have antagonized those smaller states still supporting Hammarskjold. Russian behavior in the Congo turmoil recalls similar behavior in the Spanish civil war: conflict with the international organization, failure to defy it completely, and reluctance to involve itself in war.[22]

On February 21, 1961, after several draft resolutions failed of adoption, the Council passed a resolution sponsored by the UAR, Ceylon, and Liberia. This resolution, adopted by a vote of 9–0–2, with Russia and France abstaining, was affirmed by the Assembly in April. It empowered ONUC to "take immediately all appropriate measures to prevent the occurrence of civil war in the Congo, including arrangements for cease-fires, the halting of all military operations, the prevention of clashes, and the use of force, if necessary in the last resort."[23] Other relevant provisions called for the evacuation of Belgian paramilitary and military personnel, political advisers and mercenaries, and an impartial investigation into Lumumba's death. The Council also urged "the convening of Parliament and the taking of necessary protective measures in that connection."[24] ONUC now had legal approval for pressuring Tshombe to remove Belgians from Katanga and for rendering assistance to Congolese political leaders or civilians threatened by the disorderly ANC.

The Secretary-General welcomed the new resolution as a clearer indication of the Council's attitude toward ONUC. Five countries including the United States stated that the type of force authorized in the operative paragraphs would not conflict with the Charter's prohibition in Article 2:7 and that force would not be employed to impose a political settlement. On its face the resolution seemed to accord with Hammarskjold's previously stated views on the suitable relationship between ONUC's political and military functions:

> I reject everything that would have a touch of control or direction of the Congo's internal affairs...and, second, I do not believe that the use of military initiative, or pressure, is the way to bring about the political structure in terms of persons or institutions which is at present the first need of the Congo. The United Nations can help in such a direction, but that is by the normal political and diplomatic means of persuasion and advice, not by the use of force or intimidation.[25]

But eight months after independence, the remaining Congolese de jure and de facto authorities had shown themselves incapable of resolving their

22 Alexander Dallin, *The Soviet Union at the U.N.* (New York: Frederick A. Praeger, Inc., 1962), p. 150.
23 Security Council Resolution S/4722, February 21, 1961.
24 *Ibid.*, Part B, para. 1.
25 General Assembly, *Official Records,* Fifteenth Session, 953rd Plenary Meeting, December 17, 1960, p. 1372, para. 182.

disputes by their own "normal political and diplomatic means." It was obvious that a new political structure could not be built without some form of international assistance. Authorization for active U.N. conciliation, avoided in the July and August Council resolutions, had developed first in the Assembly's September resolution and later in the Council's February resolution. Clearly, rival national influences would be a factor in determining the type of political edifice U.N. organs and field representatives would labor to construct. The tone of the February resolution accented prevention; the Council did not specify what "measures" were to be taken to secure the withdrawal of Belgian military and political advisers and mercenaries. In February it was apparent that any use of force by ONUC would invite controversial interpretations from Congolese leaders and their foreign sponsors, who could easily challenge U.N. officials' definitions of the term "last resort." Council members were unable to agree on a resolution authorizing ONUC to use the necessary force to prevent atrocities against political leaders in the various Congolese cities.

The period from July, 1960, to February, 1961, had tested ONUC's capacity to maintain sufficient order to make the host state viable and to deter national interventions. The Soviet Union had been prevented from large-scale intrusion with men and supplies, chiefly due to Washington's insistence that the Sudan and Egypt forbid Russian overflights of their territories. But in February, 1961, the host state's government lacked both viability and constitutional authorization. With its old mandate unrealized, ONUC took on additional responsibilities with a markedly inadequate force-in-being.

IV

ONUC's field representative now undertook more intensive efforts to promote a political settlement in the Congo, while the Force's attempts to stabilize the country continued. These efforts were hampered by Tshombe's assertions of "self-determination" for Katanga and by his program to secure recognition from African and non-African states. The annual payment of $40 million in royalties and taxes by the Union Minière de Haut Katanga, a mining complex controlled by British and Belgian interests, enabled Tshombe to buy arms, pay mercenaries, and maintain an international propaganda machine hostile to the U.N., the Central Government, and the U.S. The extent of UMHK's influence was apparent to U.N. field representatives:

> It is possible to accept the statement that the Union Minière as such was not promoting, actively and directly, secessionist politics in Katanga. . . . But of course such "nonintervention" in the affairs of a state whose foundations the company had encouraged, if not instigated, a state which lived on duties paid to it by the company in defiance of the law of the Congo, and which

was known to be defended on the international plane by the company's agents and money was nonintervention of a rather special kind.[26]

The efforts of the Organization to promote a political solution to the internal conflicts in the Congo were not limited to the activities of field officials. In November, 1960, a U.N. Conciliation Commission was formed under the Advisory Committee's aegis as stipulated in the Assembly's resolution of September 20. Amid the growing feeling of African leaders and Western statesmen that some form of legal government could and should be established, Nigeria's Jaja Wachuku led the Commission to the Congo and conducted interviews with major political figures there. After six weeks of observation in January and February, 1961, the group could report no headway in reconciling differences, but agreement was reached on the conditions that should prevail if a constitutional government were to be restored. The Commission concluded that a government of national unity, a federal structure, was the only from of government that could preserve the independence and political integrity of the Congo. The Commission declared in its report of March, 1961, that necessary steps toward attainment of national reconciliation should include the reconvening of parliament under proper protection, a summit conference of Congolese leaders, the drafting of a new constitution to replace the *Loi Fondamentale*, the evacuation of foreign political and military personnel, the release of political prisoners, and the reorganization of the army.[27] The Commission's recommendations were a catalogue of the Congo's political and military troubles and they furnished Hammarskjold with broadly based goals for conciliatory efforts; but these were goals suggested by outside observers. They reflected the aims of some, but not all, the leaders interviewed in the field.

By the time the Conciliation Commission's report was made available, difficulties which continued to complicate the task of finding political solutions to the Congo's post-independence chaos had emerged. Outside parties—representatives of the U.N. or national statesmen (and later, delegations from the O.A.U.)—could propose solutions to rival leaders in the Congo, but these political figures were under no obligation to accept offers of mediation or conciliation under the direction of any state or grouping of states. Yet they were susceptible to the influences of their foreign backers. Outside parties lost no time in making suggestions, but these plans for "national reconciliation," for a federal structure, often reflected a Western penchant for representative political institutions which in the perspective of the protracted strife in the Congo seems ill-suited to the indigenously African aspects of the Congo's politics—the palaver and proliferation of loyalties to entities smaller than the state.[28]

26 O'Brien, *op. cit.*, pp. 175ff.
27 See U.N. Doc. A/4711 and Add. 1 and 2, March 20, 1961.
28 See Herbert J. Spiro, *Politics in Africa* (Englewood Cliffs, N.J.: Prentice Hall, Inc., 1964), pp. 115–29.

In August, 1961, following the Tananarive and Coquihatville conferences, the reconvened Congolese parliament elected Cyrille Adoula as
premier. This accomplishment of U.N. field representatives was warmly
endorsed by the U.S. government and Hammarskjold. But the restoration
of legal government in the formal sense contributed little to the underlying
problem of national reconciliation in the substantive sense. Nevertheless
the Adoula government was an administration better equipped to deal
with the U.N. in its efforts to protect civilian personnel from attacks and
to terminate the secession, especially in view of the U.S. strengthened
support of the Leopoldville regime.

The new Central Government came into existence pledged to expel all
mercenaries and foreign officers serving in Katanga. The Adoula government's decree echoed the terms of the Council's February resolution. A
common design for Katanga's reintegration into a unitary Congo state had
taken form. Behind the U.S. and U.N. concern for the Congo's political
structure—concern leading to the events of September, 1961—lay fears
of impending economic collapse. Washington and New York officials were
agreed that the Congo could survive as an economic unit only if Katanga's
disproportionate wealth was redirected into Leopoldville coffers. Massive
bilateral U.S. aid and the U.N. civilian operation could not shore up the
tottering country permanently.

The question of ONUC's mandate, especially its use of force, and the
question of priorities for ONUC in carrying out Council directives were
now posed with particular urgency when, five months after passage of the
February resolution, the Belgian officers and the South African and other
mercenaries who had not been withdrawn pursuant to that resolution
became the chief object of concern to the Leopoldville government and
U.N. field representatives. In September, 1961, the first of three military
actions designed to end Katanga's secession was undertaken.[29]

The first military engagement between ONUC and the Katangese
gendarmerie ended in embarrassment for the U.N. and a cease-fire agreement denigrated by both the Soviet Union and Central Government
officials who regarded it as a capitulation to the rebel leader. Hammarskjold's death, coupled with the incomplete evacuation of mercenaries
and continued violence after the September fighting, resulting in greater
U.S. and Secretariat impatience with Tshombe's quixotic behavior, impatience increased by the lack of compliance with the provisional cease-fire
order of September 20. By November, 1961, the political majority behind
the February resolution had shifted. Russia now favored the U.N.'s use of
force to apprehend the remaining foreign mercenaries, as did the United
States. But the British government concurred with the French government,
whose representative insisted that "the use of force may have the opposite

[29] For details of the fighting, see O'Brien, *op. cit.*, pp. 63–330; Ernest Lefever,
Crisis in the Congo: A United Nations Force in Action (Washington: The Brookings
Institution, 1965), pp. 79–88: Arthur Lee Burns and Nina Heathcote, *Peacekeeping
by U.N. Forces, From Suez Through the Congo* (New York: Frederick A. Praeger,
Inc., 1963), pp. 100–31.

results to those intended by the Council."[30] Over the protests of the two European states, the United States led the Council to passage of a new resolution deepening the Organization's commitment to the Central Government.

V

The November 24 resolution authorized the Acting Secretary-General, U Thant,

to take vigorous action, including the use of requisite measure of force, if necessary, for the immediate apprehension, detention pending legal action, and/or deportation of all foreign military and paramilitary personnel and political advisers not under the United Nations Command, and mercenaries as laid down in paragraph A-2 of the Security Council resolution of February 21, 1961.[31]

The resolution also requested Thant "to take all necessary measures to prevent the entry or return of such elements under whatever guise and also of arms, equipment, or other material in support of such activities." The Council also declared that "all secessionist activities against the Republic of the Congo are contrary to the *Loi fondamentale* and Security Council decisions and specifically *demands* that such activities which are now taking place in Katanga shall cease forthwith."

The Council's resolution of November 24, 1961, did not refer to Articles 41 or 42 in keeping with the convictions members (except the Soviet Union) had expressed in the first four resolutions and in debates preceding their adoption that ONUC should not be construed as enforcement action against any state or interested party. The firm U.S. position plus the Belgian Foreign Minister Spaak's endeavors to bring Adoula and Tshombe together permitted Thant to counter British and French opposition to the November 24 resolution with a pledge to press for national reconciliation. Thant showed that he had different ideas, or perhaps a different style from that of his predecessor, in the conduct of the U.N.'s second military operation against the rebel province.

On November 30, Sture Linner reported from Elizabethville that increased tension and attacks on U.N. officials demonstrated Tshombe's inability to control his forces or to alter his policies toward the U.N. and its resolutions. Linner's fears of new hostilities materialized in December. The action taken by ONUC occurred before the political majority behind the November resolution could disintegrate. Although the operation involved

---

[30] Security Council, *Official Records*, Sixteenth Year, 982nd Meeting, November 24, 1961, para. 60. See also, 976th Meeting, November 17, 1961, paras. 157, 164, 166–69.
[31] Security Council Resolution S/5002, November 24, 1961.

offensive tactics and 6,000 men as compared with 1,400 employed in the September encounters, the second military action was described by U.N. officials as "defensive," as an attempt to "regain and assure our freedom of movement, to restore law and order...and to react vigorously in self-defense to every assault on our present positions."[32] As fighting spread, numerous governments pressed for a cease-fire.

What emerged from the U.N.'s second military action in Katanga was closer cooperation between U.S. authorities and ONUC's executive directors. The American role in seeking a political solution grew more obvious, as the American ambassador, in close touch with Washington, arranged a Tshombe-Adoula meeting and secured the adherence of the two leaders to the eight-point Kitona Declaration, a document affirming the *Loi Fondamentale* and the unity of the Congo under Kasavubu's control. The British and Belgian interests in Katanga helped Tshombe in his dilatory attitude toward his Kitona pledges. For six months, U.N. field representatives, operating under vague mandates, confined their roles to passive good offices, providing safe conduct for delegates to conferences and attempting to create a favorable atmosphere for negotiations between the secessionist groups and the Central Government. Sporadic talks led to acceptance of U.N. proposals in the military, monetary, transport, and communications fields, but the future relationship of Katanga to the Republic remained unsettled, as rival political leaders blamed each other for delays.

In keeping with their earlier attitudes toward the secession, the United States and Secretariat officials continued to press for a solution favorable to the Leopoldville government's interests. The submission of the Thant Plan for National Reconciliation in August, 1962, marked the beginning of a new, more active phase in peaceful settlement attempts. The Thant Plan was put forward as a nonnegotiable proposal, to be accepted or rejected by the parties in its entirety. Its provisions called for adoption of a new federal constitution to be drafted by a special U.N. commission, an interim division of Katanga's revenues from taxes, mining concessions, royalties, and other sources on a fifty-fifty basis with the Central Government, termination of the secession, currency reunification, a general amnesty, and revision of the Leopoldville administration to include representatives of all political parties and all provinces.[33] The Plan provided for the consideration of economic sanctions if Tshombe did not indicate a willingness to comply with its stipulations.

Continued unrest in the Congo stimulated Thant to ask members to consider the applicability of economic sanctions to force Tshombe's cooperation in December, 1962. The diverging attitudes of the European states with economic interests in Katanga and the United States with interests in working out federal solutions using the U.N. blocked realization of the sanctions idea. The U.S.-backed Adoula government quickly accepted the

---

[32] U.N. Doc. S/5025, December 15, 1961, p. 14.
[33] U.N. Doc. S/5053, Add. 11, August 20, 1962, pp. 16–17.

Thant Plan (of which the American government was the principal architect), while Tshombe first accepted, then procrastinated. In a short-lived attempt to placate Britain and Belgium, the U.S. submitted and then hastily withdrew the McGhee Plan which would have allowed Katanga a greater share in revenues and more autonomy vis-à-vis the Central Government than the Thant Plan. The Thant Plan, submitted to the parties as an externally sponsored solution, committed the U.N.'s prestige to a particular set of recommendations and to the fortunes of a demonstrably insecure, if legal, central regime. Technically, parties were not obligated to accept federalism as the final solution, but the pressures brought to bear on the various parties bilaterally and via ONUC were strong. The Organization, in promoting a federal rather than a confederal structure, sought to avoid the extremes of Balkanization in Africa and the repressiveness of a unitary state composed of hostile subgroups. In theory, such a solution appeared sound; but in practice, the inability of a central regime in Leopoldville to exert its authority throughout the state indicated that a federal solution could be achieved only if imposed by an outside party, by the U.S.-U.N. In terms of the Congo's long-range future, such an outside settlement might prove unacceptable to provincial groups within the country and to other African states in similar post-colonial political straits, who feared "neo-imperialism."

A year of active U.S.-U.N. involvement in promoting direct but unsuccessful negotiations between Congo disputants and a joint effort against the Orientale gendarmerie supporting Gizenga drew to a close in December, 1962, with Tshombe's failure to comply with the Thant Plan. The United States and the Soviets were now in agreement to use force against Katanga via ONUC, but for different reasons. At this juncture, the Secretary-General pressed for logistical support from the United States sufficient to terminate the secession militarily. As a result of General Truman's mission to the Congo, the U.S. supplied Thant with new aircraft, radio communications, and truck transports needed to carry out a third military action in Katanga. The fact that resistance from an estimated 20,000 mercenaries fell away, permitting the U.N. to take over the province, made the operation seem less contentious than it might have been in view of Tshombe's announced intention to pursue a scorched earth policy in the province rather than yield. Defending the action as a step needed to insure ONUC's "freedom of movement," a purpose for which the Council had not authorized the use of force in specific resolutions, Thant later placed the U.N.'s military actions in Katanga in a different light: "Other than its successful efforts to eliminate the mercenaries in South Katanga, in pursuance of the Security Council mandate, the Force took no military initiatives involving the use of force; it launched no offensive."[34]

The success of the third military action was marred by a series of events in early January, 1963. A brief pause in the U.N.'s third military action in Katanga was followed on December 30 by an announcement from

---

34 U.N. Doc. S/5784, June 29, 1964, p. 40.

Robert A. Gardiner, the U.N. operations chief in Leopoldville, that the
U.N. forces were "not going to make the mistake this time of stopping
short." "This is going to be as decisive as we can make it," Gardiner
was quoted as saying.[35] On January 1, ONUC troops entered Jadotville, an
important center of operations for UMHK, apparently ignoring an order
from Thant to refrain from entering the town. Ralph Bunche, sent to
investigate what U.N. officials described as a "serious breakdown in communications and coordination,"[36] concluded that a recurrence of the Jadotville episode could be avoided by better liaison and a thorough overhaul
of U.N. civil-military relations.[37] To some observers, "bad communications" seemed a euphemism for differences of opinion within the Secretariat
command chain over the military action.[38]

ONUC's third and decisive military action in December 1962-January
1963 ended Katanga's secession; interested outside parties and the U.N.
again turned to the political and economic problems of reintegrating the
province into the Republic. The end of the secession was accomplished
by the use of requisite force rather than by economic pressures or diplomatic
means, but the issue of self-determination for all parts of the Congo
appeared settled. With the endorsement of the left and center groups plus
the Latin American states, the U.S. had won approval for the military
operation; with the support of the right and center groups, the U.S.
received backing for its decision to maintain Tshombe as a political force
in the Congo. But the quest for a lasting political solution to the territory's
disorders was impeded by the political vacuum in Katanga after Tshombe's
flight from Elizabethville. While the end of Katanga's secession in itself
eased the situation in the Congo, it threw the remaining political problems
of the Republic into sharper relief. The Congo's future as an independent
state, capable of coping with economic and internal security demands,
appeared to depend upon whether massive aid along the lines urged by
the American-sponsored Cleveland mission could prevent a further breakdown.

VI

The future use of U.N. or other military forces in the Congo remained
an unsolved issue in early 1963. The heavy financial and political burdens
placed on the U.N. by a continuation of the field operation required that
member states reassess the status of ONUC. In February, 1963, civil war
seemed to have been averted. The Security Council, in its various resolutions, had empowered ONUC to 1) maintain the territorial integrity and

---

[35] The New York Times, January 1, 1963.
[36] U.N. Press Release, SG/1406, January 3, 1963.
[37] U.N. Doc. S/5053, Add. 14, January 10, 1963, pp. 156ff.
[38] See for example, Philip Ben, "Lessons of the Congo," The New Republic
(January 26, 1963), pp. 7–8.

political independence of the Congo; 2) assist the Congo government in restoring and maintaining law and order; 3) prevent the occurrence of civil war in the Congo; 4) secure the immediate withdrawal and evacuation from the Congo of all foreign military and paramilitary personnel and all mercenaries; and 5) render technical assistance. In February, 1963, Thant reported that civil war had been prevented and that foreign military personnel had withdrawn, but that the Congo required additional technical assistance in the retaining of its disorganized army. Moreover, the Secretary-General warned, the country's precarious state of law and order could invite external interventions threatening the territorial integrity and political independence of the Congo Republic.[39] The Secretary-General envisioned a "caretaker" role for ONUC in a transition period to last until the termination of the Force's mandate.

As the question of terminating ONUC became less theoretical, member states had to consider the alternatives open to the Organization in the light of information available. Should the U.N. continue to shoulder the burden that had threatened to topple the entire Organization? Could the U.N. pull out without additional damage to its prestige and finances, leaving the country to face an uncertain future, or take on the still heavier task of reconstruction for which it might be unequipped? The first Council resolution had left the question of termination indefinite; assistance to the Congo government would be rendered until the national security forces could perform their duties. Could the host state determine when the U.N. Force should cease to operate in its territory if a political majority in the Organization should feel that the situation constituted a threat to international peace and security? Could the host negotiate for ONUC's withdrawal or could the Force withdraw without the host state's acquiescence?

Although the ending of Katanga's secession produced a lessening of international concern for the Congo's future among those states whose primary interest in Belgian withdrawal had been satisfied, the American government persuaded Thant to accept a continuation of a reduced U.N. Force for at least six months.[40] After Thant confirmed December 31, 1963, as the deadline for the Central Government to assume responsibilities for law and order throughout the Congo, the Assembly voted sufficient funds to extend ONUC's life until June 30, 1964. The vote to extend ONUC represented a compromise between the more militant African states—Ghana and the UAR—who felt the U.N. should withdraw, and the U.S. and other Western states, who feared a collapse of governmental authority and renewed tribal fighting. In yet another ad hoc financial improvisation, the U.S. and Britain agreed to pay the additional $10 or $12 million needed to maintain 3,000 troops in the Congo for another six months.

Between January and June, 1964, the phasing out of ONUC continued. In advance of ONUC's departure, the U.N. and the Adoula government failed to conclude agreements for the reorganization of the army. Revolts

39 U.N. Doc. S/5240, February 4, 1963, pp. 98–99.
40 Lefever, *Crisis in the Congo,* p. 133.

in Kivu dramatized the obvious fact that the poorly trained, inefficient, 35,000-man army would not be able to meet the internal security requirements of the country after ONUC's termination. Plans for Canada, Norway, Israel, and others to take on responsibility for individual segments of the ANC also faltered. Although proposals for Nigerian or other African forces to render military assistance never came to fruition, the Congo government did not request an extension of ONUC beyond the June deadline.

As ONUC prepared to withdraw in mid-1964, efforts to seal Katanga's reintegration into the Republic with a new draft constitution resulted in the passage of a document emulating the French Fifth Republic's provisions. The Adoula regime, heavily dependent on U.S. diplomatic, economic, and other support, had failed to reconcile the political differences which continued to divide the country four years after independence. The new presidential system indicated that Congolese legislators had little difficulty establishing some of the forms of a representative governmental structure, but the substance, the underlying consensus needed to make such a system work, was lacking. Amid spreading rebellion in Kivu and other sections, Tshombe emerged from a palaver of the provincial authorities left in the Congo as the head of an interim government dubbed "Government of National Reconciliation." As the new administration took control, it was clear that reconciliation expressed a hope, not a reality. With the exception of Kalonji, no other regional figure of consequence was included in the Cabinet. The open hostility of other African states to Tshombe's new role suggested that the Congo's troubles were far from over.

The U.N.'s official responsibilities for political solutions, for dealing with secessionist movements, for protecting human rights in the Congo ended with ONUC's departure. The United States involvement continued as the Tshombe government relied on American and Belgian assistance in putting down challenges to central authority. The new Tshombe administration faced the need to reform the corrupt provincial administrations, to restore order, and to staff the Leopoldville government—enormous tasks in view of the elections promised after a four-year hiatus. Six months later, despite the presence of U.S. planes, white mercenary troops, and Cuban exile pilots and military instructors, the legally constituted Tshombe government in Leopoldville had not succeeded in quelling rebellions that threatened to bring down the Central regime. The U.S.-Belgian airlift in November, 1964, further demonstrated the security problems of the vast territory. The widespread political repercussions of the rescue mission pointed up a crucial aspect of the Congo's post-ONUC confusion: as the "white man's puppet" who led the secession of Katanaga province, Tshombe was vilified to the point where no military aid could be expected to come from African nations even if the former rebel leader had agreed to broaden the base of his "Government of National Reconciliation."

Similarly, expectations that the Organization of African Unity might play a constructive role in the transition period after ONUC's termination were dashed by reactions of individual African leaders to the continuing rebellion against Tshombe's Central government and the Belgian-American rescue mission. The increasing radicalism of the governments of Ghana, the U.A.R., and Algeria[41] led Nigeria's Jaja Wachuku to charge in December, 1964, that the Congo's difficulties stemmed from "the refusal of certain African states to accept the basic fact that the Congo is a sovereign state."[42] Objecting to Tshombe's "neo-colonialist" orientation, the militant African leaders minimized the massacre of white hostages in Stanleyville and played up the "imperialist intervention" and the "massacres" of Congolese by mercenaries when the Council discussed the November, 1964, Belgian-American airlift. The likelihood of additional Belgian-American "interventions" in the Congo was diminished by the outcry (largely racially tinged) from smaller states in the Council meetings of December.[43] Nevertheless, the facade of African unity was laid bare in the vituperative Council debates on the Belgian-American operation. Prior to the rescue mission, the O.A.U's Conciliation Commission failed in its attempts to negotiate the release of rebel-held prisoners, revealing the impotence of the regional body. Fissures within the membership of the O.A.U., with some states intervening in behalf of the rebels and some arguing for recognition of the legitimacy of the Tshombe government, cast doubt on the possibility of a constructive role for the O.A.U. in the remaining issues of peaceful change affecting Africa.

VII

From the standpoint of the Organization's experience in internal disorders, ONUC is a highly significant landmark for the scale and duration of the U.N.'s effort. The preceding discussion has emphasized that events quickly demonstrated the inadequacy of Hammarskjold's conceptions for the U.N.'s actions in the Congo, conceptions derived from previous experiences in Lebanon and Suez. Central to the late Secretary-General's thinking was the deeply rooted conviction that the U.N. via ONUC should neither become a party to internal conflicts nor influence their outcome. This conviction could provide operational guidance for field officials only if outside powers refrained from endorsing or aiding any rival local authorities and if the host government maintained sufficient control over the country's economic, political, and military life. But if a central government did have control over these areas there would be no need for U.N. or other interventions or interpositionary corps. The tendency of the Council's permanent members to aid factional leaders invalidated one of Hammarskjold's assumptions; the continuing constitutional crisis invalidated the other.

41 See Colin Legum, "What Kind of Radicalism for Africa," *Foreign Affairs,* XLIII (January 1965), pp. 237–51.
42 The New York *Times,* December 6, 1964.
43 See Security Council, *Official Records,* Nineteenth Year, 1170th–1173rd Meetings, 1175th–1178th Meetings, 1181st and 1183rd–1189th Meetings, December 9, 10, 15–30, 1964.

By playing up Belgian interference in the Congo rather than the Congo's internal political problems, Hammarskjold and Congolese leaders established an order of priorities relegating conciliation to a secondary role in ONUC's early stages. Later when Hammarskjold (leaning heavily on American political initiatives as well as funds) did back the Adoula government against Katanga, the unstable political majorities in the Council and Assembly favoring strengthened directives for ONUC crippled the U.N. in its dealings with Tshombe, who relied on British and Belgian economic interests to support the continued secession. Abstentions and negative votes on Council resolutions were a sign that Hammarskjold's position was becoming increasingly untenable.

The long peacekeeping effort in the Congo placed extensive responsibilities on the Secretary-General's office. The experience gained in interpreting mandates and managing a complicated field operation established a reservoir of information applicable to future internal conflicts. But just as the financial reserves of the U.N. alone were inadequate for the Congo's needs, so too the techniques of the multilateral organization alone proved insufficient to achieve what now appears to have been the too ambitious goal of national reconciliation. Grave problems developed from the expectation that ONUC could be involved in both negative and positive political and military tasks at the same time. If the Organization's negative task of preventing the escalation of local conflicts and establishing law and order were difficult to accomplish, the task of fostering national reconciliation along lines prescribed by Western states proved equally difficult. Efforts to initiate negotiations between Congolese officials were left to field personnel, who, equipped with the Secretary-General's interpretations of Council and Assembly mandates, necessarily improvised when legalistic details of resolutions failed to fit the facts of the increasingly fluid situation in Elizabethville and other outlying cities. The Congolese parties to the series of internal conflicts were incapable of resolving their own differences along Western lines of political accommodation, yet capable of sabotaging any settlement put forward by the U.N. or others, much in the same way their foreign supporters were capable of undermining Council or Assembly resolutions. The need to collaborate with the U.S. for logistical and other military support for ONUC linked the organization to American proposals for political solutions and exposed the Secretariat to hostile criticism from the excluded Soviet bloc.

While the U.N.'s political and financial over-commitment in the Congo internal conflicts was most dramatically underlined by the controversy over the military operations conducted in Katanga, in the realm of political solutions the U.N.'s activities in the Congo also bore signs of overextension; the prolonged effort to foster a political solution couched in terms of a federal structure and national reconciliation examplifies the inherent difficulties in placing the burden for selecting or implementing such settlements on the Organization. Disorders in the Congo while ONUC was deployed and the unrest since the Force's withdrawal raise questions about the capacity of an international organization to find criteria for emerging countries without political traditions linked to statehood. The inapplicability of Western federalism or parliamentary rule to the Congo's political structure is apparent. Political institutions rooted in cultural traditions with a long history cannot be grafted onto a wholly different base.

In his final report on ONUC, Thant emphasized the weaknesses which had marked the four-year peacekeeping operation. Among the weaknesses he noted was the lack of integration of national units under a U.N. Command, a factor which hampered morale and effectiveness. Of far greater consequence for future peacekeeping operations was Thant's assessment of the Congo's future. In terms applicable to other internal disorders, he remarked,

> I believe that a further extension of the stay of the Force in the Congo would provide no solution to the remaining problems of the Congo. The current difficulties in the country reflect conflicts of an internal political nature, with their main origins found in the absence of a genuine and sufficiently widespread sense of national unity among the various ethnic groups composing the population of the Congo. There is little assistance that the United Nations Force can render in that kind of situation since the solution of conflict depends entirely on the willingness and readiness of the Congolese political leaders and the traditional chiefs and their respective followers to merge their factional interests in a true effort toward national conciliation.[44]

Less than a year after ONUC's departure, its stay in the Congo appeared to have contributed to an interval, at best a hiatus, in the continuing local violence and range of external interventions by major powers and revolutionary African states determined to establish in the Congo a government to their ideological and political liking. This judgment was borne out by the attitudes interested parties adopted toward the Council's sixth resolution urging an end of all foreign intervention, a cease-fire, and withdrawal of foreign mercenaries.[45] The Council's resolution of December 30, 1964, marked a compromise between the demands of militant African states for condemnation of the U.S.-Belgian airlift and American interests in exposing the interference of others in the Congo's affairs. The ineffectuality of the resolution, which also called for the Organization of African Unity to promote efforts toward national reconciliation, became apparent as each group of interested parties announced its own interpretation. The U.S. argued that its military aid to Tshombe could not be considered "intervention" because it was sent at the request of the legitimate government. The radical African countries, Algeria, Ghana, and the U.A.R., defended their arms shipments to the rebels on grounds that as Africans they could not be considered "outsiders." And the Kasavubu-Tshombe incumbent government took the view that the cease-fire would permit the rebels to gather strength and would partition the Congo. The group of more moderate African states, including Nigeria and the Ivory Coast, while supporting

44 U.N. Doc. S/5784, June 29, 1964, p. 42.
45 Security Council Resolution S/6129, December 30, 1964.

the U.S. view on the legal aspects of intervention, decried the airlift and the use of white mercenaries by Tshombe.

In the months following U.N. discussion of the airlift, the Congo enjoyed a precarious stability under Kasavubu and Tshombe, but remained linked to competitive outside power determined to influence its political complexion. It is perhaps too early to assess the achievements and failures of the Mobutu military regime that seized control during the 1965–1966 year of coups in Africa (Algeria, Nigeria, Dahomey, Upper Volta, and the Central African Republic). Yet the coup itself, Mobutu's proclamation of a five-year presidency, and the subsequent challenges to *his* authority are additional evidence of continued political uncertainty.

VIII

An assessment of ONUC's value to the Organization and to those states concerned with enhancing the contribution the U.N. might make in other internal disorders involving a breakdown of law and order must take into account the extent to which ONUC served the needs of the international society during its four-year history. ONUC was able to function for a four-year period, although various states withdrew their troops, refused to pay assessments, or exerted bilateral pressures on the Secretary-General, field officials, and local political figures for political reasons. Although the Central Government in its successive forms argued with field personnel, no demands for ONUC's departure were issued. In fact, Russian and other moves to terminate ONUC abruptly were resisted. The conclusion emerges, as Ernest Lefever argues, that the operation served the interests of states concerned with a stable Africa, notably the United States and other Western nations together with the moderate African countries.[46] The operation did not serve the interests of states whose principal aim was to promote instability as a means of increasing national influence in the Congo—the Soviet Union, China, and the more radical African countries. Most important was the extent to which the operation served the larger international interest in peace, an interest that American, Soviet, or Belgian unilateral interventions might have failed to achieve, had such interventions been attempted in the confused days of July, 1960, or thereafter.

The dimensions of the Congo breakdown of law and order unfolded after the U.N. had become the "sole prop and hope" of the country.[47] As events shifted the balance of forces in the internal conflict from one side to the other, third parties shifted their votes in the Assembly and Council, thereby creating uncertainties about the functioning of the field operation. ONUC became a stake in factional conflicts within the Congo and the Secretary-General became a target for dissatisfied states whose national

---

[46] Lefever, *Crisis in the Congo*, p. 180.
[47] U.N. Doc. S/5784, June 29, 1964, p. 40.

interests in the internal disorder were thwarted by the U.N. Without the power to act as the sole authority in the strife-torn territory that lacked a viable, constitutional central government capable of imposing order, the U.N. was compelled to act in the service of an ill-defined, controversial policy, in cooperation with the superpower providing the Force with equipment and support. A choice was made between rival factional groups so that ONUC could perform its tasks, tasks that involved positive as well as negative facets. ONUC became embroiled in cold war politics after its use of force pursuant to Council resolutions based on a shifting political consensus. A breakdown in civil-military, headquarters-field relations further marred the operation, already seriously hampered by strained relations between U.N. field personnel and representatives of the host state.

The Organization's first peacekeeping operation in an internal disorder involving a breakdown of law and order created as many problems as it purported to resolve. Political objections, such as those voiced by the Soviet Union and later France, resulted in a grave financial crisis that threatened to wreck the entire institution. Buffers like the Advisory Committee could not shield the office of the Secretary-General from pressures affecting its direction of the field mission. The resumption of externally abetted rebellion prior to ONUC's departure underscored the "holding operation" character of the U.N.'s four-year effort and dramatized U Thant's warning that "the United Nations cannot permanently protect the Congo or any other country from the internal tensions and disturbances created by its own organic growth toward unity and nationhood."[48]

In the Congo conflict, the U.N. undertook responsibilities for finding and implementing a political solution. The type of solution advanced in the Organization's councils and in those of the O.A.U. (after 1963) reflected the views of member states with different interests in the outcome of disorder. The results of U.N. efforts led to serious controversy within the Organization. The O.A.U. served as a channel for the exchange of views and the promotion of negotiations between opposing factions, but internal dissension prevented the regional body from exerting greater influence on the course of events.

A caveat will serve to close this appraisal. In assuming responsibilities more extensive than those involved in assisting the parties to negotiate, international organizations run the risk of hindering their effectiveness in performing other political tasks. The least controversial and potentially most effective role the U.N. and regional organizations can play in promoting solutions to internal conflicts involving a breakdown of law and order is a limited one: creating circumstances favorable to negotiations between parties. By offering guidance and assistance regardless of the legal status of the parties, by refusing to assume the burden of formulating or imposing political solutions, the U.N. and regional organizations may perform acts of mediation or conciliation. The U.N., by virtue of its purposes and principles, has a vested interest in the restoration of stable conditions, but it need not have a vested

---

[48] *Ibid.*, p. 42.

interest in a particular solution to an internal disorder. So long as potential or actual threats to international peace and security are contained, even incompletely or temporarily, neither the U.N. nor regional organizations need damage their prestige by becoming committed to unworkable formulas.

DATE DUE
